IMPEACHABLE OFFENSES

OTHER WND BOOKS TITLES by AARON KLEIN and BRENDA J. ELLIOTT

FOOL ME TWICE
OBAMA'S SHOCKING PLANS FOR THE NEXT FOUR YEARS EXPOSED

THE MANCHURIAN PRESIDENT
BARACK OBAMA'S TIES TO COMMUNISTS, SOCIALISTS AND OTHER ANTI-AMERICAN EXTREMISTS

OTHER WND BOOKS TITLES by AARON KLEIN

SCHMOOZING WITH TERRORISTS
FROM HOLLYWOOD TO THE HOLY LAND, JIHADISTS REVEAL THEIR GLOBAL PLANS—TO A JEW!

THE LATE GREAT STATE OF ISRAEL
HOW ENEMIES WITHIN AND WITHOUT THREATEN THE JEWISH NATION'S SURVIVAL

IMPEACHABLE OFFENSES

THE CASE FOR REMOVING BARACK OBAMA FROM OFFICE

AARON KLEIN & BRENDA J. ELLIOTT

 WND Books

IMPEACHABLE OFFENSES

WND Books
Washington, D.C.

Book designed by Mark Karis

WND Books are distributed to the trade by:
Midpoint Trade Books
27 West 20th Street, Suite 1102
New York, New York 10011

WND Books are available at special discounts for bulk purchases. WND Books, Inc.,
also publishes books in electronic formats. For more information call
(541) 474-1776 or visit www.wndbooks.com.

First Edition

Hardcover ISBN: 9781938067198
eBook ISBN: 9781938067204

Library of Congress information available

Printed in the United States of America
10 9 8 7 6 5 4 3 2

CONTENTS

PREFACE   *i*

1   THE REAL BENGHAZI SCANDAL   1

2   FROM "FAST AND FURIOUS" TO GUN CONTROL   29

3   FORGET CONGRESS! BACKDOOR AMNESTY ALREADY HERE   59

4   REVOLVING DOOR FOR CRIMINAL ILLEGALS   89

5   EMPOWERING ENEMIES DOMESTICALLY AND ABROAD   109

6   CRONYISM, CORRUPTION, AND "CLEAN" ENERGY   133

7   BIG BROTHER OBAMA'S SURVEILLANCE REGIME   147

8   THE TRUTH ABOUT FUSION CENTERS   173

9   DHS ARMY—THE EMERGING POLICE STATE   187

10   THE DRONE NATION   219

11   OBAMACARE: UNAUTHORIZED EXPANSION OF POWER   241

12   "ANTI-WAR" PRESIDENT'S UNCONSTITUTIONAL WAR?   261

NOTES   *272*

INDEX   *321*

PREFACE

THIS BOOK IS A JOURNALISTIC INVESTIGATION into probable causes for the impeachment of President Barack Obama. Impeachment of a sitting president is certainly a matter of the utmost gravity, and it is not a charge to be undertaken for what our Founding Fathers would have called mere "factional" advantage. Just as it is remarkable that the United States Constitution provides a mechanism for the removal of the chief executive—a democratic device that developed over centuries of Anglo-Saxon politics—the fact that presidential impeachment has so seldom been attempted since our Constitution was adopted in 1789, despite almost 225 years of often tumultuous democratic self-governance, is a testament to the seriousness of this remedy.

So why do we write here of "impeachable offenses"?

Over the last five years, Brenda J. Elliott and I have written three book-length studies of Barack Obama and the radical progressive movement, in addition to hundreds of articles investigating the Obama administration. Those who study Obama and the progressive left know the low regard these ideologues have for any aspect of the Constitution that would limit the massive expansion of government, and especially the centralization of power in the hands of the executive branch. Of course, progressivism specializes in the manipulation of democratic institutions and processes—including elections, Congress, lower levels of state and local government, media "spin-control" operations, staged demonstrations by progressive constituencies, and so on—all to advance its utopian statist goals. But as we will document in this book, Obama has not hesitated to go beyond democratic, legal, and constitutional means to advance his radical agenda. As in our previous works, this is not a book of opinion. Rather, like police or court reporters, we present herein the results of our investigation into potentially impeachable offenses Obama appears to have committed against the United States Constitution and the limits of his office.

Before we probe the particulars of these offenses, let us look at definitions. What is an impeachable offense? Article II, Section 4, of the Constitution stipulates: "The President, Vice President, and all civil Officers of the United States shall be removed from Office on Impeachment for, and Conviction of, Treason, Bribery, or other High Crimes and Misdemeanors." What are these "high crimes and misdemeanors" to which the Constitution's authors referred? The phrase was well known to our Founding Fathers from the English legal tradition, which over centuries had tried to address the problem of government leaders abusing the powers of their offices. "High crimes" in the legal and common parlance of the seventeenth and eighteenth centuries signified actions by or against those who have special duties acquired by taking an oath of office that are not shared with civilians.[1]

America's Constitutional Convention of 1787 incorporated the language of "high crimes and misdemeanors" with little discussion, because the framers were already quite familiar with the term. Since 1386, the English Parliament had used "high crimes and misdemeanors" as one of the general grounds to impeach officials of the Crown. Officials accused of "high crimes and misdemeanors" were charged with offenses as varied as misappropriating government funds, appointing unfit subordinates, not prosecuting cases, not spending money allocated by Parliament (how times have changed!), promoting themselves ahead of more deserving candidates, threatening a grand jury, disobeying an order from Parliament, granting warrants without cause, and bribery.[2]

It is important to note that some of these abuses of power were actual crimes, while others were noncriminal misuses of official authority. The one common denominator in all of these transgressions was that the official had somehow abused the power of his office and was therefore unfit to serve.

After the Constitutional Convention, founding framers Alexander Hamilton, James Madison, and John Jay wrote a seminal series of essays, which became known as the *Federalist Papers*, urging adoption of the Constitution by the thirteen original states. In *Federalist* No. 65, Hamilton explained the concept of impeachment. He defined impeachable offenses as "those offences which proceed from the misconduct of public men, or in other words from the abuse or violation of some public trust. They are of a nature which may with peculiar propriety be denominated political, as they relate chiefly to injuries done immediately to the society itself."

Still, impeachment is not the final step in removing a high official from office; rather, it is the beginning of that process by bringing formal charges, i.e., an indictment. For a president to be impeached, clearly he must be accused of "injuries done immediately to the society itself," including the violation of his oath to "preserve, protect, and defend the Constitution of the United States." Typically, impeachment proceedings begin in the House Judiciary Committee, which is a subcommittee in the House of Representatives. The House Judiciary Committee considers evidence of wrongdoing and votes whether to pass the matter along to the entire body. After articles of impeachment are drawn up, the House then votes on the matter and, if a majority of the members affirm, passes the matter to the Senate. The Senate can then remove a president from office by vote of a two-thirds majority.

OBAMA'S IMPEACHABLE OFFENSES

What are President Obama's possible impeachable offenses, as documented in this book?

We will show how the president's "signature legislative achievement," popularly known as ObamaCare, not only is unconstitutional but also illegally bypasses Congress, infringes on states' rights, and marks an unprecedented and unauthorized expansion of Internal Revenue Service (IRS) power, constituting a clear case of "taxation without representation"—one of the primary reasons for the American Revolution.

We will document how Obama has already granted largely unreported de facto amnesty for millions of illegal aliens, while the US Department of Homeland Security mandated the release of immigrant suspects under the age of thirty-one. In so doing, the Obama administration bypassed Congress and used probably illegal interagency directives and executive orders, in a complete abuse of executive authority and the constitutional separation of powers. We will further show how the White House has recklessly endangered the public by releasing from prison criminal illegal aliens at a rate far beyond what is publicly known.

We present a devastating probe of the president's *personal* role in the September 11, 2012, Benghazi terrorist attacks, one of the most brazen assaults on an American overseas target in history. With new information, we show how our president and top administration officials deliberately and repeatedly lied to the American public and took decisions that denied security to our overseas' mission staff both prior to and immediately following the attacks. We will show how Obama engaged in a willful cover-up that ultimately fomented anti-American sentiment, aided an Islamist revolution, and armed our most dangerous al-Qaeda enemies. We also present new evidence about what was really transpiring at the US Benghazi mission prior to the attacks—possibly impeachable activities in and of themselves, and which likely provoked the terrorist assaults. We will further show the shocking political reasons Ambassador Chris Stevens traveled into a security vacuum in Benghazi the day of the attacks.

As Obama pushes for federal gun control legislation, we will document how he has already issued possibly illicit edicts to the heads of executive departments calling for specific gun control actions and how he has committed an impeachable offense in the form of the so-called "Fast and Furious" gun-running operation to Mexican drug gangs. This deadly scheme, we will show, was intended to collect fraudulent data and provoke attacks on Americans, all in order to push the president's gun control agenda.

Three full chapters are dedicated to Obama's gathering of intelligence on citizens and compiling massive databases of public and private records—information that is sometimes shared with foreign governments. While some of these domestic spy operations were established on a smaller scale by President George W. Bush after 9/11, we will show how they have been exponentially expanded, at times possibly illegally, under Obama. Americans are fast arriving at the stage of living under a virtual surveillance regime, featuring everything from "fusion centers" to domestic spy drones, where even businesses help the government collect information on private citizens. We will probe how Obama has expanded the Department of Homeland Security, which also appears to be seizing power in alarming ways.

On the matter of bribery and other financial crimes, we present new evidence of rank corruption, cronyism, and possible impeachable offenses related to Obama's first-term, "green" funding adventures misusing public funds.

And if that were not enough, we also probe the constitutionality of Obama's international drone campaign, as well as the legality of leading a US-NATO military campaign against Muammar Gaddafi's regime without congressional approval, coupled with the constitutionally questionable use in Libya of a globalist military doctrine unknown to most Americans—a doctrine which, according to its own founders, seeks to minimize US sovereignty while working to trivialize the concept of international state borders.

Finally, we document how Obama has weakened America both domestically and abroad by emboldening our enemies, tacitly supporting a Muslim Brotherhood revolution, spurning our allies, and minimizing the threat of Islamic fundamentalism while maintaining close and harmful associations with Islamic groups and activists of questionable character who now scandalously influence our antiterrorism policies.

It is stunning that all these "injuries to society" and the Constitution are being committed by a president who studied constitutional law at Harvard and then lectured on the subject at the University of Chicago (though the records of those years notoriously remain sealed at Obama's own insistence). Obama the constitutional lawyer, both before and after Harvard, was schooled in the techniques of progressive "community organizing," as taught to him personally in Chicago by the disciples of socialist theoretician Saul Alinsky (see our previous work, *The Manchurian President*). The two educations, as it turns out, were complementary. Obama the legal scholar needed Obama the progressive politician in order to take over the reins of government. And Obama the progressive politician needed Obama the legal scholar to massively expand and centralize executive control, and bypass Congress, once the presidency had been won.

As we were completing this book, the triple scandals of Benghazi-gate, IRS targeting of conservative groups, and the US Department of Justice obtaining private correspondence from the Associated Press and Fox News employees had begun to explode. Because we were investigating the Benghazi scandal since its origin on September 11, 2012, we have included in our chapter on Benghazi the game-changing testimony of former US deputy chief of mission in Libya Gregory Hicks and other whistle-blowers. The IRS targeting of conservative groups and DOJ targeting of journalists have not been included due to the pressure of book publishing deadlines, but these embarrassments merely add considerable weight to the basic thrust of our argument, and we have no doubt that a future printing will incorporate these and other scandals to come.

Barack Obama has done serious and sustained injury to American society and to our Constitution, the greatest document of political liberty known to man. He has fundamentally abused the powers of his office. Impeaching Obama will not, of itself, end the progressive nightmare in America. But Obama's impeachment and removal from office will go a long way toward restoring power to Congress, and to We, the People.

—*Aaron Klein*

1

THE REAL BENGHAZI SCANDAL

ONE WOULD BE HARD-PRESSED TO find a more significant impeachable offense than aiding and abetting the sworn enemies of the United States, especially when any such support includes sending weapons to our murderous adversaries. A crime on that scale would certainly be made all the more serious if those same enemies turned around and utilized the US-provided arms to kill Americans. We are not here referring to the so-called "Fast and Furious" scandal in which President Obama's Justice Department purposely allowed, with deadly consequence, licensed firearms dealers to sell weapons to illegal straw buyers with the intent of tracking the guns to Mexican drug cartel leaders. We will thoroughly investigate that possible impeachable offense, with new information, in the next chapter. Instead, we refer here to a much less reported gun-walking scandal, one you will soon regard as the "Fast and Furious" of the Middle East, the Iran-Contra of the Obama administration. It could be the White House got away not once but twice with the same misdeed of arming our foes.

In the case presented here, the enemy consists not of drug lords but of al-Qaeda, along with a witches' brew of anti-American jihadists. The results are not dead US border agents but a murdered US ambassador, along with three other diplomatic staff, in one of the most brazen assaults on an American overseas target in history. To make matters worse, we will show how our president and top administration officials deliberately and repeatedly lied to the American public while taking actions that fomented anti-American sentiment, aided an Islamist revolution currently sweeping the Middle East and North Africa, and possibly helped create, whether wittingly or not, a well-armed al-Qaeda army that is already attacking our interests and fueling conflicts worldwide. We will also show how the Obama administration engaged in a massive cover-up of the events that transpired during the Benghazi attacks, as well as the shocking reason our ambassador was sent to Benghazi on September 11, despite the many known (and ignored) security threats to the US mission there. You are about to be introduced to the real Benghazi scandal. This chapter alone should result in the immediate impeachment of Obama, as well as the toppling of other administration officials.

BENGHAZI: THE BACKSTORY

A US facility alternatively described by the news media as a "consulate" and a "mission" at Benghazi, Libya, was attacked on September 11, 2012, by a heavily armed jihadist group. The attacks consisted of assaults on two separate US compounds. The first assault occurred at the main compound, the so-called diplomatic mission (we will reveal more about what the facility really was shortly), at about 9:42 p.m. local time. The second assault took place at a CIA annex about 1.2 miles away from the "mission" at about 4 a.m. local time the following morning.[1] Four people were killed: US Ambassador J. Christopher Stevens, Foreign Service information management officer Sean Smith, and private security employees and former US Navy SEALs Glen Doherty and Tyrone Woods.

For the purposes of this chapter, we will only briefly summarize the events of the actual assaults since we are more concerned here with what was going on at the facility, an investigation that may reveal why the base was targeted in the first place. We will also address the administration's cover-up, as well as the seemingly nonsensical security decisions taken in the immediate aftermath of the attack that now must be probed in light of the new information presented in this chapter.

The initial attack on the "mission" involved between 125 and 150 gunmen who used trucks to seal off local streets, creating checkpoints leading to the main compound. According to reports, some of the trucks bore the logo of the al-Qaeda group Ansar al-Sharia, which stunningly is affiliated with the February 17 Martyrs' Brigade that was providing security at the compound. Ansar al-Sharia is believed to be linked to al-Qaeda in the Islamic Maghreb, an affiliate of the international terrorist group with origins in Algeria.[2] (That information will become relevant later in this chapter.) The Islamists used rocket-propelled grenades (RPGs), hand grenades, AK-47 and FN F2000 NATO assault rifles, diesel canisters, mortars, and heavy machine guns and artillery mounted on gun trucks in their five-plus-hour assault.[3]

According to a Pentagon time line, about fifteen minutes after the armed men began their initial assault on the US mission, an unarmed surveillance drone was directed to fly over the compound, meaning the US military had real-time video surveillance of almost the entire attack.[4] That means the Obama administration had to have known that there were no popular protests outside the mission against an obscure film about Muhammad that the White House would later blame for the Benghazi assault.

A Diplomatic Security Service agent saw the armed men attempting to breach the compound and hit the alarm, shouting, "Attack! Attack!" over the loudspeaker.[5] Phone calls were immediately placed to the relevant US agencies, including to a US quick-reaction force located at the nearby CIA annex.[6]

The militants entered the complex with cans of diesel fuel, setting the building ablaze and forcing those inside, including Stevens, to seek refuge in the bathroom until being overcome by smoke. Diplomatic Security Service special agent Scott Strickland jumped out the bathroom window, but Stevens and Smith did not follow him.[7] Later, Strickland and three other agents returned to the main building to search for survivors, finding Smith's body, but not Stevens. Stevens was reportedly somehow taken to Benghazi Medical Center, which at the time was controlled in part by Ansar al-Sharia. Reports claim that despite ninety minutes of CPR, he died from asphyxiation caused by smoke inhalation.[8]

The militants who attacked the facility clearly had inside information about the US facilities in Benghazi. At about 4 a.m. local time, the gunmen attacked the CIA annex with RPGs and a mortar that hit the annex roof, killing Doherty and Woods. Prior to the second attack, Libyan forces had escorted a group of Americans that had arrived at the Benghazi airport to the CIA annex to assist in transporting approximately thirty-two Americans at the annex back to the airport for evacuation.[9]

During US Senate hearings on February 7, 2013, outgoing defense secretary Leon Panetta testified that President Obama was absent the night of the Benghazi assault. Panetta said Obama "left operational details, including knowledge of what resources were available to help the Americans under siege, 'up to us.'"[10] Panetta further revealed he did not communicate with a single person at the White House that night and that aside from a 5:00 prescheduled meeting with the president on September 11, Obama did not call or communicate with the defense secretary that day.[11]

National Security Council spokesman Tommy Vietor confirmed to Fox News in November 2012 that Panetta, Secretary of State Hillary Clinton, and other senior officials worked on the immediate US response to Benghazi. "The most senior people in government worked on this issue from the minute it happened," he said. "That includes the Secretary of Defense, Chairman of the Joint Chiefs, Secretary of State, National Security Adviser, et cetera. Additionally, the Deputies Committee—the second in command at the relevant national security agencies—met at least once and more often twice a day to manage the issue."[12]

THE TRUE NATURE OF THE "CONSULATE"

Information surrounding the September 11 attacks against the US mission in Benghazi has been so distorted by the Obama administration and so misreported by the news media that many Americans still don't have the most basic of facts straight. Immediately following the attacks, President Obama and other White House officials notoriously blamed supposed anti-American sentiment leading to the violent events on a YouTube video that disparaged Muhammad, Islam's founder. They claimed the video was responsible for igniting popular civilian protests that they said took place outside the US mission in Benghazi—protests that allegedly devolved into a jihadist onslaught. On Sunday, September 16, 2012, US ambassador to the United Nations Susan Rice had appeared on five morning television programs to discuss the White House response to the Benghazi attacks. In nearly identical statements, she asserted that the attacks were a spontaneous protest in response to a "hateful video." Other Obama administration officials made similar claims. However, vivid accounts provided by the State Department and intelligence officials later made clear that no such popular demonstration took place. Instead, video footage from Benghazi shows an organized group of armed men attacking the compound, the officials said.[13] Despite this, the State Department spent seventy thousand dollars to air an ad on Pakistani television that featured Obama and Clinton denouncing the Muhammad video, while Obama himself denounced the film at a September 2012 address to the United Nations General Assembly.[14]

Let's start with the basics of the true nature of the Benghazi facilities. For months after the attacks, the vast majority of all news media coverage worldwide referred to the US facility that was attacked as a "consulate," even though the government itself has been careful to call it a "mission." A *consulate* typically refers to the building that officially houses a *consul*, or an official representative of the government of one state in the territory of another. Consulates at times function as junior embassies, providing services related to visas, passports, and citizen information.[15]

On August 26, about two weeks before he was killed, Ambassador Stevens attended a ceremony marking the opening of consular services at the American embassy in Tripoli, meaning the functioning US consulate

5

was working out of Tripoli.[16] The new US consul in Libya, Jenny Cordell, was stationed at the embassy in Tripoli. A search of the State Department website could find no consulate listed in Benghazi.

The main role of a consulate is to foster trade with the host government and care for its own citizens who are traveling or living in the host nation. Diplomatic missions, on the other hand, maintain a more generalized role. A *diplomatic mission* is simply a group of people from one state or an international intergovernmental organization present in another state to represent matters of the sending state or organization in the receiving state.

However, according to a State Department investigative report on the attacks, the US facility in Benghazi did not fit the profile of a diplomatic mission either. The results of the Accountability Review Board (ARB) probe, which we have read carefully, contain information indicating the US mission in Libya was involved in activities outside the diplomatic realm. The thirty-nine-page document uses phraseology and descriptions not previously utilized to describe the facility and the role it may have played in Benghazi. The report, based on an investigation led by former US diplomat Thomas Pickering, calls the facility a "U.S. Special Mission."[17] Again, until the report's release, government descriptions routinely referred to the facility as a "mission," while the news media largely and wrongly labeled the building a "consulate."

The report divulges how the mission's special "non-status" made providing security to the facility difficult. "Special Mission Benghazi's uncertain future after 2012 and its 'non-status' as a temporary, residential facility made allocation of resources for security and personnel more difficult," it said.[18]

The report contains information that clearly contradicts any claim that the special mission was to serve as a liaison office to the local government. It documents how the local Libyan government was not even informed of the existence of the mission. Noted the report, "Another key driver behind the weak security platform in Benghazi was the decision to treat Benghazi as a temporary, residential facility, not officially notified to the host government, even though it was also a full-time office facility. . . . This resulted in the Special Mission compound being excepted from office facility standards and accountability under the Secure Embassy Construction and Counterterrorism Act of 1999 (SECCA) and the Overseas Security Policy Board (OSPB)."[19]

The report relates how Stevens first arrived in Libya secretly in a cargo ship to serve as a liaison to the rebels fighting the regime of Muammar Gaddafi. It also confirms that Stevens's last official meeting was with "a Turkish diplomat."[20] Turkey is the main force behind Arab support for the opposition currently targeting the regime of Syrian president Bashar al-Assad.

Just as a side note, the report, perhaps unintentionally, contains information that may prove the facility violated the terms of the Vienna Convention on Diplomatic Relations, which governs the establishment of overseas missions. Like most nations, the US is a signatory to the 1961 United Nations' convention. Article 2 of the convention makes clear that the host government must be informed about the establishment of any permanent foreign mission on its soil: "The establishment of diplomatic relations between States, and of permanent diplomatic missions, takes place by mutual consent."[21]

But according to the State Department report, there was a decision "to treat Benghazi as a temporary, residential facility," likely disqualifying the building from permanent mission status if the mission was indeed temporary. However, the same sentence in the report notes the host government was not notified about the Benghazi mission "even though it was also a full-time office facility."[22]

Article 12 of the Vienna Convention dictates, "The sending State may not, without the prior express consent of the receiving State, establish offices forming part of the mission in localities other than those in which the mission itself is established."[23] If the Benghazi mission was a "full-time office facility," it may have violated Article 12 in that the mission most likely was considered an arm of the US embassy in Tripoli, which served as the main US mission to Libya.

Regardless, to the keen observer, the State Department report raises major unanswered questions about what was going on at the Libyan mission. Specifically, one glaring question is why the host government was not informed of the facility's existence. Was the facility being used for secretive purposes? What was happening at the facility?

ARMS TO JIHADISTS, WHITE HOUSE LIES

On multiple occasions, Middle Eastern security sources have provided author Aaron Klein with information indicating that both the US mission and the nearby CIA annex in Benghazi served as an intelligence and planning center for US aid to rebels in the Middle East, particularly those fighting the regime of Bashar al-Assad of Syria. Prior to the establishment of the Libyan mission, the United States also coordinated aid to the rebels who eventually toppled Libya's Gaddafi. That aid, the sources stated, included weapons shipments coordinated with Turkey, Saudi Arabia, and Qatar. The sources described how the weapons were carefully purchased with Arab and Turkish funds to skirt laws about the accountability of US funding for CIA and other intelligence operations.

Days after the Benghazi attacks, Klein broke the story that Stevens himself played a central role in recruiting jihadists to fight Assad's regime in Syria, according to Egyptian and other Middle Eastern security officials. Stevens served as a key contact with the Saudis to coordinate their recruitment of Islamic fighters from Libya and other parts of North Africa. The jihadists were sent to Syria via Turkey to attack Assad's forces, said the security officials.[24]

The officials also said Stevens worked with the Saudis to send names of potential jihadi recruits to US security organizations for review. Names found to be directly involved in previous attacks against the United States, including in Iraq and Afghanistan, were ultimately not recruited by the Saudis to fight in Syria, said the officials. (Take note of this detail, since it will become relevant again in a few paragraphs.)

A key issue is that until April 2013, the White House has repeatedly denied it was involved in helping to arm the rebels. Such action would be highly controversial because of the inclusion of jihadists, including al-Qaeda members, among the ranks of the Free Syrian Army and other Syrian opposition groups. Besides White House denials, other top US officials and former officials, including Hillary Clinton, have implied in congressional testimony that they didn't know about any US involvement in procuring weapons for the rebels.

Now, a starkly different picture is emerging, one that threatens the longstanding White House narrative that claims the Obama administration has only supplied nonlethal aid to the Syrian rebels. Klein's reporting on US arms coordination to the rebels has been confirmed by several major news agencies. The *New York Times* reported on March 25, 2013, that since early 2012, the CIA has been aiding Arab governments and Turkey in obtaining and shipping weapons to the Syrian rebels.[25] According to the *Times*, the weapons airlifts began on a small scale and continued intermittently through the fall, expanding into a steady and much heavier flow later in the year. The *Times* further revealed that from offices at "secret locations," American intelligence officers "helped the Arab governments shop for weapons . . . and have vetted rebel commanders and groups to determine who should receive the weapons as they arrive." The CIA declined to comment to the *Times* on the shipments or its role in them.[26]

The *New York Times* quoted a former American official as saying that David H. Petraeus, the CIA director until November 2012, had been instrumental in helping set up an aviation network to fly in the weapons. The paper said Petraeus "had prodded various countries to work together" on the plan. Petraeus did not return multiple e-mails from the *Times* asking for comment.[27]

Reuters further reported that President Obama allegedly signed a secret order in 2012 authorizing US agencies such as the CIA to provide support to rebel forces in Syria. The type of support includes helping to run a secret military communications command center in Turkey to aid rebel groups. The Reuters article also said US citizens are training rebels and possibly giving them equipment, at least since the summer.[28] While the *New York Times* report claims most of the weapons shipments facilitated by the CIA began after the 2012 presidential election, the Middle Eastern security officials speaking to Klein have said US-aided weapons shipments go back more than a year, escalating before the Benghazi attacks.

SECURITY DECISIONS

As media reports present evidence the US has played a central role in arming Syrian rebels, new questions now prompt a second look at the perplexing security decisions made by Secretary of State Clinton and other top Obama administration officials the night of the attacks on American facilities in Benghazi—the very facilities where the weapons shipments were allegedly being coordinated. One of those key decisions reportedly delayed an investigative FBI team from arriving at the Benghazi site for twenty-four days. The site was widely reported to have contained classified documents.

Remember, the Benghazi attacks took place a few weeks before the 2012 presidential election. If the arms-to-jihadist-rebels scheme had been exposed before the election, Obama may not be the current White House occupant.

Hillary Clinton seems to be at the center of the scandal. The *New York Times* report in March 2013 that since early 2012, the CIA has been aiding the Arab governments and Turkey in shopping for and transporting weapons to the Syrian rebels, is instrumental. The reported plan to arm the rebels mirrors a plan that, according to the *Times*, Clinton herself concocted. In February 2013, the *New York Times* described Clinton as one of the driving forces advocating a plan to arm the Syrian rebels. The newspaper quoted White House officials stating they rejected the plan, which was also proposed by then-CIA director David Petraeus.[29]

A comparison of the Clinton plan to arm the rebels, as first reported by the *New York Times*, and the *Times* report one month later confirming American-aided shipments to the rebels since the year before, makes clear the Clinton plan was apparently put into action. In February, the *Times* reported that the Clinton plan was to "vet the rebel groups and train fighters, who would be supplied with weapons."[30] In March, the *Times* reported that since at least November 2012, the United States has been helping "the Arab governments shop for weapons, including a large procurement from Croatia, and have vetted rebel commanders and groups to determine who should receive the weapons as they arrive."[31]

The earlier *Times* article described Clinton as having instincts that were "often more activist than those of a White House that has kept a tight grip on foreign policy." In an administration often faulted for its timidity abroad, "Clinton wanted to lead from the front, not from behind," Vali R. Nasr, a former State Department adviser on Afghanistan and Pakistan, told the *Times*.[32]

Now let's take a look at Clinton's decisions and those of the White House the night of the Benghazi attack. Remember, earlier we quoted National Security Council spokesman Tommy Vietor as confirming Clinton herself worked on the immediate US response to Benghazi, as did Obama's most senior officials.

One of the key decisions by the Obama administration and the State Department that has perplexed many security experts was the determination not to deploy an interagency rapid-response unit known as a Foreign Emergency Support Team (FEST) designed to respond to terrorist attacks. FEST teams previously "deployed immediately after al-Qaeda bombings of US embassies in East Africa in 1998 and the USS *Cole* in 2000, but they were not used for Benghazi," confounding insiders speaking to the news media.[33]

Counterterrorism officials told Fox News in November 2012 that the FEST teams could have helped the FBI gain access to the site in Benghazi faster. Again, it ultimately took the FBI twenty-four days. The site reportedly contained a large volume of classified documents related to the activities of the Benghazi facilities.[34]

Further, during the night of the attack, top counterterror officials felt out of the loop, according to e-mails shared with both Fox News and CBS News in November. Counterterrorism sources and internal e-mails reviewed by CBS News expressed frustration that key responders were ready to deploy but were not called upon to help in the attack.[35]

Besides strangely not deploying FEST, the Counterterrorism Security Group (CSG) "was never asked to meet [the night of the attack] or in subsequent days, according to two separate counterterrorism officials, as first reported by CBS News. The CSG is composed of experts on terrorism from across government agencies and makes recommendations to the deputies who assist the president's cabinet in formulating a response to crises involving terrorism."[36] It is "likely that the CSG task force, if contacted, would have recommended FEST aid," according to CBS.[37]

CBS reported that the lack of coordination with the Counterterrorism Security Group made the response to the Benghazi crisis still more confused. One official told CBS News that during the attack, the FBI received a call representing Clinton and requesting agents be deployed. But he and his colleagues explained the call was just a gesture and could not be implemented. He said his colleagues at the FBI agreed the agents "would not make any difference without security and other enablers to get them in the country and synch their efforts with military and diplomatic efforts to maximize their success."[38]

WHO SENT STEVENS INTO A SECURITY VACUUM?

In addition to the issue of what was transpiring at the US facility in Benghazi, a matter to which we will return shortly, one of the most basic questions is, what was Ambassador Stevens doing in Benghazi in the first place? Why did America's most high-profile envoy in Libya risk his life to travel into a virtual security vacuum on September 11, knowing about the many threats to the compound in general and that the 9/11 anniversary was an obvious date for further attack?

The State Department's ARB report on the attacks documents how the US diplomatic facilities in Benghazi came under direct fire twice in the months leading up to September 11, 2012. One of those cases involved a disgruntled Libyan contract guard hired by the US who allegedly threw a small improvised explosive device over the perimeter wall.[39] A Republican probe of the attacks further related how on September 8, 2012, the Ansar al-Sharia–tied February 17 Martyrs' Brigade, which had been guarding the facility, "told State Department officials the group would no longer support U.S. movements in the city, including the ambassador's visit."[40]

The threats were so serious that even the British embassy, the United Nations, and the International Committee of the Red Cross withdrew their personnel from Benghazi after armed assailants launched directed attacks against each organization. Lt. Col. Andrew Wood, who led the US military's efforts to supplement diplomatic security in Libya, stated in testimony that he personally recommended the US facility in Benghazi be withdrawn altogether.[41] (Just as a side note, Woods's testimony is at odds with Clinton's own January 23 testimony, in which she stated, "Well, senator, I want to make clear that no one in the State Department, the intelligence community, any other agency, ever recommended that we close Benghazi. We were clear-eyed about the threats and the dangers as they were developing in eastern Libya and in Benghazi."[42])

Lost in the news media coverage about the US response to the Benghazi attacks was that one day before the assaults, on September 10, 2012, al-Qaeda leader Ayman al-Zawahiri released a video calling for attacks on Americans in Libya to avenge the death of Abu Yahya al-Libi, one of the most senior al-Qaeda operatives. Released on a jihadi online forum fewer than eighteen hours before the Benghazi attack, the forty-two-minute video announced the death of al-Libi, a Libyan who was believed to have been killed in Pakistan in June 2012. Zawahiri urged jihadists, and particularly those in Libya, to avenge the killing of al-Libi. "His blood urges you and incites you to fight and kill the crusaders," he said.[43]

In other words, the leader of al-Qaeda telegraphed a specific threat against the United States in Libya, and despite this, Stevens still ventured into the viper's den.

Until around the publication of this book, the official explanation given for Stevens's mysterious September 11 Benghazi visit was that the ambassador went there of his own accord to fill a staffing gap. "The Board found that Ambassador Stevens made the decision to travel to Benghazi independently of Washington, per standard practice," said the State Department's ARB report. "Timing for his trip was driven in part by commitments in Tripoli, as well as a staffing gap between principal officers in Benghazi."[44]

However, in bombshell congressional testimony, Gregory Hicks, who was the deputy chief of mission at the US embassy in Tripoli, revealed that Hillary Clinton's desire to make Benghazi a permanent State Department facility—against a looming funding deadline—was one of the main motivations for Stevens's dangerous trip. Clinton had wanted to visit the facility just prior to her departure as secretary of state as a way to trumpet the Obama administration's supposed success in aiding in the overthrow of Gaddafi, Hicks stated. Hicks further charged that he gave this information to Thomas Pickering and the other State Department investigators and ARB report authors, but they decided not to mention this damning information in their final report.[45]

"I just want you to say it unambiguously—if that's the correct way to say it—without a flaw, one more time," stated House Oversight chairman Darrell Issa. "The reason the ambassador was in Benghazi, at least one of the reasons was X?"[46]

"At least one of the reasons he was in Benghazi was to further the secretary's wish that that post become a permanent constituent post, and also there, because we understood that the secretary intended to visit Tripoli later in the year," said Hicks. "We hoped that she would be able to announce to the Libyan people our establishment of a permanent constituent post in Benghazi at that time."

"According to [Amb.] Chris [Stevens], Secretary Clinton wanted Benghazi converted into a permanent constituent post," Hicks continued. "Timing for this decision was important. Chris needed to report before September 30th, the end of the fiscal year, on the physical—the political and security environment in Benghazi to support an action memo to convert Benghazi from a temporary facility to a permanent facility."

Rep. James Lankford (R-OK) asked, "What was the time line on trying to make this a permanent facility, or was there anything pending that had to be accomplished by a certain deadline?"

"We had funds available that we could, that could be transferred from an account set aside for Iraq and could be dedicated to this purpose," replied Hicks. "They had to be obligated by September 30th."

"OK. And where did those instructions come from?" asked Lankford.

"This came from the executive office of the Bureau of Near Eastern Affairs," Hicks replied, referring to a division of the main State Department in Washington.

Hicks told Rep. Doug Collins (R-GA) that in a discussion she'd had with him when he first became ambassador, Clinton had personally told Stevens she wanted him to make Benghazi a permanent State Department post. Hicks further stated, "Chris told me that in his exit interview with the secretary after he was sworn in, the secretary said, 'We need to make Benghazi a permanent post,' and Chris said, 'I'll make it happen.'"

"OK. Was Washington informed of the ambassador's plan to travel to Benghazi?" asked Collins.

"Yes," said Hicks. "Washington was fully informed that the ambassador was going to Benghazi. We advised them August 22nd or thereabouts."

"Were there concerns raised from that?" asked Collins.

"No, in fact—"

"Given the timing and everything?" Collins continued.

"None," said Hicks.

It must be asked whether Clinton and other Obama administration officials were so hell-bent on declaring the US and NATO intervention in Libya a success that they ignored glaring security warnings and instead allowed Stevens to travel to Benghazi, ostensibly to complete paperwork for the end-of-September deadline for funding to turn the mission into a permanent post. Libya, of course, was the template for Obama's larger policy of supporting revolutions throughout the Middle East (we will further expose this policy in chapter 5). The war against Gaddafi was also the first major test for the "responsibility to protect," or R2P, doctrine, the globalist military doctrine used to justify the NATO campaign there. It just so happens that Pickering, the lead State Department investigator on Benghazi and author of the ARB report, serves on the board of the International Crisis Group, one of the main proponents of R2P, a doctrine we will further explore and tie to Pickering and other relevant players in chapter 12.

Meanwhile, things don't get any better for Clinton. Hicks stated the former secretary of state was the only official who could sign off on Stevens's trip to Benghazi, explaining how the Benghazi post was deemed such a high security risk that only the secretary of state could issue a waiver for the ambassador to travel there. Republican lawmakers affirmed the Benghazi post did not meet the State Department's Overseas Security Policy Board (OSBP) standards, nor did the mission conform to the standards of the Secure Embassy Construction and Counterterrorism Act of 1999 (SECCA), facts also mentioned in the ARB, as quoted earlier. When asked whether Clinton was the only official with the authority to send diplomats to a facility that did not meet those government security standards, Hicks said yes.

THOSE PESKY TALKING POINTS

A major issue in Benghazi is the now infamous scrubbing of references to terrorism and al-Qaeda from the White House's Benghazi talking points. White House officials as well as CIA deputy director Mike Morell claimed those references were deleted for security reasons, a claim now contradicted by e-mails reviewed by Republican investigators who penned the forty-six-page House GOP report probing the Benghazi attacks.

In perhaps one of the most damning but largely unreported sections of the GOP report, lawmakers who penned the investigation wrote they were given access to classified e-mails and other communications that prove the talking points were not edited to protect classified information but instead to protect the State Department's reputation. We have to further ask whether any terrorism motive for the Benghazi attacks would have drawn attention to Obama's policy of arming the jihadist rebels or the wisdom of the administration's signature larger policy of supporting Middle East revolutions.

"Contrary to Administration rhetoric, the talking points were not edited to protect classified information," stated the Interim Progress Report for the Members of the House Republican Conference on the Events Surrounding the September 11, 2012, Terrorist Attacks in Benghazi, Libya.[47] "Evidence rebuts Administration claims that the talking points were modified to protect classified information or to protect an investigation by the Federal Bureau of Investigation (FBI)," the report continues.[48]

The report further charges that the talking points were "deliberately" edited to "protect the State Department." States the report: "To protect the State Department, the Administration deliberately removed references to al-Qaeda-linked groups and previous attacks in Benghazi in the talking points used by [United Nations] Ambassador [Susan] Rice, thereby perpetuating the deliberately misleading and incomplete narrative that the attacks evolved from a demonstration caused by a YouTube video."[49]

The tale of the talking points began when US intelligence officials testified behind closed doors in early November 2012 and were reportedly asked point-blank whether they had altered the talking points on which Rice based her comments about the Benghazi attacks. Again, on Sunday, September 16, 2012, Rice went on five morning television shows to claim the attacks were a spontaneous protest in response to a "hateful video."

Two congressional sources who spoke to Reuters on condition of anonymity said Morell, then acting CIA director, along with Director of National Intelligence James Clapper and National Counterterrorism Center director Matthew Olsen, each testified behind closed doors that they did not alter the talking points.[50]

On November 16, 2012, former CIA director David Petraeus testified before the same congressional intelligence committee and also denied he had changed the talking points, three congressional sources told Reuters. Then on November 27, the CIA reportedly told lawmakers that it had, in fact, changed the wording of the unclassified talking points to delete a reference to al-Qaeda, according to senators who met with Morell that day. That November 27 meeting was between Morell, Rice, and Republican senators John McCain, Lindsey Graham, and Kelly Ayotte.

A statement by McCain, Graham, and Ayotte specifically stated that Morell told the senators during the meeting that the FBI had removed references to al-Qaeda from the talking points. The senators' joint statement reads: "Around 10:00 this morning in a meeting requested by Ambassador Rice, accompanied by acting CIA Director Mike Morell, we asked Mr. Morell who changed the unclassified talking points to remove references to al-Qaeda. In response, Mr. Morell said the FBI removed the references *and did so to prevent compromising an ongoing criminal investigation* [of the attack on the US mission]. We were surprised by this revelation and the reasoning behind it."[51]

Morell's claim of changing the talking points for security reasons is now contradicted by the new Republican probe.

Further, on November 28, 2012, CBS News reported the CIA then told the news agency that the edits to the talking points were made "so as not to tip off al-Qaeda as to what the US knew, and to protect sources and methods." That same report quoted a source from the Office of the Director of National Intelligence, who told CBS News' Margaret Brennan that the source's office "made the edits as part of the interagency process because the links to al-Qaeda were deemed too 'tenuous' to make public."[52]

Meanwhile, a few hours after his meeting with the senators, Morell's office reportedly contacted Graham and stated that Morell had misspoken in the earlier meeting and that it was, in fact, the CIA, not the FBI, that deleted the al-Qaeda references. "CIA officials contacted us and indicated that Acting Director Morell misspoke in our earlier meeting. The CIA now says that it deleted the al-Qaida references, not the FBI. They were unable to give a reason as to why," Graham said in his statement.[53] "This was an honest mistake and it was corrected as soon as it was realized. There is nothing more to this," an intelligence official said about Morell's briefing to the senators.[54]

A US intelligence official further told CBS News there was "absolutely no intent to misinform." The official says the talking points "were never meant to be definitive and, in fact, noted that the assessment may change. The points clearly reflect the early indications of extremist involvement in a direct result. It wasn't until after they were used in public that analysts reconciled contradictory information about how the assault began."[55]

However, the intelligence community clearly at first portrayed the edited White House talking points as a bid to protect classified information. According to the interim House report on Benghazi, after a White House deputies meeting on Saturday, September 15, 2012, "the Administration altered the talking points to remove references to the likely participation of Islamic extremists in the attacks. The Administration also removed references to the threat of extremists linked to al-Qaeda in Benghazi and eastern Libya, including information about at least five other attacks against foreign interests in Benghazi." Charged the report: "Senior State Department officials requested—and the White House approved—that the details of the threats, specifics of the previous attacks, and previous warnings be removed to insulate the department from criticism that it ignored the threat environment in Benghazi."[56]

The report authors said that they went through e-mail exchanges of the interagency process to scrub the talking points and found that the e-mails do not reveal any concern with protecting classified information. "Additionally, the Bureau itself approved a version of the talking points with significantly more information about the attacks and previous threats than the version that the State Department requested. Thus, the claim that the State Department's edits were made solely to protect that investigation is not credible."[57]

In a particularly stinging accusation, the report states that when draft talking points were sent to officials throughout the executive branch, senior State Department officials requested the talking points be changed "to avoid criticism for ignoring the threat environment in Benghazi. Specifically, State Department e-mails reveal senior officials had 'serious concerns' about the talking points, because members of Congress might attack the State Department for 'not paying attention to Agency warnings' about the growing threat in Benghazi."[58]

DID THE OBAMA ADMINISTRATION HIDE THIS DRAMATIC EVACUATION?

Information on Benghazi released by the US government is so incomplete and misleading that the State Department may have deliberately hid the evacuation of another outpost in Libya during the Benghazi attacks, a dramatic scene in which US embassy staff four hundred miles away in

Tripoli evacuated their residential compound under possible terrorist threat. The threat was taken so seriously that, according to a key embassy staffer, communications equipment was dismantled and hard drives were smashed with an ax.

The scene was first brought to light in congressional testimony by Gregory Hicks. The incident was not mentioned in the State Department probe, nor was it previously reported in news accounts of the attack, which, as we discussed, the Obama administration first claimed was a result of popular protests over an anti-Muhammad video.

In his testimony, Hicks said that about three hours after the attack began on the US facility in Benghazi, the embassy staff in Tripoli noticed Twitter feeds asserting that the terror group Ansar al-Sharia was responsible. Hicks said there was also a call on the social media platform for an attack on the embassy in Tripoli. "We had always thought that we were . . . under threat, that we now have to take care of ourselves and we began planning to evacuate our facility," he said. "When I say our facility, I mean the State Department residential compound in Tripoli, and to consolidate all of our personnel . . . at the annex in Tripoli."[59]

Having heard that Ambassador Stevens had been killed, Hicks said he "immediately telephoned Washington that news afterwards and began accelerating our effort to withdraw from the Villas compound and move to the annex."

He recalled how his team "responded with amazing discipline and courage in Tripoli in organizing withdrawal." Continued Hicks: "I have vivid memories of that. I think the most telling, though, was of our communications staff dismantling our communications equipment to take with us to the annex and destroying the classified communications capability. Our office manager, Amber Pickens, was everywhere that night just throwing herself into some task that had to be done. First she was taking a log of what we were doing. Then she was loading magazines, carrying ammunition to the—carrying our ammunition supply to . . . our vehicles, and then she was smashing hard drives with an ax."

The vivid, nearly unprecedented scene, however, was not reported in the State Department's description of the Tripoli embassy's response the night of the Benghazi attack. The section of the State Department ARB probe titled "Embassy Tripoli Response" simply says that upon notification of the attack in Benghazi, the US embassy set up a command center and notified Washington.[60]

A later section in the State Department probe describes how a seven-person response team from Tripoli arrived in Benghazi to lend support but could not get to the Benghazi facility due to a lack of transportation. The section also says the Tripoli embassy worked with the Libyan government to have a Libyan Air Force C-130 take the remaining US government personnel from Benghazi to Tripoli.[61]

If they can cover up an evacuation, what else are we not being told?

ARMING AL-QAEDA

Let's return to the alleged use of the Benghazi mission as a place to aid the jihadist rebels. We are not here going to discuss the wisdom of toppling the Syrian or Libyan regimes, such as how Islamists have already filled the power vacuum in Libya and are likely to gain from the downfall of Assad. In chapter 5, we will thoroughly dissect Obama's relationship with the Muslim Brotherhood and his contributing to the downfall of US allies, only to have radical Islamist parties fill the power vacuum. The immediate and obvious problem with aiding the so-called rebels in Libya and Syria is that it has been credibly established by scores of mainstream news media reports that those rebels consist in large part of al-Qaeda and global jihad–linked fighters. At this point, al-Qaeda's presence among the rebels and even among the US-supported Free Syrian Army is not disputed.

Besides arming Syrian rebels, it is not in doubt that during the NATO campaign in Libya, the Obama administration coordinated foreign arms shipments via cutouts to the rebels fighting Gaddafi, and there are questions as to the nature of Obama's support for the Syrian rebels. In December 2012, the *New York Times* reported that the Obama administration "secretly gave its blessing to arms shipments to Libyan rebels from Qatar last year, but American officials later grew alarmed as evidence grew that Qatar was turning some of the weapons over to Islamic militants, according to United States officials and foreign diplomats." The article went on to say that the weapons and money from Qatar "strengthened militant groups in Libya, allowing them to become a destabilizing force since the fall of the Qaddafi government." The weapons came from Qatar and not the United States.[62]

There is more evidence of the Obama administration okaying arms to Mideast rebels. In March 2011, Reuters broke the story that Obama had signed a secret order authorizing covert US government support for rebel forces seeking to oust Gaddafi, quoting US government officials. Reuters noted that this type of order is a principal form of presidential directive used to authorize secret operations by the CIA.[63] That same month, the UK-based *Independent* reported that "the Americans have asked Saudi Arabia if it can supply weapons to the rebels in Benghazi."[64]

To be fair, it was not just the United States coordinating arms shipments to the jihadist-saturated rebels. Fellow NATO member France admitted in June 2011 that it had armed the rebels, air-dropping so-called light armaments, including guns and rocket-propelled grenades, in the Nafusa Mountains in western Libya.[65]

Aside from the possibility of arming the rebels, the United States announced in February 2013 it was providing $60 million in nonlethal aid to the Syrian opposition.[66] That was in addition to $54 million in communications equipment, medical supplies, and other nonlethal assistance to Syria's political opposition and the Free Syrian Army. Questions need to be raised about whether the transfer of these funds violates US law forbidding material support for terrorist organizations.

Just who are the rebels? Let's start with those we helped to arm in Libya. While the White House reportedly helped facilitate arms transfers, rebel leader Abdel-Hakim al-Hasidi admitted in an interview that a significant number of the Libyan rebels were al-Qaeda fighters, many of whom had fought US troops in Iraq and Afghanistan. He insisted his fighters "are patriots and good Muslims, not terrorists," but he added that the "members of al-Qaeda are also good Muslims and are fighting against the invader."[67]

A file from 2005 disclosed by WikiLeaks showed that rebel leader Abu Sufian Ibrahim Ahmed Hamuda Bin Qumu was a former Guantánamo Bay detainee alleged to be a member of the Libyan Islamic Fighting Group and that he was a "probable member of . . . Al Qaeda" and a member of the African Extremist Network."[68]

It got so bad that Adm. James Stavridis, NATO supreme commander for Europe, admitted Libya's rebel force may include al-Qaeda. "We have seen flickers in the intelligence of potential al-Qaeda, Hezbollah," he testified to the US Senate in March 2011.[69]

Former CIA officer Bruce Riedel went even further, telling the *Hindustan Times*, "There is no question that al-Qaeda's Libyan franchise, Libyan Islamic Fighting Group, is a part of the opposition. It has always been Gaddafi's biggest enemy and its stronghold is Benghazi. What is unclear is how much of the opposition is al-Qaeda/Libyan Islamic Fighting Group—2 percent or 80 percent."[70]

After Gaddafi fell, the *New York Times* reported that "the administration has never determined where all of the weapons, paid for by Qatar and the United Arab Emirates, went inside Libya." The *Times* quoted a former defense official saying some of the Arab-provided arms coordinated by the United States since have been moved from Libya to militants with ties to al-Qaeda in Mali, where radical jihadi factions have imposed Sharia law in the northern part of the country. Others have gone to Syria, according to several American and foreign officials and arms traders.[71]

It would be sufficient to conclude the chapter here. The Obama administration reportedly coordinated weapons transfers to Libyan and Syrian rebels whose ranks included al-Qaeda, and those weapons ended up with al-Qaeda and other jihadists. Weapons funneling to Syrian jihadists continues as of the publication of this book. A well-armed al-Qaeda group attacked our mission and CIA annex in Benghazi, resulting in the death of an ambassador. This alone should spark hearings on Capitol Hill. The story, however, gets worse.

ISLAMIC LAW, CHRISTIAN PERSECUTION

Another issue here is current Obama administration aid to the Free Syrian Army (FSA). The FSA is the main organized armed opposition structure operating in Syria that is targeting the regime of Bashar al-Assad. Just like the Libyan rebels, there have been scores of reports worldwide that al-Qaeda and other jihad groups are among the ranks of the Free Syrian Army, to the point where it's considered established fact among Middle East experts. Al-Qaeda groups such as the Al-Nusra Front and Ahrar al-Sham are reportedly fighting alongside the FSA, while some jihadists have also allegedly joined FSA ranks.

One need not speculate about the results of Obama's support for the Syrian opposition, including the Free Syrian Army. Even the *Huffington Post* was appalled by the US support for the Syrian opposition. The publication reported that on the outskirts of Aleppo, Syria, the US-supported FSA has "implemented a Sharia law enforcement police force that is a replica of the Wahhabi police in Saudi Arabia—forcing ordinary citizens to abide by the Sharia code." The *Huffington Post* noted the Islamist code is being enforced in secular Syria, which has never known Sharia law.[72]

Huffington Post writer Daniel Wagner further charged that Obama was tacitly supporting al-Qaeda by aiding the FSA. He wrote, "There is also evidence that the Saudis and Qataris support the al-Qaeda affiliate in the FSA (Jabhat al-Nusra) with money, and that Turkey gives JaN refuge and provides training inside Turkey. Although the US government has officially declared its opposition to JaN, there is no effective way for it to segment its financial assistance to the FSA from JaN, so it is in essence tacitly agreeing to support al-Qaeda in order to remove Assad."

Does the FSA share American democratic ideals? The FSA has been accused of summarily executing numerous prisoners whom it claims are informers.[73] Witnesses have also claimed they saw rebels conduct "trial by grave" in which an alleged informer was given a mock trial next to a premade grave and executed on the spot by members of the FSA. One rebel was quoted by the news media as saying, "We took him right to his grave and, after hearing the witnesses' statements, we shot him dead."[74]

The United Nations itself noted some credible allegations that rebel forces, including the FSA, were recruiting children as soldiers, despite stated FSA policy of not recruiting anyone under age seventeen. One rebel commander reportedly said that his sixteen-year-old son had died fighting government troops.[75]

The FSA is apparently also going around persecuting Christians. According to the Vatican news agency Agenzia Fides, 90 percent of the Christian population of Homs, about ten thousand people, were expelled from their homes by members of the FSA's Farouq Brigades.[76] The agency quoted Syrian Orthodox Christian sources saying the FSA militants went door-to-door in the neighborhoods of Hamidiya and Bustan al-Diwan, forcing Christians to flee, without giving them the chance to take their belongings. The Catholic charity organization Aid to the Church in Need supported the Agenzia Fides report, while the *Miami Herald* reported the Christians were targeted not because of their religion but due to their close ties to the Assad regime.[77]

OBAMA PAL RAISING MONEY IN DC FOR SYRIAN "REBELS"

The FSA received a major diplomatic boost when Obama recognized the leading Syrian opposition coalition as the legitimate representative of Syria in the place of Assad's regime. In July 2012, the Syrian Support Group, a Washington-based organization that supports the al-Qaeda–saturated FSA, received a waiver from the US Treasury Department authorizing it to provide logistical and financial support to the armed Syrian resistance. Brian Sayers of the Syrian Support Group said the waiver from the Treasury Department Office of Foreign Assets Control "gets us the leeway to support the Free Syrian Army in broad terms." He said the waiver would immediately allow for providing a wide range of support to the FSA, including paying for FSA salaries and provisions, as well as "communications equipment, satellite imagery, paying for satellite imagery, logistical support for transport, which could mean everything from buying a 4x4 to supporting someone's travel to Turkey." On their more intermediate-term wish list "is intelligence support, drone support, eyes in the sky, an intelligence platform," Sayers said. Syria's rebels "need both intelligence and weapons."[78]

Sayers admitted in a National Public Radio (NPR) interview that the money raised by his organization will go to weapons purchases as well. "Yes," he said when asked about weapons. "Weapons are going to be a part of the process, because if they're going to set up safe zones for the Syrian citizens . . . those safe zones have to be defended."[79]

The Syrian Support Group addresses concerns on its website about whether some of the money it raises will go to al-Qaeda organizations fighting with the Free Syrian Army. "SSG acknowledges reports of increasing Al-Qaeda and other extremist activity within Syria. SSG hopes to serve as a counterweight to this development and will only provide financial support to military councils who have adopted the Free Syrian Army's Proclamation of Principles." The proclamation outlines the FSA's commitment to a democratic Syria and also to "fight if necessary to end the tyranny and dictatorship of the Assad regime."[80]

So the Obama administration is allowing a US charity to raise money to build a virtual military for the al-Qaeda–linked Free Syrian Army while the White House itself signed off on an untold number of US-aided arms shipments to the al-Qaeda–led rebels. Tellingly, the former director of Muslim outreach for Obama's 2008 presidential campaign now is representing the Syrian Support Group charity, we have found. Mazen Asbahi, a Chicago lawyer, resigned from Obama's first presidential campaign after the *Wall Street Journal* reported that he sat on the board of an Islamic investment group called the Allied Assets Advisors Fund. Also on the board was Jamal Said, an unindicted coconspirator in the Holy Land Foundation, which raised millions of dollars for the Hamas terrorist organization.[81]

The Allied Assets Advisors Fund was itself a subsidiary of the North American Islamic Trust (NAIT), which is directed by the Islamic Society of North America (ISNA). ISNA was established in 1981 by activists from the Muslim Brotherhood–affiliated Muslim Students Association. ISNA was also named as an unindicted coconspirator in the Holy Land Foundation terrorism financing case.

ISNA was the subject of a terrorism investigation in December 2003 by the Senate Finance Committee, which looked into possible links between nongovernmental organizations and terrorist financing networks. The official court documents in the Holy Land Foundation case named ISNA among "entities who are and/or were members of the US Muslim Brotherhood." Now Asbahi is back in the spotlight as the lawyer for the Syrian Support Group. It was actually Asbahi who had applied to the US government for the license to fund the Free Syrian Army.[82]

Meanwhile, Aaron Klein reported in May 2012 there was growing collaboration between the Syrian opposition, including the Free Syrian Army, and al-Qaeda, as well as evidence the opposition is sending weapons to jihadists in Iraq, according to an Egyptian security official.[83] The official said that Egypt has received reports of collaboration between the Syrian opposition and three al-Qaeda arms networks, including one that operates in Libya: Jund al-Sham, which is made up of al-Qaeda militants who are Syrian, Palestinian, and Lebanese; Jund al-Islam, which in recent years merged with Ansar al-Islam, an extremist group of Sunni Iraqis operating under the al-Qaeda banner and operating in Yemen and Libya; and Jund Ansar Allah, an al-Qaeda group based in Gaza and linked to Palestinian camps in Lebanon and Syria.

BRAZEN ASSAULT ON WESTERN GAS COMPLEX, FUELING WORLDWIDE CONFLICT

The possibly illegal transfer of weapons and aid to Middle East rebels is clearly resulting in a newly emboldened al-Qaeda. Even the United Nations is warning that weapons delivered to Libya during the uprising there are being used to fuel conflicts in Mali, Syria, Gaza, and elsewhere.

Remember that in December 2012, the *New York Times* reported that after discussions among members of the National Security Council, the Obama administration backed arms shipments to Libyan rebels from both Qatar and the United Arab Emirates. American officials told the *Times* that the UAE "first approached the Obama administration during the early months of the Libyan uprising, asking for permission to ship American-built weapons that the United States had supplied for the emirates' use. The administration rejected that request, but instead urged the emirates to ship foreign weapons to Libya that could not be traced to the United States."[84]

"The UAE was asking for clearance to send U.S. weapons," one former US official told the *Times*. "We told them it's O.K. to ship other weapons."[85]

Earlier in this chapter, we cited more evidence of the Obama administration okaying arms to Libyan rebels. Now the United Nations reports weapons initially sent to Benghazi are spreading from Libya to extremists at an "alarming rate." The ninety-four-page report, which was dated February 15, 2013, and penned by the UN Security Council's Group of Experts, said the North African state had become a key source of weapons transfers in the region, specifically blaming Qatar and the UAE for arming the rebels. While not referencing the US support for the arms transfers, the UN experts said they had found that Qatar and the UAE had breached the arms embargo on Libya during the 2011 uprising by arming the rebels. According to Reuters, "The experts said Qatar had denied the accusation, while the United Arab Emirates had not responded."[86]

"Some 18 months after the end of the conflict, some of this materiel remains under the control of non-state actors within Libya and has been found in seizures of military material being trafficked out of Libya," the report says. The UN cites cases, both proven and under investigation, of illicit transfers from Libya to more than twelve countries and also to terror and criminal groups, including heavy and light weapons, man-portable air defense systems, small arms and related ammunition, and explosives and mines.[87] The report failed to mention the key involvement of the Obama administration, as described in mainstream media reports, in coordinating the Arab arms shipments to the rebels. In other words, Obama's policy is already spreading violence to other countries.

That Obama administration policy of support for the jihadist Libyan and Syria rebels may have already come back to haunt us in other ways. Besides questions about the arms used in the coordinated assaults against our facilities in Benghazi and the UN report on weapons proliferation, there are also claims of ties between the Benghazi attacks and a brazen assault on an Algerian gas complex where foreigners, including Americans, were employed. In the assault, a group called Al-Qaeda in the Islamic Maghreb laid siege for four days to the gas complex, with the four-day ordeal ending in the deaths of thirty-eight hostages and twenty-nine kidnappers after Algerian forces stormed the compound. The *New York Times* quoted a senior Algerian official saying several Egyptian members of the squad of al-Qaeda–tied jihadists behind the bloody gas complex siege also took part in the deadly attack on the US mission in Benghazi.[88] The Algerian official said that information was extracted during the interrogations of the jihadists who had survived the compound assault.

American counterterrorism and intelligence officials told the *New York Times* that Ansar al-Sharia, the group that carried out the attack on the diplomatic mission in Benghazi, had connections to Al-Qaeda in the Islamic Maghreb.

It is bad enough that we are supporting al-Qaeda–linked jihadists. In chapter 5, we will show how the Obama administration, using these jihadist rebels to do the dirty work, is also aiding the rise of Islamist parties throughout the Middle East and North Africa and toppling our allies while maintaining troubling relationships with Muslim Brotherhood–linked groups in the United States who are minimizing our so-called war on terrorism. The end results will be devastating for US national security.

Meanwhile, we turn next from the "Fast and Furious" of the Middle East to the original "Fast and Furious" scandal, the impeachable scheme that armed Mexican drug dealers while executive actions currently aim to push gun control on American citizens.

2

FROM "FAST AND FURIOUS" TO GUN CONTROL

They [rural Pennsylvanians] fell through the Clinton administration and the Bush administration, and each successive administration has said that somehow these communities are gonna regenerate. And they have not. . . . And, it's not surprising then that they get bitter, they cling to guns or religion or antipathy toward people who aren't like them or anti-immigrant sentiment or anti-trade sentiment as a way to explain their frustrations.[1]

—Barack Obama, April 2008

No gun control program makes people safer. When violent criminals can get their hands on any weapon they want—guns, knives, chemicals, vehicles, anything—how in the world will any gun control movement make people safer by leveraging the honest, and only the honest?[2]

—John Longenecker, LA Gun Rights Examiner, *February 7, 2009*

WE EXPOSED IN THE PREVIOUS CHAPTER how President Obama has no problem arming our jihadist enemies. Apparently arming Mexican drug dealers is okay, too, as we will discuss. However, when it comes to law-abiding American citizens, the president cannot act quickly enough to ensure against the right to bear arms. While Congress has yet to pass gun control legislation, Obama is already working on plans to bypass lawmakers with executive actions aimed at background checks, gun registries, assault rifle bans, and even a limitation on ammunition purchases. This is in addition to directives already issued to the heads of executive departments calling for specific gun control actions.[3] With the gun debate still raging, we will herein document how Obama has committed an impeachable offense in the form of the so-called "Fast and Furious" scandal, a deadly scheme, we will show, that was aimed at collecting fraudulent data to push a gun control agenda. We will also review Obama's gun policies and control attempts thus far, as well as address the reports of mass bullet purchases by the Department of Homeland Security.

"JUST ROUND ONE"

At the top of the list of President Obama's gun policies was the suggestion that Congress could require criminal background checks for all gun sales, including those by private sellers. However, Obama's "ambitious efforts to overhaul the nation's gun laws" suffered a "stunning collapse" on April 17, 2013, "when every major proposal he championed fell apart on the Senate floor."[4] The bipartisan amendment cosponsored by senators Joe Manchin III (D-WV) and Patrick J. Toomey (R-PA) fell short of the sixty votes needed to adopt legislation that would have expanded background checks to include most commercial sales. A four-month lobbying campaign by the White House and gun control advocates failed to save the bill from defeat,[5] thus for now setting aside immediate fears that expanded background checks would lead to a national gun registry.[6] It was also noted that rejection of Obama's gun control effort robbed Democrats of a wedge issue in the 2014 midterm elections.[7]

Obama had also suggested that Congress reinstate and strengthen the expired ban on assault weapons that was in place from 1994 to 2004 and limit ammunition magazines to ten rounds. Democrats pushed for both in response to the December 2012 mass shooting of twenty children and six staff at the Sandy Hook Elementary School in Newtown, Connecticut. Republicans and four Democrats countered that taking either step "would curtail the Second Amendment right to bear arms. They also argued that prohibiting the weapons would do little because assault weapons account for a small portion of gun crimes," the Associated Press reported.[8] In an expected defeat, the amendments to the 2013 gun control bill failed to gain enough votes on April 17.

In a Rose Garden presser following the defeat of his gun control efforts, a reported "visibly angry" Obama roared at the bill's opponents, "Are they serious?" He continued, "All in all, this was a pretty shameful day for Washington."[9] In fact, the liberal commentary magazine *New Republic* noted the president's "flashes of anger" that the legislation had "failed to pass" revealed the "angriest Obama we've ever seen."[10]

While Democrats blamed the National Rifle Association (NRA) for the bill's failure, "the lobby is feeding into already deeply held opposition to gun regulations and a broader sense of anxiety . . . particularly given the president's past publicized remark about 'bitter' rural voters who 'cling to their guns and religion,'" Josh Kraushaar observed at the *National Journal*.[11] Obama warned gun rights proponents, "I see this as just Round One . . . If this Congress refuses to listen to the American people and pass commonsense gun legislation, then the real impact is going to have to come from the voters."[12]

Unspoken by all was the distinct possibility that the president might strike back with unilateral gun control actions. They were right.

EXECUTIVE ACTIONS

In fact, the White House had not bothered to wait for gun control legislation to pass. On January 25, 2013, Attorney General Eric Holder began steps to fulfill Obama's executive actions with three proposals to strengthen the National Instant Criminal Background Check System (NICS).[13]

The changes would allow local law-enforcement agencies to access the NICS gun-sale database maintained by the FBI. Although the Brady Handgun Violence Prevention Act required federal background checks for gun purchases, not every firearm sale is covered under the law. Currently, law-enforcement agencies "cannot perform a NICS check when transferring, returning or selling weapons that have been confiscated, seized or recovered. The new rules would change that, allowing officials to perform a background check on people who receive those weapons to ensure that they are permitted to own a gun," *The Hill* reported.[14]

The most controversial rule goes to the heart of what we will explore further in chapter 7 on the new surveillance regime. It "would authorize the FBI to retain records on denied firearms transactions in a separate database for longer than 10 years." The last proposal is "especially irksome,"

A. W. R. Hawkins commented at Breitbart.com. It not only "increases the amount of time the government can hold on to information acquired through certain background checks," but it also "allows the creation of a de facto registry of people who have tried unsuccessfully to buy guns, and it's just common sense that this information could easily be misused."[15]

Add to this, Hawkins continued, the troubling fact that Holder "'[conceded] that the impact of [these measures] is unknown at this point,' i.e., they may not even work." In the end, he concluded, "these various gun control measures may simply be what we have all feared from the start—just another futile exercise in piling more restrictive regulations on law-abiding citizens."[16]

The following month, the NRA revealed a Department of Justice (DOJ) memorandum it had obtained that showed the Obama administration "believes its gun control plans won't work unless the government seizes firearms and requires national gun registration—ideas the White House has not proposed and does not support," the Associated Press reported.[17]

The nine-page document, produced under the name of one of the DOJ's leading crime researchers, "critiques the effectiveness of gun control proposals, including some of President Barack Obama's," the AP wrote. "The memo says requiring background checks for more gun purchases could help, but also could lead to more illicit weapons sales. It says banning assault weapons and high capacity ammunition magazines produced in the future but exempting those already owned by the public, as Obama has proposed, would have limited impact because people now own so many of those items." Also, the memorandum states that "even total elimination of assault weapons would have little overall effect on gun killings because assault weapons account for a limited propor-tion of those crimes." A DOJ official, naturally, "called the memo an unfinished review of gun violence research and said it does not represent administration policy."[18]

Only three days after the April 15, 2013, Boston Marathon terrorist bombing, Vice President Joe Biden held a conference call with gun control advocates.[19] It was unmistakable that the bombing played a significant role in the timing of his announcement. The "fight was not over and that even-tual action on gun control" would come, Biden declared. "Number one, the president is already lining up some additional executive actions he's going to be taking later this week." Other expected actions, he continued, included ways to tweak the background check system to expand the "list of prohibited purchasers" in order to increase the number of people denied the right to buy a firearm. Biden asserted that, in the long run, supporters of gun control would "win out over the NRA and its allies."[20]

To be perfectly clear, the bombers' identities—Tamerlan and Dzhokhar Tsarnaev—were not exposed until April 19, the day after Biden's conference call.[21] The young ethnic Chechen brothers, immigrants to the United States more than a decade ago and converts to Islam in recent years, had "expressed support for Jihad and al-Qaeda (although the full extent of their connections [was] not known)," professor William A. Jacobson noted on his blog *Legal Insurrection*.[22] The bomb blast that killed three and injured more than 280 bystanders was attributed to homemade improvised explosive devices (IEDs) similar to those illustrated on the Internet by al-Qaeda's *Inspire* magazine.[23] The perpetrators carried two pressure cookers filled with BB pellets and nails in backpacks and placed them near the marathon's finish line, where they were detonated.[24] At the time of Biden's conference call, these details were unknown. The use of any other weapons by the perpetrators—used in shootouts with law enforcement in the early hours of April 19, during which the older brother, Tamerlan, was killed, and later that day, after which the younger brother, Dzhokhar, was taken into police custody—had not yet occurred. The shooting death of Sean Collier, a police officer at the Massachusetts Institute of Technology, had also not taken place.

The bottom line is this: there was not yet any known connection between guns and the bombers when Biden seized the moment to hold his conference call with gun control supporters.

Regardless, on April 19, 2013, the White House made good on Biden's promise when one of Obama's twenty-three proposed executive actions was initiated. Department of Health and Human Services secretary Kathleen Sebelius announced a new "rulemaking process" as "part of President Obama's common sense plan to reduce gun violence." This action would "remove unnecessary legal barriers under the Health Insurance Portability and Accountability Act (HIPAA) Privacy Rule that may prevent states from reporting" to the NICS database "that houses information on individuals prohibited by law from possessing firearms." The

Government Accountability Office reported in 2012 that only seventeen states had submitted fewer than ten records of individuals "prohibited for mental health reasons." The public was invited to provide "input on how HIPAA may prevent some states from reporting to the NICS and ways in which these barriers can be addressed without discouraging individuals from seeking mental health services." The NICS, which we discussed earlier, "does not contain medical or mental health records."[25]

Days later, on April 22, another executive action surfaced in the form of a regulatory maneuver. The DOJ's Bureau of Alcohol, Tobacco, Firearms, and Explosives (ATF) announced a rule change regarding the United States Munitions Import List (USML) of the International Traffic in Arms Regulations (ITAR) that shifted statutory control for "defense articles or defense services for purposes of export and temporary import" and to clarify the same. Items previously controlled by the secretary of state would receive the new designation USMIL to distinguish them from the USML, and said items would now come under the control of the attorney general.[26]

"Among the speculations of what this could enable are concerns that importing and International Traffic in Arms Regulations may go forward to reflect key elements within the United Nations Arms Trade Treaty," David Codrea wrote for the *Examiner*. "The clarification in deference to the Attorney General on ITAR matters makes fair the question of why Eric Holder, then-Secretary of State Hillary Clinton, the Department of Justice Office of Inspector General and Congressional overseers were conspicuously disinterested when export violations were pointed out as matters for Fast and Furious investigators to concern themselves with."[27]

Well-known survivalist blogger James Wesley Rawles expressed deep concern for what this might mean. "Depending on how it is implemented, the implications of this change could be huge," he wrote. "With the stroke of a pen *and without the consent of Congress*, ATF bureaucrats could make **ANY** gun part or accessory (including magazines) or ammunition that were originally manufactured or perhaps even those *designed* for military use **no longer legal for importation for civilian use**. That might mean **no more milsurp parts sets. No more milsurp magazines. No more milsurp ammo. No more milsurp optics. Perhaps not even spare firing pins**." Rawles continued: "This could be ugly . . . Once an import ban is implemented, prices will skyrocket. Importation of Chinese military guns and ammunition was banned during the Clinton Administration, but importers quickly worked around that, by tapping other sources. But imagine if *all* of the channels for military surplus are cut off," he said.[28]

Obama also suggested in January that Congress could increase criminal penalties on "straw purchasers" who pass required background checks to buy a gun on behalf of someone else.[29] We discuss "straw purchasers" and "Fast and Furious" later in this chapter.

OBAMA'S SWEEPING ANTIGUN TEMPLATE

"Assault weapons are not for hunting. They are the weapons of choice for gang-bangers, drug dealers and terrorists," congressional candidate Barack Obama asserted in May 2004. Obama supported renewal of the ten-year trial ban on assault weapons due to expire September 13. The 1994 law had "banned military- and pistol-grip style, rapid-fire weapons, including nineteen models by name, like semi-automatic Uzis and TEC-9 pistols."[30]

In August 2004, an official of the Illinois State Rifle Association described Obama as "about as liberal as you can get" on the question of gun ownership.[31] Republican Alan Keyes, Obama's opponent for the Illinois seat in the US Senate, had stronger words. "His record is the record of a hard-line, academic, Marxist socialist, who wants a government takeover of health care, who voted for infanticide because of his position on taking innocent human life and so forth," Keyes said. Another example, he said, was Obama's "support for gun-control measures, adding that 'confiscation of firearms was one of the elements of the Marxist agenda.'"[32]

Quite possibly Keyes knew the details of the far-leftist federal gun control legislation Obama unveiled in December 1999 when he was running for the US House of Representatives against former Black Panther Bobby Rush.

Obama's sweeping antigun plan called for an increase to the penalties on "gun runners" who were "flooding Chicago's streets with illegal weapons"; an increase to the existing ten-year penalty in prison for the interstate transportation of firearms; making it "a felony for a gun owner whose firearm was stolen from his residence which causes harm to another person if that weapon was not securely stored in that home"; "restricting gun purchases to one weapon a month and banning the sale of firearms at gun shows except for 'antique' weapons"; banning police agencies from reselling their used weapons even if the funds were "used to buy more state-of-the-art weapons for their agencies"; restricting gun purchase or ownership to only those over twenty-one who passed a basic course; restricting federally licensed gun dealers to only selling firearms "in a storefront and not from their homes while banning their business from being within five miles of a school or a park"; banning the "sale of 'junk' handguns like the popular Saturday Night Specials"; and requiring all people who work at a gun dealer to undergo a criminal background check.[33]

Should all these measures not have been sufficient to kill gun sales and ownership, Obama incredulously asked that "gun manufacturers be required to develop safety measures that permit only the original owner of the firearm to operate the weapon purchased."[34]

When Obama proposed it, this recommendation most likely seemed like something drawn from the late 1960s television show *Mission Impossible* or a James Bond movie. However, in late April 2013, CNN's Logan Whiteside reported that "'smart guns' could be next step in gun control." The New Jersey Institute of Technology has been working for more than a decade creating so-called personalized "smart guns" with sensors that can "recognize a watch, a ring or even just a grip" of its purchaser. The company Armatix uses RFID (radio frequency identification) technology in its guns, which require a watch and PIN (personal ID number) to unlock and access. "If someone who isn't wearing the watch grabs the gun, it immediately deactivates," Whiteside said. "Anybody who picks up the handgun, whether it's a child or it's actively stolen, they can't activate the watch," Belinda Padilla, president and CEO of Armatix, told CNN. Another company, TriggerSmart, also uses RFID "to enable—and disable—guns," Whiteside added. "The chip that activates the gun can be placed in a ring, bracelet or potentially even embedded in the owner's hand."[35]

Also in 1999, Obama—without any further explanation—said he wanted increased funds for schools "to teach anger management skills for youth between the ages of 5–13."[36] Although we could not identify any particular program Obama had in mind, we did locate a possible connection. The Goals 2000: Educate America Act, signed into law in March

1994 by President Bill Clinton, specifically called for "training school personnel in programs of demonstrated effectiveness in addressing violence, including violence prevention, conflict resolution, anger management, peer mediation, and identification of high-risk youth."[37]

The intended end products had to be part of a lofty-minded, crony-centric boondoggle. For example, we found that Title VI of the act was to "help local school systems achieve Goal Six of the National Education Goals, which provides that by the year 2000, every school in America will be free of drugs and violence and will offer a disciplined environment conducive to learning, by ensuring that all schools are safe and free of violence." In order to get grant funds, schools first had to prove they were violent and drug ridden.[38] Honestly?

Ironically, in a 1995 speech to the Woman's National Democratic Club, Eric Holder, then serving as U.S. attorney for the District of Columbia, called for a public campaign to "really brainwash people into thinking about guns in a vastly different way."[39]

Obama also sought to increase federal taxes on firearms and ammunition by 500 percent. Most likely this was in reference to Federal Firearms Licenses, as there is no federal tax on the purchase of firearms or ammunition. An FFL, required for a gun dealer—including pawnbrokers, gunsmiths, and importers and manufacturers of firearms and/or ammunition or individuals or companies engaged in the interstate and intrastate sale of firearms—has been required within the United States since the enactment of the Gun Control Act of 1968.[40] The act, by the way, requires that records are kept regarding the acquisition, possession, and disposition of all firearms. Crime bills dating from 1984, 1988, and 1994 further amended the act and subsequent amendments that affect the interstate transportation of firearms, leaving the majority of gun control to state and local jurisdictions.[41]

Obama's ultraradical gun control agenda should come as no surprise. From 1994 to 2002, he served on the board of directors for the Joyce Foundation. The foundation's Gun Violence Prevention Program "seeks to drive small gun dealerships out of business by placing the firearms industry completely under consumer-product health-and-safety oversight," Discover the Networks (DTN) reports. The foundation conflates "astronomically high gun-death rates of inner-city gang members and the very low rates among the rest of the American population" to depict gun violence as a "national epidemic," DTN adds.[42] Shortly, we will reveal how Obama may have gone much farther in his attempt to concoct fraudulent statistics—so far that a US border agent is now dead possibly as a result.

OBAMA'S "GUN-GRABBING CZAR"

No discussion of gun control would be complete without a brief essay on the influential Cass Sunstein, Obama's longtime ally since their days together at the University of Chicago. Sunstein was dubbed Obama's "Gun-Grabbing Czar," someone who "couldn't care less about America's rights," on September 9, 2009, by radio talk-show host Michael Savage.[43] There is more than sufficient evidence that Savage was right on the money.

Sunstein served as Obama's regulatory czar—officially as administrator of the Office of Information and Regulatory Affairs—from September 2009 to August 21, 2012, when he resigned to return to teaching at Harvard University.

We beg your indulgence as we offer the convoluted thinking of a left-wing Harvard constitutional law professor on the topic of the Second Amendment and gun control. It will, we warn you, sound as if Sunstein's explanations and excuses are coming from several sources—and not just the one, him.

During a lecture at the University of Chicago on October 27, 2007, Sunstein called the Second Amendment the "Constitution's 'Most Mysterious Right.'"[44] He argued that "as a matter of history, the Second Amendment probably does not create an individual right, because it was designed to protect state militias." He emphatically stated that you do not have a right to own firearms. "It is striking and noteworthy," said Sunstein, "that well over two centuries since the founding, the Supreme Court has never suggested that the Second Amendment protects an individual right to have guns"—and the right to self-defense is not found in the Constitution. Sunstein also suggested that the individual right to bear arms as guaranteed in the Second Amendment would be repealed by the Supreme Court in three or four years' time.[45]

In a June 2008 interview with *Time* magazine, Sunstein said, "Obama has always expressed a belief that the Second Amendment guarantees a private right to bear arms."[46] All well and good—but what did "regulatory czar" Sunstein himself have to say on the issue? We turn to several conservative journalists who, in September 2009, explored the Sunstein positions (plural) on the individual right to bear arms.

"He's not known for being a supporter of the Second Amendment, which is the right to keep and bear arms, and that disturbs ranchers who want to protect their cattle, those who are interested to have a gun on hand to protect their family, and those who are hunters," wrote the *Examiner's* Elizabeth Delaney.[47] "In his 2005 book *Radicals in Robes: Why Extreme Right-Wing Courts are Wrong for America*, [Sunstein] writes, '[A]lmost all gun control legislation is constitutionally fine. And if the Court is right, then fundamentalism does not justify the view that the Second Amendment protects an individual right to bear arms,'" Karole Dolen-Proffit, also writing for the *Examiner*, added.[48] Constitutional law professor Ellis Washington stated at *WorldNetDaily*: "For example, here is [sic] Sunstein views on the Second Amendment right to bear arms: 'My coming view is that the individual right to bear arms reflects the success of an extremely aggressive and resourceful social movement and has much less to do with good standard legal arguments than [it] appears.'"[49]

The *Examiner's* Dave Workman pointed out the confusion about Sunstein's Second Amendment views: Sunstein "sent a letter to Sen. Saxby Chambliss of Georgia in July [2009] that stated, 'I strongly believe that the Second Amendment creates an individual right to possess and use guns for purposes of both hunting and self-defense,' and then adds, 'If confirmed, I would respect the Second Amendment and the individual right that it recognizes.'"[50]

"Well, which is it?" Workman asked. "Does the Second Amendment 'create' an individual right, or 'recognize' it? . . . In an opinion piece Sunstein authored for the *Boston Globe* on June 27, 2008, he wrote, 'For the first time in the nation's history, the US Supreme Court has ruled that the Second Amendment creates an individual right to possess guns for nonmilitary purposes.'" Workman continues (and you can almost see him rolling his eyes as his arms shoot upward in exasperation), "There he goes with that 'creation' thing again, and he clearly misrepresents what the high court ruling stated."

Workman exposed Sunstein's confusion further: "Later in the same piece, Sunstein observed, 'To be sure, everyone should agree that the Second Amendment creates some kind of individual right. But what kind? The text is unclear: 'A well-regulated Militia, being necessary to the security of a free State, the right of the people to keep and bear Arms shall not be infringed.''

"I don't know, Cass," Workman sneered (you can hear the sarcasm flowing from his keyboard). "That seems pretty clear to me, and a lot of other people. And you still don't get it about the Second Amendment."

And just in case anyone reading this is thinking Workman's next comment sounds vaguely familiar, it is. The rush to gun shops to load up on ammo and weapons did not start right after the senseless *Batman* movie theater shooting in Aurora, Colorado, or the horrific Sandy Hook school massacre in Connecticut in late 2012. "Americans voted for Obama last fall because they thought the country needed a change," Workman observed. "Yet in the aftermath, by rushing to gun shops and gun shows, they clearly demonstrated with their wallets that they don't think the country needs to abandon the Second Amendment."

Sunstein, of course, could not help himself and had to weigh in after the Sandy Hook shootings with a December 17, 2012, piece for *Bloomberg View*, for which he is a columnist. He claimed that the "rise of the Second Amendment as a serious obstacle to U.S. gun control legislation is astonishingly recent." He attributed the blame, of course, "to the skill, money and power of the contemporary gun-rights movement, which has not only exerted disproportionate influence on Congress, but also helped transform the landscape of constitutional argument." Sunstein asserted, "We should be able to have a serious national discussion uninhibited by wild and unsupportable claims about the meaning of the Constitution." In his mind, the Second Amendment is nothing more than an "ambiguous text."[51]

Keep in the back of your mind that Sunstein was Obama's close White House advisor for three years.

IMPEACHABLE—"FAST AND FURIOUS": AN IRON RIVER OF GUNS[52]

Project Gunrunner, the controversial government program that ran guns into Mexico under the Obama administration, contributed to fraudulent statistics seemingly targeting US gun owners.[53] The misleading data raised questions about the intentions of the ATF program, which some believe could be a defining scandal for the White House.

In February 2008, William Hoover, assistant director for field operations of the Bureau of Alcohol, Tobacco, Firearms, and Explosives, testified before Congress that "over 90 percent of the firearms that have either been recovered in, or intercepted in transport to Mexico, originated from various sources within the United States."[54] Hoover's statistics officially were released by the ATF and subsequently were cited in a flurry of news media pieces repeating the claim that the vast majority of illicit firearms in Mexico originate north of the border.

The US Government Accountability Office also used the ATF's 90 percent statistic in an official report to Congress about American firearms. The Justice Department even incorporated the data in several of its programs.

After a series of independent reports contradicted the ATF's claims, however, the bureau then admitted in November 2010 that its 90 percent figure cited to Congress "could be misleading" because it applied *only* to the small portion of guns verified through its eTrace system, an Internet-based firearm database around which Project Gunrunner was built.[55] The ATF admitted its statistics, collected as part of Project Gunrunner, were based on the guns it traced, all of which originated in the United States, thus skewing the data.[56]

Project Gunrunner started in 2005 as a pilot program out of the ATF's Laredo, Texas, office and was expanded nationwide in 2006. Founded under President George W. Bush, it was a bipartisan effort run by ATF in conjunction with the Justice Department and the FBI to "assist the Mexican Government in the implementation" of ATF's eTrace system.[57] In June 2007, ATF published a Project Gunrunner strategy document that proposed the expansion of the gun tracing into Mexico.[58] In June 2008, the House of Representatives passed the $1.6 billion Mérida Initiative, a "U.S. taxpayer-subsidized spending plan to help Mexico enforce its borders and get the gangs and drug smugglers under control." It authorized $73.5 million for ATF programs that targeted the smuggling of guns from the United States into Mexico.[59]

While the operation was run by a few dozen officers under Bush, it received another infusion of cash from the Obama administration. Tucked away inside the 2009 stimulus bill signed by Obama was $10 million in funding for the ATF's Project Gunrunner.[60] This is in addition to $11 million already provided to the program under Obama, and another $12 million more requested by the White House for the end of 2011.[61] Additionally, in September 2010, ATF reported it had used $37.5 million from an emergency supplemental appropriation for border security for its Gun Runner Impact Team (GRIT) initiative that deployed firearms trafficking groups to its Phoenix field office and "hubs" in Atlanta; Dallas and Brownsville, Texas; Las Vegas; Miami; Oklahoma City; and Sierra Vista, Arizona.[62]

Project Gunrunner was purportedly meant to stop the sale and export of US guns to Mexico by denying Mexican drug cartels firearms. However, the project resulted in allowing thousands of guns to cross into Mexico, where many of the weapons remain untraceable and in the hands of Mexican criminals. The same guns run into Mexico under the Project Gunrunner scheme reportedly were recovered from crime scenes in Arizona and throughout Mexico.[63]

One gun, reportedly recovered at the scene, is allegedly the weapon used to murder Border Patrol agent Brian Terry on December 14, 2010.[64] A November 2010 DOJ Office of the Inspector General report stated that ATF "did not effectively implement" Project Gunrunner, as it failed to share information ("collaboration") between ATF, US Immigration and Customs Enforcement (ICE), and the Mexican government.[65] Terry and his fellow agents probably "never had any idea of what they ultimately ran into," one observer noted.[66]

The entire project revolved around tracing the US guns that were allowed into Mexico using the eTrace system. According to ATF, eTrace technology was originally designed to trace firearms to their "legally purchased source" and to "allow law enforcement agencies to identify tracking patterns of criminal organizations smuggling firearms into Mexico."[67] ETrace does not electronically tag any of the guns; it simply serves as an online database that contains all registered information for each gun, including the personal information for all registered owners as well as whether law enforcement has information the gun was ever used in a crime. In essence, eTrace is a giant firearms monitoring database.[68] Once a gun enters the black market, the system cannot provide future information on a firearm unless the weapon is retrieved in a crime or once again enters into official registration.[69]

ETrace was thought to have been advantageous to Project Gunrunner because it could provide information on "straw purchases,"[70] meaning proxies who legally purchase a gun for a known criminal.

The ATF has repeatedly stated that its National Tracing Center eTrace system was not designed to collect statistics. Still, the agency used information it claimed to have garnered from Project Gunrunner to release what turned out to be highly misleading information about US guns.[71]

OBSTRUCTION OF JUSTICE, POSSIBLE PERJURY

Fast and Furious (F&F), launched in 2009 "ostensibly as a 'sting operation,'" was part of the program that "encouraged border-state dealers to sell thousands of guns to suspicious buyers, even after suspecting these buyers were working for Mexican drug cartels."[72] F&F came under scrutiny in 2011 with a public investigation headed by Sen. Charles Grassley (R-IO) and Rep. Darrell Issa (R-CA).[73]

Obama himself responded to the controversy in a March 29, 2011, interview with a Spanish-language television station in which he stated someone must take the fall. "There may be a situation here in which a serious mistake was made. If that's the case, then we'll find out and we'll hold someone accountable," he told Univision TV.[74]

Acting ATF director Kenneth Melson told Issa in an emergency meeting on July 4, 2011, that when he first learned about Border Agent Terry's murder and the F&F scheme, he was "sick to [his] stomach." Melson testified that, contrary to denials by the Justice Department, he "acknowledged the agents had in fact witnessed transfers of weapons from straw purchasers to third parties without following the guns any further."[75]

Melson also reportedly told Issa that those who ran the controversial project at the ATF had been reassigned, but that he couldn't tell Congress the reason for the reassignments. However, Melson stated that "Obama administration Justice Department officials directed him and other ATF officials to not communicate to Congress the reasoning behind the reassignments."[76]

Issa followed up with a letter accusing the Justice Department, headed by Eric Holder, of obstructing his investigation. "If his account is accurate, then ATF leadership appears to have been effectively muzzled while the DOJ sent over false denials and buried its head in the sand," Issa wrote. "That approach distorted the truth and obstructed our investigation."[77]

In his testimony before Issa's committee on May 3, 2011, under oath, Holder told the Judiciary Committee he had "probably" only heard about "Fast and Furious" in the "last few weeks." In July, after months of information gathering, Issa told CNSNews.com he was "convinced—'absolutely'— that Holder knew about the operation earlier than he claimed."[78]

It is also important to keep in mind that Project Gunrunner had been in operation since 2005. It is highly unlikely that outgoing attorney general Michael Mukasey, who had served in that position since November 2007, after Alberto Gonzales resigned, would not have briefed Holder about it and any other ongoing projects.

Additionally, Project Gunrunner was not a secret initiative. The *Washington Times* reported in March 2008: "During the past two years, more than 125 ATF agents and investigators have been deployed along the southwest border in Project Gunrunner to increase 'strategic coverage' of the region and disrupt firearms-trafficking corridors." In fact, Mukasey reportedly had said during a recent "State of the Border" briefing "that the ability to control 'who and what comes into and out of a country is one of the most important attributes of a sovereign government, and being able to do that is vital to our nation's security.'"[79]

And it gets even worse. You have to wonder, by the way, if it was Mexico that inspired Holder's Justice Department to launch Fast and Furious.

The Associated Press reported February 27, 2009: "Mexico blames Americans for arming the world's most powerful drug cartels, a complaint supported . . . by a U.S. government report that found nearly all of Mexico's escalating drug killings involved weapons from north of the border." Mexican president Felipe Calderón told the AP that his "police and soldiers [were] dangerously outgunned because U.S. authorities [were] failing to stop the smuggling of high-powered weapons into Mexico." Mexico's attorney general Eduardo Medina Mora "called for more aggressive prosecutions of gun smugglers, saying that the U.S. constitutional right to bear arms doesn't protect them. The Second Amendment was not put there to arm foreign criminal groups."[80]

Now here's a very disturbing issue (keep in mind this was in February 2009): Holder promised Mexico's attorney general he would "enforce a long-ignored ban on importing assault weapons, many of which are re-sold illegally and smuggled into Mexico to resupply the cartels."[81]

As for Fast and Furious, that started under Obama's and Holder's watch. Holder's by-now obviously dishonest testimony to Issa's committee was exposed in July 2011 when Andrew Breitbart's BigGovernment.com discovered a transcript of an April 2, 2009, speech on the Department of Justice's own website in which Holder boasted about "Project Gunrunner."[82]

Speaking at the Mexico/United States Arms Trafficking Conference in Cuernavaca, Mexico, Holder said, "Last week, our administration launched a major new effort to break the backs of the cartels. My department is committing 100 new ATF personnel to the Southwest border in the next 100 days to supplement our ongoing Project Gunrunner, DEA is adding 16 new positions on the border, as well as mobile enforcement teams, and the FBI is creating a new intelligence group focusing on kidnapping and extortion. DHS is making similar commitments, as Secretary Napolitano will detail."[83]

Holder's lie was exposed again in October 2012, when Fox News reported he had been "identified in documents to be aware of Fast and Furious not once but twice in 2010. One document was posted October 18, 2010, and the other was from July 2010."[84] Further damage to Holder's credibility was added in late January 2012 when a Friday night document dump revealed that Holder was aware of Fast and Furious on December 15, 2010, the date of Brian Terry's murder.[85]

It was only after Agent Terry's murder, however, that four ATF agents came forward after learning that the weapon that killed Terry "was a 'walked' weapon." Among them was John Dodson, who had worked as part of ATF Phoenix Gunrunning Group VII, "the group assigned to carry out the bulk" of F&F, and who blew the whistle and exposed the scandal.[86] "What people don't understand is how long we will be dealing with this," Dodson told Fox News in March 2011. "Those guns are gone. You can't just give the order and get them back. There is no telling how many crimes will be committed before we retrieve them." Meanwhile, an outraged Gil Guignat commented in the *Tea Party Tribune* that while Brian Terry was "killed by well-armed drug runners," he was only armed with a rubber bullet gun—Homeland Security's Janet Napolitano's "genius move," he added.[87]

Additionally, by June 2011, news of more Fast and Furious casualties had begun to roll in. Mexican officials estimated 150 of their people had been shot by F&F guns. Police "recovered roughly 700 guns at crime scenes, 250 in the U.S. and the rest in Mexico, including five AK-47s found at a cartel warehouse in Juarez . . . A high-powered sniper rifle was used to shoot down a Mexican military helicopter. Two other Romanian-made AK-47s were found in a shoot-out that left 11 dead in the state of Jalisco." Had eTrace worked? Well, the "guns were traced to the Lone Wolf Gun Store in Glendale, Ariz., and were sold only after the store employees were told to do so by the ATF."[88]

And it's no wonder people died. "ATF's own documents show it allowed just 15 men to buy 1,725 guns, and 1,318 of those were after the purchasers officially became targets of investigation." Additionally, Arizona gun store owners reported "they were explicitly told by the ATF to sell the guns, sometimes 20, 30, even up to 40 in a single day to [a] single person."[89]

But there were more guns out there that were not traced. Issa and Grassley's investigation revealed that ATF "knowingly allowed as many as 2,500 firearms to be sold illegally to known or suspected straw purchasers. One of those purchasers accounted for over 700 illegal guns." ATF agents were ordered "not to arrest illegal gun buyers or to interdict thousands of guns that were allowed to 'walk' into criminal hands." The operation was carried out with the full knowledge of senior ATF officials, who were briefed regularly and "approved of the tactics employed."[90]

GUN CONTROL MADNESS, COVER-UP

Fast and Furious was really about gun control. In December 2011, CBS News' Sharyl Attkisson reported that documents showed ATF had "discussed using their covert operation 'Fast and Furious' to argue for controversial new rules about gun sales." Whistle-blowers told CBS that ATF "secretly encouraged gun dealers to sell to suspected traffickers for Mexican drug cartels to go after the 'big fish'" by putting thousands of weapons on the street.[91]

The September 2010 DOJ Inspector General report revealed that "little fish" were not of much interest to the DOJ. The report stated: "For example, we found that 70 percent of Project Gunrunner cases are single-defendant cases, and some ATF managers discourage field personnel from conducting the types of complex conspiracy investigations that target higher-level members of trafficking rings. Federal prosecutors told us that directing the efforts of Project Gunrunner toward building larger, multi-defendant conspiracy cases would better disrupt trafficking organizations."[92]

CBS also reported that ATF officials "didn't intend to publicly disclose their own role in letting Mexican cartels obtain the weapons, but emails show they discussed using the sales, including sales encouraged by ATF, to justify a new gun regulation called 'Demand Letter 3', . . . so named because it would be the third ATF program demanding gun dealers report tracing information." Demand Letter 3 would require some US gun shops "to report the sale of multiple rifles or 'long guns.'"[93]

The CBS report continued: "Several gun dealers who cooperated with ATF told CBS News and Congressional investigators they only went through with suspicious sales because ATF asked them to. . . . Sometimes it was against the gun dealer's own best judgment. . . . 'It's like ATF created or added to the problem so they could be the solution to it and pat themselves on the back,' [said] one law enforcement source familiar with the facts. 'It's a circular way of thinking.'"[94]

Did the Obama administration ever fess up? Hardly. In September 2012, President Obama attempted to cover his tracks as well. During a reelection interview with Univision, Obama faced the studio cameras and lied to the listening audience: "I think it's important for us to understand that the Fast and Furious program was a field-initiated program begun under the previous administration. When Eric Holder found out about it, he discontinued it. We assigned [an] inspector general to do a thorough report that was just issued, confirming that in fact Eric Holder did not know about this, that he took prompt action and the people who did initiate this were held accountable."[95]

Hold on to that thought. Obama's so-called executive privilege will expire with his second term in office—there'll be no more opportunities to kick the can down the road. Clearly, the issue can also come to the forefront in the form of impeachment hearings based on this chapter.

DHS STOCKPILING BULLETS

Since spring 2012 there have been disturbing reports that the Department of Homeland Security is stockpiling massive amounts of ammunition, assault weapons, and even thousands of armored vehicles, fueling all sorts of conspiracies, not to mention the possibility DHS could use armed surveillance drones to assassinate US citizens in the future. Add to this the fevered claims after the horrific December 2012 school massacre in Newtown, Connecticut, that the federal government is preparing to violate every American's Second Amendment right to gun ownership and confiscate their weapons.[96]

Similar fears were stoked in eighteenth-century America by a despotic king on a faraway shore who refused to recognize the rights of the American colonists, resulting in our Declaration of Independence and the US Constitution. Many Americans today fear the despotic ruler in the White House who is seemingly hell-bent on eliminating those rights one by one. Where a former despot was dismissed by his colonial subjects, who formed their own separate nation, the current despot can be impeached and removed from office by America's citizens.

Alarm bells sounded in March 2012 for vigilant watchers already convinced DHS was up to no good. Defense contractor ATK was awarded a one-year contract, with four option years, to supply DHS with a maximum of 450 million rounds of .40-caliber bullets.[97] ATK was already under an open-ended contract to supply Immigration and Customs Enforcement, a DHS agency, with rounds of its HST bullet, distinctive for its ability to hold its jacket after passing through barriers. According to an ATK press release, the HST is "designed for 100 percent weight retention, limits collateral damage, and avoids over penetration."[98]

Why did DHS need 450 million rounds of this ammunition? No one purchases expensive hollow-point bullets for target practice. Practice ammo is purposely cheaper and normally it's FMJ (full-metal jacket) ammo, meaning it has a solid tip. Second, besides the cost, hollow-point bullets are "designed to shred internal organs upon impact." No other ammo beats that kind of stopping power.[99]

This controversy was confusing for people who knew nothing about how complicated the government contracting process is. Add to this the fact that DHS is a domestic agency and does not fight wars anywhere at any time. Its sole mission is to ensure the safety of the American people on American soil.[100]

So, why would DHS need so many rounds of antipersonnel ammo? Many came to the conclusion DHS was buying up 450 million rounds of hollow-point ammo to use in a war to be waged against Americans.

Just when it seemed the issue had died down, it flared up again in early August 2012, when it was erroneously reported that 46,000 rounds of .40 Smith & Wesson jacketed hollow-point (JHP) bullets for semiautomatic pistols had been ordered for delivery to the National Weather Service, a branch of the National Oceanic and Atmospheric Administration. However, a "clerical error" was discovered. The solicitation was actually intended for the National Marine Fisheries Service Office of Law Enforcement offices in Maine, Massachusetts, and Florida. Both agencies belong to the Department of Commerce, not DHS.[101]

Once explained, the whole bulk ammunition purchase issue could have settled down had it not been inflamed by word of two more solicitations. The Social Security Administration (SSA) requested 174,000 .357 Duty Carry Sig JHP bullets for its law-enforcement arm. The ammunition was to be shipped within sixty days of purchase to forty-one major Social Security offices, as well as to the administration's headquarters in Baltimore, Maryland.[102]

Had the Social Security Administration's bulk purchase not come within months of a "surprise" "random training operation" by DHS's Federal Protective Service (FPS) officers at the local SSA office in downtown Leesburg, Florida, it might have passed without notice. Visitors to the office encountered a string of blue and white SUVs encircling the building and at least one FPS official with a semiautomatic rifle posted at the door to randomly check identifications. Other officers, some with K-9 dogs, "sifted through the building."[103]

FPS launched Operation Shield, as it is called, in December 2010 to "measure the effectiveness of its countermeasures and related efforts" with unannounced inspections to evaluate the effectiveness of contract public security officers in "detecting the presence of unauthorized persons or potentially disruptive or dangerous activities in or around federal facilities," FPS director Leonard E. Patterson told a House committee in July 2011.

Operation Shield had recently been "expanded . . . to include exercises that blanket a federal facility with a significantly increased law enforcement presence," he said.[104]

This sounded the martial law alarm because within hours of the operation, the State Department announced the creation of the Bureau of Counterterrorism to coordinate US entities, such as DHS, with foreign governments to "develop civilian counterterrorism strategies and operations." Ambassador-at-Large Daniel Benjamin told reporters, "The bureau will lead in supporting U.S. counterterrorism diplomacy and seek to strengthen homeland security, countering violent extremism, and build the capacity of partner nations to deal effectively with terrorism."[105] (Benjamin described the bureau as the "next stage of implementation" of Secretary Hillary Clinton's Quadrennial Diplomacy and Development Review concluded in December 2010.[106])

The bureau's upgrade was clearly politically motivated based on Obama's "foreign policy success" in killing Osama bin Laden while he "also faced criticism over a quick withdrawal from Iraq, increasing aggression from Iran, and for negotiating with the Taliban in Afghanistan and Pakistan."[107] Perhaps the Leesburg operation was an easy target (the possible "terrorists" were mostly senior citizens, after all) and a photo op for the cameras and the international press. We could find no similar reports of FPS inspections conducted at any time at any other Social Security office. What the FPS training operation did manage to do was to feed feelings of anxiety for those already concerned with DHS's increasing intrusion into every corner of American life.

To its credit, the Social Security Administration promptly addressed the August purchase, letting the public know it had a reasonable explanation as to why it needed the ammunition. The administration explained it has 295 special agents working in sixty-six offices across the United States who have full law-enforcement authority, including issuing search warrants and making arrests, and that its investigators operate much like state or local police officers.[108] Simple math breaks the purchase down to approximately 600 rounds per special agent, or more than 2,600 rounds per Social Security office.

A second large purchase was made by DHS on behalf of its Federal Law Enforcement Training Center (FLETC) in Glynco, Georgia. The order was for the astounding number of 750 million rounds of various calibers. Delivery was to be made in thousand-round increments over a five-year period.[109] In early 2013, two more federal notices issued on DHS's behalf called for two additional purchases totaling 600,000 rounds (240,000 rounds in February and 360,000 in March) of training ammunition (.40 and 9mm JHP bullets for pistols) to be shipped to the FLETC facility in Artesia, New Mexico, setting off more speculation as to what DHS was up to.[110]

Sometimes the obvious explanation is the correct one, yet DHS did not bother to allay anyone's concerns. Had it explained the size and scope of FLETC's operations, the initial solicitation for 750 million rounds would not have sounded so threatening and all would have been well. But DHS did not—and it was not.

What DHS should have explained is that its Glynco, Georgia, facility is a residential interagency law-enforcement training organization for ninety-one federal agencies, providing training services for state, local, tribal, and international law-enforcement agencies. FLETC operates two other residential training locations, one in New Mexico, the other in South Carolina, as well as a nonresidential in-service requalification and advanced training facility in Maryland, outside of Washington, DC. Plus, the Georgia center has oversight and program management responsibilities at the State Department's International Law Enforcement Academies in Botswana and Thailand and supports training at ILEAs in Hungary and El Salvador.[111]

The general public did not know any of this, and naturally speculation ran rampant. People started to uptick the amount of ammo DHS had purchased. It was estimated that in the six months prior to September, DHS had solicited 1.4 billion rounds of ammunition: 450 million rounds of .40 hollow point, 200 million rounds of .223 rifle ammunition, and 176,000 rounds of .308 168-grain hollow-point boat tail (HPBT), ammo used almost exclusively for sniper rifles.[112]

In February 2013, DHS finally explained that bulk purchasing is cheaper. "Federal solicitations to buy the bullets are known as 'strategic sourcing contracts,' which help the government get a low price for a big purchase," Peggy Dixon, spokeswoman for the FLETC in Georgia, said. The training centers reportedly "use as many as 15 million rounds every year, mostly on shooting ranges and in training exercises," with more than

70,000 agents and officers using FLETC for firearms training in 2012, she stated. The remaining rounds "would be purchased by Immigration and Customs Enforcement, the federal government's second largest criminal investigative agency," Dixon said.[113]

This explanation for the large ammo purchases was confirmed by Larry Keane, senior vice president of the National Shooting Sports Foundation. It all comes down to the normal functioning of how the federal government does its purchasing, he said. "Because rumors are usually based on a kernel of truth that is misconstrued, exaggerated and then propagated, let's be very clear: *There is nothing out of the ordinary going on,*" Keane stated. "U.S. government procurement practices are baffling to begin with, as any federal contractor will tell you," he continued. "So, when [the] complex purchasing process is combined with an eye-popping number of up to 450 million rounds of .40 caliber to be purchased over five years by the Department of Homeland Security for its array of agencies, added to lesser amounts sought by smaller agencies with law enforcement responsibilities, it seems to some that something nefarious must be brewing."[114]

It also comes down, again, to basic math. Keane explained: "Our members confirm what we are seeing is the normal functioning of the Feds' procurement apparatus. When you do the math in the case of the DHS purchase, even the maximum purchase would add up to less than 1,400 [rounds] per year for all 65,000 DHS law enforcement personnel."[115]

Finally, near the end of March 2013, several Congressmen demanded an explanation from DHS about its ammunition purchases.[116] In November, Sen. Tom Coburn (R-OK), well known for his history of being against wasteful government spending, had asked for a similar answer. DHS responded to Coburn with information that indicated ammunition purchases had been going down, not increasing. Total ammunition purchased by DHS in fiscal year 2010 was more than 148 million rounds; in 2011 the number dropped to around 109 million rounds; and in 2012 the total purchased was around 103 million rounds. As of November 20, 2012, shortly after fiscal year 2013 began, the DHS component agencies (FLETC, the Federal Protective Service, Immigration and Customs Enforcement, Customs and Border Protection, Transportation Security Administration, and the Coast Guard) had an inventory of nearly 264 million rounds on hand.[117]

Doing the math, it is easy to calculate that this is more than the amount purchased in the previous two years. There is, of course, nothing wrong with maintaining an ammunition stockpile. At the beginning of fiscal year 2010, which began at the end of October 2009, there was also most likely a sizable inventory on hand. However, at the end of the three fiscal years, after more than 361.5 million rounds were purchased, the nearly 264 million rounds on hand (more than 73 percent) shows less than a third of those purchased were used for training or component agencies' mission.[118]

As DHS claims it does not "maintain ammunition, but uses it," conservative blogger Tim Brown, who ran the numbers on DHS's purchases, wrote, "The numbers say something different." He continued: "There is one question that stands out to me above others. Since DHS has nearly 264 million rounds on hand, why do they need to purchase ammunition at all for at least two years? After all, in 2012, they only purchased a little over 103 million rounds."[119]

Math could not explain information uncovered at the end of January 2013. Six months earlier, DHS had purchased up to 7,000 5.56x45mm North Atlantic Treaty Organization (NATO) assault rifles with "select fire" (both automatic and semiautomatic firing capabilities)—which DHS referred to in its solicitation as "suitable for personal use in close quarters and/or when maximum concealment is required."[120] The rifles were to come equipped with high-capacity thirty-round magazines, the same type antigun supporters want banned for civilian use. The 5.56x45mm NATO round is the civilian equivalent of the 200 million rounds of .223-caliber rifle ammunition DHS ordered in 2012.[121] Note that DHS made its solicitation on behalf of itself "and its components." We do not know which of its agencies received the assault weapons.

In March 2013, it was learned that not only had DHS solicited for original SIG Sauer replacement parts for duty-use SIG Sauer firearms, a contract said to be worth in excess of $4.5 million over the next five years, but also that the solicitation was nearly identical to a sole-source one issued the same week to Heckler & Koch for its H&K replacement parts.[122] The deal calls for each company to receive five equal payments of $900,000 per year—meaning ICE would receive $900,000 worth of replacement parts per year from each company, with all parts delivered to ICE. In

April 2012, DHS also purchased from H&K one hundred submachine guns with RFID installed, one hundred Picatinny 1913-style mounts for installation of optics on top of the receivers, and three hundred thirty-round detachable magazines, all to be shipped to ICE.[123]

DHS has also failed to explain its rollout in May 2012 of more than 2,700 retrofitted mine-resistant, ambush-protected (MRAP) vehicles—the vehicle of choice for fighting the counterinsurgency war in Iraq—for "service" on American streets. First reported by Ken Jorgustin at the *Modern Survival* blog, Navistar Defense, which makes an 18.9-ton MRAP for the federal government, builds its version "to withstand ballistic arms fire, mine blasts, IEDs, and other emerging threats. Its V-shaped hull helps deflect blasts out and away from the crew and its armoring can be customized to meet any mission requirement."[124]

"Why would DHS need such over-the-top vehicles on U.S. streets to withstand IEDs and mine blasts?" Jorgustin asked. "More to the point; why isn't anyone in Congress asking?"[125]

Rick Moran, blog editor at the conservative *American Thinker*, asked.[126] Perhaps it's high time that not only are these questions asked, but that some of these inquiries, particularly those related to Fast and Furious, are utilized during impeachment hearings.

DRY UP THE AMMO SUPPLY

You know a situation has reached critical mass when the politically correct *Wikipedia* allows an article about it to survive. In its opening salvo on the 2008 to 2013 shortage of civilian small arms ammunition, the article links to three significant pieces of information.[127] The first appeared weeks after President Obama's first inauguration. In March 2009, concerns surfaced that the Obama administration "could impose a new ban on some semiautomatic weapons." The Associated Press reported that, across the country, "worried gun owners [were driven] to stockpile ammunition and cartridge reloading components at such a rate that manufacturers [couldn't] meet demand." Why were they worried? Well, the month prior, Attorney General Holder had "suggested" the Obama administration favored "reinstituting a U.S. ban on the sale of assault weapons." The shortage, however, extended to all types of guns and ammunition.[128] This was confirmed in an April 2009 press release by Winchester Ammunition, which stated its ammo had been in "high demand" since fall 2008 and that production was running twenty-four hours a day, seven days a week.[129]

Additional confirmation appeared in November 2009, when Gannett Media's Ben Jones reported that gun sales had been up since Obama's election. Remarkably, Jones reported that in deeply progressive Madison, Wisconsin, background checks for handguns were running nearly 36 percent higher than in 2008, "suggesting a big increase in gun sales."[130]

It is significant that the *Wikipedia* article makes brief mention of shortages continuing into 2010 but that by September 2011, the "most scarce calibers" were once again available at retail stores and gun shops. Both claims are not sourced. As we explained earlier, the ammunition-shortage issue resurfaced with a vengeance in 2012 due to the massive purchases by DHS. Additionally, by mid-2012, economically priced ammunition was getting harder and harder to find, particularly because the US Army was the "main buyer of the lower-priced ammunition."[131]

Those concerns finally reached congressional ears. On April 25, 2013, Oklahoma Republicans Sen. James M. Inhofe and Rep. Frank Lucas introduced the Ammunition Management for More Obtainability (AMMO) Act of 2013.[132] Both bills were read and referred to committee.[133]

The legislation requires the Government Accountability Office (GAO) to "conduct a report on the purchasing of ammunition by federal agencies, except the Department of Defense, and its effect on the supply of ammunition available to the public." The act restricts agencies from "obtaining additional ammunition for a six-month period if current agency stockpiles are higher than its monthly averages prior to the Obama Administration," Senator Inhofe's press release stated.[134]

"President Obama has been adamant about curbing law-abiding Americans' access and opportunities to exercise their Second Amendment rights," Inhofe said in the release. "One way the Obama Administration is able to do this is by limiting what's available in the market with federal agencies purchasing unnecessary stockpiles of ammunition.

"As the public learned in a House committee hearing this week," Inhofe continued, the Department of Homeland Security has "two years' worth of ammo on hand and allots nearly 1,000 more rounds of ammunition for DHS officers than is used on average by our Army officers." The

AMMO Act of 2013, he asserted, "will enforce transparency and accountability of federal agencies' ammunition supply while also protecting law-abiding citizens' access to these resources."

"After hearing from my constituents about the shortage of ammunition in Oklahoma and the Department of Homeland Security's profligate purchases of ammunition," Lucas added, "we have introduced the AMMO Act of 2013 to curtail these purchases so Americans can exercise their Second Amendment rights without being encumbered by the federal government."

Lucas also said he was "surprised to find out the DHS has the right to buy up to 750 million rounds of ammunition over the next five years, while it already has two years' worth of ammo already. This is an issue that must be addressed, and I am pleased this legislation provides us the opportunity to do so."

In an April 25 hearing on the federal government's purchase of ammunition before the House Oversight and Government Reform Committee,[135] DHS chief procurement officer Nick Nayak "told lawmakers that the department buys about 100 million rounds per year and keeps about two years' worth of ammunition on hand." He explained DHS "keeps that much ammunition on hand because it is 'made specifically to our contract specifications' [and orders] can sometimes take months to come through."[136]

CBS News' Stephanie Condon claimed the legislation was inspired by the "conspiracy theory" that "the government is stockpiling ammunition as part of a gun control effort to create a shortage of bullets."[137] In his congressional testimony, Nayak asserted the claim that DHS was stockpiling ammunition was "simply not true."[138]

On May 5, Senator Inhofe told WABC talk radio show host Aaron Klein that he "believes open purchase orders from the Department of Homeland Security to buy over 1 billion rounds of ammunition are part of an 'intentional' effort by the Obama administration to 'dry up the market' for gun-owning citizens." According to WND's Drew Zahn, Inhofe told Klein, "We have in this country the Second Amendment that preserves the right to keep and bear arms, and the president doesn't believe in that."[139]

"President Obama has been doing everything he could to stop the private ownership of guns in America," Inhofe continued. "Yet he's been voted down in a big way by a large majority, and so my feeling is that he's doing this to buy up [ammunition] so honest, law-abiding citizens here in the United States, like my son, can't even buy ammunition because government is purchasing so much."[140]

"'I believe it's intentional,'" Inhofe told Klein regarding the "ammunition shortages many private and local law enforcement purchasers are experiencing . . . 'It's just another effort to restrict gun activity and ownership.'" He later added, "This has never happened in this country before. We've never had government trying to take that much control at the expense of law-abiding citizens. And we're not going to let it happen."[141]

3

FORGET CONGRESS!
BACKDOOR AMNESTY ALREADY HERE

What does President Barack Obama call a bill which has repeatedly failed in Congress? A law![1]

—Immigration expert Mark Krikorian

It will no longer use the term *illegal immigrant*, the AP announced April 2, 2013. They will now use the phrase "undocumented Democrat."[2]

—NBC Tonight Show host Jay Leno

ALL THIS TALK of future immigration reform ignores how President Obama has already overseen interagency departmental directives that have bypassed Congress and granted de facto amnesty for millions of illegal aliens. Since taking office, the president has illegally, willfully, and deliberately been derelict of his duties as the chief executive while consistently usurping the constitutional authority vested with Congress to regulate immigration. In particular, Article I, Section 8 of the United States Constitution gives Congress the power to "establish a uniform Rule of Naturalization." That clause has long been interpreted by

constitutional scholars to give Congress the power to establish immigra-
tion policy. While Article II, Section 3, states the president's role is to "take
Care that the Laws be faithfully executed," Obama's refusal to execute
Congress's immigration laws may therefore be an impeachable offense.

The Constitution states, in Article II, Section 4, that the president
"shall be removed from Office on Impeachment for . . . Treason, Bribery,
or other High Crimes and Misdemeanors." Do Obama's successive
"executive amnesties" and failure to protect America's borders against invasion by illegal immigrants, particularly criminal illegal immigrants—and
potentially terrorists—rise to the level of "high crimes and misdemeanors"?

"The deliberate failure to enforce valid immigration law and allow
hordes of foreigners to live and work in the U.S. is, arguably, 'treason,'
and doing so in an election year to appease Hispanic voters could certainly
be considered 'bribery,'" Michael Filozof, an adjunct professor of political
science at the State University of New York at Brockport, opined in
August 2012.[3] He was referring to the administrative amnesty declaration
issued June 15, 2012, and enacted two months later by Department of
Homeland Security officials—what we call the DREAM Act "Lite." We
discuss this in great detail in this chapter.

"The upshot of Obama's policy [is] not only to allow hundreds of
thousands of illegals to live and work in the U.S. during a time of 8 to
10% unemployment," Filozof continued, "but even worse, since the vast
number of illegals we're talking about are Hispanics eligible for affirmative-
action preferences, to actually get *preferential treatment* over native-born
Americans."[4] As we illustrate in the paragraphs that follow, the extent of
this preferential treatment is, simply put, mind-boggling.

"Obama has decided that he will not follow our immigration laws with
regards to people who would be eligible for the DREAM Act amnesty, a
law that never passed Congress," self-described "red meat" conservative
Daniel Horowitz, deputy political director of the Madison Project, wrote.
"If a president can disregard a law under the guise of 'executive discretion,'
what are the limits to presidential power?"[5]

When it comes to enforcing US immigration laws, the extent of
Obama's lawlessness is off the charts—unchecked by either Congress or
the American people. Speaking at the Freedom Center's February 2013
West Coast retreat, John Eastman added, "We've seen it in the DREAM

Act. The President has [used] his power not to prosecute."[6]

There is no precedent in American history for a president or any other federal official to be impeached for granting mass amnesty to criminals and lawbreakers—which is what illegal immigrants are—or handing them the keys to the kingdom at the same time. There is, however, a recent precedent on the global stage, which we will explain at the end of the next chapter. But first, let's take a look at the evidence for impeachment here in the United States.

AMNESTY TO ENSURE DEMOCRATIC RULE FOR THE LONG TERM

There is a running joke about the expiration date of Barack Obama's numerous promises. In fact, a little more than a year into his first term in office, Obama was caught reneging on his promise for comprehensive immigration reform. Jim Geraghty, writing in *National Review Online*, marked the expiration date of Obama's May 23, 2008, promise to get tough on border security with a "renewed focus on busting up gangs and traffickers" crossing the US-Mexican border, which Obama said started "at home, with comprehensive immigration reform." On March 17, 2010, the Obama administration abruptly broke that promise when it halted new work on the border's "virtual fence" after Department of Homeland Security secretary Janet Napolitano announced the diversion of "$50 million in planned economic stimulus funds for the project to other purposes."[7]

This was not the first time Obama promised immigration reform—nor is it the only time he has broken his word on the issue. During the June 3, 2007, Democratic primary debate at St. Anselm College in New Hampshire, Obama said, "We want to have a situation in which those who are already here, are playing by the rules, are willing to pay a fine and go through a rigorous process should have a pathway to legalization. . . . What [people] don't want is a situation in which there is a pathway to legalization and you've got another several hundred thousand of folks coming in every year."[8]

Two months later, speaking at the August 8, 2007, AFL-CIO Democratic primary forum, Obama modified his comments, not mentioning the probability that more illegal immigrants were busy crossing the border as he spoke. He disingenuously added that *we* have to make sure they are learning English and that *they* will have to "go to the back of the line so that they're not rewarded for having broken the law."[9]

During the December 4, 2007, Iowa-NPR radio debate, when asked what rights illegal immigrants would have come January 2009, should he be president, Obama promised a "crackdown" on people who hired illegals and stated that illegals "should not be able to work in this country." Obama also outlined his pathway to citizenship as a way to "earn a legal status." He again stated illegals would have to start to learn English—not actually have to speak or read English—adding again they would pay a "significant fine, and go to the back of the line." Most significantly, and perhaps what many people missed, he said they would not be deported from the United States. Illegals would then be able to demand a minimum wage, ensure that worker safety laws were available to protect them, and make sure they could join a union.[10] Obama was clearly dog-whistling to union leaders in particular that he was prepared to expand his party's membership with newly minted "citizens"—part of the fundamental transformation of America that Obama was offering.

This is precisely the sort of amnesty message Eliseo Medina, international secretary-treasurer of the Service Employees International Union (SEIU), openly delivered at the 2009 annual progressive conference organized by Campaign for America's Future.[11] Medina had been appointed in November 2008 by Obama to serve on his transition team committee for immigration.

The SEIU has generously backed every Obama political campaign since he first ran for the Illinois State Senate. In November 1995, the SEIU Local 880 Political Fund in Illinois contributed its first $250 to Friends of Obama.[12] SEIU 880, by the way, was then controlled by ACORN (the Association of Community Organizations for Reform Now), the disgraced-but-never-gone "community organization" with which Obama has been affiliated since his mid-1980s "community organizer" days in Chicago.[13] Obama received SEIU's endorsement for his 2004 run for the US Senate,[14] and again in February 2008, when the 1.9 million–member union endorsed his presidential candidacy.[15]

Speaking at the conference, Medina said of Latino voters, "[W]hen they voted in November [2008], they voted overwhelmingly for progressive candidates. Barack Obama got two out of every three voters that showed up."[16]

Medina continued:

So I think there's two things, very quickly, that matter for the progressive community.

Number one: If we are to expand this electorate to win, the progressive community needs to solidly be on the side of immigrants. Then we'll solidify and expand the progressive coalition for the future . . . When you are in the middle of a fight for your life, you will remember who was there with you. And immigrants count on progressives to be able to do that.

Number two: We reform the immigration laws; it puts 12 million people on the path to citizenship, and eventually voters. Can you imagine if we have, even the same ratio, two out of three? If we have eight million new voters that care about our issues and will be voting, we will be creating a governing coalition for the long term, not just for an election cycle.

Medina was boasting to a friendly audience that granting citizenship to millions of illegals would expand the *progressive* electorate and help ensure a *Democrat* governing coalition for the long term. In other words, for progressives, the issue of amnesty is not simply about so-called fairness applied to "undocumented workers." It's about stacking the electoral deck with millions of Democrat voters, changing the very tenure of the electorate. After the election, by the way, Obama rewarded the SEIU by putting Medina on his National Latino Advisory Council.[17]

Yet, comprehensive immigration legislation failed to emerge as anticipated by immigration reform groups, including left-wing organizations such as the Center for American Progress Action Fund, the Center for Community Change's FIRM (Fair Immigration Reform Movement), National Council of La Raza, and the Communist Party–affiliated National Lawyers Guild, all contributors to an immigration blueprint submitted to the Obama-Biden Transition Project in November 2008.[18] Obama's campaign promise to make it a priority during his first year in office to formulate a "plan to make legal status possible for an estimated 12 million illegal immigrants" just kept slipping into the background.[19]

As we have consistently pointed out in our previous writings, progressives never give up; they just wait for the next opportune "crisis" to push their agenda. Confronted in March 2010 by the March for America protest at the National Mall in Washington, DC, organized by the Center for Community Change, Obama delivered a video message to the more than two hundred thousand attendees.[20] Obama addressed the need for immigration reform: "In the end," he said, "our broken immigration system affects more than a single community; it affects our entire country. And as we continue to strengthen our economy and jump-start job creation, we need to do so with an immigration system that works, not the broken system we have now."[21]

Carefully avoiding any mention of a time frame, Obama said, "I have always pledged to be your partner as we work to fix our broken immigration system, and that's a commitment that I reaffirm today."[22]

The rally's main speaker, Rep. Luis Gutierrez (D-IL), claimed he was optimistic about Obama's promise. "I see a new focus on the part of this president," Gutierrez said. "That's why we are here to say we are not invisible."[23]

Clearly, Obama never intended to promote immigration reform legislation during his first term.

DIVISIVE RACE TACTICS

We described the Obama amnesty kabuki theater in some detail in our previous book, *Red Army*. While progressives and the legacy (aka leftist) media kept nudging Obama in the amnesty direction ahead of the 2012 election, it did not happen—and for good reason. Obama needed it for a campaign issue to bash about the heads of his Republican opponents.

Additionally, progressives and the Latino community had too easily forgotten that in 2007, as a US senator, Obama cast a vote that killed immigration reform.[24] We refer you to the April 2010 exchange between conservative Noel Sheppard of *NewsBusters* and liberal David Broder of the *Washington Post*. To Broder's "How Congress Botched Immigration Reform,"[25] Sheppard responded, "Broder curiously chose to ignore the fact that Barack Obama was, for all intents and purposes, the fateful deciding vote."[26]

The conversation was joined by leftist Michael D. Shear, who misdirected readers with the July 2010 *Washington Post* headline: "Republican immigration position likely to alienate Latinos, Dems say."[27] Again, a conservative journalist, Jennifer Rubin, jumped into the fray. Then with *Commentary* magazine, Rubin ignored the attempted misdirection and exposed the game of smoke and mirrors for what it was. Should Obama call for immigration reform legislation, it would be seen as supportive of the Democrat-Hispanic relationship, while the reality was, as Rubin correctly asserted, Obama was unlikely to push for it in 2010. At the same time, Obama's allies were to keep pushing Republicans in that direction.[28]

Rubin wrote, "Because, you see, if he passed a bill, the issue would go away. And then Hispanics wouldn't be mad at the GOP. It is quite a buried lode." Rubin said the headline should have read, "Obama wants divisive racial issue, not immigration reform," then added: "Hispanic activists actually wanted the president to work on comprehensive immigration reform. But during a White House meeting, they learned that's not the game here."

Again, it was okay with Obama's supporters. It was a tactic, and most knew it. Even Shear recognized that activists realized that while Obama could have been doing more, he and they were satisfied Obama would "use the immigration debate to punish the GOP and aggressively seek the Latino vote in 2012."[29] That is precisely what happened.

And as we pointed out in *Red Army*, La Raza, which was represented at the meeting, was also willing to put immigration reform on the back burner, in spite of the years it had worked diligently pushing for it, just so Barack Obama could use it as a reelection ploy to pull in Latino voters—again—in 2012. With the 2014 midterm elections on the horizon, Latinos can expect to hear many of the same promises—except, as we outline in this chapter, the script will have changed significantly.

NOTHING SUCCEEDS LIKE FAILURE

There is, of course, nothing new about the concept of amnesty for illegal immigrants. Since the radically liberalized Immigration and Nationality Act of 1965, there have been a total of seven amnesties.[30] All failed to stem the flow of illegal immigrants. The first was the Immigration and Reform Control Act of 1986 (IRCA) in which President Ronald Reagan approved amnesty for 2.7 million people, providing forgiveness for those who entered illegally and setting them on the path to citizenship. Of the

1.3 million amnesty applications that ensued, more than 90 percent were for a specialized program for agricultural workers. The number of illegal aliens seeking amnesty exceeded expectations, however, and there was reportedly widespread document fraud, with as many as a third of the applicants having been granted amnesty improperly.[31] Reagan's IRCA was an abject failure. Not only did it not stem the tide of illegal immigrants through the strengthening of border security, but it also failed to increase immigration enforcement against employers, as was intended.[32]

The 1986 amnesty provides a lesson that should have been learned long ago. An Immigration and Naturalization Service (INS) report released in October 2000 highlighted the "profound unintended consequences" of illegal immigrant amnesties—they increased the illegal immigrant population:

> Amnesties clearly do not solve the problem of illegal immigration. About 2.7 million people received lawful permanent residence ("green cards") in the late 1980s and early 1990s as a result of the amnesties contained in the Immigration Reform and Control Act (IRCA) of 1986. But these new INS figures show that by the beginning of 1997 those former illegal aliens had been entirely replaced by new illegal aliens, and that the unauthorized population again stood at more than 5 million, just as before the amnesty.[33]

What caused the numbers to increase? The relatives of the "newly legalized illegals" came to the United States to join their family members. In fact, the "flow" of illegal immigrants "grew dramatically during the years of the amnesty to more than 800,000 a year, before dropping back down to around 500,000 a year."[34]

During the Clinton administration, six more amnesties were granted. In 1994, there was a temporary, rolling amnesty for 578,000 illegal immigrants, with an Extension Amnesty in 1997. Also in 1997, there was the Nicaraguan Adjustment and Central American Relief Act, which granted amnesty for nearly one million Central American illegal immigrants. The Haitian Refugee Immigration Fairness Act Amnesty in 1998 granted amnesty for 125,000 Haitian illegal immigrants.[35]

Another significant piece of information found in the 2000 report is that 1.3 million green cards were handed out to illegal immigrants between 1987 and 1996, dwarfing immigration enforcement efforts. It was estimated that during the same period, only 335,000 illegals were deported or required to leave the country by the INS.[36]

The Center for Immigration Studies observed: "Illegal immigration can be controlled only with a strategy that combines border enforcement with efforts to turn off the magnets that attract illegal aliens in the first place—jobs and green cards."[37] That lesson is yet to be learned, especially when there is also a long history of progressives working toward full amnesty for illegal immigrants. We thoroughly documented in both *Red Army* and our most recent book, *Fool Me Twice*, how progressive legislation and research papers prepared by progressive think tanks have helped form the foundation for plans that keep resurfacing during the Obama administration. We also showed how progressive politicians strategically introduced such legislation over time, working with liberal think tanks to craft and perfect the bills.

Our review of border and immigration reform legislation and progressive research and policy papers on the topics revealed significant blueprints for future policies. Among them was the 645-page Comprehensive Immigration Reform for America's Security and Prosperity Act of 2009, which included a path to citizenship for illegal immigrants and "touch[ed] on issues of border security, foreign worker visas, employment eligibility verification, and more." The act was introduced December 14, 2009, just before Congress's winter break, by Rep. Solomon Ortiz (D-TX) and gained 103 cosponsors.[38]

The act should have sailed through the Democrat-controlled Congress wrapped in shiny paper and a big red bow, and Obama should have signed off on the amnesty gift card by Christmastime. Yet the bill gathered dust in several House committees and never made it to the floor for a vote.

It is almost unthinkable that such a monumental piece of legislation, so significant to the Democratic Party's future permanent majority, was not fast-tracked. Instead, it disappeared with nary a whimper. Why? ObamaCare. Unfazed by the extremely unpopular stimulus bill, the White House and congressional progressives pushed full steam ahead, intent on passing ObamaCare. In fact, in June 2009, in order to pass the bill, Obama pledged his support to immigration reform proponent Rep. Luis Gutierrez in exchange for the Democratic congressman's vote.[39] There was plenty of time to pass amnesty legislation—or find a work around to hand out amnesty to millions of Democrat voters-in-waiting down the road.

MINIMIZING BORDER SECURITY, STEALTH AMNESTY

The proposed legislation was not without problems, however. For example, it called for downsizing US Customs and Border Protection capabilities, including border searches and actions necessary to root out the smuggling of illegal aliens. It also mandated the creation of a Border Communities Liaison Office in each of nine border sectors along the US border with Mexico. Civilians living in those border communities—some of whom may be actively involved in illicit actions—would be warned by such "liaisons" ahead of time about the operational plans of border agents intended to curtail smuggling. Each new liaison office would be required to consult with border communities on the directives, laws, strategies, and operational issues of border patrol authorities.

If passed, the act would create new arrest-free zones for illegals. It would be illegal, for example, to apprehend "undocumented" persons in the "premises or in the immediate vicinity of a childcare provider; a school; a legal-service provider; a Federal court or State court proceeding; an administrative proceeding; a funeral home; a cemetery; a college, university, or community services agency; a social service agency; a hospital or emergency care center; a health care clinic; a place of worship; a day care center; a Head Start center; a school bus stop; a recreation center; a mental health facility; and a community center." It would also prohibit apprehension of pregnant or disabled illegals.[40] We will discuss the most recent development in this tactic shortly.

The act also identified a new class of illegals, those who are members of a newly defined "vulnerable population." This group included "individuals who have been determined by a medically trained professional to have medical or mental health needs." The so-called vulnerable population also included "individuals who provide financial, physical and other direct support to their minor children, parents, or other dependents"[41]—in other words, virtually every single illegal immigrant residing in the United States.

Perhaps the greatest beneficiaries of these new sensitivities would turn out to be the illegals themselves. Once they understood the litany of new perks they'd receive in detention in the United States under Obama, they'd be lining up to be arrested (although their arrests could be prevented under the law's antiracial profiling provisions)! The proposed bill contained many more pages of scandalous, newfound "rights" provided to all illegals held in detention centers. Each detainee, for example, would have a right to "prompt and adequate medical care, designed to ensure continuity of care, at no cost to the detainee." Included would be "care to address medical needs that existed prior to detention; and primary care, emergency care, chronic care, prenatal care, dental care, eye care, mental healthcare, and other medically necessary specialized care." This is better coverage than some of the most expensive private health plans (and most assuredly better than ObamaCare in the future). Also included in the completely free, mandated coverage for detained illegals would be "medication, prenatal care, prenatal vitamins, hormonal therapies, and birth control." Every detainee's needs would be met since, upon detention, each inmate is to get a "comprehensive medical, dental, and mental health intake screening."[42]

FORGET COSTS . . . "FUTURE FLOW" AND "W" VISAS

The Obama administration and Congress are planning ahead for a never-ending influx of illegal immigrants—amnesty or no amnesty. As we penned this chapter, new immigration reform legislation "actually being written by special interests and staffers" was being hammered out behind closed doors, with actual legislation expected to be ready for both the House and the Senate sometime in June.[43] The bipartisan Gang of Eight senators involved with the legislation "haven't seen it or read it," former South Carolina senator Jim DeMint, now president of the conservative Heritage Foundation, told Breitbart.com's Matthew Boyle. They are being told what is going to be in it, DeMint said.[44]

DeMint "drew a distinction between the average taxpayer and representatives of labor and business who are involved in drafting the legislation," Boyle wrote. "Amnesty is not a free proposition to taxpayers. So we're going to quantify that cost. I can guarantee you Heritage will be the only organization in the country that is looking at the true cost of a blanket amnesty proposal," DeMint stated.

Two items alleged to be in the bill should be of mutual concern to American citizens, legal immigrants who have spent years diligently following the path to US citizenship, the so-called "dreamers," and even illegal immigrants now being promised the fast track to citizenship: "future flow" and "W" visas.

"Future flow" refers to "the number of visas that will be given annually to guest workers," Wade Rathke explained in an April 1, 2013, post on his *Chief Organizer* blog.[45] Rathke, for those who do not know, is a former member of the 1960s radical group Students for a Democratic Society (SDS), a founder and former chief organizer of ACORN and Local 100 of the SEIU in New Orleans, a cofounder of the money funnel for wealthy progressive funders like George Soros and the Tides Foundation, and a board member of the Tides Center.

"Classically," Rathke wrote, "business wants more cheap labor, while labor resists pushing down more skilled wage rates by allowing too many foreign workers into the country. This disagreement was critical to killing the bill proposed by Arizona's Senator John McCain and others during the Bush Administration."[46]

This time around, McCain is a member of the Gang of Eight trying to avoid a similar defeat. Other members are Sens. Marco Rubio (R-FL), Jeff Flake (R-AZ), Lindsey Graham (R-NC), Dick Durbin (D-IL), Robert Menendez (D-NJ), Chuck Schumer (D-NY), and Michael Bennet (D-CO). Durbin authored the original DREAM Act, and Menendez, a member of the Hispanic Caucus, is an early proponent of the legislation.[47] We discuss the various DREAM Act proposals in the paragraphs that follow.

The new "W" visas could allow as many as two hundred thousand lower-skilled workers a year to come into the country. The annual number of W visas would depend upon "unemployment rates, job openings, employer demand and data collected by a new federal bureau pushed by the labor movement as an objective monitor of the market."[48] Already we see how this will further expand the federal bureaucracy, with more positions filled with Obama crony appointees.

The new visa status is meant, of course, to benefit employers. Contrary to the current temporary worker program, which prohibits workers from moving from one employer to another and does not include a path to citizenship, the W visa will allow workers to both change jobs and be able to seek permanent residency. Also, there is currently "no good way for employers to bring many low-skilled workers to the U.S.," as the "existing visa program for low-wage nonagricultural workers is capped at 66,000 per year and is supposed to apply only to seasonal or temporary jobs."[49]

The focus of Rathke's post was whether the "future flow" plan would benefit the labor unions. His conclusion was this: "Reports indicate that the sugar in the deal for labor was raising the minimum wages of visa workers so that a higher floor was set. This is a smart move! Given that we can no longer pretend, as our membership numbers plummet, that we are really protecting members as opposed to just being a cranky, old uncle advocate, by raising the minimum wage standards." He added that this protects the unions and helps "whatever members we have left by giving our unions more leverage at the bargaining table to push up wages by arguing about compression coming from visa workers." In the final analysis, Rathke stated, the "good deal" being struck with the Obama administration and members of Congress is a "good thing!"[50]

Pro-immigration organizations like the Immigration Policy Center (IPC) agreed that the "future flow" plan is a good idea. "If the U.S. is to thrive in the globalized 21st century economy, employment-based immigration must be seen as a strategic resource that can both meet labor market needs and foster economic growth and competition while still protecting U.S. workers and improving wages and working conditions," IPC states on its website.[51]

Others disagreed. Robert Gittelson, president of Conservatives for Comprehensive Immigration Reform, cautioned, "If labor is successful in undermining the reconstruction of America's immigration system (they reportedly are demanding that their version of a guest worker program would start at only 10,000 workers per year, and only be expanded at the behest of some kind of a politically appointed commission), we will someday—in the near future—find ourselves back in the same mess that we are currently in today."[52]

Chris Crane, an Immigration and Customs Enforcement agent and president of the union that represents ICE agents, was in total agreement. The Gang's plan, he said, "appears to be legalization, or amnesty first, and then enforcement, [and] that is a big problem for us."[53]

The Gang's plan failed to call "for stronger interior enforcement,"

Crane complained. "We fully support stronger border enforcement, but we know, *we know*, that much stronger interior enforcement is needed." It "continues to be ignored by the president and others because this is more about amnesty, or legalization, than truly addressing illegal immigration and ending it," he said.

Echoing Gittelson's concerns, Crane also "believes the nation will find itself in the same position it currently does, with millions of undocumented immigrants in the future if current laws are not enforced. That's a scenario similar to what happened after passage of an immigration policy overhaul in 1986."

Perhaps a greater cause for concern is the unknown higher economic cost of the immigration system. Individuals and businesses will be required to spend millions of man-hours filling out forms.[54] "The share of immigrant-headed households (legal and illegal) with a child (under age 18) using at least one welfare program continues to be very high," according to Steven A. Camarota, director of research at the Center for Immigration Studies. "This is partly due to the large share of immigrants with low levels of education and their resulting low incomes—not their legal status or an unwillingness to work," he added.[55] Even the White House–friendly *Politico* admitted that the "exact costs won't be clear until details of the bill are released and independent budget experts assess the impact of legalizing 11 million undocumented immigrants."[56] With luck, the reported thousand-page-plus immigration reform legislation won't be a never-ending surprise package like ObamaCare.

A LONG TIME DREAMING

The timing for the introduction of the DREAM Act (Development, Relief, and Education for Alien Minors Act) on August 1, 2001, by Sens. Durbin and Orrin Hatch (R-UT) was unfortunate.[57] The 9/11 terrorist attacks and the US war in Afghanistan launched in October 2001 were more pressing matters.[58]

A similar bill introduced in the House by Representative Gutierrez met a similar fate. Interestingly, congressional support for the bill came almost exclusively from the membership rolls of the Congressional Progressive Caucus, founded by the Democratic Socialists of America.[59] More versions of the DREAM Act were introduced in 2005, 2006, and 2007 in both houses of Congress,[60] with the 2007 version notably failing to gain enough support for debate in the Senate.[61]

Otherwise, the act would have provided a pathway to US citizenship for certain young illegals "to adjust to conditional lawful permanent resident (LPR) status." Eligible illegals were current, former, and future high school graduates under twenty-one (who had lived in the United States for at least five years) and were younger than sixteen when they first entered the country or who were GED recipients. Conditional LPR status would be valid for six years while illegals worked, attended college, or served in the armed services. A person would be removed from LPR status after six years, either after completing two years in a program for a bachelor's degree or higher degree or having served in the uniformed services for at least two years and, if discharged, received an honorable discharge. Although illegals would not be eligible for federal education grants, they would be eligible for federal work study and student loans, and individual states would be allowed to provide financial aid to them.[62]

And there is more. The DREAM Act is a "nightmare," Kris W. Kobach, a law professor at the University of Missouri–Kansas City and a visiting fellow at the Heritage Foundation, declared in September 2007. "The illegal alien who applies for this amnesty is immediately rewarded with 'conditional' lawful permanent resident (green card) status, which can be converted to a non-conditional green card in short order." In turn, the illegal immigrant could "seek green cards for the parents who brought him in illegally in the first place," Kobach wrote. Basically, he continued, the DREAM Act would reward parents for their lawbreaking behavior, providing "backdoor amnesty" for the millions of them who had illegally brought their children with them to the United States.[63]

Kobach also explained the act would allow illegal immigrants to receive in-state tuition rates at public universities, at the same time they discriminated against out-of-state US citizens and "law-abiding foreign students." The act would also have repealed a 1996 federal law that prohibited states from offering in-state tuition rates to illegal immigrants unless the state also offered in-state tuition rates to all US citizens.[64]

The Marxist publication the *Socialist Worker* blamed the bill's failure on "immigrant bashers." Meanwhile, immigrant rights activists worried "it likely would have steered more undocumented young people into the military than into higher education," the *Worker* claimed.[65]

Progressives had one last chance to pass the DREAM Act following the 2010 midterm elections that transferred control of the House to Republicans in the next congressional session. On December 8, 2010, the $6.2 billion DREAM Act passed in the House by a vote of 216 to 198.[66] Cold water was tossed on the whole business when the Congressional Budget Office (CBO) gave "an interesting read on the 'numbers' game being played in Congress," reporting the "expectation and likelihood the bill's requirements will lead to more than half of the participants who signed up to drop out." Based on data on college enrollment and graduation rates and military enlistments, the CBO expected that fewer than half of the individuals who would initially apply for conditional nonimmigrant status would qualify to apply for an extension to maintain that status for an additional five years.[67]

The absurdity of the legislation was illustrated by Tait Trussell at the conservative site *FrontPageMag*. "Now on the fourth and fifth versions of the DREAM Act, the bill would legalize between 300,000 and 2.1 million illegal immigrants—the children of illegals who were born here or came as youngsters. What is a dream-come-true to supporters is that the act would grant citizenship to these children of illegals who go to college or join the armed forces," he wrote. "But only two years of college attendance is required. So, no college degree is needed."[68]

Regarding the military service provision, Trussell added: "By existing law, the Secretary of Defense already can enlist illegal immigrants in the military if it is vital to the national interest. And the law allows such immigrants to become naturalized citizens of the U.S." because their applications are "given accelerated treatment."[69]

Victor Davis Hanson observed in *National Review* that, although the idea behind the Act sounds "noble," it would in fact grant "de facto amnesty to illegal aliens who serve in the military or who seem promising students." However, he wrote, the "logic breaks down and leads to chaos and a sort of legal anarchy." Why not, he asked with a touch of sarcasm, "extend the concept to others in violation of the law as well?"[70]

An even more startling—and less charitable—observation was made by Mike Riggs at the *Daily Caller*: the House passed legislation "aimed at denying stupid immigrants citizenship." He added: "17-year-olds, stupid kids, and pacifists will soon have to hike their happy asses back to the third-world war zones from whence they came."[71]

A more sober Roy Beck, president and CEO of NumbersUSA, the nation's largest grassroots immigration-reduction organization, commented this is "the first time in 10 years that the DREAM amnesty [had] actually passed a chamber of Congress." This was a high-water mark, Beck observed, and "ultimately the failed end" of a "10-year campaign to pass this loophole-filled, fraud-prone, overly broad amnesty that lacks any enforcement against future illegal immigration."[72]

An attempt in the Senate to bring the bill to a vote in December 2010 ended in the action being delayed, apparently indefinitely.[73]

NON-DEPORTATION, THE "NEW NORMAL"

Obviously, a legislative—and legal—remedy for illegal immigration had failed, miserably. Yet, millions of illegal immigrants remain inside the United States, and most are here to stay. Thanks to Obama's oversight of the matter from the White House and a series of documents we will discuss shortly, non-deportation of illegal immigrants is now the "new normal."

When Obama was asked during the December 2007 Iowa radio debate whether he expected Americans to turn in illegal immigrants when they came across them, he responded, "We do not deputize the American people to do the job that the federal government is supposed to do." As president, Obama continued, he would "make sure that the federal government does what it's supposed to do, which is to do a better job of closing our borders, have much tougher enforcement standards when it comes to employers, and create a pathway of citizenship for the 12 million people who are already here."[74]

We expand here on a clear example of Obama's efforts to provide the stealth amnesty we wrote about in *Red Army*. The first of two "priority memos" on immigration enforcement policies was issued June 30, 2010, by John Morton, an assistant secretary at the Department of Homeland Security and director of US Immigration and Customs Enforcement (ICE). Morton set the removal of "aliens" who posed a "danger to national security" as the highest priority, with other "Priority 1" illegal immigrants being those who are/were either engaged in or suspected of terrorism or espionage or "who otherwise pose a danger to national security," had been convicted of crimes, with a "particular emphasis on violent criminals, felons, and repeat offenders," were sixteen years of age and older but who had participated in organized criminal gangs (a group we discuss later), were subject to outstanding criminal warrants, and who otherwise posed a "serious risk to public safety."[75]

An actual footnote to this list basically says *never mind*: "This provision is not intended to be read broadly, and officers, agents, and attorneys should rely on this provision only when serious and articulable public safety issues exist."[76] It is hard to imagine a time when terrorists, violent criminals, felons, and criminal gangbangers would *not* constitute an "articulable public safety issue." The two less-urgent categories were recent illegal immigrants and fugitives or those who otherwise obstructed immigration control.[77]

A second Morton memo followed on August 20, 2010.[78] It narrowly addressed the "processing of certain cases in the immigration courts." In particular, it focused on illegal immigrants who "simultaneously [had] an application or petition for legal status pending before U.S. Citizenship and Immigration Services (USCIS) while facing removal proceedings in immigration court." The memo instructed ICE attorneys to "dismiss removal proceedings" for those thousands of people who had applications or petitions pending with USCIS and who would be eligible for "adjustment of status to permanent residence upon approval of the petition." The memo also instructed ICE attorneys to "expedite approval of applications or petitions by USCIS even where proceedings [were] not terminate."[79] In legalese, this means: "If jeopardy does not terminate at the conclusion of one proceeding, jeopardy is said to be 'continuing,' and further criminal proceedings are permitted."[80] As of July 2009, according to the memo, there were at least 17,000 individuals still subject to prosecution.

Drawing from his previous memos, Morton issued a third on June 17, 2011, which can only be characterized as a deliberate move to bypass Congress and issue backdoor amnesty for an unknown number of illegal immigrants. Morton's new memo instructed all field officers, special field agents in charge, and chief counsel to exercise *prosecutorial discretion* with civil immigration enforcement priorities in the apprehension, detention, and removal of illegals. Included were broad new factors his staff was to consider: an illegal's "contributions to the community, including family relationships; the person's age, with particular consideration given to minors and the elderly; whether the person or the person's spouse is pregnant or nursing."[81] Among scores of other disqualifications for removal, the instructions also included a mandate for leniency for "individuals present in the United States since childhood and individuals with serious health conditions." The subtext of Morton's memo was clear: stop enforcing nearly all measures against illegals.

While some may have suspected Obama as the guiding hand behind Morton's "prosecutorial discretion" memo,[82] that belief was confirmed in an August 18, 2011, post on the White House blog, written by Cecilia Muñoz (whom we discuss momentarily): "There are more than 10 million people who are in the U.S. illegally; it's clear that we can't deport such a large number. So the Administration has developed a strategy to make sure we use those resources in a way that puts public safety and national security first," she wrote. "Under the President's direction, for the first time ever the Department of Homeland Security has prioritized the removal of people who have been convicted of crimes in the United States."[83]

"People in deportation proceedings stand to benefit most from the new policy," columnist Robert Pear observed in the *New York Times*. "The new enforcement priorities also make it less likely that the government will begin such proceedings in the future against people who have no criminal records and pose no threat to national security," he said.[84]

Muñoz showed the Obama administration clearly favored "dreamers." Among those ranked at a lower priority for deportation, she said, were "young people who were brought to this country as small children, and who know no other home," and "military veterans and the spouses of active-duty military personnel." Not only did her White House post include an embedded link to Morton's June 17, 2011, memo regarding "prosecutorial discretion,"[85] but Muñoz herself had helped craft the new policy.[86] The umbilical cord between the White House and DHS and ICE—and illegal immigrant "dreamers"—could not be more obvious.

Additionally, also in August 2011, DHS Secretary Napolitano reinforced Muñoz's information. Napolitano announced a two-pronged initiative to limit deportations to those persons deemed by her department as the most dangerous to the country, rather than on the whole general population of millions of illegals.[87] The Obama administration, she said, would limit deportation proceedings on a case-by-case basis for illegals who met certain criteria, such as attending school, having family members in the military, or having primary responsibility for other family members' care.[88]

Add to this another "major shift" in deportation policy that month. The Obama administration was caught "slipping out" the news on the federal government's new approach for the three hundred thousand pending deportation cases in federal deportation courts. The lower-priority cases, "those not involving individuals considered violent or otherwise dangerous," would be *suspended*. While administration officials called it a "matter of prioritizing cases and allocating scarce resources more efficiently," critics called it what it was—backdoor amnesty, yet another "way to push through policy changes that conservatives in Congress would never agree to."[89]

The Obama administration also admitted the estimated three hundred thousand illegal immigrants could have their deportations deferred indefinitely *and* become eligible for work permits.[90] The Associated Press reported the government said it would "focus on sending back convicted criminals and those who might be a national security or public safety threat."[91] "Illegal aliens living in the United States typically don't apply for work permits for fear of deportation, but under the new policy, they could apply for work permits if granted deferred action or parole and compete with 22 million Americans who can't find a full-time job," NumbersUSA stated.[92] Jeremy Beck, also with NumbersUSA, writing about the threat Obama's administrative amnesty posed, pointed out that "almost no reporters questioned how giving work permits to illegal aliens will make it more difficult for unemployed Americans to find full or part-time jobs."[93]

In other words, in the space of three memos, a blog post, a couple of departmental directives, and carefully placed White House leaks, without any congressional approval—much less general public knowledge—the Obama administration took major steps toward comprehensive amnesty for many illegals.

"In the end," blogger Federale asserted at VDARE.com, the Obama administrative amnesty is a "serious Constitutional crisis . . . and with serious implications. . . . This crisis has evolved from the claim that limited resources restrict the Executive's ability to enforce the law, to the awarding of law violators with illegal benefits, to the latest extraordinary step—enforcing proposed legislation that failed to pass Congress on every attempt, whether with Republican or Democratic majorities."[94]

Do not be fooled: in the first three months of 2013 alone, American taxpayers footed "a $113 billion bill to ensure that illegal immigrants receive[d] free education, health care, and other services, according to a study by [the non-partisan group] Federation for American Immigration Reform (FAIR)."[95]

But there's always more.

DACA: DREAM ACT "LITE"

A clear indication his administration was working toward "executive amnesty" emerged in January 2012 when Obama appointed a longtime open-borders advocate to direct the White House Domestic Policy Council, the executive body mainly tasked with immigration issues. Cecilia Muñoz, to whom we briefly referred a few pages ago, had been a senior vice president for the National Council of La Raza, a group lobbying for open borders, mass immigration, and amnesty for illegal aliens. Muñoz also chaired the board of the Coalition for Comprehensive Immigration Reform.[96]

Six months later, on June 15, 2012, President Obama usurped the powers of Congress in yet another illegal move in his "executive amnesty" chess game. In direct defiance of Congress's unwillingness to pass the DREAM Act, Obama unilaterally announced in a Rose Garden press conference that he would allow eight hundred thousand illegal immigrants who came to the United States as children to "remain in the country without fear of deportation and able to work."[97]

Obama called it "'a temporary stopgap measure' that would 'lift the shadow of deportation from these young people' and make immigration policy 'more fair, more efficient and more just.'" The *New York Times* reported that "the group of illegal immigrants that will benefit from the policy is similar to those who would have been eligible to become legal permanent residents under the DREAM Act."[98]

It was erroneously reported by both English and Spanish nonprofit immigrant organizations and news media that Obama had signed an executive order, "leading many people to apply in the hopes of achieving legal status."[99] Obama did not sign an executive order to that effect.[100] Also, DHS secretary Napolitano made it clear in her "policy memorandum,"[101] which nearly everyone overlooked, that Obama had not signed an executive order, nor had Congress passed any relevant legislation: "This memorandum confers no substantive right, immigration status or pathway to citizenship. Only the Congress, acting through its legislative authority, can confer these rights. It remains for the executive branch, however, to set forth policy for the exercise of discretion within the framework of the existing law. I have done so here."[102]

Again invoking the immigration law term "prosecutorial discretion"—which means select immigration enforcement decisions—Napolitano provided Obama with a transparent fig leaf to hide behind. The administration's intent was not to consider a few hardship or humanitarian cases but to decide categorically for potentially hundreds of thousands of cases based on a deliberately skewed rationale that they are illegal yet deserving of amnesty. Napolitano's policy memorandum reads:

> Our Nation's immigration laws must be enforced in a strong and sensible manner. They are not designed to be blindly enforced without consideration given to the individual circumstances of each case. Nor are they designed to remove productive young people to countries where they may not have lived or even speak the language. Indeed, many of these young people have already contributed to our country in significant ways. Prosecutorial discretion, which is used in so many other areas, is especially justified here.

As part of this exercise of prosecutorial discretion, the [following] criteria are to be considered whether or not an individual is already in removal proceedings or subject to a final order of removal. No individual should receive deferred action under this memorandum unless they first pass a background check and requests for relief pursuant to this memorandum are to be decided on a case by case basis. DHS cannot provide any assurance that relief will be granted in all cases.[103]

The memo covering what has come to be known as Deferred Action for Childhood Arrivals (DACA) was sent to the heads of Customs and Border Protection (CBP), Citizenship and Immigration Services (USCIS), and Customs and Immigration Enforcement (ICE). USCIS was directed to begin implementing the process within sixty days of the memo.[104]

The DHS laid out DACA's basic criteria for consideration on its website: "Individuals who demonstrate that they meet the guidelines below may request consideration of deferred action for childhood arrivals for a period of two years, subject to renewal, and may be eligible for employment authorization."[105] Applicants should be/have: (1) under the age of thirty one as of June 15, 2012; (2) arrived in the United States prior to reaching their sixteenth birthday; (3) continuously resided in the United States since June 15, 2007, up to the present time; (4) physically present in the United States on June 15, 2012, and at the time of making a request for consideration of deferred action with USCIS; (5) entered without inspection (code for "entered illegally") before June 15, 2012, or lawful immigration status expired as of June 15, 2012; (6) currently in school, graduated, or obtained a certificate of completion from high school, obtained a general education development (GED) certificate, or an honorably discharged veteran of the Coast Guard or armed forces of the United States; and; (7) not been convicted of a felony, significant misdemeanor, three or more other misdemeanors, and do not otherwise pose a threat to national security or public safety.

"That last point," Judicial Watch noted, "shows you how easy it will be for criminals to be granted this illicit amnesty. You can have several arrests, 'insignificant' misdemeanors and two or less 'other' misdemeanors and . . . still be eligible for this amnesty."[106]

It is also hard to see how Napolitano could claim that DACA was for the benefit of "productive young people" when the application process would clearly identify those who were already or would become economic liabilities. While the application fee was set at $645 and could not be waived except in certain circumstances, those exceptions were all economic, such as an applicant being homeless or in foster care, under the age of eighteen and lacking a guardian's or parental support, or unable to care for his/herself due to chronic disability or having income less than 150 percent below the poverty level, or having debt in excess of $25,000 in the previous twelve months. Plus, the application for a fee waiver had to precede the application for deferred action.[107]

Additionally, those individuals granted deferred action by either ICE or USCIS would be eligible to apply for "work authorization" during their time of "deferred action."[108] It naturally follows that if an applicant was deemed eligible to work, he or she would need a Social Security card. According to the Social Security Administration, if USCIS and ICE granted deferred action status *and* employment authorization, an applicant was eligible for a Social Security number after receiving an Employment Authorization Card (I-766) from USCIS.[109]

DHS claimed that deferred action did not confer any legal status—not a lawful permanent resident status or a path to citizenship. The initial two-year deferment could be subject to renewal, although DHS reserved the right to terminate or renew deferred action at any time—even though its own fact sheet says extension procedures had not yet been determined.[110]

"President Obama has just opened a floodgate of opportunity for young illegal immigrants in the United States, but could it squeeze the aspirations of legal Americans in the process?" Pamela Constable asked at the White House–friendly *Washington Post*. While immigrant advocates and Hispanic youth groups "hailed Obama's decision to offer legal status to some undocumented immigrants under 30 as a watershed in U.S. immigration history and a long-sought victory for ambitious youths denied a chance to realize the American dream," Constable continued, "opponents of illegal immigration warned that the policy could create significant new competition for jobs and university slots at a time of nationwide recession and numerous states' efforts to curb public spending."[111]

Two months later, on August 15, thousands of illegal immigrant youth lined up on the streets to get their DACA applications. Judicial Watch commented: "What started as a 'top secret' Obama administration stealth initiative—illegal alien amnesty—has now become publicly and painfully obvious as millions of illegal aliens line up to receive their 'priority deferment.'"[112]

Neil Munro exposed another of the Obama administration's dirty little secrets at the *Daily Caller*. Administration officials had confirmed they expanded DACA to include "younger illegals to include low-skill immigrants who have not completed middle school or high school." The shift added "roughly 350,000 low-skill immigrants to the Department of

Homeland Security policy, which was initially portrayed as including only 800,000 people under the age of 31," Munro continued, noting that "the inclusion of middle school dropouts clashes with Obama's portrayal of the illegal immigrants as skilled workers, scientists and entrepreneurs."[113]

The numbers are important. Obama's original guesstimate of 800,000 eligibles was off by the government's own estimate by at least 90,000, meaning in the first year 890,000 would be immediately eligible for deferred deportation—ultimately meaning no deportation. Add the additional 350,000 low-skilled middle and high school dropouts and the number soars to 1.25 million or more.[114] And the cost of processing and managing applications, estimated at 3,000 applications a day, requiring more than 1,400 full-time workers,[115] and other program costs—not to mention the cost of entitlements and educational programs—were not addressed by the White House or DHS. Nor was there any discussion of how this new "deferred action" scheme would position illegals in line ahead of foreigners who have followed all the rules and applied to work in the United States. What was that Obama said in 2007 about going to the end of the line?

One item apparently overlooked in the near term was health care. Less than two weeks into the DACA application process, the Center for Medicaid and CHIP Services at the US Department of Health and Human Services (HHS) explained its policy regarding DACA applicants to state health officials and Medicaid directors.[116] For the first two weeks, however, DACA applicants had apparently enjoyed the "same access to health care and health insurance as other individuals granted deferred action." HHS's rules were explicit. For example, DACA applicants could get health insurance through their employer, if it was available. They could not, however: (1) get comprehensive health insurance under Medicaid or CHIP in their state, unless the state had a separate, state-funded program or had elected the federal option to provide prenatal care regardless of the woman's immigration status; (2) apply for the high-risk insurance pool (the Pre-Existing Condition Insurance Plan, or PCIP), unless the state where they resided had a separate state-funded program; (3) buy private, comprehensive health insurance in a health care Exchange after January 1, 2014; (4) be eligible for federal tax credits to make private health insurance affordable (even if they were paying federal taxes) in the Exchange;

and (5) be eligible for the Basic Health Plan if their state had this program. After ObamaCare comes into full force in 2014, they will "likely not be required to have health insurance under the 'individual mandate,'" although they most likely could "buy full-price health insurance outside of the Exchanges, if it is available."[117]

A full six months into the program, on February 20, 2013, USCIS published its first DACA report card.[118] Out of 936,933 eligible illegal immigrants between the ages of fifteen and thirty, an estimated 423,634 who "might immediately meet the requirements" had their applications accepted for processing. Approximately 45 percent of those "potentially eligible for the program [had] applied in the first six months." Of these, 199,460 applicants were approved for DACA and would receive two-year temporary work permits.[119]

By the end of March 2013, the approval rate for all illegal immigrants who applied for DACA reached 99.5 percent, dropping to 99.2 percent the following month. About 500,000 applications had been submitted by the end of April, with 291,859 of the total approved and a mere 2,352 denied. Reportedly, the rest were still in processing.[120]

Unsurprisingly, the majority of applicants were during September and October, when there were more than five thousand application requests a day—40 percent above expectations. Whether the Obama campaign road show played any part in those numbers is unknown; however, the number of applications dropped off sharply in November and to less than half that monthly number in December. As expected, the majority of applicants, more than 310,000, named their country of origin as Mexico.[121]

There is an alarming explanation for that significant drop-off in applications. In October 2012, Judicial Watch filed a Freedom of Information Act request with the Department of Homeland Security for "all communications, memoranda, emails, policy guidance, directives, initiatives, and any other correspondence respecting the scope and extent of background checks to be performed (or not) on aliens applying to the Obama administration's DACA program." DHS "suspended conducting full criminal background checks on illegals applying for the program and, instead, instituted a 'lean and lite' process, which allowed the applicant to continue moving through the system," Mike Flynn reported in June 2013 at Breitbart.com. He continued: "DHS staff were even informed that an immigrant's failure to produce valid identification should not be a reason to delay their application for amnesty. In an October 3 memo, agents were told, 'Biometric processing should not be refused solely because an applicant does not present an acceptable ID.'" Flynn also reported that "on November 9th, three days after President Obama won reelection, DHS staff were told to stop taking applications for the temporary amnesty. It was somehow no longer necessary to [expedite] the granting of temporary amnesty."[122]

Why is this important? Because what DACA had done was pave the way for the next move in the executive amnesty chess game—toward what the Obama administration now calls the pathway to "earned citizenship."

A "LEGAL" STATUS FOR "DREAMERS" IN 2013—AND BEYOND

While several of Obama's first-term officials moved on, Cecilia Muñoz, La Raza's fox-in-the-henhouse lobbyist, stayed put. She vowed in mid-February 2013 to "continue her push for the long-elusive immigration reform bill." Fox News Latino reported, "Sharp shifts in the political landscape have put an immigration overhaul tantalizingly close for Muñoz and the president." Ten percent of voters in the 2012 election were Hispanics, with Obama winning two-thirds of their votes.[123] Clearly, dangling the amnesty carrot one more time to entice more Hispanics to vote Democrat in the 2014 midterm elections could not hurt.

On January 29, 2013, the White House once again declared America's immigration system "broken," saying, "Too many employers [are gaming] the system by hiring undocumented workers and there are 11 million people living in the shadows." The plan provides for "earned citizenship" for illegal immigrants.[124]

Obama's "commonsense immigration reform proposal" includes a *provisional legal status* that requires illegal immigrants to "come forward and register, submit biometric data, pass criminal background and national security checks, and pay fees and penalties before they will be eligible for a provisional legal status." This also applies to agricultural workers and "dreamers," who would also be eligible for the program. This provisional status does not include eligibility for welfare or other federal entitlements, including subsidies or tax credits under ObamaCare.

As we discussed earlier, since August 15, 2012, the "dreamers" have already come part of the way with a renewable two-year deferred deportation. The new plan would go a step further, making them eligible for "earned citizenship." The Obama plan states: "By going to college or serving honorably in the Armed Forces for at least two years, these children should be given an expedited opportunity to earn their citizenship."

More recently, on February 18, 2013, "three titles of a draft White House immigration reform bill" were leaked to *USA Today* and the *Miami Herald*, which posted the white papers on the Internet. The American Immigration Lawyers Association published its own section-by-section summary of the proposals.[125] You are forewarned: you have already seen much of this before, as progressives like to recycle their musty old plans.

As had the 2009 legislation, the documents called for the establishment of a Border Communities Liaison Office in "each border patrol sector to foster and institutionalize consultation with border communities, provide information, coordinate outreach and education, and receive concerns/complaints," as well as a new Border Communities Liaison Officer.[126]

The most controversial provision is the creation of another new (legal) status for illegal immigrants—Lawful Prospective Immigrant, or LPI—under the auspices of the DHS secretary, who would be authorized to grant LPI status. The groups of people to be excluded from LPI status appear to be very limited: "(among others) people with convictions for aggravated felonies, a single offense with time served of more than 1 year, or 3 or more offenses with an aggregate time served of 90 days or more." Also excluded are Lawful Permanent Residents, "asylees, refugees, nonimmigrants and certain other individuals with lawful status."[127]

While waiting for LPI status, applicants who may acquire advance parole, but only for "urgent humanitarian circumstances," are excluded from "being considered 'unlawfully present,'" and are protected from detention or removal, unless DHS "determines the individual is or has become ineligible for LPI status." DHS must issue a receipt to acknowledge its receipt of an application and provide protection for employers who continue to employ an applicant after they learn an illegal has made an application.[128]

LPI applicants will only have to achieve an "understanding" of the English language, a much lower standard than previously required, as well as of US history and government (those under age fourteen are exempt).

Applicants must be present in the United States on the dates their applications are introduced and continue residence in the US until they are granted LPI status. This requirement allows for a single physical absence from the US of not more than six months. Applicants are required to pay their taxes and, if applicable, they are to register for selective service.[129]

LPI status, however, is not a pathway to ObamaCare—for now. Once status is granted, an individual is considered to be "lawfully present."[130] The ObamaCare law, however, "*expressly* exempts unauthorized (illegal) aliens from the mandate to have health coverage" and "bars them from a health insurance exchange." They are also "not eligible for the federal premium credits or cost-sharing subsidies" and are "barred from participating in the temporary high-risk pools."[131]

This means that illegal immigrants are "expected to make up the largest segment of some 26 million people who will remain uninsured and therefore left to seek treatment in emergency rooms," Tom Murse reported at About.com. According to the Pew Hispanic Center, he wrote, there are "more than 11 million illegal immigrants living in the country. Many do not have insurance."[132] Except that illegals need not worry; the Obama administration will ensure they are covered.

Speaking at a March 2013 seminar sponsored by Obama's progressive think tank, the Center for American Progress, on the impact ObamaCare will have on the HIV/AIDS and lesbian, gay, bisexual, and transgender communities, Mayra Alvarez, HHS's public health policy director, "urged health care advocates to carefully watch the development of immigration reform to make sure coverage is offered. . . . 'Let's keep our eyes on the prize of comprehensive immigration reform,' she said. 'I just want to emphasize that the undocumented are part of our communities. They are part of the people that many of our organizations serve. They go to school with our children, they work with us. And I think first and foremost the administration is committed to passing comprehensive immigration reform.'"[133]

As with all previous DREAM Act proposals, an individual can petition for a spouse and/or children residing outside the US or in the US in a lawful status; they are only required to pay a fee to cover the costs of processing LPI visas and for changing to LPI status. Those with LPI status may seek employment; the Social Security Administration will assign a Social Security number and issue a "fraud-resistant, tamper-resistant, and wear-resistant" Social Security card to them.[134]

LPIs are allowed travel and reentry privileges, thereby establishing the criteria for individuals seeking readmission to the United States after travel.[135] This special privilege is over and above rights allotted to American citizens, who must privately purchase and maintain individual passports to reenter the United States from Canada, Mexico, or any other country.

LPI admission is good for an initial period of four years, while DHS may adjust an LPI's status to that of an "alien lawfully admitted for permanent residence" and establish "eligibility criteria for the adjustment of status." Applicants are required to wait a minimum of six years after their initial grant of LPI status before filing for "adjustment" and to either wait eight years after enactment or thirty days after "an immigrant visa has become available for petitions filed before enactment."[136]

The proposal also provides another slush fund for pro-immigration nonprofits. USCIS will provide funding to "eligible public/private non-profit organizations to develop and implement programs to assist eligible applicants with: public education, assistance in application for LPI status, adjustment of status, and citizenship."[137]

Given the foregoing, it is impossible to see how DHS—which has failed to control the US-Mexican border and illegal immigration into the United States since 2002—plans to keep track of all the levels and ins and outs of LPI status the new plan demands. It requires an intricate flow chart just to map out the possibilities. How will DHS track millions of applicants? The simple answer is, it cannot—and that may not only be deliberate but also criminal.

Speaking of criminal, in the next chapter we will expose how Obama's policies are setting illegal alien criminals loose on our streets, wreaking havoc in cities nationwide.

4

REVOLVING DOOR FOR
CRIMINAL ILLEGALS

WHILE PRESIDENT OBAMA has been hard at work attempting to regulate legal weapons, as we documented in chapter 2, his administration has helped create perhaps the biggest armed threat within the United States, one that has allowed criminal street gangs—mostly comprised of illegal aliens—to turn our cities into their lawless fiefdoms. As we will reveal, Obama has overseen a dangerous, de facto "catch and release" policy in which illegal criminal aliens are routinely being placed back on the streets, where they pose a major threat to public safety and have already been responsible for countless violent crimes, as well as, shockingly, turning major US highways into criminal drug corridors. The FBI itself warns these illegal alien street gangs are acquiring powerful military-style weapons to potentially use against both law-enforcement members and citizens.

"Why isn't the Obama administration suing 'sanctuary cities'?" Peyton R. Miller asked more than three years ago at the *Weekly Standard*.[1] Miller was referring to the federal lawsuit filed by the Obama Justice Department against Arizona's SB 1070. While Arizona was only enforcing federal immigration law at the state level, the government's lawsuit had "nothing to do with keeping immigration policy in federal hands," Miller asserted. Sanctuary cities, which we will probe further in this chapter, generally refer to cities that do not allow municipal funds or resources to be used to enforce federal immigration laws, usually by not allowing police or municipal employees to inquire about one's immigration status.

Arizona governor Jan Brewer signed SB 1070 on April 23, 2010[2]— and for good reason: "Arizona has one of the fastest growing illegal immigrant populations in the country, increasing from 330,000 in 2000 to 560,000 by 2008. As a result, the state has become a smuggling corridor burdened by violent crime, illegal hiring practices, significant fiscal costs, ID theft, and degradation of national parks," Jon Feere, legal policy analyst at the Center for Immigration Studies, reported in April 2012.[3]

Note that in July 2010, the day before SB 1070 was to go into effect, a federal judge issued a preliminary injunction to block the law's most controversial provisions.[4] It was not until June 25, 2012, that the United States Supreme Court ruled on the case, upholding the key provision that required immigration status checks during law-enforcement stops, the "show me your papers" provision, which "came with a warning that the courts would be watching its implementation." The court struck down three other provisions as violations of the supremacy clause of the United States Constitution.[5]

Meanwhile, the federal government, namely the Department of Homeland Security's Immigration and Customs Enforcement, was in full retaliatory mode. In a May 19, 2010, interview with the *Chicago Tribune*, John Morton, ICE's director, announced that his agency "may not even process or accept illegal aliens transferred to the agency's custody by Arizona of officials." Fewer than ten days later, an ICE e-mail revealed "that 'low-risk,' short-time detainees" would be "able to have visitors stay for an unlimited amount of time during a 12-hour window, be given access to unmonitored phone lines, email, and free internet calling." Additionally, they would be "entertained with movie nights, bingo, arts and crafts, dance and cooking classes, tutoring, and computer training." By August 2010, ICE began "circulating a draft policy that would significantly limit the circumstances under which ICE would take custody of illegal aliens." ICE intended to assume custody of an illegal immigrant only after a law-enforcement agency had "independently arrested the alien for a criminal violation." In other words, ICE would no longer pick up an illegal immigrant for entering the United States illegally, for using a false ID, or for possessing false immigration documents.[6]

"Arizona is not 'regulating' immigration as its critics contend. If Arizona were unilaterally admitting or deporting aliens to and from the United States, certainly the state would be overstepping its authority," Feere continued in April 2012. "However, Arizona is simply assisting the federal government in carrying out its responsibilities. One would think that the White House would welcome the help, but that presupposes that the Obama administration actually wants the nation's immigration laws enforced."[7]

DRUG CARTELS

Nearly two years later, in a March 2013 interview, Arizona governor Jan Brewer said she had been "talking about the drug cartels on the national level" while others talked about "the 'dreamers' and those coming across the border for a better life. A very important issue that must be dealt with," she continued, is "the drug cartels who extort the illegals and have drop houses, bringing across the border the bad stuff, such as cocaine and methamphetamines."[8]

The extent of the invasion into non-border states by the Mexican drug cartels was exposed April 1, 2013, by the Associated Press's Michael Tarm, whose findings were based on a review of federal court cases and government drug-enforcement data. Although the cartels "once rarely ventured" north of the United States border, they are now "dispatching some of their most trusted agents to live and work deep inside the United States—an emboldened presence that experts believe is meant to tighten their grip on the world's most lucrative narcotics market and maximize profits," Tarm wrote. The cartels are operating in "at least nine non-border states, often in middle-class suburbs in the Midwest, South and Northeast." The well-known border states Arizona, New Mexico, Texas, and California have "long grappled with a cartel presence," he continued. Now, cases involving cartel members have "emerged in the suburbs of Chicago and Atlanta, as well as Columbus, Ohio, Louisville, Ky., and rural North Carolina. Suspects have also surfaced in Indiana, Michigan, Minnesota and Pennsylvania."

Statistically speaking, the Drug Enforcement Administration (DEA) suggested that there was a "heightened cartel presence in more U.S. cities." For example, in 2008 (before Obama), "around 230 American communities reported some level of cartel presence." In 2011, the most recent year for which information was available, the number had "climbed to more than 1,200." Tarm offered one caveat in that the increase could be "partly due to better reporting."[9] That's not necessarily true. Shutting down the Mexican drug cartels is no easy task—but not an impossible one. It's not called drug "trafficking" without reason.

For example, in October 2009, the forty-four-month Project Coronado, a nationwide crackdown on the drug cartel La Familia Michoacana, resulted in 1,200 arrests. It was pointed out that Minnesota's Twin Cities are situated at the "opposite end" of Interstate 35 (sometimes referred to as the "NAFTA Superhighway," considered a border-to-border highway beginning at the US-Mexican border at Laredo, Texas, and connecting with the US-Canadian border near Duluth, Minnesota). The Mexican drug cartels "think nothing of making the trip [northward] on a regular basis," a Minnesota state spokesman told a local news reporter. "We really are on a major supply route through the heart of the country."[10]

CRIME EXPRESSWAY AND THE "SANCTUARY CITIES"

Let's take a moment to examine the extent of that "supply route." Major east-west arterial interstate highways spanning coast-to-coast intersect with the 1,500-mile-plus I-35 trunk. Moving northward from the Mexican border, branches stretch eastward and westward: I-10 at San Antonio; I-20 and I-30 at Dallas–Fort Worth; I-40 at Oklahoma City; I-70 at Kansas

City, Missouri; I-80 near Des Moines, Iowa; and I-90 near Albert Lea, Minnesota. At their extremities, the east-west interstates connect with I-95 on the east coast and I-5 on the west. Both connect with the Trans-Canada Highway system at the northern border. A major northwesterly route begins at Kansas City, where I-29 branches off to link with I-94 at Fargo, North Dakota, and continues on to Winnipeg. Another link to the Trans-Canada Highway system north of the border is at Des Moines, with connections to Ottawa, Toronto, and Quebec, and others that reach all the way to the Atlantic provinces. On the Mexican side of the border, the highway continues to Mexico City and onward to Mexico's coasts and into Central America. While enabling the flow for commerce has been one explanation since the signing of the North American Free Trade Agreement, at what point does the drug trafficking situation get far enough out of control that the federal government, namely President Obama, recognizes that these highways promote the flow of drugs as well?

The I-35 corridor is truly worthy of the name Crime Expressway, as at nearly every major interstate hub, a sanctuary city conveniently awaits, a minor detail both Governor Brewer and the Associated Press failed to mention. The federal government and many state and city governments are complicit in providing aid and comfort to illegal immigrant criminals by providing safe havens for them. However, it is the federal government and its multitude of law-enforcement agencies that allow sanctuary cities to exist by doing nothing to eliminate them.

Just how many sanctuary cities are there? Too many, with the majority of them in California but with considerable numbers in Texas, Colorado, New Jersey, North Carolina, Ohio, and New York. Even Arizona, which is still battling the federal government for control of its own border, has four: Chandler, Mesa, Phoenix, and Tucson.

Well-known Illinois sanctuary cities Chicago, Cicero, and Evanston were represented by Barack Obama in Congress.[11] As recently as May 2012, Chicago continued to ignore federal immigration laws, thereby encouraging the "flood of illegal immigrants . . . putting enormous strains on medical and social services and bankrupting the country," the *Illinois Conservative Examiner* reported.[12] The House voted on May 10 to pass an amendment to the fiscal year 2013 Commerce, Justice, and Science Appropriations Bill that would prohibit the Justice Department from awarding funds to sanctuary cities that offered protection or assistance to illegal immigrants. Unsurprisingly, the attempt failed to gain traction in the Democrat-controlled Senate.[13]

Unless you live in or near one, you may never have heard of a sanctuary city. Sanctuary cities can be found coast-to-coast, from New York to Houston to San Diego. City officials, including police, are "forbidden from inquiring into anyone's immigration status or cooperating with immigration officials," the Claremont Institute explained in September 2005. "The police may not stop or detain persons solely due to their immigration status or even inquire into their status while making routine traffic stops or misdemeanor arrests."[14] As a result, these are safe havens for not only illegal immigrants but also for *criminal* illegal immigrants.

While sanctuary laws date from the 1980s, allegedly to "foster trust between illegal immigrants and police," the outcome has been outright lawlessness and violence. Many crimes go unreported because witnesses fear repercussions for coming forward, and illegal immigrants don't cooperate with law enforcement for fear of being deported. The policies the federal government adopted "reflect the power of immigration advocacy groups more than concerns about crime prevention," the Claremont Institute concluded. "Politicians in large cities with significant immigrant populations simply surrendered to the demands of immigrant rights groups that sought to minimize—if not extinguish—the distinction between legal immigrants and illegal aliens."[15]

The Claremont Institute also pointed out the so-called immigrants' rights groups are not the only ones promoting sanctuary cities. Businesses want a "steady source of cheap, compliant and exploitable labor; the minions of the welfare state want to magnify their power by extending the largess of the administrative state to those who will, in all likelihood, take their place in the so-called 'underclass,'" the Institute found. As a result, these policies are not only tolerant of crime—after all, illegal immigrants are lawbreakers—but also "actively abet and protect criminal activity by handcuffing the powers of the police."[16]

Eight years ago, the first year Barack Obama served in the US Senate, the Claremont Institute reported that even though a minimum of four hundred thousand illegal immigrants were given final deportation orders from a federal judge, they failed to appear for deportation. Of these, nearly one hundred thousand were convicted criminals. Shockingly, the institute reports, "in sanctuary cities police may not inquire into the deportation status of these aliens or apprehend them until they have committed another crime."[17]

Additionally, the institute's 2005 report explained that illegal immigrants constituted 25 percent of California's prison population, proportionately in "excess of their numbers in the general population." Although they were subject to deportation after completing their sentences, fewer than 50 percent of them were actually deported. Regardless, whether they were deported or not, many of them later ended up in sanctuary cities. "Such returnees naturally look to sanctuary cities as safe havens," the institute pointed out.[18]

"Numerous 'sanctuary cities' deliberately subvert federal immigration policy by preventing local law enforcement and other officials from inquiring as to the immigration status of residents. Some have gone even further by providing undocumented immigrants with local forms of identification," Peyton R. Miller wrote. "Such pro-illegal immigrant practices existed well before January 2009, but Obama did not campaign on the need to abolish them for the sake of restoring immigration policy to the federal domain."[19]

"Technically speaking, cities that designate themselves as 'sanctuaries' are in direct violation of Federal immigration law," a blogger known only as Gettysburg pointed out at the leftist *Talking Points Memo*. "Furthermore, the sanctuary designation itself is an example of a city or state supplanting Federal law, which is EXACTLY what [Attorney General] Eric Holder [accused] Arizona of doing.

"The Obama administration cannot arbitrarily decide when and when not to invoke the Supremacy Clause of the Constitution," Gettysburg continued. "To do so would be an abuse of power and a miscarriage of justice. Yet that is apparently exactly what is happening considering the administration clearly has no intention to take legal action against Sanctuary Cities."[20]

Like many others, Gettysburg got the point: "Quite simply, the Obama administration has no desire to expel the millions of illegal immigrants currently residing in this country." Why not? The answer is obvious: the ultimate goal is a *pathway to citizenship* for an estimated twelve million illegal immigrants.

Obama made this clear during the August 26, 2007, presidential debate at Dartmouth College in New Hampshire. Tim Russert asked him if he "would allow these sanctuary cities to disobey the federal law." Obama's answer was nonresponsive: "The federal law is not being enforced not because of failures of local communities, [but] because the federal government has not done the job that it needs to do." What was needed, Obama added, was "comprehensive immigration reform . . . controlling our borders but also providing a rational immigration system, which we currently don't have."[21] Obama had nothing to say on the topic of sanctuary cities.

GANGBANGERS IN THE CITIES

The sanctuary city issue is not going to go away. In fact, in view of more recent events, these cities are more significant than ever. For example, the number of criminal illegal immigrant "gangs" in US immigrant communities has proliferated since 1992. Five years later, the gangs—whose members were mostly from Mexico—were recognized as a growing law enforcement and immigration problem.[22] And that was more than fifteen years ago. Sanctuary cities serve as both the perfect hideout and easy targets for the gangbangers.

For instance, in March 2005, shortly after Obama joined the Senate, ICE made a major arrest of 103 members of the violent Hispanic gang Mara Salvatrucha, or MS-13, the most notorious street gang in the Western Hemisphere. All of those arrested, except for a handful, were illegal immigrants, and fourteen of them had been deported previously. Heather Mac Donald of the Manhattan Institute, who has written extensively on illegal immigration issues, stated the next logical step would be to "have cities like Los Angeles and New York throw out their sanctuary laws, give the police their authority to use immigration violations to target felons and get them off the street."[23] But it has not happened and is unlikely to do so.

Testifying in April 2005 before the House Judiciary Subcommittee on Immigration, Border Security, and Claims, Mac Donald said sanctuary laws were a "serious impediment to stemming gang violence and other crime. Moreover, they are a perfect symbol of this country's topsy-turvy stance towards illegal immigration." Mac Donald gave Los Angeles as an example: "Under the prevailing understanding of Los Angeles's sanctuary law (special order 40), if that officer merely enquires into the gangbanger's immigration status, the officer will face departmental punishment." To get the criminal off the street, she continued, the "cop has to wait until he has probable cause to arrest the gangbanger for a non-immigration crime, such as murder or robbery. It is by no means certain that that officer *will* successfully build a non-immigrant case against the gangster, however, since witnesses to gang crime often fear deadly retaliation if they cooperate with the police. Meanwhile, the gangbanger is free to prey on law-abiding members of his community, many of them immigrants themselves."[24]

While no one "knows for certain the percentage of illegals in gangs, thanks in large part to sanctuary laws themselves," Mac Donald continued, one thing is certain, that under LA's rules, "illegal criminals will have due process rights that citizens can only dream of: not just judicial review before they can be taken off the streets, but federal judicial review—the gold standard of all constitutional protections. Maybe home-grown criminals should renounce their citizenship and reenter the country illegally," she mocked. "It would be a constitutional windfall for them."[25]

The FBI's gang website reports there are at least "33,000 violent street gangs, motorcycle gangs, and prison gangs with about 1.4 million members criminally active in the United States today. Many are sophisticated and well organized; all use violence to control neighborhoods and boost their illegal money-making activities, which include robbery, drug and gun trafficking, fraud, extortion, and prostitution rings."[26] In October 2012, the US Department of the Treasury labeled the ultraviolent MS-13 a "'transnational criminal organization,' the first such designation for a US street gang."[27] There were then an estimated ten thousand gang members operating with impunity in forty-six US states, Canada, Mexico, and Central America.[28] The FBI further warns that gang members are acquiring high-powered, military-style weapons and equipment, which, the report says, poses "a significant threat because of the potential to engage in lethal encounters with law enforcement and citizens alike."[29]

ILLEGAL IMMIGRANT CRIMINALS? NO PROBLEM.

Kris W. Kobach, a law professor at the University of Missouri and a visiting fellow at the Heritage Foundation, explained that the "basic problem with the use of removal proceedings against these gang members is that so many of them return to the country with impunity after being removed."[30] This brings us to an early February 2013 report by Stephen Dinan in the *Washington Times* about upcoming testimony in Congress regarding the Obama administration's "prosecutorial discretion" policy. The new non-deportation policies would have allowed the September 11 hijackers to "remain in the country even if they had been picked up in the months before their deadly attacks," he reported. Additionally, ICE agents must now wait "until most illegal immigrants have three misdemeanor convictions before they can be arrested and put in deportation proceedings."[31]

"Most Americans would be surprised to know that immigration agents are regularly prohibited from enforcing the two most fundamental sections of United States immigration law," Chris Crane, an ICE agent and president of National Immigration and Customs Enforcement Council 118, the union that represents ICE agents, told Dinan. Breaking the law by being an illegal immigrant in the United States is no longer sufficient cause for arrest, according to ICE policy.[32]

"ICE is crumbling from within," Crane testified at a Senate Judiciary Committee meeting on immigration reform. "Morale is at an all-time low as criminal aliens are released to the streets and ICE instead takes disciplinary actions against its own officers for making lawful arrests. . . . New policies require that illegal aliens have a felony arrest or conviction or be convicted of three or more misdemeanors." As a result, Crane said, "many illegal aliens with criminal convictions are also now *untouchable*."[33]

Add to this an August 2012 Congressional Research Service report that stated the "decision not to deport some arrested illegal immigrants enabled a crime wave." While no specific victims were publicly identified, the CRS reported that illegal immigrants released from custody between 2008 and mid-2011 were "charged with 16,226 subsequent crimes, including 19 murders, 142 sex crimes and thousands of drunk-driving offenses, drug-crimes and felonies."[34]

Why are Americans not hearing about the violence and crime along the southern border? Both the US and Mexican media are too afraid of what the drug cartels might do to them and their families to report on their criminal activities, Judicial Watch claimed in mid-March 2013. This means, Judicial Watch explained, that "Americans will be kept in the dark about the crisis along the porous and increasingly dangerous Mexican border." This does not absolve the Obama administration, namely DHS, for not reporting about it. Secretary Napolitano, Judicial Watch continued, "insists that the region is 'as secure as it has ever been.' This delusional assessment has been repeated by Napolitano over and over again in a seemingly desperate effort to make people believe it."[35]

Judicial Watch also noted this "means no one really knows the true magnitude of the violence, though it's apparent that the U.S. government is downplaying it."[36] This was confirmed by Stephen Dinan, who headlined March 20, 2013, in the *Washington Times*, "DHS tells Congress it still can't measure border security."[37] Top DHS officials had told Congress that three years after the Obama administration "scrapped the previous yardstick" to measure the border's "operational control," top Customs and Border Protection officials said they "still [didn't] have a way to effectively measure border security—a revelation," Dinan wrote. Lawmakers have said that "could doom the chances for passing an immigration legalization bill this year" because some members want proof of a secure border before they will consider comprehensive immigration reform. There is no timetable for when a new measure will become available.

CRIMINALS AT LARGE

News of another major DHS failure began to leak out February 26, 2013, when a spokesman for Pinal County sheriff Paul Babeu told Fox News that ICE had released several hundred illegal immigrants from federal detention in local jails and planned to release up to ten thousand more. Babeu labeled the move "politically motivated—and dangerous."[38]

ICE officials confirmed they had released 303 illegals from four Arizona facilities, all in Pinal County. Spokeswoman Gillian Christensen admitted ICE had reviewed "several hundred cases and placed these individuals on methods of supervision less costly than detention." Meanwhile, all of them remained in removal proceedings and under supervision. ICE said they could be "fitted with a non-removable ankle brace that monitors their whereabouts electronically" and/or "required to show up at an ICE office at regular intervals, or routinely call ICE officials to update them on their status." Those who remained in detention were "serious criminal offenders and other individuals who pose a significant threat to public safety," ICE claimed.[39]

The action, according to ICE press secretary Barbara Gonzalez, was prompted by "the 'fiscal uncertainty' hovering over the federal government." ICE had to release the illegals "to ensure detention levels stay within ICE's current budget," she claimed. But was that true?

Let's check the numbers. ICE officials reported that as of February 23, the average daily population held in detention was 30,773,[40] while ICE is required by Congress to maintain 34,000 detention beds. If, in fact, the plan was to release ten thousand illegals—around one-third of the current inmate population—it would appear to be for other than the stated reasons.

This situation is of the Obama administration's own making. The "uncertainty" ICE claimed was the $87 billion in automatic spending cuts known as sequestration scheduled to go into effect on March 1 (when Obama doubled down, refusing any budget changes until the GOP agreed to more tax increases).[41] While Obama and Democrats blamed the cost-cutting measure on Republicans in Congress, the truth is that the plan was initiated by the Obama administration. The scheme was cooked up in July 2011 by then-budget director Jack Lew and then White House congressional-relations chief Rob Nabors, "probably the foremost experts on budget issues in the senior ranks of the federal government," Bob Woodward, author of the book *The Price of Politics*, stated in the *Washington Post*. Clearly, during his third presidential debate with Mitt Romney on October 22, 2012, Obama out-and-out lied, blaming Congress for the Budget Control Act of 2011 put together virtually under his own nose. "The sequester is not something that I've proposed," Obama declared. "It is something that Congress has proposed."[42]

Hours after word leaked out that "a few hundred illegal immigrants" facing deportation had been released from immigration jails due to budget cuts, on February 27, 2013, Gary Mead, head of enforcement and removal operations, announced in an e-mail to coworkers he was leaving ICE at the end of April.[43] Meanwhile, the White House and DHS both claimed ignorance about what they called ICE's decision. White House press secretary Jay Carney said on February 27, "This was a decision made by career officials at ICE without any input from the White House, as a result of fiscal uncertainty over the continuing resolution, as well as possible sequestration." Despite claiming the White House was "unaware," Carney described those released as "low-risk, non-criminal detainees."[44] He dismissed the situation, saying it "costs less money to release the immigrants and monitor them than it does to hold them in detention centers." Also, he claimed, it would "help ICE stay within a new lower budget that will result from the automatic across-the-board spending cuts."[45] So, it was really about the money?

By March 1, the story had changed, with DHS admitting that more than two thousand illegal immigrants facing deportation had been released from detention, and it planned to release three thousand more by the end of the month. In fact, ICE had released "roughly 1,000" illegal immigrants per week since at least February 15, and ICE field offices reported more than two thousand had been released from jails in Arizona, California, Georgia, and Texas before the plan was temporarily shut down. Secretary Napolitano claimed the sequester left her with no other choice than to release more illegal immigrants into the country.[46]

The claim that only "low-risk, non-criminal detainees" were released from detention was proven false as well. A December 2012 memorandum issued by ICE director Morton, "providing new guidance to ICE officers on when to issue detainers against non-citizens charged with crimes," listed illegal immigrant criminals charged with felonies; persons with three or more prior misdemeanor convictions; and persons charged with assault, DWI, unlawful flight from the scene of an accident, drug distribution or trafficking, or sexual abuse or exploitation. An ICE hold "can only be placed on a person who appears subject to removal or deportation." Others who may be subject to an ICE hold include persons who have been "previously deported or convicted of illegal entry."[47] In other words, illegal immigrants are not detained if they have been charged with minor misdemeanors or traffic violations and/or misdemeanor drug possession (with no allegation of distribution or trafficking).[48]

On the March 9, 2013, segment of the *Justice with Judge Jeanine* show, Pinal County sheriff Paul Babeu asserted that among those released from the Arizona jails were "criminals who had been 'convicted not just charged—convicted for weapons violations, drug smuggling (these are cartel members, these are narcotic traffickers!), drug dealers, these are people who have been in fights, and aggravated assaults against police officers . . . the worst of the worst . . . people who have been convicted of child molestation!" Babeu said he had been told by ICE agents some had even been charged with manslaughter.[49]

The Obama administration started to walk back its story on March 14 when Morton testified to Congress that ICE had released ten Level 1 offenders and had "gone out and apprehended four of them." The other six, he claimed, were nonviolent. Morton also admitted that ICE had released 2,228 illegal immigrants, 629 of whom had criminal records. He called them "low-level offenders"[50] while also admitting ICE released "many who had been convicted of drunk driving," even some who were repeat offenders.[51] Additionally, he could not say whether any of those released were (or were not) national security risks.[52]

Morton obviously fell on his sword, telling Congress he alone had made the choice to release the illegals "without any input" from the White House or Secretary Napolitano. More troubling, however, Morton was "unable to give many of the exact figures" members of Congress wanted to know. He did, however, say all those released were still subject to deportation proceedings, with all of them supposed to be under some sort of supervision, though not all were being electronically monitored. He could not provide a specific breakdown of their disposition.[53] Even more disturbing is Morton's admission that he could have avoided releasing the more than two thousand illegal immigrant detainees "by asking Congress for flexibility under sequestration, but he never made an effort to do so."[54]

MORE ILLEGAL CRIMINALS RELEASED

Next question: Is this the only time the Obama administration has released illegal immigrant criminals from jail? Of course not; in fact, more than eight thousand were released between fiscal year 2009 and May 2011 alone. ICE statistics show it had released 3,847 convicted criminal aliens in 2009; 3,882 in 2010; and 1,012 to date in 2011.[55]

A 2011 inspector general audit found that 809 recidivist Level 1 illegal immigrant criminals eligible for deportation were released from California and Texas jails in fiscal year 2009. Level 1 is the "most egregious criminal aliens, who pose a significant public safety risk." Offenses include "homicide, kidnapping, sexual assault, robbery, aggravated assault, threats, extortion, sex offenses, cruelty toward family, resisting an officer, illegal weapon possession, hit and run, and drug offenses accompanied by sentences of more than a year." Why were they released? ICE blamed it on "agent 'staffing challenges,' such as vacancies and 'increasing workload levels' created by other criminal alien identification programs." ICE may also "have missed vetting some incarcerated criminal aliens eligible for removal because agents are not required to record aliens' immigration status."[56]

And there's more: an investigation conducted by the *Boston Globe* revealed in December 2012 that "over the past four years, immigration officials have largely without notice freed more than 8,500 detainees convicted of murder, rape, and other crimes, according to ICE's own statistics, mainly because their home countries would not take them back."[57] (More than twenty governments, from Jamaica to China, routinely block deportation of their citizens.[58]) The courts are no help either; the *Globe* added, "The Supreme Court has said ICE cannot hold the immigrants forever; if immigration officials cannot deport them after six months, the court said, they should generally set the immigrants free." Additionally, the *Globe* found that "immigration officials almost never try to declare a detainee dangerous: In the past four years, immigration officials have released thousands of criminals, but court officials say they have handled only 13 cases seeking to hold immigrants longer because they are dangerous."[59] Comforting, isn't it?

Of those charged with illegal reentry, more than 96 percent were Hispanic, 85 percent of whom were Mexican. It is believed likely most of them had reentered "via clandestine crossings" along the US-Mexican border.[60] "Thus, anything that we could do to upgrade our border security would be helpful in slowing the revolving door for criminal deportees as well as curtailing illegal immigration and the smuggling of drugs into our country," wrote Peter A. Schulkin, author of the 2007 book *A Layman's Guide to the Illegal Immigration Problem.*[61]

IMMIGRATION RAIDS (OR MORE "CATCH AND RELEASE"?)

Speaking of the "catch and release" of illegal immigrant criminals, what has happened to all the illegal immigrant criminals arrested by DHS/ICE? How many new crimes have they committed and how many times have they reentered the United States? Let's look at some examples.

In a three-day raid of fifty counties in ten Midwest states in late August 2010, DHS/ICE arrested 370 illegal immigrants eligible for deportation, including some illegally in the US from Iraq, India, Kenya, Syria, Togo, Bosnia, Canada, and Vietnam. Some had been convicted of crimes, and others were immigration fugitives "wanted for being in the country illegally or people who had been deported and come back."[62]

At the end of September 2011, DHS/ICE arrested 2,900 illegal immigrants coming from all fifty states and four territories. All had at least one criminal conviction and "at least 1,282 had been convicted of multiple charges and more than 1,600 had felony convictions including manslaughter, attempted murder, kidnapping, armed robbery, drug trafficking, child abuse, sexual crimes against minors, and aggravated assault." More than 25 percent of them were immigration fugitives. Another 386 had reentered the US illegally after being removed "multiple times." However, only 146 of those arrested "during the sweep were turned over to various U.S. attorneys for prosecution on a variety of charges including illegal re-entry after deportation, a felony which carries a penalty of up to 20 years in prison." Of the total arrested, forty-two were identified as gang members.[63]

In May 2012, the Obama administration notified more than five hundred companies that it planned to audit their hiring records to crack down on the employment of illegal immigrant workers.[64] In case you missed it, at the end of April 2009, ICE issued "new enforcement guidelines for all of its agents in the field" that would effectively stop workplace raids and switch to conducting audits.[65]

Matt Mayer of the *Heritage Foundation* blog had a few bones to pick over with the audit plan. "While a quick glance would leave readers with the impression that President Obama's illegal immigration work raid policy is working, the problems with the policy sneak into the article in two places," Mayer observed. One, the audits did not lead to the deportation of the illegal workers; they all just lose their jobs, which "ultimately results in those illegal immigrants simply finding another job in the same city or in a different city. This approach just kicks the can down the road," Mayer wrote. Two, if the "silent raid" policy was working, why did the Obama administration have to come back to conduct a second audit six months later? "The employer, like the employee, knows that a return to the status quo will happen once the feds leave town," Mayer correctly assessed.[66]

The same logic applies to the Obama "catch and release" program for illegal immigrant criminals, which we discussed earlier. Why bother to "catch" if the plan is to "release" as soon as it becomes convenient?

OBAMA NEEDS TO ANSWER . . .

A number-crunching account of ten things you may not know about immigration was released April 2, 2013, by Nicholas Colas,[67] chief market researcher at BNY ConvergEx Group.[68] The report provides an eye-opening perspective on the cost and effectiveness of DHS's Customs and Border Patrol. For example, the CBP budget increased 149 percent from fiscal year 2002 to fiscal year 2012, from $1.4 to $3.5 billion. Over the same ten-year period, CBP staff more than doubled, with the biggest staff increase at northern points of entry, including Buffalo, New York; Spokane, Washington; and Grand Forks, North Dakota, where staff grew 312 percent (from 492 to 2,026). Meanwhile, apprehensions at the borders were down 62 percent since fiscal year 2002 and had fallen 78 percent after peaking in fiscal year 2000. Apprehensions for fiscal year 2012 stood at 364,768. The last time apprehensions were this low was 1972, Colas said, with "two easy explanations for the slowdown, though neither is particularly optimistic: either Border Patrol is doing a poor job, or no one is trying to cross the border.

"The latter point is corroborated by Mexican emigration estimates," he continued. "The slowdown points to a still-moribund job market in the US." According to Colas, the Pew Hispanic Center reported that Mexican migration into the United States has not only fallen to zero but also may have gone into negative numbers, what Colas called "a pessimistic sign" for the US labor market. Is it possible that the Obama administration and

Congress are desperately flailing around in an attempt to keep as many illegal immigrants as possible from fleeing the country to an ironically better standard of living south of the border?

What about the thousands of illegal immigrant criminals DHS/ICE released from detention? Recall, they claimed cost was the deciding factor. Colas reported those costs have also escalated. In fiscal year 2002, each apprehension at the border cost $1,483, which rose to $9,680 for fiscal year 2012, a 553 percent increase. The American taxpayer is getting a lot less for the money, as well. In fiscal year 2002, each CBP officer made ninety-five apprehensions, compared to only six ten years later. The cost of arresting, detaining, and deporting each person was estimated by ICE to be $12,500, while other estimates double that amount. Colas concluded that the system not only seems to be expensive but inefficient as well, what business analysts call "very high per unit costs."

Regarding those illegal immigrant–operated drug cartels, what Colas found only exposes the tip of that iceberg. While most of the marijuana comes through the Southwest (2.3 million pounds seized in fiscal year 2012, an estimated 160 pounds per seizure), the so-called coastal border (Miami, New Orleans, etc.) is "the primary seizure point for cocaine (5,962 pounds seized in 2012, 23 pounds per seizure), while most ecstasy is funneled through the northern border (199 pounds in 2012)." Based on our earlier discussion of sanctuary cities and the Crime Expressway, the I-35 north-south corridor that intersects with all major coast-to-coast interstate highways and beyond, it is easy to see how effortlessly drugs can flow in all directions. Drugs, however, are not all that the CBP has seized at the border points of entry. Add 671 firearms, 128,000 rounds of ammunition, $7.6 million in cash (not necessarily all in US currency, Colas noted), and 10,000 vehicles taken via asset forfeiture. These are not numbers to sneeze at.

Why should you care? Well, for starters, the Obama administration's policy for handling illegal immigrant criminals appears to be nothing more than "catch and release." In fact, after word got out in March 2013 that DHS/ICE was releasing detained illegal immigrants back into the US population, there was an "influx" of a large number of "migrants" from Mexico and Central America who voluntarily turned themselves in to the CBP "with the expectation that they too would be let go"—inside the

United States, that is.[69] Stupid actions can have disastrous consequences.

How about sanctuary cities? Doesn't Obama know about them and that they both provide a safe harbor for illegal immigrant criminals and enable the drug and human traffickers to ply their trade from one sanctuary city to the next? Doesn't Obama have a responsibility to do something about this dangerous situation? And how about focusing on the Crime Expressway, facilitated by the I-35 corridor that runs between the Mexican and Canadian borders and which intersects with all coast-to-coast interstate highways?

Did President Obama know that DHS and ICE planned to release thousands of illegal immigrant criminals into American society on his watch, including the most recent releases in February and March 2013? Of course he did, but it does not matter. Whether he likes it or not, Obama is the ultimate "bag holder," and for that reason alone, he is responsible for the horrible mess our immigration system has become. Comprehensive immigration *reform* does not mean letting everyone in who wants to come into the United States and allowing everyone to stay who so desires—including illegal immigrant criminals and potential terrorists. Such dereliction of duty is, in our opinion, impeachable.

IMPEACHABLE? REALLY?

Can a country's president be impeached for releasing thousands of convicted criminals back into the population? It can happen. In fact, it did happen in March 2013 in the Czech Republic in what were the country's first ever impeachment proceedings.

Members of the Senate, the Czech Parliament's upper house, "gave departing President Václav Klaus a going-away present on Monday—they voted to impeach him on charges of treason," the news media reported on March 9.[70] The treason charges were brought against Klaus after he granted a controversial "judicial amnesty" for more than six thousand inmates on January 1—to "mark the country's 20th anniversary of independence"—which "ended numerous high-profile fraud and corruption cases related to major financial scams." The punishment, if upheld in the Constitutional Court, would be loss of office, a moot point, as Klaus has already departed from it, and loss of pension. It would also render him ineligible for a third term in office in 2018.

The *Economist* reported: "It pardoned all convicts with prison terms of less than one year, those sentenced for non-violent crimes to up to two years, those aged at least 70 whose prison terms do not exceed three years and those aged at least 75 with terms of up to ten years."[71] The most egregious act, which outraged "a nation that has become increasingly angered by widespread corruption," was that Klaus "stopped criminal proceedings that have lasted for more than eight years (as long as defendants face at most ten years in prison)," which included "several high-profile cases of embezzlement, bribery and fraud dating back to the wild post-communist overhaul of the economy."[72] The overhaul was spearheaded by Klaus himself.

Are all authoritarian presidents rewarded for their imperialist acts? This one was. On March 7, 2013, former Czech president Václav Klaus started his new job as a distinguished senior fellow at the Cato Institute, a libertarian think tank in Washington, DC.[73] But he also set a global precedent when he was impeached for treason by the Czech Senate *first*.

5

EMPOWERING ENEMIES DOMESTICALLY AND ABROAD

S INCE ASSUMING OFFICE, President Obama has weakened the United States, both at home and abroad, by bolstering our foes, implying his support of a Muslim Brotherhood revolution, snubbing our allies, and playing down the very real threat of Islamic fundamentalism. At the same time, he maintains close and dangerous ties with Islamic groups and activists of dubious character who now, to our shame, are actually shaping our antiterrorism policies. In this chapter, we will show that not only has Obama aided the rise to power of major enemies of Western civilization; he has ushered those very enemies into the White

House! Serving on important US national security advisory boards are none other than members of the *Muslim Brotherhood*.

THE MUSLIM BROTHERHOOD: A BRIEF BACKGROUND

Before we thoroughly document Obama's troubling and potentially impeachable foreign and domestic policy actions, it is instructive here to briefly examine the Muslim Brotherhood, since the group plays a pivotal role in this chapter and since there are widespread misconceptions about the pan-Islamic organization and its ideology. That ideology can quite accurately and easily be summed up as being based on the worldview that Islam is the solution for every individual, social, and political problem. While there are various Muslim Brotherhood factions and political branches, each shares the defining goal of establishing a comprehensive Muslim world order by means of a long-term, multiple-stage process, with the end game being a planet run according to Islamic law.

The Brotherhood does not view the Middle East and parts of Africa as being comprised of individual countries with unique identities, but rather as one large Islamic entity waiting to be liberated. Such liberation is to come through various means, primarily by attaining political power via the election process—in some cases after first fighting "foreign" occupation. The ultimate goal is to unite this new caliphate under the banner of Islam and then spread Muslim values around the world.

Make no mistake about it: the Muslim Brotherhood seeks control over the West as well. It's just that its approach toward acquiring power in the United States and Europe differs somewhat from its strategy for the Middle East and Africa. In the latter regions, the Brotherhood has established various official branches and political parties. Some of those branches, such as Hamas in the West Bank and Gaza Strip, utilize a multi-pronged assault of violence and electoral tactics, while others mostly focus on solidifying power through political and societal influence.

In the United States, the Brotherhood quietly founded multiple organizations and networks, mostly funded by Persian Gulf states. These groups seek influence by lobbying sympathetic members of Congress and infiltrating organizations aligned with various Palestinian and Islamic causes. Identifying these organizations and exposing the agendas of the activists who run them is often difficult, since the groups repeatedly deny ties to the Brotherhood, especially after the September 11 attacks.

In Europe, the Muslim Brotherhood seeks to utilize multiculturalism to ultimately turn Islam into the main force on the continent. In a fatwa (a legal decree issued by an Islamic religious leader), Yusuf al-Qaradawi, one of the top Muslim Brotherhood leaders in Egypt, pledged the takeover of Europe by means other than war and violence. He wrote, "Islam will return to Europe as a conqueror and victor, after having been expelled from it twice . . . The conquest this time will not be by the sword but by preaching and ideology."[1] Speaking on Al Jazeera in January 1999, Qaradawi explained how the Quran predicted Islamic dominance in Europe. He declared: "The friends of the Prophet heard that two cities would be conquered by Islam, Romiyya and Constantinople, and the Prophet said that 'Hirqil [i.e., Constantinople] would be conquered first.' Romiyya is Rome, the capital of Italy, and Constantinople was the capital of the state of Byzantine Rome, which today is Istanbul. He said that Hirqil, which is Constantinople, would be conquered first and this is what happened . . . Constantinople was conquered, and the second part of the prophecy remains, that is, the conquest of Romiyya."

He then explained how such conquest need not necessarily be delivered by the sword: "[The conquest of Mecca] was not by the sword or by war, but by a treaty [the Treaty of Hudaybiyya], and by peace . . . Perhaps we will conquer these lands without armies. We want an army of preachers and teachers who will present Islam in all languages and in all dialects."[2]

One can argue that the Brotherhood is similar in certain aspects to the socialist/progressive movement in the United States—each espouses a utopian worldview that is to be achieved patiently over time, utilizing multiple means, including infiltration of universities, institutes, and major political parties. (For more on the progressive assault on the American political and economic systems, see our previous book *Red Army*.) Like progressivism, the Muslim Brotherhood understands the importance of influencing the education and political systems and forming numerous front groups that work toward a common purpose.

Interestingly, the Brotherhood does not always support terrorism as a tactic to achieve its goals. Violence is only to be used against Western "occupations" of "Islamic" lands, like Iraq, Afghanistan, and of course, Israel, which the Brotherhood views as a Western-style outpost built on Muslim territory. The Brotherhood actually opposes al-Qaeda's global terrorist tactics, seeking instead to conquer the West through nonviolent means.

The Meir Amit Intelligence and Terrorism Information Center (ITIC) at the Israeli Intelligence Heritage and Commemoration Center conducted a thorough investigation of the Muslim Brotherhood, documenting how the group is by no means monolithic. The Brotherhood has some moderate elements, including those which genuinely seek to combine pragmatism and political tolerance within Islam. However, the ITIC found that the combined weight of the more moderate elements is currently less than that of the more conservative and radical elements.[3]

Regardless, there can be no doubt that even a pragmatic Brotherhood is an ideological enemy of Western democracy and of the United States simply because the group seeks Islamic governance, and any entity run by Islamic law cannot by its very definition be a democratic and free society. One need not be a constitutional or Sharia scholar to determine that the basic tenets of Islamic law oppose those of the West. Just a few examples are the requirements that a non-Muslim cannot rule a Muslim; a non-Muslim man cannot marry a Muslim woman; non-Muslims are not allowed to publicly celebrate religious holidays; the testimony of a woman in court is half the value of a man's . . . and that's just the beginning.[4]

Take a look at the Muslim Brotherhood's official motto: *"Allah is our objective, the Prophet [Muhammad] is our leader, the Qur'an is our law, jihad is our way, death for the sake of Allah is our most exalted aspiration."*[5] This credo is routinely cited at the opening of meetings and events held by various Muslim Brotherhood–founded groups in the United States—organizations deeply tied to the Obama administration, as we will demonstrate shortly.

OBAMA AND EGYPT'S MUSLIM BROTHERHOOD

It is against this backdrop of better understanding the Muslim Brotherhood that we can now comprehend the havoc President Obama's policies have wreaked and will continue to wreak for the United States and its allies.

Let's start with Egypt. Obama called for the removal of US ally Hosni Mubarak in a country where the Muslim Brotherhood was the main and most viable opposition party and where even the most elementary observer of Middle East affairs could easily have predicted that the Brotherhood and its Islamist allies would fill any power vacuum created by Mubarak's departure.

Perhaps Obama's orientation could have been divined back in 2009, when he traveled to Cairo to deliver a historic speech to the Islamic world. Official invitations for the event were reportedly sent out by Cairo University and Al-Azhar University to ten members of the Muslim Brotherhood, including Mohamed Saad el-Katatni, head of the group's parliamentary bloc.[6] At around the same time, the Egyptian daily newspaper *Al-Masry Al-Youm* published a report claiming Obama had met with US- and European-based representatives of Egypt's Muslim Brotherhood in early 2009. The Israeli news media also ran the report.[7]

Amazingly, future Egyptian president Mohamed Morsi mocked Obama's Cairo speech. "One American president after another—and most recently, that Obama—talks about American guarantees for the safety of the Zionists in Palestine," he said on Egyptian television in reaction to the 2009 speech.[8] Yet that didn't stop the Obama administration from tacitly and directly assisting Morsi's ultimate rise to power, or from continuing to support his regime, despite its anti-Western agenda, as we shall see.

At the beginning of 2011, Mubarak faced eighteen intense days of protests targeting his regime. During that critical period, Aaron Klein spoke with Egyptian government officials who said they suspected elements of the uprising, particularly political ones, were being coordinated with the US State Department. This view was supported when the London *Telegraph* reported that in 2008 the US Embassy in Cairo had helped a young dissident attend a US-sponsored summit for activists in New York, while working to keep his identity secret from Egyptian state police. The *Telegraph* would not identify the dissident but said he was involved in helping to stir the 2011 protests against Mubarak. The report also claimed the dissident told the US Embassy in Cairo that an alliance of opposition groups had a plan to topple Mubarak's government. The disclosures, contained in US diplomatic dispatches released by the website WikiLeaks, show that American officials pressed the Egyptian government to release other dissidents who had been detained by the police.[9]

Egyptian government officials further claimed to Klein that they had information that a diplomat at the US embassy in Cairo secretly met on January 29, 2011, with a senior leader of the Muslim Brotherhood to plot the next phase in Egypt's history. An Egyptian intelligence official said the meeting took place between Essam el-Erian, a senior leader of the Muslim Brotherhood, and Frank Wisner, a former US ambassador to Egypt. The Obama administration had dispatched Wisner to Egypt a few days earlier to report to the State Department and White House a general sense of the situation in the embattled country.

The pressure from the streets and behind the scenes took its toll. On February 1, 2011, Mubarak announced he would step down at the next election, which was not scheduled until seven months later. Obama responded that while "it's not the role of any other country to determine Egypt's leaders," it was his belief that "an orderly transition must be meaningful, it must be peaceful, and it must begin now."[10] Obama's clear message was that Mubarak could not delay until scheduled elections in September but had to resign immediately.

Obama further said the transition process "must include a broad spectrum of Egyptian voices and opposition parties. It should lead to elections that are free and fair. And it should result in a government that's not only grounded in democratic principles, but is also responsive to the aspirations of the Egyptian people."[11] The *New York Times* reported two days later that the Obama administration was quietly discussing with Egyptian officials a proposal for Mubarak to immediately resign and turn over power to a transitional government.[12]

On February 5, Obama urged Mubarak "to make the right decision" to end weeks of unrest and reiterated a call for an orderly transition of power "that begins now"—another clear demand for the Egyptian president's immediate ouster.[13]

Finally, after weeks of massive international pressure led primarily by the United States, Mubarak announced his resignation from office on February 11. Obama hailed that decision, declaring, "The people of Egypt have spoken. Their voices have been heard and Egypt will never be the same. By stepping down, President Mubarak responded to the Egyptian people's hunger for change, but this is not the end of Egypt's transition. It's the beginning." He went on to say, "Over the last few weeks, the wheel of history turned at a blinding pace."[14]

There can be no doubt Obama's vocal support for the opposition in Egypt and his calls for Mubarak to resign played a pivotal role in the downfall of the secular, Western-allied Mubarak regime. While Mubarak did not exactly espouse democratic ideals, his regime at least did not promote Islamic extremism. Mubarak largely tolerated minorities, even allowing Christians into the government. He was an enemy of Iran, served as a strong US ally in the region, and promoted peace with Israel.

Whether intended or not, the Mubarak regime has since been replaced by a Muslim Brotherhood coalition that utilizes Sharia Islamic law as the basis for its constitution, routinely calls for the revocation of a critical peace treaty with Israel, reportedly persecutes Christians and other minorities while solidifying an alliance with Hamas, and is now entertaining a close relationship with Iran.

The elections that Obama called for indeed took place in stages from November 28, 2011, to January 11, 2012. However the results were not the government grounded in democratic principles that the US president had hoped for. The so-called Democratic Alliance for Egypt, which was dominated by the Muslim Brotherhood, won a plurality of the vote with 37.5 percent (their leader, Mohamed Morsi, eventually became Egypt's president). The Brotherhood party formed a coalition government with the even more extremist Islamist bloc led by the Salafist, al-Qaeda–oriented, pro-jihad Al-Nour Party, which took 27.8 percent. Not a single secular, liberal party scored in the double digits. After the Islamist parties, the liberal New Wafd Party came in third place with a pathetic 9.2 percent.[15] Most of the rest of the liberal parties received between 1 and 2 percent of the vote.

If indeed the voting was fair, the Egyptian people overwhelmingly supported Islamist candidates, a scenario evidenced in virtually every other modern election held in the Middle East to date—and a theme the Obama administration had to have known.

Upon using the electoral process to take control of Egypt, the Muslim Brotherhood wasted no time making its intentions clear. Regarding Israel, multiple Brotherhood leaders gave interviews to the news media, calling for the Egypt-Israel peace treaty of 1979 to be abrogated, a move analysts don't expect Egypt to quickly make since the Brotherhood understands any such action may end much-needed Western aid. Yet the Brotherhood did announce it will not recognize Israel and intends to bring the peace treaty to a referendum. "We will not recognize Israel under any circumstances; we are talking about an occupation entity and a criminal enemy," said Dr. Rashad Bayoumi, the deputy head of the Brotherhood.[16]

The roots of anti-Israel sentiment with the Egyptian Muslim Brotherhood go deeper than that. Morsi himself had called for children to be educated to hate Jews. "Dear brothers, we must not forget to nurse our children and grandchildren on hatred towards those Zionists and Jews, and all those who support them," he said in a 2010 television interview. "They must be nursed on hatred. The hatred must continue."[17]

One of Morsi's first official visitors as president was Khaled Meshal, the leader of Hamas, an event that shouldn't have surprised anyone since Hamas is the Palestinian arm of the Brotherhood. Hamas's official charter calls for the murder of Jews and destruction of Israel. While Mubarak largely treated Hamas as an enemy to his secular regime, Morsi stood next to Meshal as the Hamas leader hailed the Egyptian elections as the start of a "new era" between Egypt and the Palestinians.[18]

In another signal of the changing winds in the Middle East, whereas Mubarak considered Iran one of his biggest enemies, in February 2012, Iranian warships were allowed by the new Egyptian government to pass through the Suez Canal, only the second time Iranian forces had done so since the 1979 Islamic Revolution in Iran.[19] In February 2013, Iranian president Mahmoud Ahmadinejad paid a visit to Egypt, another first since the 1979 revolution.[20]

During the anti-Mubarak protests, US officials and Western analysts routinely dismissed any claim that a future Egyptian government would utilize Islamic law as the basis for the rule of law. Those officials and analysts may want to read Article 2 of the current Egyptian constitution, which retains a clause that "Islam is the state religion, and the Arabic language is its official language. The principles of Islamic sharia are the main source of legislation."[21] Secular groups wanted this article, a holdover from the earlier constitution, removed entirely, but Islamist viewpoints prevailed. This provision will now be interpreted and enforced by a government dominated by the Muslim Brotherhood.

Egypt's new constitution clearly doesn't bode well for secular Muslims or the country's Coptic Christians, a major religious minority community in Egypt whose roots date back to the origins of Christianity and who, according to medieval Arab geographer Al-Muqaddasi, once constituted the majority of the Egyptian populace.[22] While Copts were targeted by Islamists during Mubarak's regime, such persecution has increased exponentially since Mubarak's ouster. In March 2011, just weeks after Mubarak was booted, Muslim villagers reportedly set fire to a Coptic church while attacking Christians on the street. Since 2011, at least two other churches have been set on fire, one in the Imbaba neighborhood of Cairo and another in Edfu in the south of the country. Coptic Christian families were also reportedly evicted from their homes in Alexandria. When Copts attempted to protest in October 2011, security forces reportedly fired at them, killing twenty-four and wounding more than three hundred. Some reports say more than two hundred thousand Copts have fled their homes since the violence against them has escalated.[23]

Whether or not the United States played a direct role in fomenting the revolution in Egypt, there can be no excuse for Obama's continued support of the hard-line Islamic parties that now control Egypt and have made their anti-Western intentions abundantly clear. Obama's direct support now includes F-16 fighter jets and two hundred Abrams tanks as part of a foreign aid package signed with Mubarak that critics say should have been scrapped when Brotherhood-dominated parties took office.[24] In May 2011, Obama pledged $1 billion to support Egypt's new government. On March 13, 2013, Secretary of State John Kerry announced the United States would provide $250 million, the first installation of Obama's pledge, to Egypt—in other words, to the Muslim Brotherhood–controlled Egypt.[25]

ISLAMIC CALIPHATE?

Obama's support for a US ally's ouster and that leader's replacement with radical Islamic elements would be repeated numerous times in the Middle East and North Africa, to the great detriment of our country's so-called war on terror.

Even before Mubarak's departure, violent protests toppled the twenty-three-year rule of President Zine al-Abidine Ben Ali, who fled Tunisia on January 14, 2011. Ben Ali largely was seen as an ally of the West, even working behind the scenes with Israel on occasion. During the demonstrations in Tunisia, Obama publicly hailed the "courage and dignity of the Tunisian people" and called for the Tunisian government to "hold free and fair elections in the near future that reflect the true will and aspirations of the Tunisian people."[26]

Amazingly, Obama seemed to give a pass to the possibility of elections leading to something other than Western-style democracy. In his support for the revolution in Tunisia, Obama stated that "each nation gives life to the principle of democracy in its own way, grounded in the traditions of its own people" and that he had "no doubt that Tunisia's future will be brighter if it is guided by the voices of the Tunisian people."[27]

Just as in Egypt, the most organized opposition in Tunisia were Islamic parties, particularly the Ennahda Movement. Following Ben Ali's departure, which was championed by Obama, Ennahda far outdistanced its more secular competitors in the 2011 elections, winning a clear plurality of the vote and becoming the dominant governing party. It should surprise no one to learn that the Islamic Ennahda Movement was inspired by the Muslim Brotherhood and that it now advocates a more overtly Islamic identity and society for the country.[28]

Another US ally forced to step down following mass protests was Yemen's president Ali Abdullah Saleh, who was considered a crucial ally in the US fight against al-Qaeda in his country and throughout the Middle East. Was the United States involved in his ouster? On April 7, 2011, a US State Department cable obtained by WikiLeaks reported on plans of Hamid al-Ahmar, leader of Yemen's Islah Party, to organize popular demonstrations throughout Yemen, aimed at removing President Saleh from power.[29] Those protests were indeed organized, bringing the Islah Party to rule. Guess who founded the Islah Party? The Muslim Brotherhood.

During the height of the demonstrations, the Obama administration urged Saleh to sign a deal transferring power to a temporary replacement government with the goal of holding elections. Obama's then-counterterrorism adviser and current CIA director John Brennan (about whom we will have more to say later in this chapter) met Saleh at a military hospital in the Saudi capital Riyadh. A White House statement explained how Brennan called for a "peaceful and constitutional political transition in Yemen" and stated that the US "believes that a transition in Yemen should begin immediately so that the Yemeni people can realize their aspirations."[30] Those aspirations brought the Muslim Brotherhood to power in Yemen.

Islamic parties similarly saw their fortunes rise in Algeria, where Islamists joined in the government after they came in second with sixty-six parliamentary seats in May 2012 elections championed by Obama.

The United States similarly called for the king of Morocco, Mohammed VI, one of the most Western-oriented leaders in North Africa, to open his monarchy to a power-sharing agreement with a new parliament to be voted on by the people. While the king still retains vast powers, he now shares in a coalition government with the Justice and Development Party, which won a plurality of the vote, the first under the country's new constitution. The party advocates Islamism and a society governed by Islam and has been described as an offshoot of the Muslim Brotherhood.

There have been similar US calls for elections in Jordan, a key US ally where the Muslim Brotherhood is the main opposition. Already, American assistance in toppling Muammar Gaddafi in Libya has led to an Islamic rise to power there.

Are you starting to see a pattern? Just as Jimmy Carter's policies were said to have weakened the secular Shah's regime in Iran, ushering in a Shiite Islamic revolution that continues to this day to support and perpetuate acts of worldwide terrorism (soon likely to be backed up by a nuclear arsenal), so, too, Obama's policies are installing political Islam throughout the Middle East and North Africa in a tidal wave of change already reaping disastrous results for those regions as well as for US interests there.

MINIMIZING ISLAMIC TERRORISM

Not only is Obama empowering the Muslim Brotherhood overseas; he has also maintained troubling relationships with Brotherhood-founded groups in the United States while espousing policies and rhetoric that seem to dangerously minimize the threat of Islamic terrorism.

"We cannot fully know what leads a man to do such a thing," Obama stated in a Rose Garden appearance one day after a Muslim US Army psychiatrist, Major Nidal Malik Hasan, engaged in a terrorist shooting massacre at the Fort Hood, Texas, military base, in which thirteen were gunned down in cold blood and thirty others were wounded. Even though reports were quickly emerging of Hasan's Islamic radicalism, Obama urged Americans not to "jump to conclusions" about the motives behind the shooting, downplaying religion as a motive in the deadly attack.[31]

Hasan's Islamic motivations were immediately clear to anyone who bothered to look. Eyewitnesses recounted how Hasan jumped onto a desk and, like scores of other Muslim terrorist attackers, shouted "Allahu Akbar!" before firing more than one hundred rounds at soldiers and on a crowd gathered for a college graduation ceremony.[32]

Maybe Obama should have noted that Hasan attended the Dar Al-Hijrah mosque in Falls Church, Virginia, in 2001, at the same time as Nawaf al-Hazmi and Hani Hanjour, two of the hijackers in the September 11 attacks.[33] The mosque back then was led by Anwar al-Awlaki, the now assassinated Islamic cleric who had become "operational" as a senior talent recruiter, motivator, and participant in planning and training for al-Qaeda operations.[34] US intelligence officials even intercepted e-mails between Hasan and al-Awlaki in which Hasan expressed admiration for the latter's teachings and eerily wrote, "I can't wait to join you [in the afterlife]." Hasan also asked al-Awlaki when jihad is appropriate, and whether it is permissible if innocents are killed in a suicide attack.[35]

The theme of Obama seemingly minimizing Islamic terrorism inside the United States would continue. On December 25, 2009, Umar Farouk Abdulmutallab, a Muslim Nigerian citizen, attempted to detonate plastic explosives hidden in his underwear while on board Northwest Airlines Flight 253 en route from Amsterdam to Detroit, Michigan.[36] In a knee-jerk reaction, Obama immediately referred to Abdulmutallab as an "isolated extremist," while Secretary of Homeland Security Janet Napolitano claimed there was "no indication" the attack was "part of anything larger."[37] However, it emerged that Abdulmutallab had traveled to the mountainous Shabwa Province of Yemen to meet with "al-Qaeda elements."[38] Al-Qaeda in Yemen released a video, with its logo in the corner of the screen, of Abdulmutallab and others training in a desert camp, firing weapons at such targets as the Jewish star, the British Union Jack, and the letters UN. The tape included an apparent martyrdom statement in which Abdulmutallab justified his actions against "the Jews and the Christians and their agents."[39]

Obama's statements about the Hasan and Abdulmutallab incidents fit with the theme of his administration's repeated attempts to remove Islam as a motivation in Islamic terrorist attacks. In multiple speeches, Obama has referred to the phenomenon of Islamic terrorism as "violent extremism."[40] In April 2010, that reference became official policy when counterterrorism officials announced Obama's advisers will remove religious terms such as "Islamic extremism" from the National Security Strategy, the central document outlining US national security issues, and will instead emphasize that the United States does not view Muslim nations through the lens of terror.[41]

The Obama administration's shift away from associating terrorism with Islam is typified in statements from John Brennan, the White House's former top counterterrorism adviser, who now serves as CIA chief. "Our enemy is not terror, because terror is a state of mind and, as Americans, we refuse to live in fear," Brennan told an audience at the Center for Strategic and International Studies. "Nor do we describe our enemy as jihadists or Islamists, because jihad is holy struggle, a legitimate tenet of Islam meaning to purify oneself or one's community."[42]

Brennan stated that Obama's strategy "is absolutely clear about the threat we face. Our enemy is not terrorism because terrorism is but a tactic. Moreover, describing our enemy in religious terms would lend credence to the lie propagated by al-Qaeda and its affiliates to justify terrorism, that the United States is somehow at war against Islam. The reality, of course, is that we have never been and will never be at war with Islam. After all, Islam, like so many faiths, is part of America."

Then he listed an Obama national security priority: "Addressing the political, economic, and social forces that can make some people fall victim to the cancer of violent extremism." He added: "I think there's more work we need to do to understand the psychology behind terrorism. But a lot of times, the psychology is affected by the environment that has those political, social, [and] economic factors that contribute to that." Here Brennan is insisting it is our country's policies that drive terrorism, as opposed to the openly stated mission of Islamic terrorist groups to spread Islam around the world.

Such views are commonplace in the White House and Pentagon. In remarks that went unreported by the media during a 2007 Senate hearing, then senator and current secretary of defense Chuck Hagel argued that terrorism is not a belief but instead is a response to despair and a lack of hope. Obama himself claimed the 9/11 attacks were carried out because of a lack of "empathy" for the suffering of others, contending that al-Qaeda's terrorist ideology "grows out of a climate of poverty and ignorance, helplessness and despair." He went on to imply that the September 11, 2001, attacks were in part a result of US policy, lecturing the American military to minimize civilian casualties in the Middle East and urging action opposing "bigotry or discrimination directed against neighbors and friends of Middle-Eastern descent."[43]

Obama's attempts to soften and deflect a radical Islamic role in terrorist attacks can be traced to the days immediately following 9/11. In a piece about 9/11 published September 19, 2001, in Chicago's *Hyde Park Herald*, he wrote, "Even as I hope for some measure of peace and comfort to the bereaved families, I must also hope that we, as a nation, draw some measure of wisdom from this tragedy."[44]

By routinely minimizing Islamic motivation, Obama and top administration officials are making it more difficult to defeat terrorism, since its root cause—Islamic fundamentalism—is being obscured.

MUSLIM BROTHERHOOD IN THE WHITE HOUSE

Speaking in February 2010, at what became a controversial question-and-answer session with Muslim law students at New York University, John Brennan announced that the Obama administration was working to calibrate policies in the fight against terrorism that ensure Americans are "never" profiled. Profiling has long been a contentious issue. Many counterterrorism officials believe it is necessary to ensure US security, but liberal and human rights groups largely oppose the practice.[45] Brennan's words left no doubt where he and the administration stood on the matter: "We need to be looking at ourselves as individuals," he said. "Not the way we look or the creed we have or our ethnic background. I consider myself a citizen of the world." Brennan told the audience the Obama administration was trying to "make sure that we as Americans can interact in a safe way, balance policies in a way that optimizes national security but also optimizes the opportunity in this country never to be profiled, never to be discriminated against."[46]

At the session, Brennan also stated that seeing a percentage of terrorists released by the United States return to terrorist attacks "isn't that bad," since the recidivism rate for inmates in the US prison system is higher. He also criticized parts of the Bush administration's response to 9/11 as a "reaction some people might say was over the top in some areas," that "in an overabundance of caution [we] implemented a number of security measures and activities that upon reflection . . . after the heat of the battle has died down a bit we say they were excessive."[47]

While Brennan's remarks drew scrutiny in the blogosphere and in some conservative media outlets, perhaps the biggest story remains untold—that a Muslim Brotherhood–tied group arranged his controversial speech, and it has deep ties not only with other Brotherhood fronts but to the White House.

Brennan's NYU session was organized by the Islamic Society of North America (ISNA), according to the group's website.[48] ISNA, whose members asked Brennan scores of questions during the event, stated the meeting was intended to initiate a "dialogue between government officials and Muslim American leaders to explore issues of national security."[49]

ISNA was founded in 1981 by the Saudi-funded Muslim Students Association (MSA), which itself was founded by the Muslim Brotherhood.[50] The two groups are still partners, and their complementary ideologies are still evident to those who look. In 2003, Aaron Klein attended an MSA event at New York's Queensborough Community College, at which violence against the United States was urged by speakers. "We are not Americans," shouted one speaker, Muhammad Faheed. "We are Muslims. [The United States] is going to deport and attack us! It is us versus them! Truth against falsehood! The colonizers and masters against the oppressed, and we will burn down the master's house!"[51]

ISNA is known for its promotion of strict Saudi-style Islam in mosques throughout the United States, notes the website Discover the Networks. Through its affiliate, the North American Islamic Trust—a Saudi government–backed organization—ISNA reportedly holds the mortgages on 50 to 80 percent of all mosques in the United States and Canada. "Thus the organization can freely exercise ultimate authority over these houses of worship and their teachings," states DTN.[52]

Islam scholar Stephen Schwartz describes ISNA as "one of the chief conduits through which the radical Saudi form of Islam passes into the United States."[53] According to terrorism expert Steven Emerson, ISNA "is a radical group hiding under a false veneer of moderation." It publishes a bimonthly magazine, *Islamic Horizons*, that "often champions militant Islamist doctrine." Emerson says the group also "convenes annual conferences where Islamist militants have been given a platform to incite violence and promote hatred," citing an ISNA conference at which Muslim Brotherhood leader Yusuf al-Qaradawi, discussed earlier in this chapter, was invited to speak.[54]

Discover the Networks notes that ISNA has held fund-raisers for terrorists. When Hamas leader Mousa Marzook was arrested in 1995 and eventually deported in 1997, ISNA raised money for his defense. The group also has condemned the US government's post-9/11 seizure of Hamas's and Palestinian Islamic Jihad's financial assets.[55] The Justice Department named ISNA an unindicted coconspirator in its case against the Holy Land Foundation in Texas, which was found guilty of raising money for the Hamas terrorist organization.[56] In 2009, Holy Land Foundation founders were given life sentences for "funneling $12 million to Hamas."[57]

Brennan is not the only Obama official to address the radical ISNA. In May 2011, Obama's deputy national security adviser, Denis McDonough, was hosted by an ISNA-affiliated mosque to give a speech touted as part of a White House initiative to reach out to Muslims. McDonough's speech received widespread media attention, yet not a single article we reviewed mentioned he was visiting an official affiliate of ISNA.

ISNA itself was less discreet. It filed a press release announcing, "Yesterday afternoon, ISNA President Imam Mohamed Magid hosted an event at ISNA affiliate organization, the All Dulles Area Muslim Society, of which Imam Magid serves as Executive Director." Continued the release, "The event, entitled, 'Our Collective Security,' featured Deputy National Security Advisor to President Obama, Mr. Denis McDonough, as he outlined the many contributions of Muslims to maintain national security and the White House's five point strategy to continue collaborations with the Muslim and interfaith community and to overcome extremism in all forms."[58]

During his speech, McDonough focused on Obama's initiatives for the Muslim community. "Here in Virginia and across the country,

Muslim Americans are our neighbors and fellow citizens," he said. "You inspire our children as teachers. You strengthen our communities as volunteers, often through interfaith projects, like the President's 'United We Serve' program."[59]

In another sordid example, in July 2011 Obama's faith adviser, Eboo Patel, spoke at the main event of a three-day convention held by the Muslim Students Association (which, as we noted, was founded by the Muslim Brotherhood). Patel appeared on a panel alongside Tariq Ramadan, grandson of the notorious founder of the Muslim Brotherhood, and Siraj Wahhaj, who was named as a possible coconspirator in the 1993 World Trade Center bombing, has defended the convicted WTC bomb plotters, and has urged the Islamic takeover of America.[60]

ISNA's extensive relationship with the Obama administration started even before Obama took office in 2009. One week before Obama's inauguration, Sayyid Syeed, national director of the ISNA Office for Interfaith and Community Alliances, was part of a delegation that met with the directors of Obama's transition team. The delegation discussed a request for an executive order ending "torture."[61]

ISNA president Ingrid Mattson represented American Muslims at Obama's inauguration, where she offered a prayer during the televised event.[62] In June 2009, Obama's top aide, Valerie Jarrett, invited Mattson to work on the White House Council on Women and Girls, which Jarrett leads.[63] That July, the Justice Department sponsored an information booth at an ISNA bazaar in Washington, DC.[64] Also that month, Jarrett addressed ISNA's forty-sixth annual convention. According to the White House, Jarrett attended as part of Obama's policy of outreach to Muslims.[65]

ISNA's Mattson was present at Obama's August 14, 2010, White House dinner that marked the start of the Islamic Ramadan month of fasting.[66] (She also represented ISNA at Obama's Ramadan dinner at the White House in 2009.[67]) It was at that dinner that Obama famously expressed support for the rights of an Islamic organization, the Cordoba Initiative, to build an Islamic cultural center and mosque two blocks from the area known as Ground Zero in Lower Manhattan.[68]

RADICAL ISLAMIST TIES TO US COUNTERTERROR AGENCIES

How close are radical Islamists to our counterterror agencies? In April 2009, Homeland Security secretary Janet Napolitano swore in Mohamed Elibiary as a member of her agency's Advisory Council. Elibiary, president and CEO of the Freedom and Justice Foundation of Carrollton, Texas, fervently endorses the teachings of Egyptian writer Sayyid Qutb, who is widely considered the father of the modern Islamic terrorist revolution.[69] Osama bin Laden and terror groups worldwide rely on Qutb for their fatwas and ideology.[70]

Qutb, executed in 1966 on charges of attempting to overthrow the Egyptian government, called for the creation of a worldwide Islamic state. He declared, "There is only one place on earth which can be called the home of Islam (Dar-ul-Islam), and it is that place where the Islamic state is established and the Shariah is the authority and God's limits are observed." Qutb labeled the non-Muslim world the Dar-ul-Harb—the house of war. "A Muslim can have only two possible relations with Dar-ul-Harb: peace with a contractual agreement, or war," wrote Qutb. "A country with which there is a treaty will not be considered the home of Islam," he said.[71]

Elibiary has regularly upheld Qutb's teachings. He has written that he sees in Qutb "the potential for a strong spiritual rebirth that's truly ecumenical allowing all faiths practiced in America to enrich us and motivate us to serve God better by serving our fellow man more."[72]

After *Dallas Morning News* editorial page editor Rod Dreher criticized Qutb's writings, Elibiary engaged in a lengthy, published e-mail feud in which he repeatedly defended Qutb. In one exchange, Elibiary wrote, "I'd recommend everyone read Qutb, but read him with an eye to improving America, not just to be jealous with malice in our hearts."[73]

Elibiary has strongly criticized the government's persecution of fundraisers for Hamas and is a defender of the Hamas-linked Council on American-Islamic Relations (CAIR).[74] He has criticized the US government's prosecution and conviction of the Holy Land Foundation and five of its former officials for providing more than $12 million to Hamas.[75] He wrote an op-ed in the *Dallas Morning News* suggesting the convictions were part of a US government policy of "denying our civil liberties and privacy at home" while pursuing antiterror policies that have "left thousands of Americans dead, tens of thousands maimed, trillions of taxpayer dollars squandered and our homeland more vulnerable than ever."[76]

In 2004, Elibiary was one of seven advertised speakers at an Irving, Texas, conference titled "A Tribute to the Great Islamic Visionary," celebrating the sixteenth anniversary of the death of the anti-US founder of the Iranian Islamic Revolution, Ayatollah Khomeini.[77] The main ad for the event, listing Elibiary as a speaker, declares, "'Neither east nor west' is the principal slogan of an Islamic revolution . . . and outlines the true policy of non-alliance for the Islamic countries and countries that in the near future, with the help of Allah SWT, will accept Islam as the only school for liberating humanity."[78] Under the heading "Selected sayings of Holy Prophet," another advertisement read, "Allah has made Islam to prevail over all other religions."[79]

The local CBS News affiliate in Texas reported on the event. CBS reporters Todd Bensman and Robert Riggs reported that one speaker at the conference was a Washington, DC, imam, Muhammad al-Asi, known for his radical views. At the event, CBS reported, Asi issued a strongly worded anti-American, anti-Jewish speech in which he said American imperialism and pro-Israel Zionism are "diabolical, aggressive, bloodthirsty ideologies that are trying to take over the world and destroy Islam." Another speaker at the conference, a ten-year-old boy, opened the tribute by praising Khomeini for reviving "pure" Islamic thinking and saving the religion from being conquered by the West, reported CBS. The boy called President Bush "the greatest enemy of the Muslim Ummah."[80]

Elibiary told CBS he did not know the event at which he was an advertised speaker was a tribute to Khomeini until after he arrived. He claimed he arrived at the event before hearing the first speakers, which included the boy and Asi. "I didn't attend the whole thing," he said, calling Asi an "extremist."[81]

DEPARTMENT OF STATE PENETRATED?

Questions need to be raised about whether the Obama administration exposed national security information to US enemies via an individual who had close personal access to Obama's first-term secretary of state,

Hillary Clinton. Huma Abedin, Clinton's deputy chief of staff, had deep personal and family associations with Islamic extremists and even terrorist organizations.

Some have raised concerns about the ties of Abedin's parents to the Muslim Brotherhood. But let's start with Abedin herself. It has emerged that she worked on the editorial board of a Saudi-financed Islamic think tank alongside a Muslim extremist accused of financing al-Qaeda fronts. The extremist, Abdullah Omar Naseef, is deeply connected to the Abedin family.

Naseef is secretary-general of the Muslim World League (MWL), an Islamic charity known to have spawned terrorist groups, including one declared by the US government to be an official al-Qaeda front. As we will soon demonstrate, Abedin's mother, Saleha Abedin, was the official representative of Naseef's terror-stained Muslim World League in the 1990s. Also, Huma's father, Professor Syed Abedin, was active in the Institute of Muslim Minority Affairs, a Saudi group that was founded by Naseef.

Saleha is currently the editor of the *Journal of Muslim Minority Affairs*, the publication of Syed's institute. The institute bills itself as "the only scholarly institution dedicated to the systematic study of Muslim communities in non-Muslim societies around the world." Now it has emerged that Huma herself served on the editorial board of the *Journal of Muslim Minority Affairs* from 2002 to 2008.[82]

Documents obtained by author Walid Shoebat reveal that Naseef served on the board with Huma from at least December 2002 to December 2003.[83] Naseef's sudden departure from the board in December 2003 coincides with the time at which various charities led by Naseef's Muslim World League were declared illegal terrorism fronts worldwide, including by the US and UN.

We have found that Saleha Abedin has been quoted in numerous press accounts as both representing the Muslim World League and serving as a delegate for the charity. In 1995, for example, the *Washington Times* reported on a United Nations–arranged women's conference in Beijing that called on governments throughout the world to give women statistical equality with men in the workplace. The article quoted Saleha Abedin, who attended the conference as a delegate, as "also representing the Muslim World League based in Saudi Arabia and the Muslim NGO Caucus."[84]

The UN's website references a report in the run-up to the Beijing conference that also lists Abedin as representing the Muslim World League at the event. The website posted an article from the now-defunct United States Information Agency quoting Abedin and reporting she attended the Beijing conference as "a delegate of the Muslim World League and member of the Muslim Women's NGO caucus." In the article, Abedin was listed under a shorter name, "Dr. Saleha Mahmoud, director of the Institute of Muslim Minority Affairs." We have confirmed the individual listed is Huma Abedin's mother. (The report misspelled part of her name. Her full professional name is at times listed as Saleha Mahmood Abedin S.)[85]

How bad is the Muslim World League? Founded in Mecca in 1962, it bills itself as one of the largest Islamic nongovernmental organizations. But according to US government documents and testimony from the charity's own officials, it is heavily financed by the Saudi government. The MWL has been accused of terrorist ties, as have its various offshoots, including the International Islamic Relief Organization (IIRO) and the Al-Haramain Islamic Foundation, which was declared by the US and UN as a terror-financing front. Indeed, the US Treasury Department, in a September 2004 press release, alleged Al-Haramain had "direct links" with Osama bin Laden.[86] The group is now banned worldwide by United Nations Security Council Committee 1267.

There long have been accusations that the IIRO and MWL repeatedly funded al-Qaeda. In 1993, bin Laden reportedly told an associate that the MWL was one of his three most important charity fronts. An Anti-Defamation League profile of the group accuses it of promulgating a "fundamentalist interpretation of Islam around the world through a large network of charities and affiliated organizations." The profile further states that "its ideological backbone . . . is based on an extremist interpretation of Islam, and several of its affiliated groups and individuals have been linked to terror-related activity."[87]

In 2003, *US News and World Report* documented that accompanying the MWL's donations, invariably, are "a blizzard of Wahhabist literature." The report continued: "Critics argue that Wahhabism's more extreme preachings—mistrust of infidels, branding of rival sects as apostates, and emphasis on violent jihad—laid the groundwork for terrorist groups around the world."[88]

In 1988, the MWL founded the Al-Haramain Islamic Foundation, developing chapters in about fifty countries, including for a time one in Oregon, until it was designated a terrorist organization. In the early 1990s, evidence began to grow that the foundation was funding Islamist militants in Somalia and Bosnia, and a 1996 CIA report detailed its Bosnian militant ties. The US Treasury designated Al-Haramain's offices in Kenya and Tanzania as sponsors of terrorism for their role in planning and funding the 1998 bombings of two American embassies in East Africa. The Comoro Islands office was also designated because it "was used as a staging area and exfiltration route for the perpetrators of the 1998 bombings."[89]

The *New York Times* reported in 2003 that Al-Haramain had provided funds to the Indonesian terrorist group Jemaah Islamiyah, which was responsible for the 2002 Bali bombings that killed 202 people.[90] Al-Haramain's Indonesia office was later designated a terrorist entity by the US Treasury.

In February 2004, the US Treasury Department froze all of Al-Haramain's financial assets pending an investigation, leading the Saudi government to disband the charity and fold it into another group, the Saudi National Commission for Relief and Charity Work Abroad. Despite that move, the United States designated Al-Haramain a terrorist organization in September 2004. In June 2008, the Treasury Department applied the terrorist designation to the entire Al-Haramain organization worldwide.

In August 2006, the Treasury Department also designated the Philippine and Indonesian branch offices of the MWL-founded IIRO as terrorist entities "for facilitating fundraising for al-Qaeda and affiliated terrorist groups." The *New York Post* reported the families of the 9/11 victims filed a lawsuit against IIRO and other Muslim organizations for having "played key roles in laundering of funds to the terrorists in the 1998 African embassy bombings" and for having been involved in the "financing and 'aiding and abetting' of terrorists in the 1993 World Trade Center bombing."[91]

Despite its offshoots being implicated in terror financing, the US government never designated the Muslim World League itself as a terror-financing charity. Many have speculated that the United States has been trying to not embarrass the Saudi government.

Meanwhile, Huma Abedin's mother, Salaheh, reportedly acted as one of sixty-three leaders of the Muslim Sisterhood, the de facto female version of the Muslim Brotherhood. Salehah served alongside Naglaa Ali Mahmoud, the wife of Mohamed Morsi, Egypt's new president. Saleha Abedin and Morsi's wife both were members of the Sisterhood's Guidance Bureau, Walid Shoebat found.[92]

Saleha Mahmood Abedin is an associate professor of sociology at Dar Al-Hekma College in Jeddah, Saudi Arabia. In February 2010, Hillary Clinton spoke at the college, where she was first introduced by Abedin and then praised the work of the terror-tied professor: "I have to say a special word about Dr. Saleha Abedin," Clinton said. "You heard her present the very exciting partnerships that have been pioneered between colleges and universities in the United States and this college. And it is pioneering work to create these kinds of relationships." Clinton continued, "But I have to confess something that Dr. Abedin did not, and that is that I have almost a familial bond with this college. Dr. Abedin's daughter, one of her three daughters, is my deputy chief of staff, Huma Abedin, who started to work for me when she was a student at George Washington University in Washington, DC."[93]

From aiding the rise of anti-Western Islamism overseas to developing troubling relationships with Muslim Brotherhood–linked groups in the United States, the Obama administration has been undermining US security at nearly every turn. Many questions need to be raised about Obama's role in the downfall of US allies and about his seemingly deliberate, dangerous campaign that is creating a worldwide Brotherhood beast already at odds with the United States.

6

CRONYISM, CORRUPTION, AND "CLEAN" ENERGY

DURING HIS STATE OF THE UNION address on February 12, 2013, President Obama announced plans for something called an Energy Security Trust, which, he told the nation, will "drive new research and technology to shift our cars and trucks off oil for good."[1] The president did not divulge more details about the composition of such a trust during his speech. However, we are quite familiar with the scheme. In our most recent book, *Fool Me Twice*, we dedicated an entire chapter section to revealing plans for the trust. We showed how the fund would serve as a de facto federal "green" bank that would borrow billions from the federal treasury to provide low-cost financing to private-sector investments in "clean energy." Our chapter further divulged plans for a second-term "green" stimulus.[2]

While Obama moves ahead with these and multiple other new clean-energy financing schemes, including some potentially shady deals, as we will soon show, the president has yet to be held accountable for the rank corruption, cronyism, and possible impeachable offenses related to his first-term green funding adventures using our taxpayer dollars. We recommend that Congress immediately convene hearings based on the information presented in this chapter.

To start with, lawmakers should look into possible corruption related to the authorship of the American Recovery and Reinvestment Act of 2009, also known as the "stimulus," and how activists who helped craft key sections of the bill are themselves quite close to companies that received billions from the very legislation they helped write.

We begin our journey with BrightSource Energy, a solar energy company attempting to build the world's largest solar power plant amid concerns such a venture might be too risky an investment for the federal government. BrightSource received a $1.37 billion federal loan guarantee, the largest the Department of Energy has ever provided for a solar power project.[3] The loan guarantee was for the construction of a gigantic California desert solar plant known as the Ivanpah Solar Electric Generating System, featuring mirrors that reflect sunlight toward a massive central tower that is then heated to produce steam, spinning turbines that, in turn, produce electricity.[4] During a national address in October 2011, Obama mentioned the possible benefits of BrightSource Energy's "revolutionary new type of solar power plant."[5]

The news media has entirely ignored the fact that BrightSource's chairman at the time of the federal loan guarantee was John Bryson, who stepped down from the energy company before being sworn in on October 21, 2011, as the thirty-seventh secretary of the Department of Commerce.[6] (Bryson resigned on June 21, 2012, after an unusual hit-and-run accident that he blamed on seizures.) Questions should already be raised about how the former employer of Obama's commerce secretary received the Energy Department's biggest loan guarantee. But it gets worse. Bryson also cofounded the Natural Resources Defense Council, an environmental activist group belonging to the controversial Apollo Alliance, which helped craft the "green" portions of the 2009 stimulus, the legislation that underwrote BrightSource's loan. No conflict of interest there?

ANTI-AMERICAN EXTREMISTS

Just so we can get a better concept of who was behind the stimulus—to see that there is supposedly radical ideology at play alongside the corporate pirating—let's stop for a minute and take a closer look at the Apollo Alliance, since this extremist-led group has been key in writing much environmental legislation that has so far redistributed billions of dollars in US taxpayer funds to questionable companies. The Apollo Alliance changed its name to the BlueGreen Alliance in May 2011, following a slew of publicity about the group's radicalism, including numerous major exposés by Aaron Klein. So as not to confuse readers, we will continue to refer to the group as the Apollo Alliance.

Apollo boasted in its own promotional material that it helped craft portions of the $787 billion stimulus legislation (officially called the American Recovery and Reinvestment Act, or ARRA) that Obama signed into law in early 2009. It was involved in writing the "clean energy and green-collar jobs provisions" of the bill, for which $86 billion in funds were earmarked, including public money "to build new transit and high speed rail lines, weatherize homes, develop next generation batteries for clean vehicles, scale up wind and solar power, build a modern electric grid, and train a new generation of green-collar workers."[7]

Apollo also recommended the stimulus bill allocate $11 billion for the development of a so-called "Smart Grid," which would use digital technology to deliver electricity from suppliers to consumers. Ultimately, the bill allocated precisely that amount to Smart Grid–related projects, including a $100 million provision for job training related to Smart Grid technology.[8] Soon we will look at some of these Smart Grid recipients.

In addition to its influence over stimulus funds, the Apollo Alliance was also instrumental in helping draft a "clean technology" bill known as the Investments for Manufacturing Progress and Clean Technology Act of 2009, or IMPACT. That legislation was sponsored by Sen. Sherrod Brown (D-OH). The act died in Congress but is likely to be resurrected after the 2014 midterms. It seeks to establish a $30 billion revolving loan fund to help small and midsized manufacturers restructure their factories to produce so-called clean technologies and become more energy efficient.[9] The Apollo Alliance documented how the act was based on the group's "GreenMAP" or Green Manufacturing Action Plan, which laid out aggressive steps to scale up production of American-made clean energy systems and components while making US factories more energy efficient.[10]

When Senator Brown formally introduced the act in June 2010, he was joined by Apollo Alliance chairman Phil Angelides and other notable business, labor, and clean energy leaders.[11] One year earlier, Angelides served as chairman of Obama's Financial Crisis Inquiry Commission.

Yet another piece of legislation that bears Apollo's fingerprints is the Consolidated Land, Energy, and Aquatic Resources Act of 2009, or the CLEAR Act, which passed 209 to 193 on July 30, 2010. It still requires Senate confirmation. The bill is somewhat ambiguous, so federal agencies will need to determine how it is implemented. It is being sold as a government response to the Gulf oil spill crisis, but the bill itself stretches far beyond addressing that tragedy to include page after page of provisions that are unrelated to the oil spill.[12]

Why should you care? Well, aside from how some of its personalities are tied to stimulus funds, the Apollo Alliance is led by a slew of radicals, including Van Jones, Joel Rogers, and Jeff Jones.[13] Van Jones, of course, is famous for resigning in 2009 as Obama's "green" jobs czar after it was exposed that he founded a communist revolutionary organization and suggested President Bush may have been involved in the 9/11 terrorist attacks.

Jeff Jones, meanwhile, cofounded the Weatherman domestic terrorist group, later known as the Weather Underground Organization, with Bill Ayers and Mark Rudd. The three signed an infamous statement calling for a revolution against the American government inside and outside the country to fight and defeat what the group called US imperialism. Jones went underground after he failed to appear for a March 1970 court date to face charges of "crossing state lines to foment a riot and conspiring to do so."[14] He moved to San Francisco with Ayers's wife, Bernardine Dohrn. That year, at least one bombing claimed by the Weathermen went off in Jones's locale at the Presidio army base. Jones's Weatherman infamously took credit for multiple bombings of US government buildings, including attacks against the US Capitol on March 1, 1971; the Pentagon on May 19, 1972; and the State Department on January 29, 1975.

Apollo member Joel Rogers is a founder of the socialist-oriented New Party, a 1990s political party that listed Barack Obama as a member in the organization's own newsletters. Obama's campaign later denied he was ever a member. Rogers is a professor of law, political science, public affairs, and sociology at the University of Wisconsin–Madison. He directs the Center on Wisconsin Strategy (COWS) and its projects, including the Center for State Innovation, Mayors Innovation Project, and State Smart Transportation Initiative.

Rogers is also the cofounder of something called Emerald Cities Collaborative. That group in 2009 worked with its fellow member, CoLab, to author a report on how stimulus funds could be leveraged to "achieve sustainable, empowered, prosperous, and equitable communities."[15] The report highly recommended that the Obama administration fund Smart Grid projects, funding we will soon tie to possible corruption.

If we want to bring it full circle, the Apollo Alliance is a project of the Tides Center, which is a spin-off of the Tides Foundation, a George Soros–funded organization founded in 1976 by antiwar activist Drummond Pike.[16] The Tides Center's board chairman is Wade Rathke, best known as the founder and chief organizer of the Association of Community Organizations for Reform Now, or ACORN. Rathke is also president of the New Orleans–based Local 100 of the Service Employees International Union. Tides also funds a who's who of radical groups, from MoveOn.org to the Ruckus Society, which trains radical Occupy activists in the tactics of direct action and confrontation.

BIG DONORS, BIG TAKERS

Let's get back to the rank corruption in the Apollo-crafted stimulus and other related green schemes. Obama's "science" czar, John Holdren, was coauthor of a 2004 energy policy paper tied to Apollo, titled "Ending the Energy Stalemate: A Bipartisan Strategy to Meet America's Energy Challenges" that recommended "cap and trade" legislation, including "clean coal" technology and $2 billion from the federal budget for construction of one or two new nuclear facilities. We found that the coauthor of the paper with Holdren is John Rowe, a financial bundler for Obama's 2008 campaign who, until his retirement in March 2012, served as chairman of Exelon, the mega utility owning 30 percent of all US nuclear plants.

Rowe has financial ties to several members of the Obama administration and previously boasted how his company stands to gain financially from the regulation of high-carbon-emitting plants—the very recommendations Rowe set forth in his paper with Holdren. Susan Tierney, another author of the paper, is now the number-two official at the Energy Department.[17]

Among the paper's key recommendations were:

- Establish a mandatory, economy-wide tradable-permits program to limit greenhouse gas emissions while capping initial costs at $7 per metric ton of $CO2$-equivalent reduction.

- Provide $4 billion over ten years in public incentives for integrated-gasification combined-cycle coal technology and for carbon capture and sequestration.

- Provide $3 billion over ten years in public incentives to demonstrate commercial-scale carbon capture and geologic sequestration at a variety of sites.

The paper further recommended "$2 billion over 10 years from federal energy research, development, demonstration and deployment budgets for demonstration of one to two new advanced nuclear facilities." In February 2010, the Obama administration announced a conditional $8.3 billion loan guarantee to support the construction of two nuclear reactors in Georgia, which would be the first new US nuclear plants in more than three decades.[18]

While Rowe's Exelon did not get the Georgia plant contracts, it gained massively from the stimulus. Exelon provides power to more than 6.6 million customers in at least sixteen states and the District of Columbia. It was chosen as one of only six electric utilities nationwide for the maximum $200 million stimulus grant from the Energy Department. Exelon also landed a Treasury commitment for up to $646 million, allowing it to finance one of the world's largest photovoltaic solar projects on what the

New York Times described as "extremely generous financial terms."[19]

Exelon is deeply tied to the Obama administration. The *New York Times* documented how Exelon's top executives were early and frequent supporters of Obama from his days in the Illinois State Senate to the White House. Exelon board member John W. Rogers Jr. is a friend of the president and one of his top fund-raisers. Obama's political strategist, David Axelrod, once worked as an Exelon consultant, and Obama's former chief of staff, Rahm Emanuel, originally helped found Exelon through an $8.2 billion corporate merger in 2000 while working as an investment banker. That deal was described as the biggest financial transaction in which Emanuel was ever involved. Rowe reportedly sought out Emanuel personally, stating he believed Emanuel would offer a different dimension, providing wisdom on what might pass muster at the governmental level.[20]

What the *Times* missed is that several coauthors of Holdren's 2004 energy policy paper have links to the Apollo Alliance. Coauthor Ralph Cavanagh is an attorney with the Natural Resources Defense Council, an Apollo affiliate. Another coauthor, Leo Gerard, is the international president of the United Steelworkers, which is on the Apollo board and has worked closely with Apollo's initiatives.[21]

STRONG-ARMING US NAVY TO ADVANCE OBAMA CRONIES?

Here's another Obama crony we found playing a key role in developing the energy provisions of the stimulus bill while occupying the boards of several companies recently receiving federal funds, including hundreds of millions in stimulus money. T. J. Glauthier served on Obama's 2008 White House transition team. Along with Apollo, he is widely credited with helping craft the energy provisions of the 2009 stimulus. In addition to serving on the boards of multiple major energy companies, Glauthier previously held two presidential appointments during the Clinton administration. He was the Energy Department's deputy secretary and chief operating officer, its second-highest-ranking official. Earlier, he served in the White House for five years as the associate director for natural resources, energy, and science in the Office of Management and Budget.

Unsurprisingly at this point, Glauthier is tied to several energy companies that benefited from the stimulus bill that he himself helped write.[22]

One such company that we investigated is GridPoint Inc., where Glauthier was appointed to the board in March 2008.[23] GridPoint provides utilities with software solutions for electrical grid management and electric power demand and supply balancing. The stimulus provides a whopping $4.5 billion for so-called Smart Grid projects and, as we reported in our previous book *Fool Me Twice*, GridPoint got paid from scores of Smart Grid deals funded by the stimulus. The company partnered with the Electric Transportation Engineering Corporation (eTec), Nissan, the Idaho National Laboratory, and others in a project to deploy electric vehicles (EVs) and their charging infrastructure in five states.[24] The Energy Department had awarded eTec almost $100 million in stimulus funds to support the project. GridPoint's role in the eTec project was to supply smart charging and data logging capability to utilities located in strategic markets of eTec's program in Arizona, California, Oregon, Tennessee, and Washington.

GridPoint also benefited from stimulus funds when it provided home energy management, load management, and electric vehicle management software solutions for a Green Impact Zone SmartGrid demonstration put on by KCP&L in Kansas City, Missouri.[25]

GridPoint helped the Sacramento Municipal Utility District (SMUD) manage power from its customers' rooftop solar panels.[26] SMUD had won $127.5 million in stimulus funds from the Department of Energy to carry out the project, which also included deploying six hundred thousand smart meters in its service territory. Again, in early 2009, the Energy Department awarded Argonne National Laboratory nearly $2.7 million in stimulus funding for three solar energy–related research projects. Argonne reportedly shared another $5 million in stimulus funding for projects with GridPoint and other companies and the Illinois Sustainable Technology Center.[27]

Besides benefiting from stimulus grants, GridPoint in 2010 won a separate $28 million contract with the US Postal Service to install energy management systems in selected post office locations across the United States.[28] At the same time, GridPoint's founder, Peter L. Corsell, contributed the $50,000 maximum donation allowable to Obama's inauguration.[29]

Did the Obama administration push a T. J. Glauthier company on the US Navy? Fox News reported the US Navy had purchased 450,000 gallons of biofuel for about $16 a gallon, or about four times the price of its standard marine fuel, JP-5, which had been going for under $4 a gallon. *HotAir* first noticed that Glauthier is a "strategic advisor" to Solazyme, the California company that is selling a portion of the biofuel to the Navy.[30] *HotAir* reported how Solazyme received a $21.8 million grant from the 2009 stimulus package. Also, writing at BigGovernment.com, Whitney Pitcher found that prior to serving as advisor to Solazyme and after his time as part of Obama's transition team, Glauthier served on the advisory board of SunRun, a solar financing company. In October 2010, just a few short months after Glauthier joined SunRun's advisory board, SunRun secured a $6.73 million grant from this Treasury Department stimulus program.[31] The company was the ninth largest recipient of such programs through December 2010.

WHITE HOUSE "IDEA FACTORY" TIED TO STIMULUS GRANTS

Anyone who has read our previous works is fully aware of the enormous influence the Center for American Progress holds over the White House. It is fair to say CAP, led by John Podesta, is the de facto policy nerve center of the Obama administration. *Time* magazine called CAP Obama's "idea factory," noting that "not since the Heritage Foundation helped guide Ronald Reagan's transition in 1981 has a single outside group held so much sway."[32] *Time* reported it is "difficult to overstate the influence in Obamaland of CAP." Podesta himself codirected Obama's transition into the White House in 2008 and has been one of the most frequent visitors to the White House ever since. The Center was quite influential in crafting the "stimulus." Many CAP fellows also serve on the board of the Apollo Alliance.

A little searching on our part uncovered that Podesta's sister-in-law served as the lobbyist for a wind power firm recently awarded a $135.8 million loan guarantee from the Department of Energy. The company is Brookfield Asset Management. It has a board of nine directors, including New York mayor Michael Bloomberg's longtime girlfriend.[33] The grant was finalized to build the 99-megawatt Granite Reliable Power Windpark project in New Hampshire's Coos County, making it the state's largest wind plant. Seventy-five percent of the new wind project is owned by BAIF Granite Holdings, which was created earlier this year by Brookfield Renewable Power, a subsidiary of Brookfield Asset Management of New York.[34]

Since 2009, Brookfield Management has been represented by the lobbying firm of Heather Podesta and Partners, LLC.[35] Podesta, a top financial bundler for Democrat politicians, is wife of lobbyist and art collector Tony Podesta, who is John's brother. Heather Podesta and her husband, in July 2011, topped the Federal Election Commission's lobbyist bundler database, raising more money by far in the six prior months than any other lobbyists. Their fund-raising was largely for Democrats.[36] According to White House visitor logs, Heather Podesta visited the White House eight times in Obama's first six months alone.[37]

Another example of questionable ties to the Obama administration and public financing is Duke Energy. Besides three nuclear power plants, two in South Carolina and one in North Carolina, Duke Energy operates fourteen so-called coal-fired energy plants, as well as several traditional hydro plants, oil- and gas-fired plants, and pumped-storage hydro plants.[38]

Duke stepped up in this latest election cycle to subsidize the Democratic National Convention to the tune of a $10 million line of credit." Duke's CEO, Jim Rogers, has given more than $30,000 toward Obama's reelection and has contributed more than $210,000 to Democrats since 2008. Duke "pocketed $230 million in taxpayer money from Obama's stimulus" for so-called green energy projects and has "lobbied for and stands to profit from the sort of cap-and-trade policies President Obama supports, as well as other Obama green-energy subsidies."[39]

MONEY DOWN THE CLEAN DRAIN

Besides probing the issue of corruption, there are also questions about whether the Obama administration violated the public trust by utilizing taxpayer money for highly risky ventures, many of which failed miserably. There are so many companies that received stimulus grants only to later go bankrupt that we don't even know where to begin and we cannot effectively cover the issue in a small chapter section. Solyndra is only the tip of the iceberg. How humiliating for Obama that just two days after his January 24, 2012, State of the Union address in which he singled out his stimulus grants to battery makers, the government-funded battery manufacturer Ener1 went bankrupt. It had approval for $118.5 million in grants from the Energy Department but had received only about half of that when it entered bankruptcy.[40]

Another battery company, A123 Systems, was described by the *New York Times* as the "centerpiece of the government's electric-vehicle program, opening two factories in Michigan and securing contracts to supply batteries to automakers including General Motors and the start-up firm Fisker Automotive." A123 was awarded a $249 million stimulus grant to establish battery manufacturing operations in Michigan. It had received about $132 million of the grant before filing for bankruptcy in October 2012.[41]

Speaking of waste, the LG Chem Michigan, an advanced battery plant funded by the stimulus faced some nasty accusations from the Energy Department's own inspector general. The inspector announced that federal auditors found LG Chem improperly used $842,000 of its $150 million federal grant to pay employees who volunteered at local nonprofits, played games, and watched movies.[42] In another of so many examples, Rentech Inc., which received $23 million from the Department of Energy for a Colorado refinery for its "green fuel" technology, announced on February 28, 2013, it was ceasing operations.[43]

The "green fuel" issue deserves a closer look. Be warned, however, we're about to enter the theater of the absurd. Scores of companies have received federal loans and grants from President Obama's 2009 stimulus to manufacture an experimental fuel called cellulosic ethanol, which has not been successfully produced in the United States and might not even work. The fuel, which is supposed to come from wood chips, was first pushed and funded by the George W. Bush administration. Despite the fact that no company has been able to produce the fuel, Congress previously passed a law imposing mandates on oil companies to mix the nonexistent cellulosic fuel into gasoline. Some companies have even been fined by the Environmental Protection Agency for failing to use the nonexistent fuel.

A George Soros–financed company attempted to cash in on the government mandate that all oil companies utilize a certain percentage of cellulosic ethanol, which is said to be environmentally friendly. Qteros, the private Massachusetts company backed by Soros Fund Management, closed last year due to lack of further investment, while other firms, some backed by stimulus money, are scaling back their production efforts.[44]

Cellulosic ethanol is a biofuel that is supposed to be produced from wood, grasses, or the inedible parts of plants. The 2007 Energy Security and Independence Act signed into law by President Bush mandated that oil companies use five hundred million gallons of biofuel in 2012, three billion in 2015, and sixteen billion annually by 2022. Of those numbers, a significant percentage must be made from so-called lighter environmental stocks, including cellulosic ethanol.[45]

The *Wall Street Journal* reported some seventy million gallons, or 70 percent of the cellulosic supply to meet the never-reached 2012 mandate, was to come from Alabama-based Cello Energy.[46] In 2009, a jury in a civil fraud case ruled that Cello had lied about how much cellulosic fuel it could produce.[47]

As the EPA quietly scaled back the 2011 cellulosic fuel requirement to just 6.6 million, there is much speculation about when the fuel can actually be produced. A Congressional Research Service study recently conceded that the US government "projects that cellulosic bio fuels are not expected to be commercially available on a large scale until at least 2015."[48] However, in a strange turn of events, the Obama administration's EPA has actually been fining oil companies for not utilizing the biofuel.

"As ludicrous as that sounds, it's fact," said Charles Drevna, who represents oil refiners in a suit against the EPA. "If it weren't so frustrating and infuriating, it would be comical," Drevna told Fox News.[49] Tom Pyle of the Institute for Energy Research, also speaking to Fox News, characterized the cellulosic biofuel program as "the embodiment of government gone wild."

The Soros-backed Qteros company was created for the very purpose of producing cellulosic ethanol in the United States. The company's closure due to lack of further investment may be indicative of whether the fuel can be produced. Another oil firm, Codexis, recently announced its cellulosic ethanol research collaboration between Iogen and Shell will be terminated.[50]

Scores of firms to produce the fuel were funded by Obama's "stimulus." US energy secretary Steven Chu announced in July 2010 his agency was providing a $105 million loan guarantee to support the construction of a cellulosic plant by POET LLC, the largest US ethanol company. The Energy Department also finalized a $132 million loan guarantee to Abengoa Bioenergy to support the development of a commercial-scale cellulosic ethanol plant.[51]

Perhaps most stunning is that despite the wild failures of Obama's clean energy ventures, despite the cronyism and corruption that need to be further investigated, the largely unchecked White House is now moving ahead with more "clean" funding projects. The latest venture is a $2 billion energy security project that Obama says is dedicated to fueling research into technologies that would result in a new generation of cars and trucks running on clean energy. We guess Obama has no interest in looking into the status of his wood chip fuel ventures before further wasting our public funds. It is time our lawmakers probe this waste, cronyism, and corruption that is a breach of the public trust and the ethics supposedly governing the office of the presidency.

7

BIG BROTHER OBAMA'S SURVEILLANCE REGIME

U NDER THE LEADERSHIP OF PRESIDENT OBAMA, the US government and private firms are quietly eavesdropping on our e-mails and phone conversations, gathering intelligence on citizens, and compiling massive databases of public and private records, information that is at times shared with foreign governments. High-tech, science fiction–like identification systems replete with major constitutional problems are being deployed while the government now says it is mining our private data not only to stop terrorism, an already sketchy excuse, but amazingly, also to predict *future* criminal activity. While some of these spy systems were established on a smaller scale by President Bush after 9/11, we will show how they were expanded exponentially and at times possibly illegally under Obama. It is to the point where we now live under a virtual surveillance regime, a country where Big Brother is watching us and where even private companies can easily obtain nearly unrestricted information on We the People.

UNCONSTITUTIONAL STROKE OF PEN

Would people be surprised to learn that on December 30, 2012, Obama extended the Foreign Intelligence Surveillance Act (FISA), an unconstitutional law that openly allows for warrantless surveillance of Americans' overseas communications, for five more years, with a stroke of the pen? Add that this is not the first time Obama had the opportunity to put an end to such actions but failed to do so.

Would they be disturbed to learn that, after a single day of rushed debate, the Democrat-controlled Senate shamefully voted for the FISA extension a brief two days prior? Or that amendments brought to the floor four days before could have brought a modicum of transparency and oversight to the government's activities but were hastily rejected?

Would they be upset that Justice Department reports on the "use of 'pen register' [outgoing data] and 'trap and trace' [incoming data] surveillance powers" revealed "federal law enforcement agencies [were] increasingly monitoring Americans' electronic communications, and doing so without warrants, sufficient oversight, or meaningful accountability"? The ACLU reported last September that between 2009 and 2011, the "combined number of original orders for pen registers and trap and trace devices used to spy on phones" had increased from 23,535 in 2009 to 37,616 in 2011.[1]

It is all true. Also, in a move reminiscent of the 2010 ObamaCare legislation—although the Senate had had months to consider them—the proposed amendments to the bill were not brought up for a vote until after the 2012 presidential election, and at a time when Congress would normally have been on its winter break. There was simply not enough time allotted for the amendments to have been properly discussed or passed.[2]

FISA—in force since 1978 and last renewed in November 2008 during the Bush administration, again with the help of a Democrat-controlled Congress—has critics on both sides of the aisle who claim that, with its "suspicionless" searches, it is a serious threat to both the privacy and constitutional rights of Americans.

"It's a tragic irony that FISA, once passed to protect Americans from warrantless government surveillance, has mutated into its polar opposite due to the FISA Amendments Act," Michelle Richardson, legislative counsel at the ACLU, said after Obama signed the renewal. "The Bush administration's program of warrantless wiretapping, once considered a radical threat to the Fourth Amendment, has become institutionalized for another five years."[3]

Curiously, Obama's renewal of FISA did not set off the same degree of alarm or public outcry that followed the December 2005 revelations by the *New York Times* that President Bush had violated the Fourth Amendment to the Constitution, which protects citizens against unwarranted search or seizure. It should be remembered that Obama began serving in the US Senate in January 2005 and was well aware of what the renewal of FISA would mean. Not only was he a party to the FISA renewal in 2008 but was also at the center of his own FISA vote controversy. As you will see, Obama's objections to the many unconstitutional aspects of the law were fleeting—if they ever existed at all—and should have been a warning of how he would manipulate the law once he was the chief executive on both this and many other key issues.

We begin with the January 26, 2006, appearance by Obama and then senator Chuck Hagel (D-NE), Obama's secretary of defense in his second term, on *ABC's This Week with George Stephanopoulos*. In response to the suggestion by White House aide Karl Rove that national security was a partisan issue, both Obama and Hagel assured Stephanopoulos that both Republicans and Democrats were "equally committed" to fighting terrorism.[4] "I think that I can make certain that we have the tools that are necessary to monitor calls from al-Qaeda to US citizens without going overboard and creating a situation in which, randomly, we are rifling through the e-mails and cell calls of ordinary American citizens," Obama asserted.[5]

Ironically, it is worth keeping in mind that, with straight faces, Obama and Hagel also told Stephanopoulos they were "uncertain that a president could have broad 'blank check' authority."[6] Speaking of impeachable offenses, it is equally ironic that, in March 2006, when Sen. Russ Feingold (D-WI) called for Bush to be censured "for allegedly breaking the law regarding domestic surveillance," Obama was among Democrats quick to distance themselves from the suggestion ahead of the midterm election. "It's not impeachment, but it's not something you apply lightly," Obama said. "And whether we want to start applying censure motions or impeachment when there are questions about a president's authority in national security [it] is something that you have to be judicious about."[7]

Nearly as soon as the Orwellian-named RESTORE Act of 2007 (Responsible Electronic Surveillance That Is Overseen, Reviewed, and Effective Act) was introduced,[8] the George Soros–funded MoveOn and as many as a "dozen top progressive blogs" launched an all-out campaign to pressure Obama and Sen. Hillary Clinton (D-NY), the top two Democratic presidential candidates, to publicly declare support for the vow by Sen. Chris Dodd (D-CT) that he would "place a hold on and filibuster the bill."[9]

"If Hillary and Obama don't comply," MoveOn spokesman Adam Green told Greg Sargent of Talking Points Memo on October 23, 2007, "it would send an unfortunate signal to Democratic voters about whether they're willing to stand up to George Bush. The idea is to get Democrats to stand on principle and exercise the powers of their office to stop Bush from covering up how far he went in illegally spying on the private emails and phone calls of innocent Americans."

The following day, Obama spokesman Bill Burton told Sargent, "To be clear: Barack will support a filibuster of any bill that includes retroactive immunity for telecommunications companies." Upon hearing the news, Green told Sargent, "Excellent—this is the kind of leadership we need to see from the Democratic candidates."[10] When the vote on the FISA bill was held in February 2008, Obama missed it while campaigning. He issued a statement declaring his support for Senators Dodd and Feingold, and members of the "grassroots movement."[11]

However, Obama changed his tune by the time Congress finally struck a deal in June to "overhaul the rules" on the government's wiretapping power. The deal provided what amounted to legal immunity for the phone companies that participated in Bush's warrantless eavesdropping program. The deal allowed the government to use "broad warrants to eavesdrop on foreign targets and conduct emergency wiretaps without court orders on American targets for a week if it is determined important national security information would be lost otherwise," Eric Lichtblau reported in the *New York Times*. Retroactively, it was believed the courts would have to see that the wiretaps had been necessary.[12]

Regarding Obama's deeply disappointing role in the act's passage, we turn to Yale law professor and critical legal studies–friendly Jack M. Balkin.[13] Balkin is an editor of the 2009 book *The Constitution in 2020*, the publication of which was supported by Yale University, George Soros's Open Society Institute (now known as Open Society Foundations), and the American Constitution Society for Law and Policy.[14] *The Constitution in 2020* conference held at Yale in 2005 was led by Balkin and Obama's former regulatory czar, Cass Sunstein. This is the Sunstein who holds that "interpretation of federal law should be made not by judges but by the beliefs and commitments of the U.S. president and those around him."[15]

Balkin noted in June 2008 that Obama had been "missing in action" on the FISA compromise bill passed by the House. When he did surface, Balkin noted, the Obama campaign "sent a lukewarm endorsement of the measure: As to the key reforms of FISA, the bill is an acceptable compromise, not perfect but the best one can do under the situation. As to the retroactive immunity for telecom companies, Obama [said he would] work to change that in the Senate." Balkin, however, had the correct interpretation for Obama's silence; the answer was simple: "Barrack [sic] Obama plans to be the next President of the United States. Once he becomes President, he will be in the same position as George W. Bush: he wants all the power he needs to protect the country."[16]

Only hours after the House approved the legislation, Obama issued a statement that angered the left: "Given the legitimate threats we face, providing effective intelligence collection tools with appropriate safeguards is too important to delay. So I support the compromise, but do so with a firm pledge that as president, I will carefully monitor the program."[17]

"It's becoming clear even to the Left that Obama has no real firm principles, only ambition," conservative blogger Ed Morrissey noted at HotAir.com.[18] The FISA package was much the same as that supported by Democrats in February, except Morrissey noted it required a court "to certify that telecoms meet the prerequisites for immunity that the first bill granted outright." What had changed? Obama no longer needed the hard left to get past Hillary Clinton in the election. Obama had "tossed them under the bus with as much consideration as he did Jeremiah Wright and

Jim Johnson," Morrissey noted.

Why *would* Obama oppose the FISA compromise bill? Jack Balkin had the answer to that as well: if done on Bush's watch, Obama wouldn't have to worry about "wasting political capital" on it after the election. Although the act gave a "bit too much power to the executive," Obama "plans *to be the executive*," he stated.[19]

The FISA compromise also expanded the executive's "ability to wiretap and engage in much broader searches of communications" than previously allowed. Balkin wrote, perhaps with a note of sarcasm, "President Obama will *like* having Congress authorize these new powers. He'll like it just fine. People aren't paying as much attention to this part of the bill. But they should, because it will define the law of surveillance going forward. It is where your civil liberties will be defined for the next decade."[20]

WARRANTLESS SPYING ON STEROIDS

An equally brutal assessment of the FISA legislation had appeared on June 19, 2008, the day before the act passed in the House. Jim Cook of the far-left *Irregular Times* wrote, "Americans will be stripped of the legal standing to challenge the constitutionality of warrantless searches and seizures. Don't let the authoritarians in Washington, DC distract you with some kind of claim that this is about protecting citizens by watching foreigners with funny names like Ahmed and Abdul . . . [the Act] specifically authorizes the U.S. government to spy on American citizens without a warrant too."[21]

The new FISA was not just about intercepting phone calls. Without a warrant or even the prior approval of a FISA judge, the administration could now conduct a physical search as long as it later informed a judge it had done so, merely stating that the information was gathered in the name of "public safety." Therefore, Cook wrote, the government "can go ahead and engage in ANY physical search, ANYWHERE, WHENEVER it wants—then use the information as it sees fit, even if some judge later on says that the search was unjustified."[22]

Another valuable assessment was published June 22, 2008, by Martin "Marty" S. Lederman. This new all-inclusive global FISA legislation, he concluded, provided for "vacuum-cleaner" surveillance when there was "no way of knowing in advance which calls are wholly international" and "which of the targets of such vacuum-cleaner surveillance are foreign powers or their agents."[23]

Lederman, currently on leave from his position as associate professor of law at the Georgetown University Law Center, was appointed in January 2009 by Obama as a deputy assistant attorney general in the Department of Justice's Office of Legal Counsel. More recently, Lederman coauthored the 2010 paper *The National Security Agency's Domestic Spying Program.*[24]

When the bill passed in the Senate in July 2008, an outraged ACLU press release asserted that it "essentially legalize[d]" Bush's unlawful warrantless wiretapping program.[25] Caroline Fredrickson, director of the ACLU Washington Legislative Office, deemed the bill a constitutional "nightmare." "With one vote, Congress has strengthened the executive branch, weakened the judiciary and rendered itself irrelevant," she said. "The government can listen in without having a specific reason to do so. Our rights as Americans have been curtailed and our privacy can no longer be assumed."[26]

Echoing Lederman's line of thought, Balkin wrote a year after the bill's passage that now Obama has "the authority to run surveillance programs similar in effect to the warrantless surveillance program . . . That is because New FISA no longer requires individualized targets in all surveillance programs. Some programs may be 'vacuum cleaner' programs that listen to a great many different calls (and read a great many e-mails) with any requirement of a warrant directed at a particular person as long as no U.S. person is directly targeted as the object of the program."[27]

Now that we know how we got here, let's look at today's concerns. A big one, of course, is that unsuspecting Americans could "get swept up in an investigation if officials think they are in contact with a terrorism suspect." A prevision states that intelligence officials cannot "intentionally target a specific American, nor intentionally acquire communications that are 'known at the time of acquisition' to be wholly domestic."[28]

The key word here is "intentionally." How likely is it that innocent Americans might not get "swept up" when trillions of phone calls and e-mails can be reviewed by the National Security Agency, the government's chief eavesdropping agency, without a warrant? Not very.

"INTENTIONALLY": CASE IN POINT

On June 5, 2013, Glenn Greenwald of the UK's *Guardian* newspaper shook things up when he exposed just how "intentionally" the National Security Agency had been manipulating FISA to conduct its mass surveillance programs.[29]

A top secret court order issued by FISA judge Roger Vinson, of the Northern District of Florida, had granted the NSA a ninety-day window between April 25 and July 19 to collect "the telephone records of millions of US customers of Verizon, one of America's largest telecoms providers."[30]

The order "[required] Verizon on an 'ongoing, daily basis' to give the NSA information on all telephone calls in its systems, both within the US and between the US and other countries," Greenwald reported. The document, he wrote, "shows for the first time that under the Obama administration the communication records of millions of US citizens are being collected indiscriminately and in bulk—regardless of whether they are suspected of any wrongdoing." Greenwald continued: "Under the terms of the blanket order, the numbers of both parties on a call are handed over, as is location data, call duration, unique identifiers, and the time and duration of all calls. The contents of the conversation itself are not covered."[31]

The records to be produced are numerical in nature: "'session identifying information,' such as 'originating and terminating number,' the duration of each call, telephone calling card numbers, trunk identifiers, International Mobile Subscriber Identity (IMSI) number, and 'comprehensive communication routing information.'" Greenwald explained that this type of information is classified "as 'metadata,' or transactional information, rather than communications, and so does not require individual warrants to access." The document also "specifies that such 'metadata' is not limited to the aforementioned items." Such collected data would "allow the NSA to build easily a comprehensive picture of who any individual contacted, how and when, and possibly from where, retrospectively," he added.

Greenwald also explained how this differs from data collection by the Bush administration: "Under the Bush administration, officials in security agencies had disclosed to reporters the large-scale collection of call records data by the NSA, but this is the first time significant and top-secret documents have revealed the continuation of the practice on a massive scale under President Obama."

Andy Greenberg at *Forbes* emphasized that the Verizon "spying order" only targets Americans, not foreign communications. It would seem that the FBI made an end-run around the law on the NSA's behalf by obtaining a "top secret order" which "demanded that Verizon turn over all metadata for phone records originating in the United States" to the NSA. Greenberg confirmed: "The order specifically states that only data regarding calls originating in America are to be handed over, not those between foreigners."[32]

Why should you care? This April, in its first-quarter earnings report, Verizon Communications Inc. "listed 121 million customers . . . 98.9 million wireless customers, 11.7 million residential phone lines and about 10 million commercial lines," the Associated Press reported. However, remember that under the terms of the FISA order, "the phone numbers of both parties on a call are handed over, as are location data, call duration, unique identifiers, and the time and duration of all calls."[33] This is a huge slice of the American populace. Do the math: the total estimated US population in 2012 was in the neighborhood of 319 million.[34]

Additionally, the "law on which the order explicitly relies is the so-called 'business records' provision of the Patriot Act, 50 USC section 1861," Greenwald reported. FISA critics view this as an "extreme interpretation of the law to engage in excessive domestic surveillance."[35] The Electronic Frontier Foundation (EFF) and others point out that the Obama administration has committed an unconstitutional act in its violation of the Patriot Act by manipulating Section 215, "the legal authority the government was relying on to perform this type of untargeted surveillance." "These recent events reflect how profoundly the NSA's mission has transformed from an agency exclusively devoted to foreign intelligence gathering, into one that focuses increasingly on domestic communications," the EFF stated.[36]

The Obama administration immediately became defensive. Aboard *Air Force One*, on the president's trip to North Carolina, reporters were given the White House talking points, including the claim that "a 'robust legal regime' is in place to ensure civil liberties aren't violated by government use of powers under the Patriot Act." White House spokesman Josh Earnest said: "That regime has been briefed to and approved by the court. And activities authorized under the Act are subject to strict controls and procedures under oversight of the Department of Justice, the Office of the Director of National Intelligence, and the FISA [Foreign Intelligence Surveillance Act] Court to ensure that they comply with the Constitution and the laws of the United States, and appropriately protect privacy and civil liberties."[37]

Verizon was not the only major telecommunications company to be on the receiving end of a FISA mass surveillance warrant. Fewer than twenty-four hours after Greenwald's revelation, on June 7, 2013, the *Wall Street Journal* reported that AT&T, with "107.3 million wireless customers and 31.2 million landline customers," and Sprint Nextel, with "55 million customers in total," were also included. This was in addition to the "records from Internet providers and purchase information from credit-card providers," the *Journal* reported. Unsurprisingly, the *Journal* reported, the "credit-card firms, phone companies and NSA declined to comment."[38]

And it gets even worse. Eli Lake, the national security correspondent for the *Daily Beast*, reported June 7, 2013, that "sensitive" data "secretly collected" from US phone companies was shared with at least one foreign government. The NSA shared the data with "its British counterpart, the Government Communications Headquarters (GCHQ)," Lake wrote.[39]

Lake further reported that an agreement between the US and the UK provides for the sharing of "signal intercepts and electronic intelligence through a pact known as the United Kingdom United States of America Agreement." That agreement, he added, "has been expanded to include Australia, Canada, and New Zealand." Lake also learned from US intelligence officials that, while UK intelligence officials were not allowed hands-on direct access, GCHQ "received unredacted analysis of targeted searches, according to these sources."

Surely the seizure of domestic phone records from three major phone carriers for more than an estimated 300 million users is unconstitutional on two obvious counts. It is a First Amendment assault on freedom of speech and the Fourth Amendment right against unreasonable search and seizure.

It is also worth noting that there will soon be a new mega-facility in the United States expressly to handle the massive data the NSA is collecting. Plans for the $1.2 billion "data farm" were announced in 2007 and the "heavily-fortified" facility is expected to open in September 2013.[40]

It was not until July 2009, however, that the project was "enabled" when Obama signed a funding bill.[41]

The center's purpose is "to intercept, decipher, analyze, and store vast swaths of the world's communications as they zap down from satellites and zip through the underground and undersea cables of international, foreign, and domestic networks," James Bamford wrote at Wired.com.[42] It is projected that the center will be able to store yottabytes of information. Rich Trenholm explained a yottabyte at the UK tech website c|net: "As well as scoring 17 points in Scrabble, a yottabyte is equal to 1,000,000,000,000,000GB. We don't know how to even say that out loud." He also observed that it will take an "electricity bill the size of Salt Lake City's" to power the estimated "million square feet" facility.[43]

A "top official" "involved with the program" told Bamford that the NSA had "made an enormous breakthrough several years ago in its ability to cryptanalyze, or break, unfathomably complex encryption systems employed by not only governments around the world but also many average computer users in the US." The "upshot," the official said, is that "Everybody's a target; everybody with communication is a target."[44]

This should dispel any notion that the yottabytes of data to be stored and analyzed will only be focused on identifying the activities of foreign terrorists. The center—officially called the Community Comprehensive National Cybersecurity Initiative Data Center, and code-named "Bumblehive"—falls under the purview of the NSA's Domestic Surveillance Directorate. The center's website clearly explains its mission (note the use of the word "exploited"): "The steady rise in available computer power and the development of novel computer platforms will enable us to easily turn the huge volume of incoming data into an asset to be exploited, for the good of the nation."[45]

James Bamford pointed out that the NSA now has all its ducks in a row: It "has turned its surveillance apparatus on the US and its citizens . . . established listening posts throughout the nation to collect and sift through billions of email messages and phone calls, whether they originate within the country or overseas . . . created a supercomputer of almost unimaginable speed to look for patterns and unscramble codes . . . [and built] a place to store all the trillions of words and thoughts and whispers captured in its electronic net." Of course, he wrote, "it's all being done in secret. To those on the inside, the old adage that NSA stands for Never Say Anything applies more than ever."

An inconvenient fact, Greenberg wrote, is that the NSA is deeply enmeshed in domestic surveillance even though its "charter specifically [disallows] surveillance of those within the United States."[46] Add to this a second inconvenient fact: the NSA is an agency of the Department of Defense and is headed by a general officer. Like the TALON program we discuss shortly, this is most likely a military intelligence-gathering operation carried out against US citizens in violation of the Posse Comitatus Act of 1878. The act expressly forbids direct participation by the military in a "search, seizure, arrest, or other similar activity" on the federal government's behalf.[47]

"LIKE SCIENCE FICTION"

How can innocent Americans avoid being swept up in the FBI's Next Generation Identification (NGI) program, an intelligence database implemented in "unidentified locales" across the United States? NGI is described as a "compilation of initiatives" that includes a state-of-the-art facial recognition project and updates to its automated fingerprint identification system that "keeps track of citizens with criminal records" and is used to "accumulate and archive information about each and every American." The federal government is "linking a database of images and personally identifiable information of anyone in their records with departments around the world thanks to technology that makes fingerprint tracking seem like kids' stuff," *Russia Today* reported in September 2012.[48]

The FBI said the "technology could be used for 'identifying subjects in public datasets,' as well as 'conducting automated surveillance at lookout locations' and 'tracking subject movements,' meaning NGI is more than just a database of mug shots mixed up with fingerprints," *Russia Today* continued. The FBI has admitted that its "intent with the technology surpasses just searching for criminals but includes spectacular surveillance capabilities. Together, it's a system unheard of outside of science fiction."[49]

And don't forget the "old adage in computing and data processing: Garbage in, garbage out. How much is the incompetence driven violation of your rights costing us? No one seems to be sure," lawyer and political blogger Gene Howington observed.[50]

If you think that the government's "vacuum cleaner" programs only sweep your phone calls and e-mails, face, and fingerprints, then you'd be very wrong. There are several other ways Americans might find themselves "swept up" in surveillance activity without their knowledge.

It was revealed in February 2006, more than a year after Obama was sworn as a US senator, that the "supposedly defunct" Total Information Awareness data-mining and profiling program had been acquired by the NSA.[51] It should come as no surprise that the Obama administration has continued the Bush administration program—and its progeny—to new depths of intrusion.

After 9/11, the number of federal, state, and local organizations gathering information in the "war on terrorism" steadily increased. In 2004, the General Accounting Office conducted a survey of more than one hundred federal departments and agencies regarding their use of data mining from personal information and other federal agencies. Ultimately, the GAO found that nearly two hundred data-mining efforts used personal information (including student loan application data, bank account numbers, credit card information, and taxpayer identification numbers). The Department of Defense reported the largest number of efforts, including analyzing intelligence and detecting terrorist activities, although efforts for detecting criminal activities or patterns were spread "relatively evenly."[52] Additionally, the Department of Homeland Security pledged to share all data maintained by the FBI and the CIA with state and local officials.[53]

The GAO also found collection and mining of large amounts of data culled from commercial sources. Agencies were not only using data for investigations of known terrorists but also attempting to "discern potential terrorist activity by unknown individuals."[54]

TOTAL INFORMATION AWARENESS TOWARD TOTALITARIAN STATE

In a January 2010 *Human Events* editorial, Jed Babbin recommended that the government's "Terror Lists" be merged to prevent another attack similar to those on Christmas day 2009 by "underwear bomber" Umar Abdulmutallab or the November 2009 massacre at Fort Hood by US Army major Nidal Hasan.[55] (The Obama administration yet refuses to admit that the latter was an act of terrorism, preferring to call it "workplace violence" by virtue of the fact it was carried out by a soldier who gunned down other soldiers on a military installation.)

But if the government were to merge its lists, which lists should those be? Babbin singled out two. The first is the TIDE (Terrorist Identities Datamart Environment) list,[56] which supports the US government's screening and watch lists and gathers information about people who "may be connected to terrorism."[57] In December 2012, there were more than five hundred thousand "identities suspected of terror links." Some of the names are "known or suspected terrorists; others are terrorists' friends and families; still more are people with some loose affiliation to a terrorist."[58] The second is the "no-fly" list of people deemed to be a threat to aviation or national security and who have allegedly been barred from US flights.

TIDE, by the way, was built upon the US government's TIPOFF program, which dates to 1987.[59] Originally created to alert consular officials as to whether individuals applying for visas for entry to the United States were known or suspected terrorists, TIPOFF was expanded in 1991 to assist Immigrations and Customs inspectors at ports of entry into the United States. It then excluded information on domestic terrorism.[60] The FBI's Terrorist Screening Database, a subset of the TIDE database, was created to serve as the US government's main database for international terrorism.[61] The TIDE database was unique in that it consolidated terrorist information missing from various incomplete identity records. It included: "names, aliases, dates and places of birth, identification and travel documents, unique or distinguishing physical features, biometric data [fingerprints and DNA records], and individuals' affiliation with terrorist acts or groups."[62]

As the federal government constantly reinvents and rebrands its missions, make no mistake: these are only a few of the many databases that have been created and maintained by various government agencies and organizations. The more things change, as the saying goes, the more they stay the same.

The idea of merging terrorist watch lists did not escape John Poindexter, the former national security advisor in the Reagan administration and the chief architect of the Iran-Contra affair. In early 2002, Poindexter came up with Total Information Awareness. The TIA system ran the innovative computer-based statistical and recognition techniques used by scientists and marketers. It is simply known as data mining. Although military and intelligence agencies had never before been permitted to spy on Americans "without extraordinary legal authorization," Poindexter argued that the government needed "broad new powers to process, store and mine billions of minute details of electronic life in the United States."[63]

(This sounds exactly like the sort of justification the Obama administration has used on a number of occasions. Why does no one question what "broad new powers" means?)

TIA was overseen by the Orwellian-sounding Information Awareness Office established as a branch of the Defense Department's Defense Advanced Research Projects Agency, best known as DARPA. The Office website spelled out how it planned to carry out its mission in purposely broad strokes.[64] It was to gather and merge all the databases. Put simply, the Office's mission was to "gather as much information as possible about everyone in a centralized location for easy perusal by the United States government."[65]

Left-wing, right-wing, and libertarian critics alike claimed the Office's very existence "disregards the concept of individual privacy and liberties and is far too invasive and prone to abuse . . . [and is] another step farther down the slippery slope to a totalitarian state."[66]

The Office and the Awareness system were targeted early in January 2003. Democratic senators Russ Feingold (WI) and Ron Wyden (OR) introduced legislation that would shut them both down. The Awareness system was unfunded and said to have been ended. But was it? Not if you believe in the power of successively cranked-out acronyms.[67] The most prominent of the Awareness system's successors was TALON (Threat and Local Observation Notice reports). The TALON format was developed in 2001 by the Air Force Office of Special Investigations for its Eagle Eyes program, a neighborhood watch program "to detect and report suspicious activity of possible targeting of Air Force interests by terrorists."[68]

A May 2003 memorandum from deputy secretary of defense Paul Wolfowitz to Pentagon top brass directed the heads of military departments and agencies to immediately begin producing TALON reports related to domestic threats.[69] A TALON report consisted of raw, nonvalidated information that was to be passed on to analysts and incorporated into the Department of Defense's process for warnings against terrorism. The memorandum also ordered that TALON reports be directed to the Counterintelligence Field Activity, or CIFA.[70]

The information gathered was dispersed even wider. CIFA, which had been created by a presidential directive signed in January 2001 by President Clinton, was to provide full access to the entire TALON database to the Defense Intelligence Agency for its terrorism warning function. Details such as CIFA's size and budget remain classified.[71] By 2005, the TALON database and other counterintelligence reports were designated as Cornerstone.[72] The system for sharing TALON and other reports was known as the Joint Protection Enterprise Network. JPEN belonged to the US Northern Command, which used TALON reports to assist in its homeland defense mission.[73] However, in June 2006, funding dried up for JPEN, and all TALON reports were transferred directly to the US Northern Command.[74]

Had TALON accomplished its mission to date? Not quite. A June 2007 Department of Defense Office of Inspector General investigation of more than a thousand deleted reports included 263 reports related to domestic antiwar or counter-military recruitment groups' protests and demonstrations. Only seventy-five of these involved criminal actions, followed by arrests, court action, violence, and destruction, and required police intervention. Although the inspector general asserted this demonstrated the "value" of the TALON reports for law enforcement and force protection purposes,[75] it should be noted that none of the reports had anything to do with terrorists or terrorism, the purpose for which the program was created.

The new undersecretary of defense for intelligence, Lt. Gen. James R. Clapper Jr., who went on to become Obama's director of national intelligence, wanted the TALON program terminated and called upon Secretary of Defense Donald Rumsfeld to do so.[76] The number of reports diminished after reporting activity was restricted to "possible international terrorist activity only" and the results were found inconsistent with the program's original intent.[77]

Does this mean that TALON disappeared? Even though the Department of Defense announced the database was to be terminated in September 2007, the DOD was expected to develop new threat reporting procedures and facilities. Meanwhile, threat reports were to be transmitted to the FBI database known as Guardian.[78]

WHY SHOULD I CARE?

Why is this important? First of all, it is significant because it illustrates how the insatiable government "vacuum cleaner" has continued to suck up information and carried out its data mining of US citizens, illegal immigrants, and foreigners dating at least to the TIPOFF program in 1987. While Congress "ostensibly killed" the Total Information Awareness project, legislators reportedly preserved the program's funding for the project's "component technologies" if—or when—they were transferred to other government agencies.[79]

In other words, Congress ensured that Total Information Awareness lived to fight another day. Also, if all this alphabet soup of surveillance and data mining programs sounds like something from a Robert Ludlum novel or a Jason Bourne spy movie, it is.

A second reason the TALON program is significant is that it also was a military intelligence operation carried out against US citizens in violation of the Posse Comitatus Act.[80]

The contents of the TALON database were quite possibly turned over to the FBI as well to add to its massive database. Although we were told that TALON reports had been destroyed, the Defense Department inspector general had access to what may have been duplicate reports for its June 2007 investigation. The question remains, what happened to those reports, with their nonterrorism-related information allegedly destroyed by US Northern Command in 2005?

Also, the constant shuffling, reshuffling, copying, sharing, and passing around of government databases calls their integrity—not to mention the security of the information they contain—into question. The ACLU was sufficiently concerned in August 2004 that it released a detailed forty-seven-page report, *The Surveillance-Industrial Complex*. Jay Stanley, the report's author, wrote that the "drive to access ever more information about ever more people" has "practical limits" on the "resources, personnel and organization needed to extend the government's surveillance power to cover hundreds of millions of people." There are limits to the number of people who can be hired, as well as to the right "ratio of watchers to the watched." The US security establishment sought to overcome this obstacle by "enlisting individuals and corporations as auxiliary members of its surveillance networks."[81]

By engaging private partners, the government gained access to private-sector databases. The government could also "carry out privacy-invading practices at 'arm's length' by piggy-backing on or actually cultivating data collection in the private sector that it could not carry out itself without serious legal or political repercussions," Stanley wrote.[82]

One program detailed in the ACLU report is TIPS (Terrorism Information and Prevention System), a program launched in January 2002 by the Justice Department. The plan called for a nationwide roving network of untrained and unaccountable government informants, including "millions of American truckers, letter carriers, train conductors, ship captains, utility employees and others." The pilot program aimed for one million informants in ten cities. The plan failed; faced with a "storm of outrage," the program was at first reduced to eliminate visits to Americans' homes before it was shut down completely by Congress.[83]

If this sounds like shades of the Cold War–era Soviet Union, it is. Are similar programs being carried out by the Obama administration? You betcha.

In fact, TIPS and all its urgency to turn ordinary citizens into neighborhood spies made a recent comeback as "If You See Something, Say Something," a Department of Homeland Security campaign. "Homeland Security Begins with Hometown Security," the campaign's website reads. DHS is also looking to cast a wide net for reports that "document behavior reasonably indicative of criminal activity related to terrorism" by partnering with "transportation systems, universities, states, cities, sports leagues and local law enforcement."[84]

Another program, First Observers, is the Transportation Security Administration's highway security program that "engages truckers as watchdogs." Lisa Simeone explained on *TSA News* that First Observers is funded by FEMA and DHS and run by the TSA, which "recruits truckers from an organization called OOIDA, Owner-Operator Independent Drivers Association. OOIDA, in turn, partners with a security firm called HMS."[85]

As you can see, TSA and the Obama administration learned a valuable lesson from TIPS: don't disperse an untrained army of informants around the country; train them first. "It's hard to figure out exactly who does what," Simeone wrote, "but it appears that HMS trains truckers to 'observe, assess, report' for OOIDA, which then sends its observations, assessments, and reports to the TSA. In other words, it's DHS chief Janet Napolitano's 'If You See Something, Say Something' program writ large."[86]

There is no question that Napolitano thinks big. "See Something, Say Something" was "originally implemented by New York City's Metropolitan Transportation Authority and funded, in part, by $13 million from DHS' Transit Security Grant Program." In December 2010, the program was launched nationwide at Walmart stores, with a total of 588 stores in twenty-seven states expected to be participating within weeks.[87]

BIG BROTHER, BIG BUSINESS

The number of state and local "watch" programs and "tip centers" proliferated after 9/11, as did the number of private companies the government brought into the surveillance-industrial fold. The Privacy Act of 1974, "riddled with exceptions and loopholes," was no match for a government determined to circumvent its restrictions. As Jay Stanley wrote in his 2004 ACLU report, the abilities of these private entities to gain access to "dossiers" on private individuals were unrestricted by law. They could buy and transfer private data that the government could not.[88] The same holds true today.

In February 2013, the Australian newspaper the *Sydney Morning Herald* exposed how the Massachusetts-based multinational corporation Raytheon—the world's fifth largest defense contractor—had developed a "Google for Spies" operation. Ryan Gallagher wrote that Raytheon had "secretly developed software capable of tracking people's movements and predicting future behaviour by mining data from social networking websites" like Facebook, Twitter, and Foursquare.[89]

The UK *Guardian* obtained a four-minute video that shows how Raytheon's RIOT (Rapid Information Overlay Technology) software uses photographs on social networks. The images, sometimes containing latitude and longitude details, are "automatically embedded by smartphones within so-called 'exif header data.' Riot pulls out this information, analysing not only the photographs posted by individuals, but also the location where these images were taken," the *Guardian* reported.[90]

Raytheon told the *Sydney Morning Herald* it has not sold RIOT to any clients but admitted that in 2010, it had shared the program's software technology with the US government and "industry" as part of a "joint research and development effort . . . to help build a national security system capable of analysing 'trillions of entities' from cyberspace."[91]

"Using RIOT it is possible to gain a picture of a person's life—their friends, the places they visit charted on a map—in little more than a few clicks of a button," the *Herald* reported.[92]

Privacy advocates are not thrilled by the prospects of RIOT's "vacuum cleaner" technology. "This sort of software allows the government to sur-veil everyone," said Ginger McCall, attorney and director of the Electronic Privacy Information Center's Open Government program. "It scoops up a bunch of information about totally innocent people. There seems to be no legitimate reason to get this, other than that they can." As for RIOT's ability to help catch terrorists, McCall called it "a lot of white noise."[93]

What may not be "white noise" is the top secret data-collection program PRISM that was authorized by federal judges "working under the FISA Act." Because most of the world's communications flow through the United States, it is a target-rich cyber environment. PRISM "collects a wide range of data" directly from the central servers of nine US-based companies—Google, Microsoft, Yahoo!, AOL, Apple, Skype, PalTalk.com, YouTube, and Facebook—although "the details vary by provider," according to the *Washington Post*, which exposed the program on June 6, 2013.[94]

Drawing some of their information from an April 2013 set of briefing slides, the *Post*'s Barton Gellman and Laura Poitras reported that Micro-soft was the first to join PRISM in September 2007, followed by Yahoo! in March 2008; Apple was the most recent, joining in October 2012, more than a year after AOL.[95] Interestingly, Google—which is closely allied with the Obama administration—did not join until January 2009, just ahead of the inauguration. Data gathered includes e-mail, VoIP, chat (video and voice), video conferencing, videos, photos, stored data and file transfers, and online social networking "details." Additionally, collection includes "notification of target activity," to include logins.[96]

The question that naturally follows is whether Congress and the president know about PRISM. The answer is, of course, that they do. Gellman and Poitras reported: "Even late last year, when critics of the foreign intelligence statute argued for changes, the only members of Congress who knew about PRISM were bound by oaths of office to hold their tongues." Last year, PRISM data—the "most prolific contributor"—was cited in 1,477 articles for the President's Daily Brief, the journalists added.[97]

Why should you care? Gellman and Poitras explain: "Firsthand experience with these systems, and horror at their capabilities, is what drove a career intelligence officer to provide PowerPoint slides about PRISM and supporting materials to The *Washington Post* in order to expose what he believes to be a gross intrusion on privacy. 'They quite literally can watch your ideas form as you type,' the officer said."[98]

And there is more. Ever heard of the code name "Perfect Citizen"? Siobhan Gorman of the *Wall Street Journal* was first to report in June 2010 about the Orwellian-named government program. Perfect Citizen, she wrote, would place sensors on computer systems to "detect cyber assaults on private companies and government agencies running such critical infrastructure as the electricity grid and nuclear-power plants."[99] Raytheon won the classified $100 million (or more) contract.[100]

A Freedom of Information Request filed with the NSA by the Electronic Privacy Information Center finally got results in January 2013. The response clearly showed that Perfect Citizen is not simply an R&D (research and development) project, as the NSA claimed. The documents indicate that the program is operational.[101] The "190 pages of dry legalese" also confirms that a "statement of work was first released back in September of 2009, with Raytheon being awarded the government contract in June of 2010—just before the *Wall Street Journal* published its story on the project."[102]

How does Perfect Citizen impact individuals? It is not clear right now. However, we do know that the month after the June 2010 report, the NSA issued a brief statement claiming the program did not "involve the monitoring of communications or the placement of sensors on utility company systems." It also claimed it was "not engaging in any illegal or unauthorized monitoring."[103] But do not forget that this is the NSA—the government's chief eavesdropping agency—we are talking about.

CAN BIG BROTHER GET ANY "BIGGER"? YES, YES IT CAN!

In August 2010, President Obama issued a new directive, Executive Order 13549, "aimed at easing the sharing of classified information about terrorist threats." This "elevated the role" of the "little-known but long-established" DHS-run Homeland Secure Data Network (HSDN), the US government's "primary non-defense, secret level classified information network" initiated in 2005 by then DHS secretary Michael Chertoff.[104]

The move goes beyond blurring the lines between nonmilitary and military intelligence gathering. In fact, it erases them. HSDN, DHS's major domestic intelligence information network, is now directly linked with one operated by the Department of Defense, including use of the military's Secret Internet Protocol Router Network (SIPRNET). In March 2012, DHS secretary Janet Napolitano released an implementing directive "to align security standards for accessing classified data across all levels of government and in the private sector."[105]

No longer is anything safe from prying eyes who want to see.

EXECUTIVE ORDERS; BIG BROTHER TO MONITOR "SOVEREIGN CITIZENS"

With almost no news media coverage, on February 5, 2013, the White House announced its new Interagency Working Group to Counter Online Radicalization to Violence that will target not only Islamic terrorists but also so-called violent "sovereign citizens."[106] The FBI defines "sovereign citizens" as "anti-government extremists who believe that even though they physically reside in this country, they are separate or 'sovereign' from the United States."[107]

The law enforcement agency noted such citizens believe they don't have to answer to any government authority, including courts, taxing entities, motor vehicle departments, or police. Without providing any proof to back its claims, the FBI warned that sovereign citizens commit murder and physical assault; threaten judges, law-enforcement professionals, and government personnel; impersonate police officers and diplomats; and engineer various white-collar scams, including mortgage fraud and so-called redemption schemes.

The new online working group will be chaired by the national security staff at the White House with input from specialists in countering what the Obama administration calls violent extremism. Also included in the group, according to a White House release, will be "Internet safety experts, and civil liberties and privacy practitioners from across the United States Government."[108]

The new working group says its initial focus will be on raising awareness about the threat and "providing communities with practical information and tools for staying safe online." The group says it will also coordinate with the technology industry to "consider policies, technologies, and tools that can help counter violent extremism online" while being careful not to interfere with "lawful Internet use or the privacy and civil liberties of individual users."[109]

A week later, Obama issued an executive order aimed at thwarting cyber-attacks against critical infrastructure. Such a move was predicted in November 2012 when Democrats failed for a second time to get the sixty votes needed under Senate rules to bring the bill up for passage. The cybersecurity legislation backed by Obama had also failed in August.[110]

The executive order establishes a voluntary program in which companies operating critical infrastructure would elect to meet cybersecurity best practices and standards crafted, in part, by the government.[111]

The question arises as to exactly which citizens are considered threats by the government amid previous troubling ideology from some Obama administration officials.

Aaron Klein broke the story about how Obama's regulatory czar, Cass Sunstein, wrote a lengthy academic paper suggesting the government should "infiltrate" social network websites, chat rooms, and message boards. Sunstein stepped down last year. Such "cognitive infiltration," he argued, should be used to enforce a US government ban on "conspiracy theorizing." Among the beliefs Sunstein classified as a "conspiracy theory" is advocating that the theory of global warming is a deliberate fraud.[112]

In January 2012, Reuters revealed a government document indicating the Department of Homeland Security's command center routinely monitors dozens of popular websites, including Facebook, Twitter, Hulu, and WikiLeaks, and news sites such as the *Huffington Post* and Drudge Report.[113]

Reuters reported that a "privacy compliance review" issued by DHS in November 2012 confirms that since at least June 2010, the department's national operations center has been operating a "Social Networking/Media Capability" which involves regular monitoring of "publicly available online forums, blogs, public websites and message boards."[114]

How long has this Internet monitoring been going on? At least since August 2009, when an unnamed federal contractor conducted an early test of the program using Twitter, Facebook, and three different blogs to gather information, Charlie Savage reported in the *New York Times*.[115]

Monitoring social media sites is not as tricky a feat for the government as you might think. A wiki of publicly accessible social media "monitoring solutions" includes a list of more than two hundred private websites in the United States and worldwide that watch any or all blogs, forums, and news sites; social media such as Twitter, Facebook, YouTube, Google Analytics, bitly, MySpace, Google+, Flickr, and LinkedIn; and review sites like Amazon reviews, Yelp, and Travelocity.[116] How hard would it be for the government to outdo these sites? Not very.

THERE IS ALWAYS MORE

Although we could fill this whole book with examples of active and suspected government intrusion into the private affairs of American citizens, illegal immigrants, and foreigners, perhaps these few examples explain why the appearance of awareness-like possibilities was so disturbing in March 2012. With the stroke of his pen, Attorney General Eric Holder accommodated US intelligence officials who wanted to create a government dragnet that could "[sweep] up millions of records of U.S. citizens—even people suspected of no crime." In spite of resistance, Holder revved up the "vacuum cleaner" and signed off on the request that relaxed restrictions on "how counterterrorism analysts may retrieve, store and search information gathered by government agencies for purposes other than national security threats."[117]

In a concept ripped from the pages of Steven Spielberg's 2002 script for *Minority Report*, the changes call for data sharing on a massive scale to help predict future crime activities. The new rules allow the National Counterterrorism Center (NCTC) to "examine the government files of

U.S. citizens for possible criminal behavior, even if there is no reason to suspect them." The NCTC now has eye-popping access to—and may copy unimpeded—any and all government databases. It also has permission to store data about innocent US citizens for as long as five years and analyze it at will for "suspicious patterns of behavior."[118]

The new rules allow the NCTC to run a dragnet through government files of US citizens to look for "possible criminal behavior, even if there is no reason to suspect them," Julia Angwin reported in December 2012 after the *Wall Street Journal* filed Freedom of Information requests with numerous government agencies. Previously, the center was barred from "storing information about ordinary Americans unless a person was a terror suspect or related to an investigation." It can now copy "entire government databases—flight records, casino-employee lists, the names of Americans hosting foreign-exchange students and many others," Angwin wrote.[119]

The data.gov website includes publicly available databases for thirty-nine states and thirty US cities and counties.[120] Searchable nonpublic databases could include every record or application filed with and/or maintained by the federal government regarding criminal background checks and all arrest data; federal employment, military service, immigration and naturalization; passports and visas; IRS, Social Security, Medicare, Medicaid, and electronic medical records; federal housing programs (loan applications and mortgage records and national flood insurance files); student loans and grants; US Census files; and small business loans. The possibilities are nearly endless.

The Obama administration–endorsed changes are a definite threat to Americans' Fourth Amendment rights prohibiting unlawful search and seizure. Counterterrorism officials promised they would be "circumspect" with the data. (Where have we heard this before? Ah, yes: "Trust us. We're from the government.") Also, the "probable cause" clause, they claimed, "doesn't cover records the government creates in the normal course of business with citizens."[121]

It should be obvious by now that government agencies are out of control in their thirst for intelligence on "terrorists"—and now nonterrorists—while innocent Americans are ever more at risk of getting swept up in the surveillance "vacuum cleaner." Where's the outrage?—especially since the NCTC will also allow foreign governments to look for "clues that people might commit future crimes."[122]

The ACLU is keeping an eye on the Obama administration and is particularly concerned with the FBI's national security surveillance powers. In a January 22, 2013, report, the ACLU stated, "The potential for abuse is once again great, particularly given that the lines between criminal investigations and foreign intelligence operations have been blurred or erased since 9/11. As a result, intrusive surveillance tools originally developed to target Soviet spies are increasingly being used against Americans."[123]

In particular, the ACLU references COINTELPRO, the domestic intelligence/counterintelligence program run by the FBI during the Cold War. COINTELPRO, the ACLU writes, "quickly evolved from a legitimate effort to protect the national security from hostile foreign threats into an effort to suppress domestic political dissent through an array of illegal activities."[124]

And just how are the Terrorist Identities Datamart Environment and other information gathered and stored in databases being used today? As you are about to read, in ways the majority of people residing in the United States will find difficult to believe. In the following chapter, we are going to take a trip inside those deeply troubling fusion centers.

8

THE TRUTH ABOUT FUSION CENTERS

NOW THAT WE HAVE THOROUGHLY DOCUMENTED how the Obama government is invading our privacy by collecting data on private citizens, it is time to address how that information is utilized and by whom. Specifically, we will expose what is really going on inside fusion centers and how these spy centers represent a government completely drunk on its own usurped power.

Fusion centers are single locations where all that data mining we previously discussed will come in handy. They are not and will not become detainment or concentration camps, as some people believe. Instead, fusion centers are analysis-driven, information management and logistics operations under the control of the Department of Homeland Security, although with many troubling aspects. The centers jointly share facilities with several law-enforcement operational centers; many are housed within federal law-enforcement agencies or state and local police departments.[1]

These data-mining and surveillance-aggregation "spy" hubs were created by, operate cooperatively with, and are funded not only by federal, state, local, and tribal law-enforcement agencies but also, in some cases, in part by private contractors, who also help mine the data. Yes, that's right. Private companies may be sifting through your personal business. Fusion centers "contain large data warehouses that collect information from all 16 US intelligence agencies, including the CIA, FBI, NSA, the military, state and local police agencies, as well as privately owned corporations and organizations," Gregory Patin explained at Examiner.com.[2] This allows fusion centers to tap into and feed a voluminous number of public and private databases and data streams such as NASDAQ (financial data) and the Centers for Disease Control and Prevention (emerging disease information), allowing them to pry into and exchange information on the public and private life of every American.

"Fusion centers invite reports from public employees such as firemen, ambulance drivers, and sanitation workers as well as from private-sector sources such as hospitals and neighborhood watch groups. They often operate tip hotlines; this means a 'suspect's' name could be submitted by a disgruntled employee, a hostile neighbor, or an ex-spouse who seeks child custody," Canadian anarchist and individual feminist Wendy McElroy wrote in February 2010.[3]

Yes, fusion center operations are definitely something to be feared. "An apt analogy," lawyer and political blogger Gene Howington writes, "would be they are a large part of the brain behind the brawn, not wearing jackboots themselves but certainly responsible for informing their marching orders. No one from a Fusion Center is ever going to kick in your door."[4]

IMPEACHABLE?

"Violation of privacy rights, excessive secrecy, lack of congressional oversight, the inevitability of inaccurate and non-correctable information, the lack of due process for the accused, the encouragement of racial/ religious profiling, the creation of a 'snitch' nation, the political abuse of dissidents—the objections scroll on," McElroy wrote.[5]

This is the case for impeachment in a nutshell—and the left knows it well. It screamed the loudest when Congress quickly passed and President George W. Bush signed into law the PATRIOT Act shortly after the September 11 attacks.[6] Bush reauthorized the act in 2005. In one of many repeated power grabs by the Imperial President, in May 2011, Barack Obama signed a last-minute four-year extension containing three key provisions: roving wiretaps, searches of business records, and conducting surveillance of "lone wolves" (individuals suspected of terrorist-related activities not linked to terrorist groups).[7] The act has been unfavorably compared to the emergency Reichstag Fire Decree issued in February 1933 by German president Paul von Hindenburg that nullified many of the key civil liberties of German citizens.[8]

Add to this the unconstitutional FISA Act discussed in the previous chapter, which grants permission for warrantless, "suspicionless" surveillance of US citizens,[9] illegal immigrants, and foreigners alike by agents of the government. First signed in 1978, it was renewed by Bush in November 2007 and extended for another five years by Obama in December 2012.

Countless local police and other first responders have been turned into domestic surveillance agents at the beck and call of the Department of Homeland Security. An untold number of massive databases have been created and shared by numerous government, public, and private sources, such as those we discussed earlier in this chapter.

In fact, the tentacles of the domestic surveillance state are now so widespread they are literally everywhere you turn. More than seventy fusion centers scattered around the United States connect federal, state, local, and tribal agencies, serving as hubs to coordinate an endless stream of intelligence. Dozens of drone command centers remotely control the spies in the skies—as well as other real and imaged functions, which we detail later in chapter 10.

As unbelievable as it may seem, some Americans live in a constant state of anxiety, even to the point of paranoia, worried that the POTUS will deploy an armed DHS surveillance drone, when there is no imminent threat, to assassinate US citizens—or worse, others might become collateral damage—on US soil. Is this any way for Americans to live? We say *no!* We the People have not given the US government permission to usurp our constitutionally-guaranteed rights and President Obama needs to be held accountable.

A LITTLE FUSION CENTER HISTORY

Although we cannot pinpoint an exact date, we do know fusion centers have been around for decades and are not a new concept. What is new is their likely unconstitutional expansion under Obama. The June 14, 1985, hijacking of TWA Flight 847 from Cairo to London by members of Hezbollah and the Islamic Jihad, and the horrific drama of the two-week hostage ordeal that followed, was the motivating event for the evolution of a strategy to combat terrorism—and none too soon. Between February 2 and December 31, 1985, twenty-three Americans were killed and 160 wounded in terrorist actions in Greece, Spain, El Salvador, West Germany, Italy, Austria, and Lebanon, as well as over the Atlantic Ocean and on the Mediterranean Sea near Egypt.[10]

In mid-July, President Ronald Reagan signed a national security directive establishing a cabinet-level task force headed by Vice President George H. W. Bush.[11] The task force submitted forty-four recommendations in its report. Several, such as a full-time position on the National Security Agency to monitor terrorism and the establishment of a major intelligence community-oriented counterterrorism center, were implemented.[12]

Director of Central Intelligence Bill Casey set up a standalone multi-disciplinary center that "brought together analysts, clandestine intelligence officers, technical support officers, and collection officers." According to Charles E. Allen, Casey's principal substantive advisor, the center established an intelligence fusion center "which brought synergy to the intelligence efforts communitywide." "Because of this," Allen stated, "we were able to engage in proactive operations worldwide to disrupt terrorist groups and to thwart terrorist attacks. I think the integrated approach avoided numerous terrorist incidents."[13]

DHS'S FUSION CENTERS

The Department of Homeland Security, which now supports dozens of fusion centers, resulted from the Homeland Security Act of 2002 signed into law by Bush that November. While the act created DHS, it did not mention fusion centers at all, let alone mandate them—or give DHS the "sweeping responsibilities to gather, fuse and share terrorism-related information with federal, state and local entities" it has assumed for itself.[14]

In a June 2002 Heritage Foundation policy paper, Michael Scardaville set forth principles for creating an effective Department of Homeland Security. Included was the recommendation for a fusion center for "all terror-related intelligence" as an "important first step in correcting some of the intelligence deficiencies that existed before September 11, 2001." The center would be a special office to coordinate "intelligence-sharing on matters related to the war on terror and terrorist threats to the United States between the federal government and state and local governments and [analyze] intelligence related to those threats." Previously, Scardaville, pointed out, this had been the responsibility of Office of Homeland Security's director, Governor Tom Ridge. However, state and local officials wanted more support from the federal government than it received from OHS in its advisory capacity, Scardaville wrote. In his opinion, DHS would be able to do the job.[15]

In an interview with *Insight on the News*, Scardaville said a top priority should be better information sharing within government. He suggested an "intelligence fusion center" similar to that of the Reagan era that would "use advanced information technology and data-mining systems to ensure that all federal officials are up to speed on critical security matters."[16]

DHS opened its doors in March 2003 and within months Bush created two terrorism centers. The interagency Terrorist Threat Integration Center was to centralize threat information, and the Terrorist Screening Center, an interagency operation administered by the FBI, was to consolidate the federal government's many terror watch lists. By 2004, state and local fusion centers began to multiply even though they had not been officially mandated.

The final report by the 9/11 Commission, released in July 2004,[17] "highlighted the failure of public officials to 'connect the dots,' or share key terrorism-related intelligence in time to prevent the attack." It did not mention fusion centers in its recommendations. Rather, DHS and other advocates of fusion centers chose to interpret the panel's recommendations to improve information-sharing as a call for increased federal support for fusion centers.[18]

Bioterrrorism expert Daniel M. Gerstein concurred. In 2004, he wrote that it was insufficient to have an interagency process that would bring in "representatives for specific coordination at discrete points in time." The US government, he asserted, "must develop a fully manned, full-time Interagency Fusion Center to address the day-to-day business of coordinating efforts as well as crisis action management." The center, he wrote, should include all cabinet-level departments and such specialized organizations as the Centers for Disease Control and Prevention, the CIA, and the FBI.[19]

DHS was already working with eighteen state and local intelligence and fusion centers. Two years later, Charles E. Allen, then-DHS's intelligence chief, submitted a detailed fusion center plan to then-DHS secretary Michael Chertoff, in which he highlighted the potential of fusion centers to aid federal counterterrorism efforts. Allen called fusion centers "critical sources of unique law enforcement information and threat information" and "the natural entry point into the State and Local 'systems' for critical threat information from the National Intelligence Community." DHS officials stressed to Congress and other agencies that local police, because they conducted interrogations every day, could be used as "intelligence sources" through the fusion centers. The plan did not end with using local law enforcement as community spies: firefighters would be included as well because they were "one of the few people who can enter your home without a warrant." Chertoff approved the plan and, by the end of 2006, fusion centers had begun operations in Connecticut, Delaware, Indiana, Maine, and North Carolina.[20]

Significantly, Congress did not get around to specifically authorizing fusion centers until 2007, after there were already thirty-seven state and city centers in operation. While Congress emphasized the fusion centers' counterterrorism function, many of the states that had fusion centers were "not likely to be targeted by foreign terrorism," prominent left-wing blogger Marcy Wheeler observed.[21]

This observation is borne out, by the way, by a recent analysis by the right-leaning London think tank the Henry Jackson Society, which profiled 171 "homegrown" terrorists convicted for terrorism-related offenses in US federal (97 percent) or military (3 percent) courts, or who had participated in suicide attacks against the United States between 1997 and 2011. The selection criteria required that each subject must have been a member of al-Qaeda or motivated primarily by a belief in al-Qaeda ideology.[22]

The detailed statistical report includes a map indicating the town or city in which an individual lived at the time of arrest or a suicide attack, even if the perpetrator may have lived in multiple locations in the US prior to arrest. In descending order, the number of arrests for 27 states and the District of Columbia are: New York, 20; Florida, 16; New Jersey, 13; Virginia, 9; California and Minnesota, 8; Illinois and North Carolina, 7; Texas, 6; Maryland, Ohio, and Oregon, 5; Pennsylvania and Massachusetts, 4; Colorado, 3; Alaska, Washington, Missouri, Tennessee, and Georgia, 2; and Arizona, Wyoming, Oklahoma, Arkansas, Kentucky, Connecticut, and Washington, DC, 1.[23] Not a single arrest took place in the remaining states, many often dismissed collectively as "fly-over" country. Plus, of all the factors discussed in the 107-page analysis, there is absolutely no mention of fusion center operations connected to terrorist detection and arrests since their inception—a factor worthy of even passing notice.

The 2007 legislation introduced by Rep. Bennie Thompson (D-MS) and signed into law in August by Bush implemented recommendations of the 9/11 Commission. The act authorized the DHS and the Transportation Security Administration to provide support and coordinate federal involvement in the various fusion centers.[24]

DHS was to provide the fusion centers with "operational and intelligence advice," conduct training and field exercises with them, and provide management assistance. It was also supposed to review information, particularly "homeland security information, terrorism information, and weapons of mass destruction information" gathered by state, local, and regional fusion centers, as well as to incorporate "such information, as appropriate, into the Department's own such information," a subject we discuss in some detail momentarily.[25]

But first, there is an interesting side note. The act was sponsored and passed by the House Democratic majority. Thompson's bill had 205 cosponsors: 204 Democrats—a large number of which were Democratic Socialists—and only one Republican, Christopher Shays of Connecticut. The final vote was 299 "aye" votes (231 Democrat, 68 Republican) and all 128 "nay" votes coming from Republicans. The Democrats own this legislation and everything it contains. It should come as no surprise Obama did not vote on the bill's conference report in the Senate.[26] His Illinois counterpart, Sen. Dick Durbin, reported Obama was "necessarily absent" on July 26, 2007. And where was Obama when discussion and his input were required for this important vote? The Campaigner-in-Chief was in Columbia, South Carolina, delivering a campaign speech to the College Democrats of America, the official youth branch of the Democratic National Committee.[27]

In 2009, Bart Johnson, then the acting undersecretary of DHS intelligence and analysis, proposed that DHS secretary Janet Napolitano issue a "Secretarial declaration of recommitment" to robustly support "establishment and sustainment of a nationwide network of fusion centers." Napolitano approved the proposal, making fusion centers one of the department's top priorities. In his 2010 National Security Strategy, Obama publicly embraced fusion centers as part of DHS's antiterrorism strategy.[28]

BEYOND COUNTERTERRORISM

Mission creep was evident in Secretary Napolitano's March 2012 testimony before the Senate in which she stressed that fusion centers work beyond counterterrorism: "Their mission is terrorism prevention, but it's also much broader than that . . . And as [Arizona] governor I started one of the first fusion centers in the country. It is an ideal place to co-locate, to share information. We use them in a variety of ways."[29]

That variety apparently does not include finding and catching terrorists. DHS has been unable to identify a single "clear example in which a fusion center provided intelligence which helped disrupt a terrorist plot." Meanwhile, local and federal law enforcement agencies have allegedly "thwarted dozens of attacks on U.S. soil and against U.S. interests in the past decade."[30]

DHS's fusion centers have many problems, beginning with who is really in charge of their terrorist-hunting operations.

PRIVATE CONTRACTORS

We gain insight into how out of control DHS's data-mining operations—including trolling social media—have become from a February 2012 article found on the Federal Emergency Management Agency (FEMA) website: "Vast amounts of social media data pour into state and local fusion centers—and companies are hard at work trying to distill what's truly significant."[31]

We'd like to tell you how many "companies" (code for defense contractors) there are, where they are, who they are, and what they do. It seems that DHS does not know. One blogger snarked, "If you understand bureaucracies and contractors, you will realize that these people need to justify their paychecks by finding terrorists. And that probably already includes you because you are on the Internet and have opinions."[32]

The October 2012 Senate report we discuss below failed to discuss DHS's contractors. "The centers rely on private contractors, and it isn't clear that contractors should be playing such a big role in this sensitive work," Neil Gordon, an investigator with the independent nonprofit watchdog Project on Government Oversight (POGO) noted.[33]

This is a major problem. It is the government's responsibility to direct and control contractors, not the other way around. DHS was so dependent upon its contractors that the contractor employees sometimes outnumbered the government employees, while some of the contractor employees were found to be "under-trained or poor performers." Gordon opined this meant contractor employees were "directing and controlling" some, if not all, aspects of fusion center operations and "therefore illegally performing inherently governmental functions."[34]

This is just the tip of the proverbial iceberg. Senate investigators ran into a brick wall when DHS balked at sharing a 2010 assessment of the fusion centers. The ACLU reported that DHS did so only after the DHS obtained "consent" from the National Fusion Center Association (NFCA), a private, nongovernmental organization. The NFCA supposedly had "the authority to represent the 68 centers subject to review." Created in 2009, the NFCA, as it turns out, is led by a former DHS grants official who lobbies on behalf of the association's clients for increased federal funding for fusion centers. Plus, the NFCA receives funding from corporate clients wanting business with fusion centers.[35]

NFCA's executive director, W. Ross Ashley III, is an excellent example of how the government-industry revolving door works. Ten years prior to his Senate confirmation in December 2007 to serve as assistant administrator for grant programs at FEMA, Ashley was founder and president of the Templar Corporation, a "commercial partner with State, local, and tribal first responders, specifically in the areas of information sharing, incident management, and communications interoperability." Prior to Templar, Ashley was the director of law-enforcement technologies for the ISX Corporation, where he managed all of National Institute of Justice–funded research and development projects for ISX. NIJ is part of the Department of Justice. He currently works as an advisor for IxReveal, Inc., which works on behalf of its government clients to cut "'Big Data' down to size."[36]

Apparently, the irony of a Big Government contractor pimping itself out to cut down the vastness of Big Government's "Big Data" escapes notice. Unsurprisingly, as the ACLU reported, "the fusion center network, in short, has become a funding conduit for the national security industrial complex."[37]

Another prime example surfaced within weeks of the October 2012 Senate investigative report's release. ICF International announced it had won an $18.1 million contract—with a one-year base and four option years—from DHS to "help sustain and improve the integrated national network of state and major urban area fusion centers." ICF described the services to be provided as "high-end policy analysis, planning and program management."[38] Not mentioned is in how many fusion centers ICF would operate.

Private contractors operating in fusion centers are not a new concern for the ACLU. In December 2007, the ACLU noted that the mission for the fusion centers had quickly changed from covering "all crimes and hazards" to seeking information for analysis to "include not just criminal intelligence, but public and private sector data, and participation in these centers [had] grown to include not just law enforcement, but other government entities, the military and even select members of the private sector."[39] Everyone, it seemed, wanted a piece of the fusion center pie.

The ACLU also questioned the "very serious privacy issues" raised by the fusion centers, which comes "at a time when new technology, government powers and zeal in the 'war on terrorism' [are] combining to threaten Americans' privacy at an unprecedented level."[40]

That "zeal" was revealed in the March 6, 2013, protest filibuster over the vote on Obama's nominee for director of the CIA, John Brennan, by Sen. Rand Paul (R-KY), who provided insight into one fusion center's misguided broadcasting to local law enforcement what sounds a lot like a hit list. "The one in Missouri a couple years ago came up with a list and they sent this to every policeman in Missouri," Senator Paul said. "The people on the list might be me. The people on the list from the fusion center in Missouri that you need to be worried about, that policemen should stop, are people that have bumper stickers [that] might be pro-life, who have bumper stickers that might be for more border security, people who support third-party candidates, people who might be [members of] the Constitution party."[41]

SO, WHAT ELSE IS WRONG WITH DHS'S FUSION CENTERS?

The question, perhaps, should be, what is right with them? Speaking in the vernacular, DHS's oversight of its fusion centers is a hot mess. Let us count the ways.

The Senate investigation initiated by Senators Carl Levin (D-MI) and Tom Coburn (R-OK), covering the thirteen-month period from April 1, 2009, to April 30, 2010, outlined the glaring failure of DHS's fusion centers. For starters, the centers had failed to identify any "reporting which uncovered a terrorist threat, nor could it identify a contribution such fusion center reporting made to disrupt an active terrorist plot." It was also found that the fusion centers lacked basic counterterrorism capabilities. Also, after promising to do so for more than two years, DHS never got around to assessing fusion center performance. Even more disturbing, although DHS had conducted its own investigation and found the fusion centers lacking, it did not share its report with Congress or make it public.[42]

The October 2012 report revealed that fusion center reporting was often flawed and included "irrelevant, useless or inappropriate intelligence" unrelated to terrorism. Most fusion center reporting related to drug smuggling, illegal alien smuggling, or other criminal activity, while some reports were deemed to have "nothing of value." Some fusion centers "produced no intelligence reporting whatsoever," while nearly one-third of all reports were never published at all. Terrorism-related reporting was often "outdated, duplicative, and uninformative, or based on older published accounts."[43] Some draft reports, had they been published, could have violated civil liberties or the Privacy Act of 1974, with inappropriate records also retained contrary to DHS policies and the Privacy Act.[44]

There's an explanation for this. Most of the reporting came from three border states "with significant drug and human trafficking issues but—except for CA—not really significant international terrorism issues." Second, most of the reports were vetted for "privacy and relevance" related to drugs and human trafficking. Third, most of the reports came from six individuals whom it was suggested "were reflecting their own issues, not actual issues of concern." Most important, the majority of the other states hadn't reported anything.[45]

That DHS had had "success stories" was mostly a myth. DHS did not, in the investigators' opinion, demonstrate the centers' value to counterterrorism efforts. The DHS website includes a list of twenty-four alleged "success stories" dating from August 2007 through August 2012, all predating the Senate investigation. Examples include responding to a Colorado wildfire, supporting drug seizures, assisting in the return of a runaway teen, contributing to a decrease in auto theft, responding to facial recognition queries, and coordinating security for the 2008 Republican and Democratic national conventions.[46] This is not much "success" for a five-year stretch and billions of dollars expended to identify terrorists.

DHS was also caught fudging its claims. The subcommittee report named four instances where DHS credited fusion centers as having provided key information when they had not. On the other hand, it was found that fusion centers may have gotten in the way of federal counterterrorism efforts. Two examples cited are the Russian "cyberattack" in Illinois that was not a cyberattack at all, and the shooting of former Democratic congresswoman Gabby Giffords and eighteen others in Arizona. That report provided erroneous and misleading information about the shooter, Jared Loughner.[47]

Making matters worse, DHS exhibited personnel management problems. Intelligence reporting officials who repeatedly violated guidelines were not sanctioned. The fusion centers were short-staffed and relied upon underqualified, underperforming contract employees, as noted above, which hampered reporting efforts. DHS failed to sufficiently train its fusion center detailees to legally and effectively collect and report intelligence. Intelligence officials were only trained by DHS for a single week before being sent to state and local fusion centers "to report sensitive domestic intelligence, largely concerning U.S. persons." Late reporting delayed the review process by months due to hasty implementation and poor coordination. Shockingly, reporting officials escaped evaluation on the quality of their reporting entirely.[48]

DHS had also failed in its fiduciary responsibility to the American taxpayer. It had no idea how much money it had spent to support the fusion centers. It had also failed to oversee how its fusion center grant funds were expended, particularly since grant requirements did not ensure states spent their fusion center funds effectively. On DHS's behalf, FEMA distributed hundreds of millions of taxpayer dollars to support state and local fusion centers. However, DHS admitted it was "unable to provide an accurate tally of how much it had granted to states and cities to support fusion centers efforts." Instead, DHS gave broad estimates for fusion center activities from 2003 to 2011, ranging from $289 million to $1.4 billion.[49]

The ACLU found it even more remarkable that the "funds kept flowing no matter what was produced." And, according to the ACLU, DHS had still "made no attempt to keep track of who is getting how much and what they are using DHS funds for."[50]

How pathetic is the record keeping? ACLU reported: "FEMA—the DHS agency that distributes the funds—has to do a keyword search using terms like 'information sharing' and 'data collection' when it tries to find out how much of taxpayers' money has gone from the DHS to fusion centers."[51]

A DHS internal assessment conducted in 2010 discovered that four of its claimed seventy-two fusion centers did not exist. Meanwhile, DHS officials "kept using the 72 figure publicly with Congress."[52] As if this was not bad enough, the Senate investigators identified at least two DHS-recognized fusion centers—one in Wyoming and the other in Philadelphia—that not only did not exist but also had been counted and allegedly received funding. Meanwhile, others that did exist failed to prioritize counterterrorism efforts.[53]

There is no doubt that the Senate investigation was thorough. The report describes the process plainly: "Over a period of two years, the Subcommittee reviewed more than 80,000 pages of documents, including reviews, audits, intelligence reports, emails, memoranda, grant applications, news accounts, and scholarly articles; conducted a nationwide survey of fusion centers; and interviewed over 50 current and former DHS officials, outside experts, and state and local officials."[54]

Obama and the fusion centers were "shifting their focus so they can pretend to meet a need," progressive blogger Marcy Wheeler stated. "As a result of the apparent fact that there's no actual need for fusion centers [as they are] currently defined, both the Administration and fusion centers themselves are redefining their mission."[55]

There are other ways to view this situation as well. Jack Kenny, who writes for LewRockwell.com and TheNewAmerican.com, observed, "It's hard to fail or be inefficient, when you don't even have a mission."[56] In other words, as commenters of all political persuasions have made clear, the fusion centers lack a clear antiterrorism mission. Problem easily solved—the Obama administration will simply make one up.

What should now be obvious is that Barack Obama has picked up the unlit Molotov cocktail handed to him by George W. Bush and is holding it in one hand while holding a match in the other. Obama is playing fast and loose with our country's information gathering and data mining, all the while ready to set off a firestorm that would sweep away citizens' constitutionally guaranteed right to privacy and protection against unwarranted search or seizure. This surveillance and data mining is troubling enough. However, as you will read in the next chapter, the theme continues and becomes far more concerning when seen through the lens of a largely unreported DHS expansion taking place mostly under the radar—the creation of a virtual domestic army, a federal power grab that could alter the balance of power while placing enormous, unconstitutional authority in the executive branch.

9

DHS ARMY—
THE EMERGING POLICE STATE

America will never be destroyed from the outside. If we falter and lose our freedoms, it will be because we destroyed ourselves.[1]

—Abraham Lincoln

N OUT OF CONTROL Transportation Security Administration expanding its invasive authority beyond airports. "Freeze" drills. VIPR teams. The declared objective of a civilian security force that is just as powerful as the US military. Is it any wonder American citizens are increasingly of the belief that the federal government is plotting against them and the Department of Homeland Security, in violation of the Constitution,[2] is in the throes of a power grab to create an alternative federal police force? As many see it, this move not only incorporates state and local law enforcement into the DHS fold but also seizes unconstitutional powers by usurping the sovereign rights granted by the Tenth Amendment to the states while shifting the balance of power toward an emerging police state.

Where *do* the fear and anxiety come from? Why is it that some Americans are convinced that heavily armed jackbooted thugs will break down doors to round up dissident citizens and unceremoniously haul them off to illegal indefinite detention in secret locations known only to shadowy agents of the government? What would make people believe that the president is creating his own private civilian army to rule the land? And why is it so many are willing to accept the much-bandied-about conspiracy theory that federally operated fusion centers are gulag-style concentration or reeducation camps in disguise, as we discussed in the previous chapter? Or, that the government has a fleet of killer drones watching their every move that is, without warning, ready to obliterate them, their loved ones, and their homes, which we cover in detail in the next chapter?

These are not idle questions dreamed up by a loony conspiracy-minded citizenry. There is, sadly, a lot more fact than fiction to support their fears. Since at least the 9/11 attacks, the federal government is largely to blame for allowing such wild rumors to endure. More recently, natural disasters like Hurricane Katrina in September 2005 and Hurricane Sandy in October 2012 shook peoples' sense of security to the very core, as these storms not only forced families from their homes, some of which were completely destroyed or rendered uninhabitable, but also demonstrated how quickly life can turn from daily routine to total chaos. People are conflicted, afraid their government will not be there when it is needed—or fear that it *will* be there to completely uproot their lives.

Take for example the brief white paper, "Homeland Security and Intelligence: Next Steps in Evolving the Mission," prepared by the Aspen Homeland Security Group, cochaired by former DHS chief Michael Chertoff, and presented in January 2012 to the House Permanent Select Committee on Intelligence. The Aspen Institute group recommended DHS evolve away from its terrorism-based mission and refine its focus to work with state, local, and private sector partners and use its tools to secure the borders and analyze travel, protect critical infrastructure, and prevent cyber intrusions by "emerging adversaries." DHS, the group explains, uniquely has access to many different agencies "looking at similar problems to ensure that we miss no new perspective, no potentially valuable data source."[3] We discussed this aspect in the previous two chapters.

Many are arriving at the very uncomfortable conclusion that DHS is building its own militarized force to fight US citizens on US soil. On his February 15, 2013, talk radio show, Mark Levin, former Reagan Justice Department official and author of *Ameritopia: The Unmaking of America*, speculated the government was simulating multiple scenarios for collapse of the US economic system. "I'm going to tell you what I think is going on. I don't think insurrection. Law enforcement and national security agencies—they play out multiple scenarios. They simulate multiple scenarios. I'll tell you what I think they're simulating: the collapse of our financial system, the collapse of our society and the potential for widespread violence, looting, killing in the streets, because that's what happens when an economy collapses," Levin said. "I'm talking about a collapse when people are desperate, when they can't [afford] food and clothing, when they have no way of going from place to place, when they can't protect themselves. There aren't enough police officers on the face of the Earth to adequately handle a situation like that."[4]

While Levin may be correct, it's not due to the federal government's lack of effort. In 2009, a study prepared by the RAND Arroyo Center investigated the need for a US Stability Police Force, or SPF. The investigation was carried out at the behest of the US Army's Peacekeeping and Stability Operations Institute (PKSOI) headquartered at the US Army War College in Carlisle, Pennsylvania.[5]

The RAND Corporation is "the establishment's go-to think tank for the pseudo-scientific justification for both the planned and perfidious expansion of government and the corresponding contraction of liberty," lawyer Joe Wolverton II commented in January 2010 in the *New American*. The report, he wrote, is "over 200 impenetrable pages long and proclaims loudly the urgent need" for an SPF.[6]

The report's authors describe an SPF as "a high-end police force that engages in a range of tasks such as crowd and riot control, special weapons and tactics (SWAT), and investigations of organized criminal groups" with the ability to operate in stability operations similar to those of such European forces as the Italian *Carabinieri* and the French *Gendarmerie Nationale*. The SPF would focus on high-end tasks "fundamentally different from UN or other civilian police, who deal with more routine law and order functions." The SPF would also differ from "most military forces, which are generally not trained and experienced to conduct policing tasks in a civilian environment."[7]

Other considerations included what an SPF should look like if it was necessary; what its objectives, tasks, speed of deployment, and institutional capabilities should be; and more practically, where it should be headquartered.[8]

"The study goes on and on attempting to coat its government-expanding agenda in a patina of urgency," Wolverton wrote, "but despite the academic meanderings, the paper ends where you imagine it would, with a plan for the establishment of a new domestic, federal police force to respond to worldwide calamities and conflicts." Ultimately, the study recommends the US Marshals Service as the "most likely to successfully field an SPF."[9] The reason given for the selection of the Marshals Service is not, Wolverton wrote, because its officers are "abler or better trained, not that they possess some strain of especially potent skill set perfectly matched to the mission for which they would be deployed." While options had included the Departments of Defense, Homeland Security, Justice, and State, the "most desirable option"—the Military Police Corps—was out of reach because of the Posse Comitatus Act, which prohibits the US military from acting as a police force on US soil. This is important to keep in mind as you continue to read this chapter. The US Marshals Service, you see, is part of the Department of Homeland Security.

"CIVILIAN NATIONAL SECURITY FORCE"

In his July 2, 2008, "New Era of Service" address delivered at the University of Colorado at Colorado Springs, presidential candidate Obama famously said, "We cannot continue to rely only on our military in order to achieve the national security objectives we've set . . . We've got to have a civilian national security force that's just as powerful, just as strong, just as well funded."[10] Note that Obama's preaddress prepared remarks did not include this passage.

Senator Obama's inspiration for this idea came by way of George W. Bush's secretary of defense, Robert M. Gates. In the July 7, 2008, issue of *Defense News*, John T. Bennett and Tobias Naegele reported on the "most extensive interview to date exclusively on military matters" with Senator Obama, writing, "Obama did appear to back a soft-power vision Gates began advocating in a series of speeches last fall: a more modern State Department and 'civilian national security force' that could 'deploy teams that combine agricultural specialists and engineers and linguists and cultural specialists who are prepared to go into some of the most dangerous areas alongside our military.'"[11]

"If we've got a State Department or personnel that have been trained just to be behind walls, and they have not been equipped to get out there alongside our military and engage, then we don't have the kind of national security apparatus that is needed," Obama said. "That has to be planned for; it has to be paid for. Those personnel have to be trained. And they all have to be integrated."[12]

We fast forward to January 23, 2009, when Obama revised President Bill Clinton's 1992 Defense Department Directive 1404.10, Emergency-Essential (E-E) DOD US Citizen Civilian Employees.[13] The original directive was rescinded. The new directive states that a Civilian Expeditionary Workforce "shall be organized, trained, cleared, equipped and ready to deploy in support of combat operations by the military; contingencies; emergency operations; humanitarian missions; disaster relief; restoration of order; drug interdiction; and stability operations."[14] As conservative blogger Doug Ross noted, the old directive addressed the overseas deployments of civilian personnel. It did not use language such as "restoration of order" or "stability operations," which, Ross observed, are "prominently featured in the new directive." Ross also pointed out that, while the 1992 directive "uses the term 'overseas' no fewer than 33 times," the 2009 directive "does not mention the term 'overseas' in the body of the directive *even once*."[15]

Note also the new directive was issued a mere two days after Obama's inauguration, meaning that it had been sitting in somebody's hip pocket just awaiting a signature. This fact by itself is interesting. Secretary of Defense Robert M. Gates continued in office and did not have to be reconfirmed. (The directive was actually signed by Deputy Defense Secretary Gordon England, who also did not have to be reconfirmed.) Was the Civilian Expeditionary Workforce part of some grand bargain for Gates to stay on into Obama's first term? Also ask yourself why such a force was needed with the many thousands of defense contractors already in theater in Afghanistan, for example.

While the new directive may indicate one thing, as Ross pointed out, a Department of Defense press release states the case quite differently, specifically stating that the Civilian Expeditionary Workforce would "be trained and equipped to deploy overseas in support of military missions worldwide."[16]

In January 2009, when the ink on the directive had barely dried, the inaugural class of sixteen students completed its training course. They underwent a comprehensive one- to two-week course at Muscatatuck Training Range and the Camp Atterbury Joint Maneuver Training Center in Indiana. Training conducted by the contractor, the McKellar Corporation, took place in the classroom and at the range, where students "progress to interactive sessions that include traveling in a convoy and aircraft and taking part in vignettes designed to fully immerse students in deployment scenarios."[17]

The answer is yes if you are wondering whether the "volunteers" are armed while deployed in places like Afghanistan. If the job requires it, training and authorization to carry a weapon in "conflict zones" follows.[18]

Let us be perfectly clear: this is a little-known jobs program and perhaps the first one that was "shovel ready" under Obama. The "volunteers" are holding down high-paying ($70,000–$100,000 per annum) taxpayer-funded federal jobs. A list of occupations sought by the Department of Defense includes civil engineers, lawyers, financial administrators, IT management, intelligence experts, language specialists, and many more professional positions.[19] The compensation includes such items as locality pay or a market supplement, a cost-of-living allowance (COLA), danger pay, imminent danger pay, hardship duty pay, hazardous duty pay/environmental differential pay, as well as sick leave, annual leave, paid holiday leave, compensatory time for travel, medical care, and all the usual federal employee perks.[20]

While this program and these jobs are not currently on US soil, the expertise and training invested in the thousands of individuals who have worked for the Department of Defense in Afghanistan or other countries could just as easily be put to a different use right here at home.

Yes, Obama—and Gates—got their "civilian national security force" and Congress and the American citizenry were none the wiser, and that's exactly the problem.

Next question: How will the Department of Homeland Security explain the privacy-invasive operations like those carried out by the Transportation Security Administration?

TSA: OVERREACHING, IMPERIOUS, AND A THREAT TO LIBERTY

Claims of TSA mission overreach and imperiousness are not exaggerated. On a daily basis, TSA invades the constitutionally guaranteed right to privacy of everyone—American citizen, illegal immigrant, and foreigner alike.

The TSA was placed under the Department of Homeland Security in March 2003. Statistically speaking, TSA carries a hefty workload: nearly fifty thousand of its agents operate security checkpoints for the "safety and security of the traveling public," with approximately 1.7 million passengers passing through 450 US airports daily, and all cargo subjected to 100 percent screening for domestic and international-outbound passenger aircraft.[21]

As you will see, the real escalation in TSA's operations began in the first few months of the Obama administration. In March 2009, for example, the TSA was guaranteed a healthy portion of the $3.5 billion in Economic Recovery Act ("stimulus") funds earmarked to support various DHS programs, including $1 billion for explosive detection systems and enhanced checkpoint screening equipment at airports[22] and $1 billion more for "aviation security projects."[23] In July 2010, DHS was still receiving and spending endless millions of stimulus funds for airport and border security.[24]

In the beginning, the TSA mission was simple. Its expansion from an airport safety and security agency to the domestic surveillance operation it has become is beyond overreach—it is repugnant to freedom-loving Americans.

There have been countless complaints of excessive groping, harassment, and humiliation delivered at the hands of TSA agents. Such incidents have been reported even for private screenings by a same-gender TSA agent with another TSA agent or companion present. This is not to mention complaints by flyers claiming they were racially or ethnically profiled by TSA agents—and they were, as the TSA deploys thousands of behavior detection officers at airports across the country—or were singled out or maltreated because of a disability or a medical condition or were prohibited from bringing or checking common nonthreatening items on an airplane or caught up in one of TSA's occasional "Simon Says" freeze drills.[25]

The variety of issues is boundless. Passengers have consistently been irritated by changing or seemingly meaningless rules. In April 2012, for example, TSA screeners refused to explain why travelers had to remove their laptops from their bags but were allowed to leave Kindles, iPads, iPhones, and/or iPods "nestled snugly away."[26]

The evidence is overwhelming. Sordid tales of invasion of travelers' privacy by TSA agents have repeatedly made local and national news and frequently receive star billing online, often mocked in such YouTube video classics as software engineer John Tyner's "Don't Touch My Junk."[27] (Tyner had refused a TSA pat-down at the airport in San Diego.) Or such outrageous antics as the "wildly inappropriate" scribbled note *Feministe* blogger Jill Filipovic found in her checked luggage—"Get Your Freak On Girl"—courtesy of a TSA employee who felt compelled to comment on a vibrator among her personal belongings.[28]

Is this, as some ask, security or "security theater"?[29]

TSA regulations have also produced a number of unintended consequences. The administration ranks as the number two most hated government organization—right after the IRS. The airport ordeal became so distressing for many travelers that a 2011 survey by the US Travel Association revealed two out of five travelers boycotted airports and their ever-present invasive checkpoints to travel by train or automobile.[30] Taking to the roads or using rail or bus travel, however, is not the answer.

TSA is not just for airports anymore.

THE VIPRS

The stage was set for two of the most invasive "security" operations of our time by two pieces of legislation. Embedded within the Aviation and Transportation Security Act, signed into law in November 2001 by President Bush (but taken much further under Obama), was authorization for the Transportation Security Administration, tasked with securing all modes of transportation.

In turn, the TSA operates the cryptically named Visible Intermodal Prevention and Response (VIPR) program. Even though VIPR operations had been underway for nearly two years, which we discuss below, they were not officially authorized until August 2007 by the same act that implemented the recommendations of the 9/11 Commission[31] and directed the TSA to put more focus on surface transportation security.[32]

The 2007 act also authorized the TSA to use any DHS asset for its VIPR teams, including federal air marshals, transportation security officers, surface transportation security inspectors, canine detection teams, explosives detection specialists, behavior detection officers, and federal, state, and local law-enforcement officers. As an extension of the TSA, VIPR teams may be found screening passengers, looking for suspicious behavior, and acting as a "visible deterrent for potential terrorist acts."[33]

This is the official version of what the VIPR program and its teams are and are supposed to do. While VIPR teams were intended to augment local, state, and federal entities, the mobile SWAT teams have become a law-enforcement franchise in their own right.

In his 2012 book, former TSA administrator Kip Hawley, who created the TSA in 2005, left a lot of unanswered questions about the advent of the VIPR team. He pegs the date for the first VIPR team to November 27, 2005, ten days after Operation Glidepath, "a plot hatched at the highest levels of al-Qaeda and aimed at targets in the United States and the United Kingdom . . . Glidepath's intelligence suggested that we expect an attack on transportation but TSA didn't know when, why, or how," Hawley wrote. "VIPRs came together as a way to combine different force packages of TSA assets and deploy them unpredictably." Hawley also described Operation Glidepath as an August 2006 plot and connected it with "CIA personnel [who had] laid out a series of tiny information snippets, each a puzzle piece that meant little by itself. Some of these bits of data were from human sources; some from electronic surveillance or intercepted e-mails and phone calls. But as the fragments piled up over the next twenty minutes, a picture slowly emerged."[34]

We could not locate any other mention of this operation from any other source than Hawley's book. Any direct connection with the VIPR program is unclear. What is clear, however, is that whatever the DHS and TSA admit VIPR is, it is a whole lot more.

How many VIPR teams are there? No one knows for sure. An August 2012 report claims there were thirty-seven VIPR teams. This is up from the fifteen existing plus twelve anticipated new teams reported eight months earlier. It is obvious that the number of VIPR teams exploded when the threat had not.[35]

How often have VIPR teams been deployed? We cannot say with any certainty, and we're not sure if the TSA knows. Let's look at some official information first.

We examined several reports and the answer is unclear. For example, a June 2008 report stated that the number and frequency of VIPR operations began to increase a year earlier, and exercises had grown from an average of one per month to one or two per week.[36] A few months later, at an August 2008 TSA oversight hearing in the Senate, Hawley told Congress that, to date, VIPR teams had deployed more than one hundred times at "key commuter and regional passenger rail facilities, Amtrak stations, ferries, and airports."[37] That number is at variance with an earlier claim for twice that number. An April 2008 slide show presented by Francine Kerner, TSA chief counsel, claimed that, to date, TSA had conducted more than two hundred VIPR exercises, with approximately 10 percent of them involving searches.[38]

A June 2009 report presented to the House Committee on Homeland Security claimed that, since late 2005, TSA had deployed more than eight hundred teams. If this is true, there had been a major escalation in the number of deployments in less than a year's time.[39] This time period also coincides with the first five months of the Obama administration when, as we noted earlier, DHS began receiving billions in stimulus funds for its domestic security and surveillance programs.

Yet another report drafted for unnamed "Congressional requesters" makes it clear that there is no definitive answer. The General Accounting Office reported TSA officials told them they did not know how many VIPR deployments had specifically addressed the airport perimeter and "access control security," although the TSA could confirm that from March 2008 through April 2009, it had performed exactly 1,042 commercial and general aviation airport or cargo VIPR operations. If this report only included airport-based operations, how do we square this with an October 2009 claim that VIPR teams had executed more than 3,500 operations since 2007, with half of them carried out in 2009?[40] Hawley also claimed there were more than 8,000 VIPR deployments in 2011.[41]

The reason for the uncertainty may be explained in the GAO report. TSA officials admitted that as of May 2009, the agency was "enhancing" its VIPR database to "more accurately capture and track specific operational objectives."[42]

While the TSA may have been doing a very poor job of monitoring and documenting (or concealing) its VIPR operations, it wasted no time cranking out official press releases to be repeated by the media. To be fair, local law-enforcement officials did toot their own horns whenever possible and local media was glad to oblige.

Anecdotal reports date from mid-December 2005 when the *Washington Post* announced the appearance of the VIPR teams replete with undercover air marshals and uniformed law-enforcement officers who would "fan out to bus and train stations, ferries, and mass transit facilities across the country." Readers were told the "new test program" was to "conduct surveillance and 'counter potential criminal terrorist activity in all modes of transportation.'"[43]

The *Post* reported that VIPR teams were stationed in the public areas along Amtrak's Northeast Corridor and Los Angeles rail lines, at the ferries in Washington state, and in the mass transit systems in Atlanta, Philadelphia, Baltimore, and Washington, DC. In particular, air marshals looked for "individuals attempting to avoid or depart areas upon visual observation of the VIPR teams." Each VIPR team included six or seven individuals: "two air marshals, one TSA bomb-sniffing-canine team, one or two transportation security inspectors, one local law enforcement officer, and one other TSA employee."[44]

The only noted objection to the operation came from Douglas Laird, a security consultant and former head of security for Northwest Airlines, who called the air marshals' participation in the VIPR missions "absurd." "This is clearly a responsibility of the local jurisdictions," he said. "They don't have enough air marshals to carry out the mission they are supposed to do. To spread them even thinner dilutes the reason they are there in the first place." David Adams, the spokesman for the Federal Air Marshal Service, countered that the TSA is "charged with overseeing all modes of transportation—not just aviation."[45] Apparently, the significance of the word air in Air Marshal Service had somehow lost its meaning.

In this, as in all subsequent press releases or news reports, the TSA was careful to make it clear that the exercises had not been prompted by "new intelligence indicating that terrorists [were] interested in targeting transportation modes."[46] As some might put it, *move along, there's nothing to see here.* The gradual introduction of VIPR teams, however, also had the impact of turning them into a routine presence for travelers.

As indicated in the *Washington Post* article, initial VIPR team exercises were explained as experimental. The frequency of the exercises increased slowly from once per month to once or twice per week until fall 2007 when the newly passed act loosed the TSA and the Air Marshal Service to expand beyond airport security.

Hawley noted that, by late 2006, he "could see that each measure [TSA took] had a specific reason and provided some serious security value," although he viewed the TSA as "still too reactive and dependent on regulatory prohibitions to parry the very real threat stalking us." He said the TSA was "making progress with better training and the introduction of new proactive security measures like document checking, pop-up patrols of VIPRs, and behavior detection, but . . . needed to accelerate our pace to keep up with the pipeline of oncoming plots."[47]

Early in March 2008, TSA conducted its first surprise inspection of Seaborne Airlines' seaplane passengers in the Virgin Islands. The size of the VIPR team numbered about thirty officers drawn from Customs and Border Protection (joined by two canine units to sniff for drugs and bombs), the Coast Guard, and the Air Marshal Service, joined by local Virgin Islands police and its Port Authority Marine Unit. The Drug Enforcement Agency, Immigrations and Customs Enforcement, and the US Attorney's Office were on standby during the operation.[48]

About one hundred passengers were screened during the six-hour operation under the airline's blue-and-white-striped tent. The VIPR team hand-searched bags and used hand wands for metal detection. Meanwhile, a special Customs van outfitted with X-ray machines was parked nearby. Mel Vanterpool, Virgin Island territorial Homeland Security director, said the VIPR program was designed to be "a deterrent to any person trying to move illegal substances such as drugs, firearms, any types of explosives through the seaplane. We do know that these things are shuttled back and forth by the seaplane."[49]

Is it any wonder no terrorists showed up? The VIPR team had set up a three-ring circus to welcome passengers at the dock.

The following day, a VIPR team of about thirty officers conducted another local surprise screening. Ferry passengers traveling between St. Thomas and St. John were screened at the marine terminal in Red Hook. The team took seven people with invalid immigration status into custody, and officers confiscated at least three bags of drugs.[50] Note that again there were no terrorist sightings.

By September 2008, the VIPR operations were becoming more grandiose. The Amtrak Office of Security Strategy and Special Operations, Amtrak Police Department, TSA personnel, and officers from approximately one hundred commuter rail, state, and local police agencies "mobilized" for the "largest joint, simultaneous Northeast rail security operation of its kind, involving 150 railway stations between Fredericksburg, Virginia, and Essex Junction, Vermont."[51] (The multiforce security "surge" returned in September 2009 for Operation ALERTS [Allied Law Enforcement for Rail and Transit Security] to repeat the operation.[52])

Amtrak police chief John O'Connor announced that the operation—with "hundreds" of law enforcement officers across thirteen states and Washington, DC, monitoring an estimated seven hundred thousand travelers—was the "longest wall of security ever mobilized along the East Coast." O'Connor asserted, "We are one team, with one mission, and that is to protect rail and mass transit passengers, patrons and employees from harm, manmade or otherwise."[53]

While the TSA and Chief O'Connor may have seen the operation as remarkable, the reality is it also proved that government agencies could mobilize and demonstrate a "highly visible police and security presence" never seen before.

This reality was reinforced by TSA assistant administrator John Sammon, who claimed, "It is critical that we continue to expand and exercise our collective ability to respond to a terrorist threat or incident." The operation had been an "opportunity to demonstrate in dramatic fashion the force potential and security enhancement value of regional collaboration as TSA joins its professional colleagues throughout the Northeast to increase familiarization with the local stations and provide a highly visible security presence during rush hour," according to Sammon. The TSA and Amtrak also announced (or warned) it would carry out similar operations across the country.[54]

It is clear there would now be no limitations to what the TSA and its VIPR teams could pull off. In February 2009, teams simultaneously actively patrolled eight general aviation airports and three commercial airports, including Tampa International, Sarasota-Bradenton International, and St. Petersburg-Clearwater.[55]

And the event requiring this high level of security was—*ta da!*—the Super Bowl! (Apparently, VIPR teams love NFL football. In December 2012, teams patrolled the game between the Green Bay Packers and the Minnesota Vikings.[56])

Also in February 2009, CBS News noticed that federal air marshals were no longer confined to the air and had joined TSA/VIPR team operations by launching "counterterror surveillance at train stations and other mass transit facilities in a three-day test program." While some team members wearing jackets with the TSA emblem on the back would be obvious to the traveling public, others were plainclothes air marshals "scanning the crowds for suspicious individuals." Air marshal spokesman David Adams explained, "We just want to develop the capability to enhance security outside of aviation."[57]

Black helicopters—often attributed only to conspiracy theorists' imaginations—were involved with VIPR team operations the following month. A pair of black helicopters was noted flying low over the perimeter at Charleston, West Virginia's, Yeager Airport as part of a two-day VIPR operation. Also reported was "an abundance" of uniformed and plainclothes TSA officers going through the terminal and inspecting delivery trucks.[58]

The purpose of this operation? So the TSA could "spot check security procedures and increase safety." Did the black helicopters only fly over the airport perimeter? Of course not! They reportedly made "wide loops over the city, moving slowly over several neighborhoods."

Also, according to Yeager Airport director Rick Atkinson, VIPR teams visited every airport at least once a year, with a VIPR team at "an airport or two somewhere in the country every day." Without question, this was a far cry from the once monthly or once- or twice-weekly VIPR exercises of 2005.

TSA kept the VIPR teams rolling with ever bigger, broader, and bolder operations. In June 2009, VIPR patrols were on Chicago-area Metra commuter trains with the expectation that teams would operate on all eleven lines.[59] The Greyhound Bus terminal in Orlando went through a TSA random check—the first time for the company in Florida—coordinated in October.[60] Later in the month, VIPR teams carried out the TSA's largest operation to date at the Chesapeake Bay Bridge-Tunnel, even though a VIPR operation had recently been done at the James River ferry, cruise ship terminal, and rail stations. Eight agencies were represented at the Bridge-Tunnel, stopping traffic and checking drivers' licenses, while explosives- and drug-sniffing dogs checked vehicles. Two Coast Guard boats and a Virginia Beach police boat patrolled the bay.[61] (The exercise was repeated in 2010 with vehicles stopped at "safety checkpoints" at the tollbooths.[62])

The following month, a "deliberately conspicuous" VIPR operation in Memphis can only be described as a combination of domestic spying and profiling. Armed officers, including federal agents and local officers from Memphis and throughout the Southeast, watched for "suspicious conduct" at the Memphis Area Transit Authority's transportation terminals, as well at the Greyhound Bus terminal and Amtrak station downtown where "bomb dogs [also] sniffed luggage."[63] Memorial Day weekend 2010, a VIPR team at the Sault Ste. Marie international bridge border crossing in Michigan, where eight thousand travelers crossed over the weekend, yielded non-terrorism-related-yet-interesting contraband: thirty-two narcotic pills and fourteen Cuban cigars. Border Patrol marine interdiction agents searched a private sailing vessel, which yielded the discovery of two grams of marijuana and a used marijuana pipe. In other incidents, they seized more "contraband and drug paraphernalia."[64] Not found were any signs of terrorists.

By now it should be clear that the VIPR teams had failed to encounter anything even remotely terrorism-related. It's not for lack of trying, however.

In what could be called the MacDaddy of VIPR extravaganzas to date, in mid-June 2010, the TSA pulled out all the stops with an operation that incorporated terrain in three states—Ohio, Kentucky, and West Virginia. More than three hundred law-enforcement and military personnel representing eighty-three agencies swept through a one-hundred-mile stretch of the Ohio Valley with the alleged goals of familiarizing themselves with the area's industrial infrastructure and learning how other agencies responded to emergencies. It is difficult to see how much real information participants gleaned from the "brief visual inspections of power and chemical plants, rail and riverboat terminals, lock and dam complexes and natural gas pipelines."[65]

Note that the inclusion of military personnel in this surveillance activity is a violation of the Posse Comitatus Act, which expressly forbids direct participation by the military in a "search, seizure, arrest, or other similar activity."[66]

An unbelievable number of agencies and a variety of equipment were called into play. VIPR teams "used helicopters, emergency vehicles, reconnaissance aircraft, Coast Guard patrol boats and watercraft from the Divisions of Natural Resources in West Virginia and Ohio." Three mobile command centers were set up at the complex at Gallipolis Ferry by the TSA, the West Virginia Division of Homeland Security and Emergency Management, and the Ohio State Highway Patrol to coordinate communications and collect data from the field. A total of 124 TSA employees were stationed in West Virginia. TSA officers were stationed at all West Virginia airports with commercial service, and TSA inspectors checked airport cargo. Three helicopters were used for "aerial inspection." The Ohio State Highway Patrol used the powerful camera aboard its Cessna Caravan aircraft to send "color and thermal images of power plants and other key infrastructure items . . . back to the command center at Gallipolis Ferry from more than fifteen miles away."[67]

Michael Cleveland, federal security director for TSA operations in West Virginia, boasted this was his "biggest VIPR ever." People and resources had been pulled from both Ohio and West Virginia, with federal air marshals borrowed from Pittsburgh. "We wanted to get as many key players together as possible to have a visible presence and let people know we're out here. It can be a deterrent," Cleveland declared.[68]

Any terrorists in the area would surely have known the "biggest VIPR ever" was going on and only had to wait for the teams to pack up and go home to carry on business as usual.

This massive exercise, of course, had to be topped. The TSA outdid itself a year later, in June 2011, when it created an event deemed the "largest of its nature in the country." The all-day field exercise encompassed five thousand square miles along the Ohio River transportation corridor that covered parts of Ohio, Kentucky, Pennsylvania, and West Virginia, including air, water, and ground resources.[69]

The widespread VIPR operation included Coast Guard boats on the river, Ohio Air National Guard Black Hawk helicopters with multijurisdictional teams on board and the West Virginia Air National Guard and other aircraft in the air, and law-enforcement vehicles "visible at various 'targets' (industrial plants, pipelines, surface or road assets) and other general infrastructure, including the Willow Island Locks and Dam," and Ohio State Highway Patrol on the ground.

The possible volume of information gathered and shared by the various agencies participating is mind-boggling. "We have the ability to link up with other agencies, the TSA in Washington, D.C., with videos, the decision-makers who need to have real-time information," James M. Fotenso, public affairs manager with the TSA, said. Local law enforcement, the West Virginia National Guard, and several other agencies utilized West Virginia's interoperable radios, and pictures "pushed" from the helicopters were e-mailed to the command vehicle and the state commander.

Not everyone was as pleased with the increasingly more invasive exercises as the TSA and VIPR team members appear to have been. One blogger remarked, "Americans must decide if, in the name of homeland security, they are willing to allow TSA operatives to storm public places in their communities with no warning, pat them down, and search their bags. And they better decide quickly."[70]

Both VIPR and a similar program, THOR (Target Hardening Operational Response), possess obvious "paramilitary titles, connotations, and descriptions, [raising] legitimate questions about the missions and goals of the agencies participating in them," former Georgia congressman Bob Barr wrote in March 2011 in his "Barr Code" column for the *Atlanta Journal-Constitution*. THOR, operated by Atlanta's MARTA public transit system, uses a "surge sweep" with an "overwhelming presence of law enforcement personnel." Barr continued: "More important, they tend to cause significant disruption to, and concern among, the public. Such concerns, however, appear not to register with the government agencies themselves."[71]

Even the left-wing publication *Mother Jones* reacted to the threat to civil liberties. "Think you could avoid the TSA's body scanners and pat-downs by taking Amtrak? Think again," Jen Quraishi wrote. "Even your daily commute isn't safe from TSA screenings. And because the TSA is working with Immigration and Customs Enforcement (ICE) and Border Patrol, you may have your immigration status examined along with your 'junk,'" Quraishi continued.[72]

Never satisfied, in October 2011 the TSA literally took its operation on the road with its "first ever instance [of] simultaneous statewide VIPR operations" held in seven locations. In partnership with the Tennessee Office of Homeland Security and "several other federal and state agencies"—allegedly for a "safety enforcement and awareness operation"—the TSA set up checkpoints at five weigh stations on Tennessee's interstates and at regional bus terminals in Nashville and Knoxville. Federal and state agents inspected trucks and other vehicles to "identify security threats."[73]

Tennessee Department of Safety and Homeland Security commissioner Bill Gibbons said, "Where is a terrorist more apt to be found? Not these days on an airplane; more likely on the interstate."[74] On Examiner.com, Cynthia Hodges asked, "Is there evidence to support the claim?" She continued: "The VIPR program is a serious blow to freedom-loving Americans. Many civil rights organizations believe that the government is steadily increasing the VIPR program in order to test how much the American public is willing to tolerate before the line is drawn."[75]

In June 2011, TSA chief John Pistole told a Senate committee the TSA had conducted eight thousand sweeps across the country in the past year alone.[76]

EMERGING POLICE STATE

Recall earlier in this chapter when we called attention to the belief by some that the Department of Homeland Security is working toward the creation of an alternative federal police agency that would not only incorporate state and local law enforcement but also usurp their position to shift the balance of power toward an emerging police state. Former FBI deputy director John Pistole supported our point in July 2010 soon after he took over as TSA administrator.

Pistole clearly exposed the TSA agenda when he told *USA Today* he wanted to take the TSA to the "next level," to make it a "full partner in U.S. counterterrorism efforts." The TSA and its employees would operate as a "national-security, counterterrorism organization, fully integrated into U.S. government efforts."[77] What he did not explain is how his TSA VIPR operations and teams already incorporate a large number of federal, state, and local law-enforcement agencies—and, at times illegally, the military—in "exercises."

Pistole's 2012 TSA budget called for expanding VIPR programs by 50 percent, meaning more searches but not necessarily "more safety." The Government Accountability Office noted the TSA had "measured the progress of its VIPR program in terms of the number of VIPR operations conducted, but had not yet developed measures or targets to report on the effectiveness of the operations themselves. That's a nice way to say that TSA is acting for action's sake," the *Washington Times* noted in late October 2011.[78]

The more recent DHS-run VIPR event, the second inauguration of President Barack Obama, on January 21, 2013, drew little attention. It was declared a National Special Security Event by the Secretary of Homeland Security, Janet Napolitano, on September 12, 2012, allowing "the full force of the federal government to be brought to bear in the development of the event security and incident management plans."[79]

VIPR teams provided support near regional airports and rail stations, and the TSA deployed security officers to assist Secret Service agents in screening participants along the parade route and at select inaugural events. The Coast Guard had primary responsibility to coordinate "maritime security planning and maritime domain awareness to protect critical transportation infrastructure." It conducted "waterside security patrols; security sweeps at marinas located within the protected region, and other operations including enforcement of airspace restrictions." Immigration and Customs Enforcement provided pre-event planning, participated in event command centers, and provided response capability when needed. Customs and Border Protection provided "multiple aerial assets to assist federal, state, and local agencies and assist with perimeter security."[80]

While that was the official version for the media and public, it was dubbed "the American Lockdown State" by leftist Tom Engelhardt: "Washington, after all, was in a lockdown mode unmatched by any inauguration from another era—not even Lincoln's second inaugural in the midst of the Civil War, or Franklin Roosevelt's during World War II, or John F. Kennedy's at the height of the Cold War."[81]

Engelhardt quotes from the *NBC Nightly News* report:

> [T]he airspace above Washington . . . [will be] a virtual no-fly zone for 30 miles in all directions from the U.S. capital. Six miles of the Potomac and Anacostia Rivers will be shut down, with 150 blocks of downtown Washington closed to traffic, partly out of concern for car or truck bombs . . . with countersnipers on top of buildings around the capital and along the parade route . . . [and] detectors monitoring the air for toxins . . . At the ready near the capital, thousands of doses of antidotes in case of a chemical or biological attack . . . All this security will cost about $120 million dollars for hundreds of federal agents, thousands of local police, and National Guardsmen from 25 states.[82]

In all fairness, DHS had had more than four months to plan for the National Special Security Event, in addition to the experience it had gained from several years of VIPR team operations. True to his leftist roots, Engelhardt just couldn't help himself and affixed the blame for the "post-9/11 National Security Complex" on President Bush: "[Osama] Bin Laden, of course, is long dead, but his was the 9/11 spark that, in the hands of George W. Bush and his top officials, helped turn this country into a lockdown state and first set significant portions of the Greater Middle East aflame." Bin Laden, Engelhardt wrote, "helped facilitate the locking down of this society in ways that should unnerve us all."[83]

TSA's mission creep has also caught the attention of the American trade magazine *Government Executive*, which noted an extra fifty-five TSA screeners "on hand to help the Secret Service check delegates at the Democratic National Convention in Charlotte last summer. That's a real stretch of the agency's mandate," it wrote, "even for the most security-obsessed traveler." TSA insiders assert it is not mission creep; TSA is "just fulfilling its objectives." Pistole states on the TSA website that his agency's mission is "to secure transportation systems."[84]

"Defenders of the agency say that it is precisely because of its broad mandate that it has (together with other law enforcement agencies) pre-vented another 9/11," Christopher Elliott reported in the March/April 2013 issue of *National Geographic Traveler*.[85]

Critics like Fred Cate, a law professor at Indiana University, claim "there's no causal relationship between a TSA with a sprawling mandate and the absence of a terrorist attack." It's the "law-enforcement equivalent of a clumsy police dragnet," Cate said. Edward Hasbrouck, a privacy advocate and one of the leading voices against TSA overreach, said, "But we can't defend freedom by adopting measures that prevent us from exercising the rights we profess to believe in."[86]

What Engelhardt and many others fail to ask is why Americans are allowing Obama and his DHS/TSA/VIPR team storm troopers get away with locking down America and endangering our freedoms. Who is going to stop this insanity?

EXECUTIVE INTERROGATORS

In a January 31, 2010, *Washington Post* article, former CIA director Michael V. Hayden discussed the error of the Obama administration's ways in its handling of the Christmas Day Detroit-bound Umar Farouk Abdulmutallab, the "Underwear Bomber."[87]

In the very last paragraph, Hayden noted that, in August 2009, the Obama administration had "unveiled" the High-Value Detainee Interrogation Group (HIG) to question al-Qaeda operatives and had announced the FBI would begin questioning CIA officers about the alleged abuses outlined in the 2004 inspector general's report on CIA-run prisons. While interrogations of the CIA personnel were "well underway," the administration had yet to get the HIG "organized" and ready to conduct the al-Qaeda interrogations.[88]

It is unclear what Hayden did or did not know. It would appear that his January 2010 article may have helped to spur sufficient interest to kick-start the HIG into action. As for not knowing what the Obama administration's right and left hands were doing, he was not alone. Stay close as we attempt to navigate our way through another fine Obama White House mess.

In August 2009, according to "senior White House officials," Obama "approved the creation of an elite team of interrogators to question key terrorism suspects, part of a broader effort to revamp U.S. policy on detention and interrogation." Incredibly, the White House would be in complete control of the interrogation operation. The new unit, comprised of "experts from several intelligence and law enforcement agencies," was to be housed at the FBI and overseen by the National Security Council, effectively "shifting the center of gravity away from the CIA and giving the White House direct oversight," Anne E. Kornblut reported in the *Washington Post*. The HIG director was expected to come from the FBI, and not the CIA, while a deputy would be chosen from another intelligence agency, possibly from the CIA.[89]

Former senator Kit Bond (R-MO), vice chairman of the Senate Intelligence Committee, called the move "an 'odd lack of faith in their own intelligence community' and a 'bizarre vote of no confidence' in the director of the CIA," CNN reported. Bond said he was "really concerned," because he believed that "if the White House is involved in this at all, that it will really politicize the entire process, could hurt national security in the long run." The White House disagreed, stating it would not be "involved in any operational activities of the unit."[90]

HIG (the Beltway loves acronyms) was not totally new news. In mid-July 2009, the *Wall Street Journal* reported Obama was "considering overhauling the way terror suspects are interrogated by creating a small team of professionals drawn from across the government." A *Journal* source said that one of the new team's tasks would be to "devise a new set of interrogation methods," using techniques possibly "drawn from sources ranging from scientific studies to the psychology behind television ads." If adopted, the article continued, HIG "would represent the Obama administration's effort to sweep away a contentious counterterrorism issue that has dogged the CIA and Justice Department since a U.S. network of secret prisons was revealed in 2005. The team would reduce the CIA's controversial role in interrogations, but the agency remains at odds with Congress."[91]

In late June 2009, Spencer Ackerman of the *Washington Independent* was the first to report about the creation of a task force stemming from the January 22, 2009, Executive Order 13493 on interrogations issued by Obama. Ackerman wrote, "The task force charged with fleshing out President Obama's ban on torture in interrogations is likely to recommend the creation of small, mixed-agency teams for interviewing the most important terrorist targets. Representing an implicit demotion of the CIA, which currently has responsibility for interrogating high-level terrorists, the teams would report jointly to the attorney general and the director of national intelligence, according to officials familiar with the proposal."[92]

Ackerman reported that the interrogation teams were the "brainchild of three members of the Intelligence Science Board, a panel that reports to the director of national intelligence": forensic psychologist Robert A. Fein; former deputy attorney general Philip B. Heymann, now a law professor at Harvard; and former CIA official N. John MacGaffin III. The trio had begun to conduct research three years prior on all "available social science literature concerning interrogations in a variety of nations, including the United States, France, the United Kingdom and Japan, in order to inform a humane and effective interrogation regimen." The two reports that followed "both repudiated torture and attributed interrogation-related abuses in part to a 'shortfall in advanced, research-based interrogation methods at a time of intense pressure from operational commanders to produce actionable intelligence from high-value targets,'" Ackerman wrote.[93]

In March 2009, J. Douglas Wilson, a Justice Department official who headed the Obama administration's Special Task Force on Interrogation and Transfer Policies, a group created by the January executive order banning torture, presented Intelligence Science Board members with recommendations. One recommendation was the "creation of 'an organizational structure that could draw' on the experience of a small corps of the best interrogators currently working for the government who 'could produce what would very likely be the best non-coercive interrogation or interviewing capacity in the world,'" Ackerman wrote. This "corps would serve as the first wave of interrogators under the new structure while preparing a syllabus on proper interrogation guidelines for new recruits to the teams."[94]

According to Ackerman, Heymann said small teams of three to five interrogators would be "mobile and go where it needed to go," only dealing with "major interviews and major occasions to get information from a terror suspect." Heymann also said the teams "would 'report both to the Justice Department and to the intelligence world' . . . to ensure that interrogations [did] not compromise prosecutions of detainees."[95]

The task force, then officially chaired by Attorney General Eric H. Holder Jr. and co-vice-chaired by former director of national intelligence Dennis C. Blair and former secretary of defense Robert M. Gates, had "embraced the proposal," Ackerman learned from an unnamed official. It was also learned that the Intelligence Science Board had "recommended that ahead of the deployment of the interrogation teams, senior administration officials should decide whether or not the substance of the interrogation ought to be used as evidence for a criminal prosecution."[96]

Jake Tapper, now with CNN, and Sunlen Miller reported for ABC News in mid-July 2009 that the Special Task Force on Interrogation and Transfer Policies and the Detention Policy Task Force would not meet as scheduled and had also failed to meet the deadline designated in the January executive order. The task force asked for and was granted a two-month extension and was reportedly "working to determine who will interrogate detainees and what the rules of engagement will be moving forward." Tapper and Miller asked, "Why the delay?"[97]

The Detention Policy Task Force did release a preliminary document stating it had focused thus far on "options for the lawful disposition of detainees" held at Guantanamo Bay. However, the task force explained it had yet to determine future policies regarding "apprehension, detention, and treatment of suspected terrorists," including what personnel would be involved, how to "work together more effectively to plan and execute" activities, what rules and boundaries should be set for "any future detention under the law of war," how to make the federal courts and military commissions "more effective for prosecuting terrorists," how international law would apply in the future, whether to revise detention policies in Afghanistan, and other key issues.[98]

It appears that Abdulmutallab's case was almost immediately handed off to the federal criminal courts because it was determined to be "feasible."[99] Who made the determination is unknown. Was Eric Holder the de facto head of HIG?

The task force report declared that military commissions were "no less legitimate" than civilian courts," Tom Eley noted at the World Socialist website. However, unlike criminal courts, military commissions "can allow for the protection of sensitive sources and methods of intelligence-gathering . . . and take into account the realities of the battlefield and the particular challenges of gathering evidence during military operations overseas." It would seem that "methods of intelligence-gathering" and "challenges of gathering evidence during military operations" referred to evidence extracted through torture, Eley observed. The third option offered in the report was "indefinite detention without trial." Importantly, Eley noted, the report does not distinguish between alleged terrorists captured abroad and US citizens, as "the same methods could be used against those deemed domestic 'enemies' of the state."[100]

In a November 2009 article, Spencer Ackerman stated it would be unlikely that HIG would interrogate Nidal Hasan, the active-duty Army major who committed the Fort Hood massacre, because HIG's jurisdiction did not include acts committed on US soil. Ackerman wrote that FBI Special Agent Andrew McCabe, HIG's director (although not previously identified as such in the press), "referred all questions about the Hasan case to the FBI's public affairs office and said he would not be able to elaborate on HIG operations beyond an August statement by Attorney General Eric Holder announcing the group's creation."[101]

Again, it appears that Eric Holder—overseer of the FBI—was the de facto head of the HIG.

WHO'S IN CHARGE?

As for FBI Special Agent Andrew McCabe, he was identified in January 2010 when the *Wall Street Journal* reported the HIG was still months in the future. McCabe, a "veteran FBI counterterrorism investigator" in the FBI's Washington field office, told the *Journal* "it will take several more months to establish teams that could question high-profile suspects," although "the bureau can currently cobble together an ad-hoc team of interrogators if the need arises."[102]

Further into the *Journal* article, we find that DNI Dennis Blair made what was deemed "an apparent gaffe" when he criticized the FBI for not using the HIG, a "new panel charged with designating so-called high-value terrorism suspects for special interrogations." Blair reportedly "used the expression 'duh' to emphasize his point." Later that day, he backtracked, claiming his comments were "misconstrued." In an obvious attempt to recover, Blair added that the FBI's "expertise in interrogation [would be] available in the HIG once it is fully operational."[103]

Blair, allegedly involved with the task force that created HIG, and presumably knowledgeable about what had been going on, was not aware that HIG was not authorized to operate on US soil? Or was Ackerman's intel incorrect? Perhaps Blair should have had a chat with Holder—or McCabe, HIG's purported leader.[104]

However, McCabe's comments to the *Journal* revealed nothing, as he focused only on HIG's interrogation methodology in general, basically that the interrogations would continue to rely on methods being used by the FBI and "other agencies." Also, he stated Obama had ordered that the interrogators adhere to only the nineteen questioning guidelines,[105] i.e., the nonviolent methods outlined in the US Army field manual on interrogation.[106]

McCabe had nothing to say about Abdulmutallab. Justice Department spokesman Matthew Miller did say Abdulmutallab had been questioned by the FBI—and had provided intelligence that had "already proved useful in the fight against al-Qaeda"—before he was Mirandized. Abdulmutallab was not read his "rights as a criminal defendant until after he stopped cooperating." Miller did not say whether McCabe or HIG had been involved.[107]

The *Journal* article also made it clear that HIG qualified as another Obama administration fairy tale. The National Security Council was "still reviewing operational details of how the teams will operate," while McCabe and the deputies from the CIA and Defense Department were "seeking office space in Washington's Virginia suburbs and preparing to pick members of the interrogation teams." HIG's initial plans were reserved for overseas use only, although the administration hadn't ruled out using them on US soil "for incidents such as the Christmas bomb plot."[108]

It would appear that the HIG can was again kicked down the road in 2011. Exactly when HIG went fully operational, and *what* it did *when* it did, remains unclear. In the report for the fiscal year 2012 Appropriations Bill for the Commerce, Justice, Science, and Related Agencies is a request for $16.8 million and funding for eighteen positions to support HIG. Included in HIG's responsibilities was the "conduct of scientific research to determine the effectiveness of current interrogation techniques, and develop new effective, lawful techniques." A status report was due to the committee by January 15, 2012, "detailing the research activities conducted under the auspices of the HIG, the results of such research, and any recommendations for the development of new techniques."[109]

The HIG had been deployed in fourteen "instances" to conduct interrogations over the past two years, FBI director Robert Mueller told a House appropriations subcommittee in March 2012. While Mueller did not list any specific cases in which the HIG was used, an unnamed law enforcement official told CNN that the HIG could "be deployed both overseas and in the United States and can be used in interrogations with U.S. citizens as well as non-citizens."[110]

CNN reported that, based on comments made in May 2010 by John Brennan, Obama's counterterrorism adviser, the HIG was "used when Pakistani-American Faisal Shahzad attempted to detonate a car bomb in Times Square on May 1."[111] Writing in the *Daily Beast*, Mark Hosenball reported that, according to a number of unnamed US law-enforcement and intelligence personnel, the HIG had played "only a limited role in the investigation." Hosenball commented that this "raises new questions about just what the HIG's mission is and when the unit is supposed to be deployed."[112]

While "elements" of the HIG who participated in the interrogation of Shahzad report to the Justice Department, they are also "supervised by a subcommittee of the National Security Council at the White House." Two officials said their understanding was that HIG personnel provided "intelligence support" to the FBI agents who were "doing the actual questioning" of Shahzad but were not part of the HIG itself. Two officials, perhaps not the same ones, also said the HIG was "playing little to no role in the questioning of multiple presumed associates of Shahzad who were detained by authorities in Pakistan following the failed Times Square attack" because Pakistani authorities "declined to invite HIG personnel into their country to participate in the interrogations."[113]

Moreover, HIG personnel were not deployed to Pakistan "after authorities there captured Mullah Abdul Ghani Baradar, military commander of the Afghan Taliban and perhaps the most important terrorist leader captured since the arrest [in 2003] of 9/11 mastermind Khalid Sheikh Mohammed." Why? Hosenball reported that "one of the main reasons officials said at the time that HIG had not been sent to question Baradar after his capture was because of Pakistani unwillingness to allow the unit into the country."[114]

What good was the newly minted elite interrogation unit when it was unwanted and unloved in Pakistan? Why the HIG was not wanted is unknown.

Unnamed officials told CNN that "elements of the HIG were used when Umar Farouk Abdulmutallab, a Nigerian citizen, tried to set off a bomb hidden in his underwear on a Christmas Day flight to Detroit in [December] 2009." While the HIG was "not fully operational at that time," a HIG team was deployed "to provide support." There had been a delay, Brennan stated, because Abdulmutallab was read his Miranda rights and had a lawyer.[115]

CRITICS, ALWAYS CRITICS

More evidence emerged in January 2010 that the Obama administration had not only been derelict of its duty in handling the Abdulmutallab case but also had failed to use the HIG, which it had specifically created to replace CIA interrogators. It was a major intelligence fail-fail.

Sen. Kit Bond, a vocal critic of the Obama administration's treatment of terrorists as common criminals, said in a January 20, 2010, statement that the administration had fumbled the terror case, "shutting the intelligence community out of the vital decision making process on how to question the terrorist." Bond said, "It's clear the Administration's own intelligence officials think they fumbled the Christmas Day terrorist case. That this Administration chose to shut out our top intelligence officials and forego collecting potentially life-saving intelligence is a dangerous sign." He continued, "Unlike the foolhardy plan to treat terrorists like common criminals, we need to recognize they are enemy combatants in a war."[116]

Also, in their January 20 testimony before the Senate Homeland Security Committee, DNI Blair, Secretary of Homeland Security Janet Napolitano, and Michael Leiter, chief of the National Counterterrorism Center, "all revealed they were not consulted" on whether Abdulmutallab "should have been questioned" by the HIG or charged in federal court.[117] "That unit was created exactly for this purpose," Blair told the committee. "We did not invoke the HIG in this case. We should have."[118]

A joint statement by Senators Bond and Dianne Feinstein (D-CA), chairman of the committee, declared the Christmas Day bombing attempt had "thankfully failed. But it only failed because the bomb didn't explode.

Otherwise, the event was a major intelligence failure," they said. Realistically, they were basically saying Obama's HIG gambit had failed: it was "not yet operative" and "there was no process in place for Intelligence Community officials to be consulted before the individual was Mirandized."[119]

Of course, this begs the question, who did make the decision? US Senate Republican Leader Mitch McConnell asked the same thing January 21 from the Senate floor: "At what level of authority was this decision taken to treat him as a criminal defendant instead of an unlawful enemy combatant? Who made this decision? . . . I asked this question last night of John Brennan, the president's senior counterterrorism adviser, three times and he refused to answer." McConnell continued: "I think that the Senate is entitled to know precisely who authorized this. . . . A year ago the president decided to revise the nation's interrogation policies, and to restrict the CIA's ability to question terrorists. The administration created a High Value Detainee Interrogation Group to question terrorists. Why wasn't his group brought in once this terrorist was taken into custody?"[120]

Rep. Joe Pitts (R-PA) was equally blunt: "Upon taking office, President Obama scrapped the Bush Administration procedures to interrogate terrorists and constructed a new process known as the High-Value Detainee Interrogation Group. Over a year after taking office, this group is still not running. Furthermore, the Interrogation Group cannot be used for terrorists apprehended in the United States." Pitts stated, "Terrorists didn't stop plotting as our federal government changed chief executives."[121] Former senator Judd Gregg (R-NH), then ranking member of the Appropriations Subcommittee on State, Foreign Operations, and Related Agencies, added, "The manner in which we interrogate terror suspects is debatable, but the failure to have systems in place to interrogate them at all is inexcusable."[122]

WHO ASKED CONGRESS? NOBODY!

Another not-so-small matter is that Obama did not consult Congress about his unilateral decision to create the HIG. Rep. Pete Hoekstra (R-MI), the ranking Republican on the House Intelligence Committee, slammed the Obama administration on its failure "to implement another flawed policy—developed without transparency or consultation with Congress—to put federal law enforcement in charge of intelligence collection" via the HIG. "The Obama administration's failures on Guantanamo Bay, Fort Hood, and Detroit show the consequences of politically motivated, haphazard, national security decision-making without implementation plans," Hoekstra said.[123]

In a February 2, 2010, letter to National Security Advisor Gen. James L. Jones, Rep. Frank Wolf (R-VA), the top Republican on the House appropriations subcommittee that funds key counterterrorism programs, including the FBI and HIG, sought answers about the interrogation of Abdulmutallab. He sent two similar letters earlier to John Brennan, Jones's deputy; they failed to get any response. "There has been considerable confusion among agencies as to what their role was, what their role should have been, whether the HIG should have been involved, whether the HIG is intended to operate inside the United States, and even whether the HIG exists," Wolf stated.[124]

Progress of sorts was made at the end of January 2010. In his February 4 testimony before Congress, DNI Blair announced that the classified charter for HIG, a "special unit to interrogate terrorists," had been signed the week before. HIG was miraculously "fully operational." Curiously, the *Washington Post*'s Walter Pincus and Carrie Johnson had the inside scoop that HIG was not "formally authorized" until January 28, "under a previously unreported 14-page memo" signed by General Jones.[125]

The memo made it clear that "more than 100 preexisting Joint Terrorism Task Forces set up by the FBI [would] take the lead in national security incidents within the United States," Pincus and Johnson reported. Intelligence analysts and interrogators participating in the HIG "mobile teams can help with potentially deadly but previously unidentified suspects," they wrote. The "primary objective" for the HIG mobile interrogation units will be "to gather intelligence to prevent terrorist strikes against the United States or its allies," they explained. "But 'where possible,' the high-value units will collect information 'in a manner that allows it to be used in a criminal prosecution.'" The HIG units are "limited to interrogation strategies contained in the Army Field Manual, which explicitly repudiates waterboarding and other methods employed in the early years of President George W. Bush's administration that critics have likened to torture."[126]

It is unsurprising that the Obama administration wants to expand its federal employee rolls. Positions in the HIG units will be filled by federal employees, and not contractors, who will "participate in the teams, unless there is a special need for linguistic expertise."[127]

The *WaPo* article also makes it clear as to why the Obama administration wanted control over terrorist suspects: "FBI agents are allowed to interrogate people in the United States without informing them of their constitutional rights to remain silent and to secure an attorney if the agents want to gather intelligence and protect public safety." There was one unresolved matter, though: it remained "unclear who will decide when Miranda warnings come into play in cases related to national security."[128] Plus, we still don't know who gave the green light to Mirandize Abdulmutallab.

Did anything actually move forward for the HIG? Well, it, or perhaps we should say the FBI, was tasked with submitting a progress report by March 17, 2012, in which it outlined HIG's research activities and provided "any recommendations for developing new interrogation techniques," although it was unclear whether the report would be publicly available or classified.[129]

The March 2012 CNN report also revealed that the line between the intelligence community, both foreign and domestic, and homeland security had been erased. The HIG, CNN reported, "provides key research and cultural background on alleged terrorists," and its regionally focused mobile interrogation teams, known as MITs, comprised of FBI agents, CIA officers, and "others in the intelligence and homeland security community," could "question suspects."[130]

The HIG mission appears to be alive, but we are not so sure about the kicking part. It appears to be an agency mired in White House bureaucracy. As recently as February 2013, the FBI issued a detailed presolicitation "for behavioral science research to advance the science and practice of intelligence interviewing and interrogation to advance the [HIG] mission."[131]

10

THE DRONE NATION

WOULD IT SURPRISE YOU to learn that the Department of Homeland Security maintains its own domestic law-enforcement air force that operates surveillance drones on US soil using militarized equipment?[1] What if we told you that the same agency overseeing President Obama's overseas drone warfare currently eliminating suspected al-Qaeda members also helps collect data on American citizens domestically inside the controversial fusion centers? Would it further surprise you to find out that DHS is now almost definitely the largest dedicated homeland security air and marine force in the world?[2]

Before we cover the constitutionality of Obama's international drone campaign, let's start with an issue closer to home for most Americans—the emerging drone state in our country. It all started on a small scale with the Bush administration, but Obama took it much further to the point where Americans are deeply concerned. To understand how we got here, let's first trace the DHS drone program back to when it got its start in 2006.

DHS took delivery of its first drone—officially known as an unmanned aerial vehicle (UAV).[3] DHS's late entrance into launching its drone operations can be traced to the department's major problems similar to those we described in chapter 8 regarding its mismanaged fusion centers. A March 2006 in-depth article described DHS as an "unwanted child" with its "22 ill-fitting and at times ill-tempered agencies [being forced] to act like one organization."[4]

The man tasked in 2005 with straightening out the mess DHS had created, and "appeasing critics," was former Air Force pilot and NASA senior executive Michael C. Kostelnik.[5] Ordinarily, we might not spend much time with a single individual's history, but it is key to understanding the direction DHS's surveillance drone program took and, based on his influence, where it might be headed in the future.

Maj. Gen. Michael Kostelnik served in 1999 as commander of the Air Armament Center at Eglin Air Force Base in Florida. During his time serving in Bosnia, he sought another way to use the Predator drone—to "arm it with a weapon so new it didn't exist yet, a 250-pound, GPS-guided, nine-inch-diameter munition called the Small Smart Bomb (later renamed the Small Diameter Bomb)." In 1995, Kostelnik watched a Predator video beamed to the Pentagon from an exercise conducted at Fort Huachuca, Arizona. Later that year, he visited the General Atomics Aeronautical Systems Incorporated (GA-ASI) flight center at El Mirage, California, where he literally fell in love with the Predator drone after seeing it fly.[6]

Based on his conversations with GA-ASI, Kostelnik proposed a "Combined Development Force" whose "goal would be to drop a live Small Smart Bomb from a Predator by May 2001." Although the smart bomb did not make it onto the Predator,[7] ten years later, Kostelnik told *Air Force Magazine*, "If we had the [Small Diameter Bomb] in numbers in Kosovo, it would have been the star."[8]

Miniaturization was considered critical to next-generation platforms that would only be "capable of carrying a limited number of existing and planned munition systems," the Air Force predicted in summer 2011. A drone must be capable of multiple kills per pass while causing minimal collateral damage; able to locate and destroy small and mobile targets in real time; and resistant to camouflage, concealment, deception, and countermeasures.[9]

Is it any wonder, as we fast-forward to September 2006, we find Kostelnik's domestic Office of Air and Marine (OAM) taking delivery of its first GA-ASI Predator B drone? The OAM is an agency of Customs and Border Protection (CBP) and operates under the auspices of DHS. Kostelnik told a defense industry journal he had personally chosen the Predator for OAM's fleet because he had been involved with it since its "earliest days as a classified program." He justified the sole-source purchase from GA-ASI, arguing he had "leveraged a decade of development, procurement and proven operational experience including over a million flight hours," which "vastly reduced OAM's risk in the procurement." He also felt OAM should "take advantage of the Air Force's existing operating and support infrastructure to help OAM . . . [allowing it] to ride the coattails of the USAF's investments" in both the Predator itself and future "payload improvements."[10]

Obviously, Kostelnik was planning ahead. He noted that deployment of the remotely piloted, hand-flown Predator made for "seamless interoperability" with existing Department of Defense "force structure in the event of national emergency." While the majority of Defense's assets were deployed overseas, he said, OAM was in the position of having its fleet and operators "in the homeland." Should the need arise, the CBP fleet and well-trained operators could, he offered, "at a moment's notice, be 'CHOPed'—Change in Operational Command" to come under the Department of Defense's control.[11]

The Air Force also boasted in September 2006 that the Predator, now known as the MQ-9 Reaper, is "the Air Force's first hunter-killer UAV." The MQ-9 was larger and more powerful than its predecessor and is "designed to go after time-sensitive targets with persistence and precision, and destroy or disable those targets with 500-pound bombs and Hellfire missiles."[12]

"We've moved from using UAVs primarily in intelligence, surveillance and reconnaissance roles before Operation Iraqi Freedom, to a true hunter-killer role with the Reaper," Air Force chief of staff Gen. T. Michael Moseley boasted. "Today, the Air Force can launch a UAV from a remote field on the other side of the globe, then pilot that aircraft from a base in the United States. These systems and the Airmen who operate them offer unprecedented flexibility to combatant commanders world-wide," Moseley added.[13]

By now you're perhaps wondering, why in the world *would* DHS need hunter-killer drones for "intelligence, surveillance, and reconnaissance?" Good question.

Two years later, in April 2008, OAM—which by then deployed the world's largest law-enforcement air force—dedicated its very own national training center at Will Rogers World Airport in Oklahoma City. Kostelnik succeeded in his plan for OAM to "train its own pilots and pay-load operators and organically operate its own assets." The center would bring "advanced personnel from throughout the nation . . . to spearhead specialized training" for all OAM pilots and air crews, to train them and train them to train others.[14]

This was a huge milestone for an agency that had barely existed for two years, reportedly was short on personnel and funding,[15] and belonged to a department that was still in search of an identity. Although Predator drones had flown along the southwest border since 2005, OAM extended its operation with the arrival of its first "virtually piloted" MQ-9 at Grand Forks Air Branch in North Dakota, along the northern tier on the Canadian border, in December 2008. Opened in 2007, this was the fourth of five branches on the northern border. Operational flights were to start as early as January 2009.[16]

A year later, in December 2009, with the Obama administration fully at work at expanding the DHS, the agency's OAM launched a new unarmed Predator marine drone, about the size of a small turboprop commuter airplane, "loaded with special radar, cameras and sensors" to track drug smugglers from the southwestern border. Its wide-range radar gave a "more sweeping view of the ocean than any of the government's fleet of manned aircraft." Set to take off in January 2010, the first drone was scheduled to be joined by a second taking flight by summer 2010 in the Gulf of Mexico. They joined a small but growing fleet of five MQ-9s flying along the south-west border from a base in Arizona and the Grand Forks location.[17]

The OAM fleet was still small, yet by fall 2010, OAM was flying Guardian drones, as well as other manned aircraft operations, from Cape Canaveral to the Bahamas/Key West area of operation, while feeding imagery to the US Southern Command and the US Coast Guard's District 7. Remember, the Coast Guard also comes under control of the DHS. It had test-flown war drones for "maritime border monitoring" as long ago as 2003 and 2004.[18] In fact, OAM partnered with the Coast Guard in the land-based operation of the Predator for a number of years. A cooperative OAM-Coast Guard joint program office managed Guardian drone deployments and fed imagery directly to District 7. Kostelnik indicated in fall 2010 that OAM was training Coast Guard officials to operate the Guardian drones at the Cape Canaveral site.[19]

It was pointed out by T. J. Bonner, president of the union for Border Patrol agents, that the marine drones are limited by visual flight rules. In other words, the weather has to be clear enough for the remote controllers to see where the drone is going. Bad weather, on the other hand, limits a drone's use. The union also deemed the drones as costly and inefficient, preferring agents and equipment on the ground to drones in the air. "Unmanned aircraft serve a very useful role in military combat situations, but are not economical or efficient in civilian law enforcement applications," Bonner said.[20] Another thought to keep in mind.

At a 2010 symposium, Kostelnik provided an update on the progress of the drone surveillance program. The OAM had been operating in the US National Airspace System since 2005 and was then the world's second largest operator of MQ-9 Reapers.[21] The Cape Canaveral Air Force Station was the first operational site, and operations in South Texas had been launched from the Naval Air Station Corpus Christi base. OAM anticipated it would have ten operational drones in service in 2011.[22]

The most significant thing he shared was information about what Kostelnik called "Big Pipe Video Operations." This web-based "real time data distribution system," with "streaming full motion video" in high resolution with metadata, had more than 250 simultaneous users for MQ-9, Guardian, and P-3 feeds. The P-3 Airborne Early Warning Aircraft is the Border Patrol's detection and surveillance plane for long-range patrols along the entire US border, in "source" and "transit zone countries," and throughout Central and South America.[23]

Kostelnik also reported that in spring 2011 OAM planned a deployment of the Guardian drones to an unnamed Central American country in association with Joint Interagency Task Force South and anticipated the Coast Guard would be "fully involved."[24] Indeed it should, since the task force, based at Naval Air Station Key West in Florida, is subordinate to US Southern Command and is commanded by a Coast Guard flag officer. Its operation dates from the 1980s' "war on drugs." It is a "cross-functional, interagency team" that includes four branches of the military, the Coast Guard, three federal law-enforcement and five federal intelligence agencies, and eleven partner nations.[25]

In other words, the lines between civilian law-enforcement and civilian intelligence agencies and the US military were obliterated decades ago. It is just the American public that has been unaware of it. Add to this the reality that DHS is operating its own intelligence fusion centers and becoming increasingly more militarized, and you have a very troubling prospect indeed. In fact, the reality is, DHS has already become the "homeland" branch of the military.

SEE ALL, TELL ALL, KILL ALL?

In a spring 2012 interview for *Inside Homeland Security*, Kostelnik eagerly described the synthetic aperture radar used by OAM as one of the "most powerful technologies in the Predator portfolio," as it "creates high-quality images from radar." While conventional radar images are typically "blips and fuzzy shapes," he said, synthetic aperture radar not only provides "clear, sharp images, [but] also provides the means to capture images of precise locations at different times." This capability, he explained, is used to "perform before-and-after analysis to detect changes in specific areas."[26]

"So, if you have a database, and then you have an event, you go back and take another radar shot from the same geospatial location, then you can compare the before and after with analysis in this radar spectrum, and you can determine if something has changed," Kostelnik said. He claimed FEMA and the US Army Corps of Engineers had both used the technology "during floods in North Dakota, Minnesota, and the Mississippi River Valley, as well as hurricanes in the Gulf of Mexico and the Atlantic coast." It is also frequently used for border security.[27]

Now for something really scary: Kostelnik also boasted that the images are of "such high quality that we can tell when there's been footprints on the ground. So analysts can take these high definition images and, with analysis, provide intelligence that there's a problem with [a border] fence, there's people moving in this area."[28]

Kostelnik also noted that not only can the MQ-9 fly at high altitudes ("typically 19,000 feet") where they cannot be seen or heard from the ground, but also, when on night missions, they are usually flown unlighted.[29] That is a modest assessment. Another report disturbingly brags the MQ-9 is "powerful enough" to identify a tennis shoe at 60,000 feet.[30]

But this, too, is misleading. DHS is not in the business of simply tracking footprints or tennis shoes on the banks of the Rio Grande or near an illegal border crossing—although that information might be useful to determine if people have been where people should not be. It is the drones' surveillance capabilities, such as identifying people legally going about their business, whether carrying weapons or carrying cell phones on their person, that are worrisome.[31]

FACIAL RECOGNITION

A fairly new surveillance module being tested in 2011 by the US Army for the drone tool kit not mentioned by Kostelnik is facial recognition. "It's not enough for the U.S. military to be able to monitor you from afar," *Popular Science* contributor Clay Dillow wrote in September 2011. "The U.S. Army wants its drones to know you through and through . . . and it is imbuing them with the ability to recognize you in a crowd and even to know what you are thinking and feeling. Like a best friend that at any moment might vaporize you with a Hellfire missile."[32]

The Army had at least one contract to "arm drones with facial recognition software that can remember faces so targets can't disappear into crowds," Dillow continued. Accomplishing this feat is not as easy as it may sound. Testing required the subject to be as close to the drone as possible, which then could not be done from 19,000 or 60,000 feet up. It also required as little movement by the subject as possible, optimally standing still, and the subject should also be looking toward the drone, not downward or while wearing head gear.[33] Facial recognition technology will also allow drones to "recognize and track individuals based on attributes such as height, age, gender, and skin color."[34]

Additionally, DHS's standards now require drones "'capable of identifying a standing human being at night as likely armed or not,' meaning carrying a shotgun or rifle," Declan McCullagh reported in February 2013 at the tech site CNET.[35]

Even with the ability to collect and store facial recognition and similar files, there has to be a database for comparison. Enter the FBI. In September 2012, it launched its $1 billion Next Generation Identification program to update its national fingerprint database. In addition to facial recognition files, the FBI will add biometrics such as iris scans, DNA analysis, and voice identification. States have already begun scanning and sending mug shot photos for the pilot project.[36]

Civilian photos were not part of this pilot project, but adding driver's license photos to the database cannot be far away. For example, states such as Ohio and Florida have made millions selling their citizens' info for years, although Florida claims it does not sell photos and Social Security numbers.[37] In July 2010, Ohio admitted it sold information from driver's licenses, vehicle registrations, and vehicle titles, while Social Security numbers were included for "some records sold, but only for verification" purposes.[38] More than likely, this information has already found its way into the numerous private databases we discussed in chapter 7 exposing Obama's surveillance regime.

The FBI would take the information and "run an algorithm to perform an automatic search and return a list of potential hits." The human element then comes into play as law-enforcement agencies—or DHS-run fusion centers—could then use it for identification purposes and possible leads.[39]

Another US Army contract, Dillow reported, is for a "human behavior engine [that] mashes up all kinds of behavioral data into a system that churns out an assessment of adversarial intent, determining if a subject has enough built up resentment" toward the United States to make the subject a "potential threat." After all, he wrote, "what good is tracking if you don't know who your enemies are?" So, he concluded, "pretty soon the drones may know who you are, where you're going, and what you're planning to do when you get there."[40]

DHS also specified "'signals interception' technology that can capture communications in the frequency ranges used by mobile phones, and 'direction finding' technology that can identify the locations of mobile devices or two-way radios."[41] Kostelnik, the agency's godfather, is no longer with OAM. Before leaving, however, he testified that the drones' direction-finding ability is part of a set of Department of Defense capabilities "being tested or adopted" by OAM to "enhance" drone performance for homeland security.[42] In other words, you can run with that GPS tracking device embedded in the cell phone in your pocket, but you cannot hide—anywhere.

The Electronic Privacy Information Center examined documents that "clearly evidence" that DHS is "developing drones with signals interception technology and the capability to identify people on the ground," Ginger McCall, director of EPIC's Open Government Project, stated. "This allows for invasive surveillance, including potential communications surveillance, that could run afoul of federal privacy laws."[43]

A September 2012 report compiled for the Congressional Research Service by legislative attorney Richard M. Thompson II states, "The relative sophistication of drones contrasted with traditional surveillance technology may influence a court's decision whether domestic drone use is lawful under the Fourth Amendment." The report "expresses a view that in most cases, using drones to spy on people in their homes would have to fall within the legal 'plain view' doctrine (which means police can only carry out surveillance of someone's home from a 'lawful vantage point'). However, areas nearby the home—say, in a driveway or at a gate—receive a much more ambiguous protection," Richard Chirgwin noted in the *Register*. According to Chirgwin, the report also points out that the "falling cost of drones could, in itself, exacerbate privacy concerns, noting that: 'access to inexpensive technology may significantly reduce budgetary concerns that once checked the government from widespread surveillance.'"[44]

And then we have that pesky Fifth Amendment. During his March 6, 2013, filibuster, Sen. Rand Paul—concerned that the Obama administration would not commit to never using drones to assassinate US citizens on US soil—asked, "What does the Fifth Amendment say? The Fifth Amendment says that no person shall be held to answer for a capital or otherwise infamous crime unless on presentment or indictment of a grand jury. It is pretty explicit. The Fifth Amendment protects you, it protects you from a king placing you in the tower, but it also should protect you from a president that might kill you with a drone. We were granted due process. It's not always easy to sort out the details of who is a threat."[45]

THERE'S ALWAYS MORE

Let's recap. The MQ-9 Reapers have been used on the southwest border, in the Caribbean, off the Florida coast, near the Bahamas, and over Central America and along the northern tier to track drug traffickers, look for illegal immigrants crossing the border, and reportedly to monitor and help out in natural disasters. But they are also hunting-killing machines—or can be commandeered by the Department of Defense to become so—which Kostelnik boasted was one of the reasons he chose Reapers for the Border Patrol.

Recently, we learned, DHS put out a solicitation on behalf of OAM for fourteen additional MQ-9 Reapers, more than doubling OAM's fleet. It was estimated it would cost $237 million to purchase the drones and the operating systems they require. It was unknown whether OAM would receive sufficient funding, Andrew Becker noted in November 2012 at California Watch. Congress had not appropriated funding for more than the drone OAM had recently received, its tenth, which was set to fly from Cape Canaveral, Florida. OAM had not asked for funding for any more drones in the 2013 fiscal year budget, Becker wrote.[46]

According to a document justifying GA-ASI as a sole-source provider for the MQ-9 Reapers, OAM operates two drone variants. OAM's MQ-9 fleet includes five Predator Bs and five Guardians, as well as five ground control systems (GCS) for ground equipment and maintenance or support services. Four GCSs are on contract for future delivery.[47]

To be perfectly clear, the cost involved is not just for the price of an individual drone; it is part of a larger system.[48] Also, although the solicitation went out around the same time testing finished on communication upgrades to the remotely controlled MQ-9, we do not know if any, all, or none of the new design options will be procured by OAM. For example, the new design includes "dual ARC-210 VHF/UHF radios with wingtip antennas that allows for simultaneous communications between multiple air-to-air and air-to-ground parties, secure data links, and an increase in data transmission capacity."[49]

Other operational upgrades include a "new high-capacity starter generator" to provide an increase in electrical power capacity over the current design. Also, there is a backup generator "sufficient to support all flight critical functions" to improve "the reliability of the electrical power system by providing three independent power sources." GA-ASI also offers "field retrofitable capabilities—lengthened wings, wing-borne fuel pods, and new heavy-weight landing gear—that greatly extend Reaper's already impressive endurance and range while further increasing its operational flexibility."[50] Longer wings, stronger landing gear, and the ability to fly longer and possibly faster would enable OAM to do what? Add more surveillance equipment? Add weapons?

Next question: What makes OAM so certain that it will get this massive funding and build its fleet to twenty-four or more hunter-killer drones? Read on.

CONSTANT SURVEILLANCE, PRIVACY CONCERNS

In the not-too-distant future, state and local law enforcement will be using surveillance drones to monitor US citizens, which, Declan McCullagh asserted in February 2013, "raises privacy concerns" because drones are "far cheaper than manned helicopters or fixed-wing planes and can stay aloft far longer," enabling law enforcement to "monitor Americans in their backyards, cars, or at political gatherings in ways that would not have been possible before."[51]

While a few law-enforcement agencies have used drones in recent times, it is the federal government, namely Congress, we have to thank for this new development. On February 14, 2012, Obama signed the Federal Aviation Administration's Modernization and Reform Act, "accelerating the timetable for unmanned air vehicle use in U.S. skies." The bill "greenlighted both public and private UAVs—or drones—for domestic liftoff by September 2015," *Boston Globe* political correspondent David Uberti wrote.[52]

"Opponents of the FAA bill," Uberti continued, "don't dispute drones' policing capabilities. But they say the same components that allow drones to stalk and strike terrorists in the Middle East and South Asia will be used to scout crime scenes, follow suspects and patrol wide areas. Thermal imaging, for example, makes it easy to look at suspects inside buildings. And high-resolution cameras let operators follow several subjects simultaneously."[53] We will shortly connect the overseas drone assassination war to the domestic monitoring.

Alan Gottlieb, founder and executive vice president of the Second Amendment Foundation, voiced his concerns about the new law: "I am very concerned that this technology will be used against law-abiding American firearms owners. This could violate Fourth Amendment rights as well as Second Amendment rights."[54]

The ACLU also responded with alarm: "'Drones greatly increase the capacity for domestic surveillance' . . . noting that the devices could carry not just high-resolution video cameras, but also infrared cameras, heat sensors and automated license plate scanners, and be programmed to track dozens of targets." Drones not only "present a unique threat to privacy," the ACLU wrote, but also are "designed to undertake constant, persistent surveillance to a degree that former methods of aerial surveillance were unable to achieve."[55]

A possible measure of protection for Americans' Fifth Amendment rights is legislation introduced in February 2013 by Reps. Zoe Lofgren (D-CA) and Ted Poe (R-TX). The Preserving American Privacy Act would "establish due process protections" for Americans against government-operated drones in US airspace because an individual has a reasonable expectation of privacy. In particular, it would require a warrant to use government-operated drones to "collect information that can identify individuals in a private area," and it would require a "court order and . . . public notice beforehand to collect information that can identify individuals in defined public areas" (although warrant and court order requirements would be subject to exceptions for emergencies, border security, and consent). Furthermore, state laws regarding the use of drones would not be preempted by federal law, and, perhaps most important, private and law-enforcement drones could not be used or operated "equipped with firearms or explosives" inside US airspace.[56]

The drones can see all and tell all—but you can't see or hear them—or defend yourself against their intrusion into your privacy. And that is precisely the problem.

DRONE KILL CAMPAIGN TIED TO DOMESTIC SPYING

Most people who learn about President Obama's international drone assassination campaign against al-Qaeda and other terrorists likely assume the distant remote control warfare is unconnected to the domestic drone program. However, we will reveal major concerns on that front while documenting possible constitutional issues related to an international drone campaign deliberately shrouded in mystery by the Obama administration.

While the international drone campaign began on a small scale under President George W. Bush in Yemen in 2002 and then later in Pakistan, the campaign expanded rapidly under Obama, with the drone killing of alleged terrorists becoming so routine it is now streamlined into a formulaic process. Drones have been the Obama administration's tool of choice for taking out terrorists outside of Iraq and Afghanistan—from Yemen to Somalia and beyond, with a new drone base being considered in northwest Africa as of this writing.[57]

Just how are Obama's targets chosen? A series of articles based largely on anonymous comments from administration officials have given a partial picture of how the United States picks targets and carries out drone strikes. Previously, the White House approved proposed targets, with Obama signing off on any sensitive military drone missions himself. However, since last year, the process has evolved to the point where the White House no longer needs to directly approve every drone strike carried out in Pakistan by the CIA.

The *Washington Post* got an inside look at how the process has become streamlined, with the National Counterterrorism Center (NCTC) developing and overseeing something called the "disposition matrix" to determine targets for drone strikes. The *Post*'s Greg Miller describes this matrix as a "single, continually evolving database in which biographies, locations, known associates and affiliated organizations are all cataloged. So are strategies for taking targets down, including extradition requests, capture operations and drone patrols . . . The database is meant to map out contingencies, creating an operational menu that spells out each agency's role in case a suspect surfaces in an unexpected spot."[58]

The NCTC prepares its lists of potential targets, which are reviewed every three months by a panel of intelligence analysts and military officials.

The synthesized list is then passed to a panel at the National Security Council, currently helmed by CIA director John Brennan, and then to Obama for final approval. The general criteria for addition to the list are determined personally by Obama himself. In other words, what is happening is that based on Obama's guidelines, this "matrix" serves as a centralized clearinghouse for determining who will be assassinated. The killing of militants overseas by drones has become so routine that the Obama administration needed to create a whole new system for running the ever-expanding program.

Before we analyze the legality of the drone war, one immediate issue is that the same NCTC overseeing the drone campaign is also involved in mining data on US citizens domestically, including synthesizing data collected at DHS fusion centers. Responding to the reports revealing Obama's "disposition matrix" kill process, Chris Calabrese of the ACLU noted how his legal advocacy group has long warned against what it claims is the NCTC's true role—the "massive, secretive data collection and mining of trillions of points of data about most people in the United States." Calabrese contended the NCTC operates a gigantic data-mining operation in which all sorts of information about American civilians is systematically monitored, stored, and analyzed. This includes "records from law enforcement investigations, health information, employment history, travel and student records. Literally anything the government collects would be fair game."[59]

Calabrese, writing at the ACLU's online blog, further complained that "once information is acquired, the new guidelines authorize broad new search powers. As long NCTC says its search is aimed at identifying terrorism information, it may conduct queries that involve non-terrorism data points and pattern-based searches and analysis (data mining). The breadth and wrongheadedness of these changes are particularly note-worthy. Not only do they mean that anytime you interact with any government agency you essentially enter a lineup as a potential terrorist, they also rely on a technique, data mining, which has been thoroughly discredited as a useful tool for identifying terrorists. As far back as 2008 the National Academy of Sciences found that data mining for terrorism was scientifically 'not feasible' as a methodology, and likely to have significant negative impacts on privacy and civil liberties." The ACLU charged that the information gathered by the NCTC is in many cases shared with "'a federal, state, local, tribal, or foreign or international entity, or to an individual or entity not part of a government' . . . That sharing can happen in relation to national security and safety, drug investigations, if it's evidence of a crime or to evaluate sources or contacts. This boundless sharing is broad enough to encompass disclosures to an employer or landlord about someone who NCTC may think is potentially a criminal, or at the request of local law enforcement for vetting an informant . . . All of this is happening with very little oversight."[60]

VIOLATING CONSTITUTION, INTERNATIONAL LAW?

The Obama administration has somewhat attempted to legally justify its use of drone warfare, including the controversial killing of at least four US citizens. Anwar al-Awlaki, an American-born al-Qaeda operative in Yemen, was killed in a drone strike in 2011 along with his American-born seventeen-year-old son. Also killed by drone was Samir Khan, a North Carolina resident who died in the same strike as the elder al-Awlaki. Under the Bush administration in 2002, Ahmed Hijazi, an American citizen based in Yemen, was killed in a drone strike.

The Justice Department's Office of Legal Counsel has reportedly authored classified memos on the targeted killings, purportedly providing authoritative legal advice to the president and all executive branch agencies on the legality of the drone strikes. The only problem is we don't know how Justice is fully justifying the drone campaign since the White House has refused to turn all of the memos over to Congress or release them publicly. Instead, we are to largely divine the Obama administration's legal arguments from public speeches and proclamations on the subject.

The memos took center stage during the confirmation hearings for CIA director John Brennan, prompting the administration to at least release a number of secret memos to only the Senate Intelligence Committee. Members of the Judiciary Committee have been demanding access to the memos, as well. "Congress has a significant role to play in conducting oversight of national security matters," said Sen. Charles E. Grassley of Iowa, the ranking Republican on the Judiciary Committee. "We have the right to ask for and receive classified information—through appropriate channels and subject to protections—to determine if the activities of the executive branch are appropriate."[61]

To clarify the Obama administration's policy on killing Americans without a trial, Attorney General Eric Holder in March 2013 wrote a letter to Sen. Rand Paul stating, "It has come to my attention that you have now asked an additional question: 'Does the President have the authority to use a weaponized drone to kill an American not engaged in combat on American soil?' The answer to that question is no."[62] One year earlier, Holder sang a different tune when he delivered a speech at Northwestern University in which he alluded to circumstances where the president might order attacks against American citizens without specific knowledge of when or where an attack against the United States might take place. "The Constitution does not require the president to delay action until some theoretical end-stage of planning, when the precise time, place and manner of an attack become clear," he said.[63]

In January 2013, US district court judge Colleen McMahon recognized the constitutional problems inherent in Obama's drone campaign in response to a lawsuit brought by the *New York Times* and the ACLU seeking access to the secret Justice Department memos under the Freedom of Information Act. McMahon, describing herself as being caught in a "veritable Catch-22," said she was unable to order the release of the documents given "the thicket of laws and precedents that effectively allow the executive branch of our government to proclaim as perfectly lawful certain actions that seem on their face incompatible with our Constitution and laws while keeping the reasons for the conclusion a secret." McMahon criticized Obama administration officials for holding discussions of the legality of targeted killings "in cryptic and imprecise ways, generally without citing . . . any statute or court decision that justifies its conclusions."[64]

Following intense political pressure, the Justice Department in February 2013 finally leaked a confidential, sixteen-page memo in which it gave us a clearer picture of its justification for the drone killings of US citizens. The so-called white paper on drone strikes was said to mirror legal arguments made by the Justice Department in other classified memos. The white paper, however, may have exposed the White House to new questions by revealing that an "informed, high-level" official of the US government—not necessarily the president or CIA chief—can determine that the targeted American has been "recently" involved in "activities" posing a threat of a violent attack and "there is no evidence suggesting that he has renounced or abandoned such activities." The memo does not define "recently" or "activities."[65]

The memo concludes that the US government can order the killing of American citizens if they are believed to be "senior operational leaders" of al-Qaeda or "an associated force"—even if there is no intelligence indicating the targets are engaged in an active plot to attack the United States, as NBC News revealed. "The condition that an operational leader present an 'imminent' threat of violent attack against the United States does not require the United States to have clear evidence that a specific attack on U.S. persons and interests will take place in the immediate future," the memo states.[66]

"This is a chilling document," commented the ACLU's deputy legal director, Jameel Jaffer. "Basically, it argues that the government has the right to carry out the extrajudicial killing of an American citizen. . . . It recognizes some limits on the authority it sets out, but the limits are elastic and vaguely defined, and it's easy to see how they could be manipulated." In particular, Jaffer said, the memo "redefines the word imminence in a way that deprives the word of its ordinary meaning."[67]

Other legal issues may revolve around the controversial contention that the United States government has been killing some so-called terrorists whose names they don't even know. ProPublica reported:

While administration officials often have frequently framed drone strikes as going after "high-level al Qaeda leaders who are planning attacks" against the U.S., many strikes go after apparent militants whose identities the U.S. doesn't know. The so-called "signature strikes" began under Bush in early 2008 and were expanded by Obama. Exactly what portion of strikes are signature strikes isn't clear.

At various points the CIA's use of signature strikes in Pakistan in particular have [sic] caused tensions with the White House and State Department. One official told the *New York Times* about a joke that for the CIA, "three guys doing jumping jacks" was a terrorist training camp. In Yemen and Somalia, there is debate about whether the militants targeted by the U.S. are in fact plotting against the U.S. or instead fighting against their own country.[68]

The *New York Times* documented how in Yemen, some strikes apparently launched by the Obama administration killed suspects who were preparing to attack not America but Yemeni military forces.[69] Micah Zenko, a fellow at the Council on Foreign Relations who has been critical of the drone program, charged that the United States is essentially running "a counterinsurgency air force" for allied countries.[70] ProPublica also notes that at times, strikes have relied on local intelligence that later proves faulty.

OBFUSCATION, MYSTERY

We are not exactly sure how many have been killed until now by Obama's drone program. In November 2012, the *New York Times* put the number at some 2,500 people killed in more than three hundred strikes by the CIA and the military since Obama first took office. Sen. Lindsey Graham estimated the death toll of the drone program is 4,700, while Zenko of the Council on Foreign Relations produced a report that estimated the death toll to be closer to 3,500.[71]

The administration's continued obfuscation of its drone program makes it difficult to determine the legality of such drone strikes. The *Wall Street Journal* reported on debates within the Obama administration about the legal justification of the drone war in Pakistan. State Department legal adviser Harold Koh, the former dean of Yale Law School, reportedly concluded that the drone assassination campaign "veers near the edge" of illegality but does not go over the cliff.[72]

Writing at CNN.com, international law specialist Mary Ellen O'Connell argued the question of the legality of drone strikes must be answered in terms of international law. "When the United States kills people in foreign, sovereign states, the world looks to international law for the standard of justification. In war, enemy fighters may be killed under a standard of reasonable necessity; outside war, authorities are far more restricted in their right to resort to lethal force."[73]

O'Connell relates that independent scholars confirm many drone attacks are occurring outside of the war zones of Iraq and Afghanistan, thereby utilizing a set of rules outside those that govern war. She claims targeted killing with drones in Yemen, Somalia, and Pakistan "have generally violated the right to life because the United States is rarely part of any armed conflict in those places. The human right to life that applies is the right that applies in peace."

The human right to life to which O'Connell refers is codified in the International Covenant on Civil and Political Rights to which the United States is a party. It prohibits the "arbitrary" deprivation of life, but does not prohibit absolutely all taking of life. She writes:

> The military may use lethal force against enemy fighters during an armed conflict if the use of force meets the requirements of military necessity, and if it will not have a disproportionate impact on civilian lives and property. Countries may lawfully initiate armed conflict in self-defense if the state is the victim of a significant armed attack, as long as the self-defense is carried out against the state responsible for the armed attack.

Continues O'Connell:

> Targeted killing with drones in Yemen, Somalia, and Pakistan have generally violated the right to life because the United States is rarely part of any armed conflict in those places. The human right to life that applies is the right that applies in peace.
>
> Today, the United States is engaged in armed conflict only in Afghanistan. To lawfully resort to military force elsewhere requires that the country where the United States is attacking has first attacked the United States (such as Afghanistan in 2001), the U.N. Security Council has authorized the resort to force (Libya in 2011) or a government in effective control credibly requests assistance in a civil war (Afghanistan since 2002).

The United Nations itself claims the drone strikes are illegal, at least as far as international law is concerned. The leaked Justice Department white paper memo detailed earlier cites the UN Charter, which allows states to make war in the interest of self-defense. But the UN's terrorism and human rights envoy issued a statement calling the US drone strikes in Pakistan a violation of international law.

"The position of the government of Pakistan is quite clear: It does not consent to the use of drones by the United States on its territory and it considers this to be a violation of Pakistan's sovereignty and territorial integrity," said Ben Emmerson, the UN's special rapporteur on counterterrorism and human rights. "As a matter of international law, the U.S. drone campaign in Pakistan is . . . being conducted without the consent of the elected representatives of the people or the legitimate government of the state," said Emmerson, who is British and has been investigating the impact of US drone attacks in Pakistan's tribal areas on the civilian population.[74]

Slate's Eric Posner also views the drone war through the lens of international law and concludes the killings "probably aren't legal—not that they'll stop." Posner points out the UN Charter permits countries to use military force abroad only with the approval of the UN Security Council, in self-defense, or with the permission of the country in which military force is to be used. "The U.N. Security Council never authorized the drone war in Pakistan," he writes. "Self-defense, traditionally defined to mean the use of force against an 'imminent' armed attack by a nation-state, does not apply either, because no one thinks that Pakistan plans to invade the United States. That leaves consent as the only possible legal theory." Posner writes that while Pakistan, for example, has not given any public consent to the drone war, the Pakistani military clears airspace for drones and doesn't interfere with the assassination campaign. Yet Posner claimed such behavior by Pakistan may be "coerced consent" since the United States acts in a way that may not give Pakistan much choice.[75]

Poster further argues the UN Charter "does not permit states to use military force to unilaterally address long-term threats in this way. It is too easy for states to characterize other states as long-term threats regardless of whether they are."

Washington Post columnist Charles Krauthammer, however, argued the drone war is legal, but he says it needs to be codified. He uses the laws of war to define al-Qaeda as legally existing in a perpetual state of war against the United States. Writes Krauthammer:

> We are in a mutual state of war. Osama bin Laden issued his fatwa declaring war on the United States in 1996; we reciprocated three days after 9/11 with Congress's Authorization for Use of Military Force— against al-Qaeda and those who harbor and abet it. (Such resolutions are the contemporary equivalent of a declaration of war, as evidenced in the 1991 Persian Gulf War and the 2003 Iraq War.)

Regarding al-Qaeda, therefore, imminence is not required. Its members are legitimate targets, day or night, awake or asleep. Nothing new here. In World War II, we bombed German and Japanese barracks without hesitation.[76]

Krauthammer contends Anwar al-Awlaki could lawfully be killed by drone "because he was self-declared al-Qaeda and thus an enemy combatant as defined by congressional resolution and the laws of war." The prominent columnist wrote that once anyone, even a citizen, takes up arms against the United States, "you become an enemy combatant, thereby forfeiting the privileges of citizenship and the protections of the Constitution, including due process. You retain only the protection of the laws of war—no more and no less than those of your foreign comrades-in-arms."[77]

11

OBAMACARE: UNAUTHORIZED EXPANSION OF POWER

President Obama's health care legislation is riddled with constitutional problems.[1]

—Ken Klukowski, Director of the Center for Religious Liberty at the Family Research Council

The Constitution is violated more than sixty-five times by [ObamaCare] . . . What the vast majority of people do not realize is the unbelievable number of sections that invade individual liberty.[2]

—10th Amendment Foundation

THE OBAMA ADMINISTRATION has been attempting to paint the Supreme Court's decision to uphold ObamaCare as final evidence the healthcare legislation is constitutional and legal. However, we will document how President Obama's "signature legislation," the Patient Protection and Affordable Care Act of 2010, is not only unconstitutional but illegally bypasses Congress, infringes on states' rights, and marks an unprecedented and unauthorized expansion of IRS power that constitutes a clear case of "taxation without representation"—one of the primary reasons for the American Revolution in the first place.

At the end of March 2012, after the US Supreme Court had heard three days of vigorous oral arguments on whether the whole of the act would be struck down as unconstitutional or only the individual mandate deemed unlawful,[3] it was obvious Obama's legislative accomplishment was in deep trouble. Some acknowledged that oral arguments in favor of ObamaCare had gone badly, while others generously deemed its fate "uncertain."

We predicted in our most recent book, *Fool Me Twice*, that, should the Supreme Court strike the whole law, or only the mandate, the huge messaging efforts under way to prevent its repeal would immediately shift to pushing for a single-payer health care plan—to be touted as a legitimate tax. Former Clinton advisor Dick Morris suggested March 28, 2012, on Fox News Channel's morning news program, "If ObamaCare fails, Obama will move directly to single-payer health care—which he wants—which will be designated as a tax. He will be forced to move to the left on health care."[4]

Ironically, in its ruling released on June 28, 2012,[5] the Supreme Court ruled in a five to four vote, with conservative chief justice John Roberts siding with the majority, that the requirement that the majority of Americans would have to obtain health insurance or pay a penalty was constitutional, authorized by Congress's power to levy taxes. "The Affordable Care Act's requirement that certain individuals pay a financial penalty for not obtaining health insurance may reasonably be characterized as a tax," Chief Justice Roberts wrote in the majority opinion. "Because the Constitution permits such a tax, it is not our role to forbid it, or to pass upon its wisdom or fairness."[6]

The bottom line is this: the Supreme Court said it was okay for the government to tax people for not having done something, namely buy health insurance.

In a second five to four vote, again with Justice Roberts joining the majority, the court rejected the administration's most vigorous argument in support of the law, that Congress held the power to regulate interstate commerce. The Commerce Clause, the court ruled, did not apply. "Five justices accepted the argument that had been at the heart of the challenges brought by 26 states and other plaintiffs: that the federal government is not permitted to force individuals not engaged in commercial activities to buy services they do not want," the *New York Times* reported.[7]

Also, seven justices on the court "substantially limited the law's expansion of Medicaid, the joint federal-state program that provides health care to poor and disabled people." Congress, they agreed, had "exceeded its constitutional authority by coercing states into participating in the expansion by threatening them with the loss of existing federal payments." The *Times* continued: "The restrictions placed on the Medicaid expansion may also have significant ripple effects. A splintered group of justices effectively revised the law to allow states to choose between participating in the expansion while receiving additional payments or forgoing the expansion and retaining the existing payments. The law had called for an all-or-nothing choice."[8]

Obama's victory speech should have been a warning: "The highest court in the land has now spoken. We will continue to implement this law. And we will continue to improve on it where we can."[9] While the court's rulings had settled all issues for some, the rulings quickly gave birth to several new problems for ObamaCare, which is scheduled to come into full force in 2014.

"What do you do when you wrote, passed, and defended to the death in a Supreme Court steel-cage match a law that doesn't quite work—and you no longer have the votes to make any new changes?" Peter Suderman asked in August 2012 at Reason.com. "You cross your fingers, let the Internal Revenue Service rewrite it through the rulemaking process, and hope that the words 'IRS rulemaking process' cause eyes to glaze over before too many people start to care."[10]

We will next discuss the issues of overstepping the office of the presidency.

ILLEGALLY BYPASSING CONGRESS? BRIBING STATES?

Like the rest of the nation, the Obama administration wants a different health-care law than the one we got. But that doesn't give it the authority to rewrite the law by fiat," Jonathan H. Adler of the Case Western Reserve University School of Law and Michael F. Cannon of the Cato Institute observed in November 2011 in the *Wall Street Journal*.[11]

One of the major glitches in the ObamaCare law had surfaced. While married couples would only get 14 percent of the law's tax credits, more than seven million people would cease paying income taxes altogether. A twenty-two-page staff analysis based on new information provided by the nonpartisan Joint Committee on Taxation had been released in October 2011 by the House Oversight Committee, led by chairman Darrell Issa (R-CA). "While the intent of the [health care reform law] was probably not to penalize marriage and take millions of people off the tax rolls," the report concluded, "it will be the result."[12]

The following month, in response to regulations proposed by the Treasury Department in September, several ObamaCare advocates clamored for the Internal Revenue Service to "allow workers' spouses and dependents to qualify for tax credits if employer-sponsored family plans [proved to be] unaffordable," *The Hill*'s Julian Pecquet reported. The department had proposed granting subsidies to workers and their families in cases when the employer coverage costs too much for the employee only but not when family coverage is "out of reach." The issue, which Pecquet first reported in July, risked "blowing up in Democrats' face in 2014 when the subsidies for coverage in state-based insurance exchanges become available." While the proposed rule would not penalize families that couldn't afford insurance, advocates said it was not enough.[13]

This was an obvious attempt by the Obama administration to illegally bypass Congress and allow the IRS to make up its own rules. Advocates backed the move, repeatedly claiming that the Treasury Department had the authority to change the law. The liberal Center on Budget and Policy Priorities "downplayed the cost of fixing the problem."[14]

Another "glitch" was also revealed in November 2011 by Adler and Cannon. This one is so problematic that it threatens ObamaCare's "basic functioning," they asserted. Behind the scenes, the Obama administration was again "brazenly trying to rewrite the law without involving Congress," they noted.[15]

The "premium assistance"—tax credits and subsidies—promised in the health care act to households purchasing coverage through new health-insurance exchanges was "designed to hide a portion of the law's cost to individuals by reducing the premium hikes that individuals will face after ObamaCare goes into effect in 2014," Adler and Cannon stated. In an aside they added, should (or perhaps when) "consumers face the law's full cost, support for repeal will grow."[16]

Here's the "glitch" they found: "The law encourages states to create health-insurance exchanges, but it permits Washington to create them if states decline . . . ObamaCare authorizes premium assistance in state-run exchanges (Section 1311) but not federal ones (Section 1321). In other words, states that refuse to create an exchange can block much of ObamaCare's spending and practically force Congress to reopen the law for revisions."[17]

This is the good news. The bad news is that the Obama administration was furiously at work in an attempt to avoid a "legislative debacle," Adler and Cannon wrote. The administration proposed an IRS rule to "offer premium assistance in all exchanges 'whether established under section 1311 or 1321.'" The Treasury Department, they continued, was "confident" that the IRS had the authority to offer premium assistance where Congress had not authorized it and that this overreach was "consistent with the intent of the law and [its] ability to interpret and implement it."[18]

"Such confidence is misplaced," Adler and Cannon asserted. "The text of the law is perfectly clear. And without congressional authorization, the IRS lacks the power to dispense tax credits or spend money."[19]

In spite of opposition and reason, in May 2012, the IRS released its final regulations that would "provide guidance to individuals who enroll in qualified health plans through Affordable Insurance Exchanges and claim the premium tax credit, and to Exchanges that make qualified health plans available to individuals and employers." Free-market advocate Phil Kerpen called the regulations an "outrageous edict that attempts to up-end the ability of states to opt out of [Obama's] health care law's new entitlement."[20]

This is a classic example of an Obama bait and switch, as well. Kerpen continued: "When the law was written, its supporters assumed states would be eager to participate and get access to enormous subsidies from federal taxpayers. Instead, more than half the states challenged the constitutionality of the law in court, and at least that many are likely to refuse to set up the so-called exchanges through which the new entitlement subsidies flow."[21]

Kerpen called the Obama administration out for what it was obviously attempting to do, to "bribe states to participate by manipulating language in the law that is meant to authorize start-up grants to instead fund years of operating expenses." A July 2012 announcement from the

Department of Health and Human Services (HHS) offered states six full years of funding. Kerpen commented: "Even that bribe isn't convincing many states that are flatly refusing to implement exchanges—which are subject to onerous regulatory control by HHS."[22]

Kerpen was correct. By mid-February 2013, only seventeen states and the District of Columbia had decided to run their own exchanges, another seven chose to "share the duties with the federal government," and twenty-six states had completely opted out of state-run exchanges—"leaving the Obama administration to handle the details—and the costs—itself," Kirsten Anderson observed at LifeSiteNews.com.[23]

The IRS, Kerpen continued, "likely at the direction of an Obama White House increasingly concerned that the whole law will crumble due to the number of states opting out, is scrambling to bureaucratically rewrite the law and allow subsidies to flow through federal exchanges." Moreover, he wrote, "because employers can be taxed $3,000 per subsidy-eligible employee, the IRS is literally attempting taxation without representation. The new IRS tax will whack companies in states that already opted out and therefore shouldn't lawfully be taxed."[24]

Was this maneuver constitutional? Hardly. Kerpen continued: "It's an affront not just to principles of federalism but to the very first thing our founders put in the Constitution after the famous 'We the People' preamble. Article I, Section 1 states: 'All legislative Powers herein granted shall be vested in a Congress of the United States, which shall consist of a Senate and House of Representatives.'" It goes without saying, Congress does not vest the power to write and rewrite laws in HHS and IRS, nor can unelected bureaucrats impose taxes on states that "legitimately opted out of a federal program," he continued.[25]

An outline of the scope of this "latest example of skullduggery by Obama's apparatchiks," David Catron noted in the *American Spectator*, is found in a legal case study by Adler and Cannon, published in July 2012, *Taxation without Representation*. The IRS, the authors asserted, "is attempting to create two entitlements not authorized by Congress, and in the process, to tax employers whom Congress did not authorize the agency to tax." Initially, Adler and Cannon thought they had uncovered an error, hence calling it a "glitch," but later changed their minds: "[O]ur further research demonstrates this feature of the law was intentional and purposeful, and that the IRS's rule has no basis in law."[26]

On August 1, 2012, Adler and Cannon explained the issue again on the *Health Affairs* blog: "To advance the PPACA's goal of expanding access to health insurance, Section 1311 directs states to establish health insurance 'exchanges' where residents may purchase qualifying insurance plans. Section 1321 authorizes the federal government to create Exchanges where states do not. . . . [Qualifying] health plans offered through the Exchanges will be rather expensive. Thus the Act authorizes tax credits that shift much of the cost of those plans to the federal government. Those tax credits trigger additional 'cost-sharing' subsidies (which further shift costs to taxpayers) as well as penalties against employers under the law's employer mandate." The dispute is whether the health care act authorizes the IRS to provide tax credits only in exchanges established by the states or also in exchanges established by the federal government.[27]

Adler and Cannon concluded that, contrary to the "plain language of the statute," the IRS had gone ahead in May 2012 and finalized "a rule that will issue tax credits—and therefore will trigger cost-sharing subsidies and employer-mandate penalties—through federal Exchanges." They contended that the rule is illegal.[28] The day after the blog article appeared, on August 2, they testified before the House Committee on Oversight and Government Reform and reaffirmed their position that the rule "exceeds the IRS's statutory authority under the PPACA and is illegal."[29]

The IRS's rule, they told the committee, "issues tax credits in health insurance 'exchanges' established by the federal government. It thus triggers a $2,000-per-employee tax on employers and appropriates billions of dollars to private health insurance companies in states with a federal Exchange, also contrary to the clear language of the statute and congressional intent. Since those illegal expenditures will exceed the revenues raised by the illegal tax on employers, this rule also increases the federal deficit by potentially hundreds of billions of dollars, again contrary to the clear language of the statute and congressional intent."[30]

Not only is the rule illegal, but it also lacks any statutory authority and cannot be justified on other legal grounds, they stated. The rule is also a "large net tax increase." They further asserted, "For every $2 of unauthorized tax reduction, it imposes $1 of unauthorized taxes on employers, and commits taxpayers to pay for $8 of unauthorized subsidies to private insurance companies. Because this rule imposes an illegal tax on employers and obligates taxpayers to pay for illegal appropriations, it is quite literally taxation without representation."[31]

Robert Book, a contributor to Forbes.com, discovered an employer loophole in another IRS regulation that "could make it possible for most employers to completely, or in some cases nearly, avoid the employer mandate altogether." Theoretically, he wrote, the "law requires employers to either offer 'qualified' coverage or pay a penalty, with another penalty if the coverage they offer is 'unaffordable.' But as it turns out," he wrote, "the section of the law covering the employer mandate is not so simple."[32]

Book continued: "One of the most curious provisions in the entire health reform law is the one that requires employers to pay a penalty if they hire workers with a family income . . . below a variable threshold—but only if the employer does offer them health coverage." Again, without congressional approval, the IRS had "issued proposed regulations designed to fix this manifestly unfair and unworkable provision by essentially rewriting the statute." Employers will inevitably ask, "How are we supposed to know our employee's family income?" The answer, Book wrote, is, "based on the legislative language . . . basically, 'You aren't supposed to know—the IRS will tell you when they figure out your penalty.'"[33]

Good policy or not, Book concluded, it is "debatable at several levels." But," he added, "what is clear" is that "this debate is supposed to be settled through the democratic process in Congress—not through executive fiat by the IRS."[34]

In an August 22, 2012, meeting of the House Oversight and Government Reform Committee, Chairman Issa reported that a month-old legal analysis of the IRS rule by the American Law Division of the Congressional Research Service (CRS) raised "serious doubt that the IRS 'implemented the law that was written' when it issued its rule or that the law contained language that authorized credits to federal exchange enrollees." CRS also "noted that the original text of the law would create an issue should the law be challenged in court."[35]

There was a growing consensus that the IRS had clearly and deliberately usurped powers granted only to Congress. "First the Supreme Court rewrote President Barack Obama's signature health reform law to save it from the Constitution. Now the Internal Revenue Service claims its new rule can interpret the law in a way that violates its text and history," Ashton Ellis wrote in September 2012 at the Center for Individual Freedom. "By rewriting ObamaCare without statutory authorization, the IRS is engaging in an illegal power grab that will cost taxpayers billions."[36]

According to the CRS, Issa told his committee, "a court reviewing the legality of the rule might not 'limit itself to consideration of only the plain text of the provision,' and might also look at 'legislative history, legislative purpose, and context.'" Based on the opinions of "two noted health care and legal experts," most likely Adler and Cannon, Issa said "neither the structure, history nor other indicia of congressional intent support the IRS position." The IRS rule is, he stated firmly, "thus 'illegal.'"[37]

TAXATION WITHOUT REPRESENTATION: UNCONSTITUTIONAL

ObamaCare is unconstitutional under Article 1, Section 9 of the Constitution: "No capitation, or other direct, Tax shall be laid, unless in Proportion to the Census or Enumeration herein before directed to be taken." This section is clarified in the Sixteenth Amendment: "The Congress shall have power to lay and collect taxes on incomes, from whatever source derived, without apportionment among the several States, and without regard to any census or enumeration."

The Supreme Court ruled that the mandate is a tax. However, this tax does not satisfy any one of the three types of taxes—income, excise, or direct—that are listed as valid in the Constitution. Because the penalty is not assessed on income, it is not a valid income tax. Because the penalty is not assessed uniformly or proportionately and is triggered by economic inactivity, it is not a valid excise tax. Finally, because ObamaCare fails to apportion the tax among the states by population, it is not a valid direct tax.[38]

Days before the Supreme Court issued its decision on June 28, 2012, in reference to the role the IRS would play should the law survive the court's ruling, Jonathan Adler and Michael Cannon wrote, "Under the guise of implementing the law, the Internal Revenue Service has announced it will impose a tax of up to $3,000 per worker on employers whom Congress has not authorized a tax. To make things more interesting: If the IRS doesn't impose that unauthorized tax, the whole law could collapse."[39]

"The Act's 'employer mandate,'" they continued, "taxes employers up to $3,000 per employee if they fail to offer required health benefits. But that tax kicks in only if their employees receive tax credits or subsidies to purchase a health plan through a state-run insurance 'exchange.'"[40]

The final IRS rule created in May 2011, contrary to the "express language" of the ObamaCare statute that restricted tax credits available through state exchanges, also made them available through federal exchanges. "Because those credits trigger penalties against employers," Adler and Cannon wrote, the IRS is "literally taxing employers and spending billions without congressional authorization."[41]

Estimates by the leftist Urban Institute indicated that, Adler and Cannon continued, "had this rule been in effect in 2011, it would have cost at least $14.3 billion for [the Department of Health and Human Services] to run exchanges for 30 states," with approximately 75 percent of that amount in new federal spending.[42]

The IRS "doesn't have a leg to stand on here," they concluded. "It has not cited any express statutory authority for its decision, because there is none. The language limiting tax credits to state-established exchanges is clear and consistent with the rest of the statute." Taxation without representation, they asserted, is "a difficult position to defend. If that approach fails, states that have refused to establish a health insurance exchange, and large employers the IRS will hit with this unauthorized tax, could challenge the rule in court."[43] Adler and Cannon explained their position at great length in a paper published in spring 2013. "Because tax credit eligibility can trigger penalties on employers and individuals, affected parties are likely to have standing to challenge the IRS rule in court," they stated.[44]

Expectedly, immediate objections followed the Supreme Court's ruling. "What was not described as a tax by anyone during the debates over the law—not by Congress, not by the President, not by media—has been retroactively turned into a tax," Trevor Burrus,[45] a research fellow at the Cato Institute's Center for Constitutional Studies, commented. "As a result, the Court has given a dangerous new power to Congress."[46]

In fact, Barack Obama has consistently stated that the individual mandate was not a tax. Speaking in September 2009 with George Stephanopoulos on ABC News, Obama famously denied the mandate was a tax. "Note that Obama does not merely deny that ObamaCare is a tax," John Hayward wrote at HumanEvents.com. During the interview, Obama not only ridiculed the idea but also suggested "that anyone who says it's a tax is engaged in sophistry," Hayward continued. Obama "compares ObamaCare to the concept of purchasing auto insurance, and says 'nobody considers that a tax increase.'" Additionally, Obama accused anyone who disagreed with him "to be 'making up language,'" Hayward said.[47]

Again, speaking in 2009, Obama insisted that forcing citizens to buy health insurance was "absolutely not a tax increase." He had previously assured the public that "raising taxes on the middle class to support his health care plan was 'the last thing we need in an economy like this,'" an *Investor's Business Daily* editorial noted. "Folks are already having a tough enough time," Obama added. And yet, as *IBD* pointed out, Obama's plan "subsidizes some 30 million uninsured, [which] amounts to a $1.8 trillion whammy on working families. And that's just for starters"—plus there are at least twenty "other new taxes that are embedded in the law."[48]

"Congress knows how to use the word *tax*," Burrus continued. "They also know that every time they use that word they face strong political backlash. People don't like to be taxed. We fought a revolution in this country over 'no taxation without representation.' Now, if Congress does not want to represent something as a tax, they certainly won't, thus creating a new type of 'taxation without representation.'"[49]

STATES' RIGHTS VIOLATED

The Tenth Amendment to the Constitution reads: "The powers not delegated to the United States by the Constitution, nor prohibited by it to the States, are reserved to the States respectively, or to the people." The Tenth Amendment Center, which was among the plaintiffs who took ObamaCare to the Supreme Court, clarifies that the amendment was "written to emphasize the limited nature of the powers delegated to the federal government. In delegating just specific powers to the federal government, the states and the people, with some small exceptions, were free to continue exercising their sovereign powers."[50]

As we stated earlier, as of February 2013, only seventeen states and the District of Columbia plan to run their own exchanges, while another seven opted for state-federal exchanges. The twenty-six states that have chosen to opt out entirely challenged the law in the Supreme Court.[51]

In January 2010, Ken Klukowski explained that the Tenth Amendment does not apply here in the way that many people have thought—although it does apply in a more serious manner. Klukowski coauthored with former Ohio secretary of state Kenneth Blackwell the 2010 book *The Blueprint: Obama's Plan to Subvert the Constitution and Build an Imperial Presidency*.

Citing two cases from the 1990s, Klukowski wrote that the Supreme Court "shocked the legal world" by striking them down for violating the Tenth Amendment. The first case was in 1992, *New York v. United States*, "where the Court struck down a federal law requiring states to pass state laws for the disposal of radioactive waste, and to issue regulations for implementing those laws." In the second case, *Printz v. United States* in 1997, the court "struck down a provision of the Brady Act—a federal gun-control law—that required state and local law enforcement to run background checks on handgun purchasers."[52]

From these two cases, Klukowski explained, "emerged the anti-commandeering principle, holding that the Tenth Amendment forbids the federal government from commandeering—or ordering—any branch of state government to do anything. The states are sovereign and answer only to their voters, not to Washington, D.C."[53]

The commandeering principle is the real problem for ObamaCare, which "requires each state to pass laws setting up statewide non-profit insurance exchanges," Klukowski wrote. "It then requires the states to pass regulations for implementing those laws. And it further requires the states to dedicate staff and spend state money to administer those programs." In his opinion, ObamaCare is a "straight-out repeat of those 1992 and 1997 cases. The main difference is that Obamacare violates the anti-commandeering principle in a far more severe and egregious way than those previous laws ever did," Klukowski concluded.[54]

A new challenge for the states emerged in late March 2013 when Obama said he was not going to wait on the states to enforce ObamaCare. "In fact, his administration has said that in states where they refuse to comply with federal healthcare mandates that agents from the Department of Health and Human Services will assume absolute control over the state's health insurance industry," blogger Tim Brown wrote in the *Freedom Outpost*. This was confirmed by *Politico*, which reported that officials in Missouri, Oklahoma, Texas, and Wyoming had received letters from the federal Center for Consumer Information and Insurance Oversight, part of the Centers for Medicare and Medicaid Services (CMS), after those states told the Department of Health and Human Services "they couldn't or wouldn't implement the new rules."[55]

In the letter that Oklahoma insurance commissioner John Doak received, "it was clearly stated that the Oklahoma Insurance Department does not have the authority to enforce federal law." Doak said that "it is unfortunate that health insurers are being forced into a system of dual regulation by the overreaching Obama administration. My position on this has never wavered, and I welcome every opportunity to try to overturn Obamacare," he said. It was also reported that health insurance companies doing business in Oklahoma had also received letters from Cohen "telling them that enforcement of the law's requirements will be handled by the federal agency." As part of its oversight, CMS demanded in the letter that insurance companies "submit all group and individual health insurance policy forms, certificates, riders, endorsements, and amendments, as well as any other requested material pertinent to the market reforms" called for in ObamaCare to CMS for it to review. The letter also declared that "a filing with the Oklahoma Insurance Department does not constitute a filing with CMS for these purposes."[56]

In other words, Tim Brown wrote, the Obama administration couldn't "care less about the boundaries of the Constitution, the Tenth Amendment or anything else regarding the law. They believe they are above the law and will seek to force unlawful laws upon a law abiding people. This is a tyrannical Federal government that is seeking to usurp state constitutions and the will of the people in those states, including nullification legislation that has passed through state legislatures."[57]

DIGGING DOWN TO OBAMACARE'S FINANCIAL ROOTS

Article 1, Section 7 of the Constitution states: "All bills for raising Revenue shall originate in the House of Representatives." The Sacramento,

California–based Pacific Legal Foundation filed a challenge to ObamaCare that contends it is unconstitutional because the bill originated in the Senate, not the House. The foundation claims that under the Origination Clause of the Constitution, "all bills raising revenue must begin in the House." The tip to follow this course of action came from the Supreme Court itself. In his June 28, 2012, ruling, it was noted that Chief Justice Roberts "took pains in the majority opinion to define Obamacare as a federal tax, not a mandate," which is when the "foundation's attorneys had their 'aha' moment."[58]

Using its usual convoluted logic, the Justice Department claimed that the bill did not originate as a spending bill and therefore it does not violate the Origination Clause. The bill, which began life as House Resolution 3590, then called the Service Members Home Ownership Tax Act, was stripped of its contents after it passed in the House (in a process known as "gut and amend"), replaced entirely with the thousands of pages of what eventually became ObamaCare, and given a new name. The Obama government's position is that while using the resolution as a "'shell bill' may be inelegant . . . it's not unconstitutional."[59]

The foundation's response was that "it is undisputed that H.R. 3590 was not originally a bill for raising revenue . . . Unlike in the prior cases [cited by the Justice Department], the Senate's gut-and-amend procedure made H.R. 3590 for the first time into a bill for raising revenue. The precedents the government cites are therefore inapplicable." While the Justice Department contended that raising revenue was incidental to ObamaCare's "central purpose"—to improve the nation's health care system—the foundation's attorney, Timothy Sandefur, disagreed. "What kinds of taxes are not for raising revenue?" he asked.

CREATING COMMERCE

The Commerce Clause, as stated in Article 1, Section 8 of the Constitution, grants Congress "the rights to regulate interstate commerce, not intrastate commerce. Health insurance is not interstate commerce since you cannot buy it across state lines. Secondly, not buying insurance is not commerce."[60] The purpose of Congress's power to regulate commerce among the states was "to end interstate protectionist measures and establish a national free trade pact. The Constitution does not give Congress the power to create commerce in order to regulate it."[61]

"Since the 1930s, Supreme Court decisions have interpreted the commerce clause broadly," Ilya Somin, an associate professor of law at George Mason University School of Law and coeditor of the *Supreme Court Economic Review*, wrote in March 2013. "But every previous case expanding the commerce power involved some sort of 'economic activity,' such as operating a business or consuming a product. Failure to purchase health insurance is neither commerce nor an interstate activity. Indeed, it is the absence of commerce," Somin added.[62]

Georgetown University Law Center professor Randy Barnett, a former student of Harvard Law School professors Charles Fried and Laurence Tribe, "both of whom argued for the constitutionality of the [economic] mandate," has been referred to as "the 'mastermind' of the legal challenge" against ObamaCare. Barnett opined in a March 2011 debate with his former teachers, "Though Congress can compel people to be drafted into the military or sit on a jury, those activities relate to, as the Supreme Court put it, the 'supreme and noble duty' of citizenship . . . There is no supreme and noble duty of citizens to enter into contracts with private companies." Barnett added that "the mandate would result in a 'fundamental alteration in the status of American citizens.'"[63]

Even the Congressional Budget Office weighed in, stating in January 2010, "A mandate requiring all individuals to purchase health insurance would be an unprecedented form of federal action. The government has never required people to buy any good or service as a condition of lawful residence in the United States."[64]

SOCIAL ENGINEERING

ObamaCare affixes a financial penalty on Americans who fail to purchase health insurance in order to regulate behavior. "The Constitution does not grant Congress an independent power to tax for the general welfare and may not use taxation as a means to regulate activity, unless that regulation is authorized by the Constitution."[65]

The most candid assessment of ObamaCare came in October 2012 from Debra Smith of the Western Center for Journalism. "They are missing the main point of it all," she declared. "If someone broke into your home, would you stand there arguing with him as to what is okay for him to take and what is not? Of course you wouldn't," she wrote. "And yet that is what is happening with the health care law. People are arguing about what is in the law instead of the fact that the law is there to begin with and shouldn't be.

"There is no power given to Congress that allows them to take over the privately-owned health insurance industry and turn it into a government-run health care system. The health care law is basically saying that there is no longer any such thing as health insurance," she continued. ObamaCare is "a health 'care' act, not a health 'insurance' act. Hence the reason that no one can be turned down."[66]

"It is not insurance," Smith insisted. "Insurance insures us in case something happens, not after it happens. We don't get house insurance after our kitchen burns down. . . . It is now health care, a government-run entity, in which everyone has to put [money] into the pot. And it is beyond socialism. It is out-and-out communism because of the government's takeover of an industry, the dissolving of it, and the forcing of those who were in that industry to now work for a government-run entity."[67]

"So how can the federal government do this?" Smith asked. "Legally, it cannot. It can only do it illegally. And this is how it is doing it, illegally."[68]

LIMITLESS POWERS

Limitless government grants unto itself limitless powers. The individual mandate, now that it has been designated to be a tax by the Supreme Court, lays the groundwork for limitless legislative and regulatory powers in violation of the Constitution—which enumerates for Congress "few and specific legislative powers."[69] "Conservatives were rightly disturbed with [Chief Justice] Roberts and his decision, given that it massively expanded the government's power to use taxes to accomplish anything it wants," researcher and writer R. Cort Kirkwood understated in September 2012 in the *New American*.[70]

Scott P. Richert commented after the Supreme Court ruling, "Congress has been given the green light to do something that even the most imaginative interpretation of the Commerce Clause would not allow: to

compel the supposedly free citizens of the United States to purchase anything that Congress deems in those citizens' best interest—or to compel
them to purchase one thing rather than another." Richert, who is executive
editor of *Chronicles*, the monthly magazine published by the conservative
think tank the Rockford Institute, continued: "All Congress has to do is
to pass legislation levying a tax on those who, say, fail to purchase smoke
detectors for their homes, or who insist on purchasing a car that runs on
gasoline over one that runs on electricity."[71]

The legal issues swirling around ObamaCare originated in the proverbial back halls of Congress and gained notoriety status on March 9,
2010, when then House Speaker Nancy Pelosi told the 2010 Legislative
Conference for the National Association of Counties that not only was the
passage of the bill going to be "very, very exciting," but also that Congress
had to pass the bill "so you can find out what's in it, away from the fog
of controversy."[72] Missing from media reports about her statement is the
context. Peter Roff, contributing editor of *U.S. News & World Report*,
wrote that Pelosi ended the "windup of her healthcare pitch by alluding
to the controversies over the healthcare bill and the process by which it
[had] reached its current state." It was at that point Pelosi delivered her
now-famous words.[73]

Roff was appropriately wary. The bill had been passed in the Senate
at Christmas 2009 and had been posted on the Internet for "well over 72
hours." Roff explained that the bill had been "discussed and dissected by
healthcare policy experts repeatedly over the last two months." If this was
the case, he pondered, why was Pelosi telling the National Association of
Counties that the bill "had to pass before they—and the rest of us 'can
find out what's in it'"? He bluntly asked, "What is she hiding?"[74]

What *was* Nancy Pelosi hiding? We are still finding out.

RATIONING, DEATH PANELS INSIDE OBAMACARE TEXT?

Already, Aaron Klein went through the entire text of the Patient Protection and Affordable Care Act, finding the foundations for health-care
rationing and even so-called death panels may have been quietly laid in
largely unreported sections of President Obama's health-care legislation.
There is also concern for preferential treatment based on race, ethnicity,

and so-called life preferences.[75]

The text of ObamaCare calls for the establishment of a Patient-Centered Outcomes Research Institute. The new institute's purpose, according to the legislation, is to carry out "comparative clinical effectiveness research," which is defined in the law as evaluating and comparing "health outcomes" and "clinical effectiveness, risks and benefits" of two or more medical treatments or services.

In other words, the purpose of the research is purportedly for the government to determine which treatments work best so that money is not spent on less-effective treatments. Such research was already previously allotted $1.1 billion in Obama's 2009 stimulus package. That legislation first created a Federal Coordinating Council for Comparative Effectiveness Research.[76] ObamaCare now allows for about $3.8 billion in additional funding for effectiveness research, with the establishment of the new Patient-Centered Outcomes Research Institute.

The institute is to be governed by a "board" to assist in identifying research priorities and establishing the research project agenda. Also weighing in will be an "expert advisory panel" of practicing and research clinicians, patients, and experts in scientific and health services research and health services delivery.

A section of ObamaCare makes clear the secretary of health and human services may not use research data from the new institute in a manner that treats the life of an elderly, disabled, or terminally ill individual as lower in value than that of an individual who is younger, non-disabled, or not terminally ill. However, the dictate comes with a qualifier we find concerning.

ObamaCare contains text that allows the health secretary to limit any "alternative treatments" of the elderly, disabled, or terminally ill if such treatments are not recommended by the new research institute.

Reads that qualifier: "Paragraph (1) shall not be construed as preventing the Secretary from using evidence or findings from such comparative clinical effectiveness research in determining coverage, reimbursement, or incentive programs under title XVIII based upon a comparison of the difference in the effectiveness of alternative treatments in extending an individual's life due to the individual's age, disability, or terminal illness."

Paragraph (1) refers to the section that bars the health secretary from valuing the life of an elderly, disabled, or terminally ill patient as lower than that of the younger or nondisabled patient. The qualifier leaves the health secretary with the power to use government-provided research data to determine whether "alternative treatments" are effective in extending the life of the elderly, disabled, or terminally ill.

Another section of ObamaCare calls for the new institute to study the effectiveness of treatment in "subpopulations," including "racial and ethnic minorities, women, age and groups of individuals with different comorbidities, genetic and molecular sub-types, or quality of life preferences."

The effectiveness of such research has been widely called into question. In a 2009 study, the Cato Institute raised concerns about such government-funded research being politicized or influenced by lobbying. "Unlike market-generated research, a federal comparative-effectiveness agency would be subject to political manipulation, which could block the generation of any useful research," wrote Cato.[77]

Continued Cato: "Such research necessarily poses a direct threat to the incomes of pharmaceutical manufacturers, medical device manufacturers and millions of providers. If a government agency produces unwelcome research, those groups will spend vast sums on lobbying campaigns and political contributions to discredit or defund the agency."

During the stimulus debate, Sen. Jon Kyl (R-AZ) fought the $1.1 billion spending on effectiveness research, spotlighting countries like Britain as cautionary tales. "Think about this a moment," Kyl said on the Senate floor. "Do you want Washington bureaucrats, such as those who brought you the AIG mess, making your health care decisions for you and your family?"[78]

Writing in *Forbes*, Sally Pipes, president of the Pacific Research Institute, slammed effectiveness research under ObamaCare as a "recipe for cook-book medicine, where the government can pressure doctors into prescribing treatments according to average results rather than an individual patient's needs and preferences."[79]

Even some close to the Obama administration are admitting ObamaCare will lead to rationing. Writing in the opinion pages of the *New York Times*, Steven Rattner advocated that such rationing should target elderly patients, while stating, "We need death panels."

Rattner was the so-called "car czar," the lead auto adviser, to the Treasury Department under Obama. Rattner serves on the board of the New America Foundation (NAF), a George Soros–funded think tank that was instrumental in supporting ObamaCare in 2010. Soros's son, financier Jonathan Soros, is also a member of the foundation's board.[80]

Rattner penned a September 2012 opinion piece in the *New York Times* titled "Beyond Obamacare" in which he argued rationing must be instructed to sustain Obama's health-care plan. "We need death panels," began Rattner. "Well, maybe not death panels, exactly, but unless we start allocating health-care resources more prudently—rationing, by its proper name—the exploding cost of Medicare will swamp the federal budget."

Continued Rattner: "But in the pantheon of toxic issues—the famous 'third rail' of American politics—none stands taller than overtly acknowledging that elderly Americans are not entitled to every conceivable medical procedure or pharmaceutical." Rattner lamented how Obama's Affordable Care Act "regrettably includes severe restrictions on any reduction in Medicare services or increase in fees to beneficiaries."

Rattner said the numbers don't add up unless ObamaCare utilizes rationing. "If his Independent Payment Advisory Board comes up with savings, Congress must accept either them or vote for an equivalent package," stated Rattner. "The problem is, the advisory board can't propose reducing benefits (aka rationing) or raising fees (another form of rationing), without which the spending target looms impossibly large."

Rattner singled out elderly patients for benefit cuts. He wrote: "No one wants to lose an aging parent. And with price out of the equation, it's natural for patients and their families to try every treatment, regardless of expense or efficacy. But that imposes an enormous societal cost that few other nations have been willing to bear. Many countries whose health care systems are regularly extolled—including Canada, Australia and New Zealand—have systems for rationing care." He continued: "At the least, the Independent Payment Advisory Board should be allowed to offer changes in services and costs."

Rattner concluded that, "We may shrink from such stomach-wrenching choices, but they are inescapable."[81]

Alas, we agree.

12

"ANTI-WAR" PRESIDENT'S UNCONSTITUTIONAL WAR?

"**W**E CAME, WE SAW, HE DIED," Hillary Clinton joked with a TV news reporter moments after she learned that Muammar Gaddafi had been killed in Libya.[1] Clinton was preparing for an interview with CBS News in Kabul, Afghanistan, when her Muslim Brotherhood–linked senior aid, Huma Abedin, handed her a BlackBerry with the first news of Gaddafi's death.

We will not here launch into an analysis of the wisdom of toppling Gaddafi's secular, albeit dictatorial, regime in light of the almost certain rise of political and militant Islam in its place, since that aspect was thoroughly covered in chapter 5. Instead, we must begin with the question of the legality of leading a US-NATO military campaign against Gaddafi's regime without congressional approval, coupled with the constitutionally questionable use in Libya of a globalist military doctrine unknown to most Americans that, according to the doctrine's own founders, seeks to minimize US sovereignty while working to trivialize the concept of state borders.

"At my direction," President Obama told Congress, "U.S. military forces commenced operations" in Libya. Obama argued the use of force in Libya was intended "to prevent a humanitarian catastrophe and address the threat posed to international peace and security by the crisis in Libya."[2] The claim of a so-called humanitarian crisis utilized as the impetus for the NATO campaign was itself quite murky since the facts on the ground were unclear, with both the jihadist-led rebels and Gaddafi's regime accused of atrocities. Despite this, we aided the side of the rebels in their advances.

CONSTITUTIONAL OFFENSE?

An immediate issue is Article I, Section 8 of the United States Constitution, which specifically states that "Congress shall have the power . . . to declare war." Legal scholars have long debated whether the stipulation means Congress must approve every use of military force abroad and whether the president maintains the flexibility to use force as long as hostilities do not become a "war," a word that itself has many definitions. Indeed, previous declarations of war by Congress came at times after hostilities had already begun. Constitution framer James Madison informed that in the Federal Convention of 1787, the phrase "make war" was changed to "declare war" in order to leave to the president the decision to repel sudden attack but not to commence war without the explicit approval of Congress.[3]

John Samples, director of the libertarian Cato Institute's Center for Representative Government, noted how Obama and Vice President Joe Biden both previously interpreted the Constitution in a manner that would have made Obama's use of hostilities in Libya illegal.[4] In a speech on the Senate floor on July 30, 1998, Biden lectured that only one framer of the Constitution, Pierce Butler of South Carolina, thought the president should have the power to initiate war. Biden concluded that under the Constitution, the president could not use force without prior authorization unless it was necessary to "repel a sudden attack."[5] Obviously, the use of force in Libya did not fit Biden's expressed definition. Obama himself agreed with this premise in a 2007 interview with the *Boston Globe*, stating, "The President does not have power under the Constitution to unilaterally authorize a military attack in a situation that does not involve stopping an actual or imminent threat to the nation."[6] Clearly, the conflict in Libya posed no immediate or actual danger to US national security.

Biden expounded on the framers' reasons for limiting presidential ability to launch hostilities: "The rationale for vesting the power to launch war in Congress was simple. The Framers' views were dominated by their experience with the British King, who had unfettered power to start wars. Such powers the Framers were determined to deny the President."[7]

Concluded Cato's Samples: "The framers did not empower the president to initiate war to prevent humanitarian catastrophes, deal with threats to international peace and security, or protect the lives of foreign nationals. The framers stated that the Constitution was instituted to provide for the common defense of We, the People, not the defense of people everywhere."[8]

Jack Goldsmith of *Slate* took the other side, arguing that Obama's use of force in Libya was constitutional, citing other similar conflicts as helping to set a precedent that provides the president with broad military powers. Goldsmith noted how the Korean War was launched by President Harry Truman in 1950 without congressional authorization, as was Bill Clinton's intervention in Kosovo in 1999. "An important principle of constitutional law—especially when the allocation of power between the branches is at issue—is that constitutional meaning gets liquidated by constitutional practice," wrote Goldsmith. "Congress has known about this pattern of presidential unilateralism for some time and done little in response. It has never impeached a president for using force in this way."[9]

Sen. Rand Paul was among those calling the war in Libya unconstitutional. He contended the Libya conflict was prohibited by the War Powers Resolution passed by Congress during the Vietnam War in an attempt to rein in some of the president's military powers. That act specifically states: "The constitutional powers of the President as Commander-in-Chief to introduce United States Armed Forces into hostilities, or into situations where imminent involvement in hostilities is clearly indicated by the circumstances, are exercised only pursuant to: (1) A declaration of war; (2) Specific statutory authorization; or (3) a national emergency created by attack upon the United States, its territories or possessions, or its armed forces."

Paul argued that "not only is Mr. Obama's lack of congressional authority for war unconstitutional," but that "the war also is not in our best interest. Our country is in the midst of an economic crisis, and we do not have the funds to subsidize the rest of the world."[10] Paul noted that during the campaign in Libya, the United States provided 93 percent of the cruise missiles, 66 percent of the personnel, 50 percent of the ships, and 50 percent of the planes. Perhaps he should have also questioned exactly how aiding Islamist rebels in Libya would advance our country's position in Africa.

Michael Lind, cofounder of the New America Foundation, argued at the left-leaning *Salon* magazine that the hostilities in Libya were both "unconstitutional" and "illegitimate." He posited that by taking part in a war "unrelated to American defense on the basis of a U.N. Security Council resolution, without asking the House and the Senate for a joint resolution as the basis of his authority, President Obama has validated the fears of the critics that U.S. participation in the United Nations would informally amend the Constitution, by transferring authority to initiate all kinds of wars from Congress to the president."[11]

Obama's attitude of informing Congress of his decision to use force as part of an international coalition was further illustrated by then secretary of defense Leon Panetta, who argued "international permission" provides a legal basis to initiate hostilities. (Note that in our previous book, *Red Army*, we documented Panetta's longstanding ties to troubling globalist groups as well as to the Marxist-oriented, antimilitary Institute for Policy Studies.)

Under question from Sen. Jeff Sessions (R-AL) at a Senate Armed Services Committee hearing, Panetta was asked whether it would be legal for Obama to repeat his decision in Libya by initiating a similar no-fly-zone in Syria without congressional approval. Panetta stated, "Again, our goal would be to seek international permission and we would come to the Congress and inform you and determine how best to approach this. Whether or not we would want to get permission from the Congress, I think those are issues we would have to discuss as we decide what to do here."

Sessions fired back, "I'm almost breathless about that, because what I heard you say is, 'We're going to seek international approval, and tell Congress what we might do, and we might seek Congressional approval.'"[12]

Panetta went on to suggest the president has the authority to "act in the defense of the nation" without congressional approval. He did not bother to explain how intervening in Syria or Libya would serve to defend the United States.

After the hearing, Sessions told the CNN blog *Security Clearance* in an interview that Panetta's comments were "very revealing of the mindset" of the administration. Panetta "seemed so natural in expressing it as if he didn't understand this went against" the fundamentals of our government. The Pentagon felt the need to clarify Panetta's remarks after the comments stirred controversy. "He was re-emphasizing the need for an international mandate. We are not ceding U.S. decision-making authority to some foreign body," a defense official told CNN.[13] However, we found information that suggests Obama's Libya war utilized a military doctrine that seeks just that—to cede some US authority to a foreign body.

GLOBALIST DOCTRINE USED IN LIBYA

It is critical to take a closer look at that very military doctrine used by Obama in Libya so that perhaps we can better understand some of the motivation for intervening to topple Gaddafi while raising major constitutional issues. The doctrine, crafted by some highly controversial figures, as you will soon read, seeks to minimize the sovereignty of nations. The same doctrine is likely to be used again in the future, perhaps soon in Syria.

"Responsibility to protect," or R2P, was the military doctrine cited repeatedly by Obama as the main justification for US and international airstrikes against Libya. Indeed, the Libya bombings have been widely regarded as a test of R2P.[14] In *Red Army, Fool Me Twice*, and throughout Aaron Klein's reporting, concerns about the origins of the responsibility to protect doctrine have been raised, with connections that go directly to George Soros's Open Society Institute (now Open Society Foundations), as well as to Samantha Power, senior director of multilateral affairs at the National Security Council. Power is also the wife of Obama's controversial former regulatory czar, Cass Sunstein. Last year, Power took on the additional role of chief of the new White House Atrocities Prevention Board, which is tasked with formulating a response to so-called war crimes, crimes against humanity, and mass atrocities.

Responsibility to protect, or responsibility to act, as cited by Obama, is a set of principles, now backed by the United Nations, based on the idea that sovereignty is not a privilege but a responsibility that can be revoked if a country is accused of "war crimes," "genocide," "crimes against humanity," or "ethnic cleansing."[15] The term "war crimes" has, at times, been used indiscriminately by various UN-backed international bodies—including the International Criminal Court (ICC), which has applied it to Israeli antiterror operations in Gaza. There is also concern the ICC could use the term to prosecute US troops.[16]

Soros's Open Society Foundations is one of only three nongovernmental funders of the Global Centre for the Responsibility to Protect, the main body behind promoting the doctrine. Government sponsors include Australia, Belgium, Canada, the Netherlands, Norway, Rwanda, and the United Kingdom.[17]

The R2P center's patrons include former UN secretary-general Kofi Annan, former Irish president Mary Robinson, and South African activist Desmond Tutu.[18] Robinson and Tutu have made solidarity visits to the Hamas-controlled Gaza Strip as members of a group called the Elders, which includes former US president Jimmy Carter.[19] Annan once famously stated: "State sovereignty, in its most basic sense, is being redefined—not least by the forces of globalization and international co-operation. States are . . . instruments at the service of their peoples and not vice versa."[20]

The Carr Center for Human Rights Policy served on the advisory board of a 2001 commission that originally formulated R2P. The center was led at the time by Samantha Power, who is reported to have heavily influenced Obama in consultations leading to the decision to bomb Libya.[21] That 2001 commission, named the International Commission on Intervention and State Sovereignty, invented the term "responsibility to protect" and defined its guidelines.[22]

Also on the advisory board of the commission that founded R2P was Arab League secretary-general Amr Moussa, as well as Palestinian legislator Hanan Ashrawi, a virulent denier of the Holocaust who long served as the deputy of late Palestinian Liberation Organization chairman Yasser Arafat.[23]

Yes, you read that correctly. The deputy to a terrorist whose PLO is a notorious human rights violator helped found a military doctrine claiming to protect human rights. That factoid alone should set off alarm bells about the doctrine's true intent.

Soros himself outlined the fundamentals of responsibility to protect in a 2004 *Foreign Policy* journal article titled "The People's Sovereignty: How a New Twist on an Old Idea Can Protect the World's Most Vulnerable Populations." In the article, Soros wrote:

> True sovereignty belongs to the people, who in turn delegate it to their governments.
>
> [. . .]
>
> If governments abuse the authority entrusted to them and citizens have no opportunity to correct such abuses, outside interference is justified.
>
> [. . .]
>
> By specifying that sovereignty is based on the people, the international community can penetrate nation-states' borders to protect the rights of citizens.
>
> In particular, the principle of the people's sovereignty can help solve two modern challenges: the obstacles to delivering aid effectively to sovereign states, and the obstacles to global collective action dealing with states experiencing internal conflict.[24]

The cofounder of the R2P doctrine is a guy named Ramesh Thakur, an activist who recently advocated for a "global rebalancing" and "international redistribution" to create a "new world order." In a piece in the March 2010 issue of the *Ottawa Citizen*, Thakur wrote, "Toward a new world order, Westerners must change lifestyles and support international redistribution."[25] Here he was referring to a UN-brokered international climate treaty of which he argued, "Developing countries must reorient growth in cleaner and greener directions."

Thakur also discussed recent military engagements and how the financial crisis has impacted the United States. "The West's bullying approach to developing nations won't work anymore—global power is shifting to Asia . . . A much-needed global moral rebalancing is in train," he wrote. "Westerners have lost their previous capacity to set standards and rules of behavior for the world. Unless they recognize this reality, there is little prospect of making significant progress in deadlocked international negotiations."

Further, he contended, "The demonstration of the limits to U.S. and NATO power in Iraq and Afghanistan has left many less fearful of 'superior' western power."

Thakur invented R2P along with another fellow named Gareth Evans, president emeritus of the International Crisis Group, a Soros-funded "crises management" firm where Soros himself sits on the small board. ICG is one of the main proponents of the international responsibility to protect doctrine.

The International Crisis Group is particularly relevant here because along with Soros on the board sits former ambassador Thomas Pickering, who was appointed as the lead investigator into the September 11, 2012, Benghazi attacks. The ICG, as Aaron Klein's reporting thoroughly documented, has long-standing ties to the opposition in Libya, Egypt, Tunisia, Algeria, and other countries that saw their leaders deposed, only to be replaced by Islamists.

R2P founders Evans and Thakur served as cochairmen on the advisory board of the International Commission on Intervention and State Sovereignty, which invented the term "responsibility to protect." In his capacity as cochairman, Evans also played a pivotal role in initiating the fundamental shift from sovereignty as a right to "sovereignty as responsibility." Evans officially presented the responsibility to protect doctrine at the July 23, 2009, United Nations General Assembly, which was convened to consider the principle.

We are not here necessarily arguing that Obama's use of R2P is itself an impeachable offense. However, questions do need to be raised about the president's motivation for the doctrine's promotion in Libya and beyond and what R2P means for the future of state sovereignty as well as for the future of internationalist warfare that may not serve the defense interests of our country. We have in this chapter raised additional challenges regarding the constitutionality of the war in Libya, questions that until now remain unanswered.

***

As this book was going to press, in mid-June of 2013, a series of scandals continued to shake the Obama administration. Each of these scandals displayed the president's contempt for the US Constitution. As Texas senator Ted Cruz put it in a radio interview: the Obama administration "essentially views the Constitution and the Bill of Rights as a pesky obstruction to carrying out their agenda."[26]

From going after journalists and media organizations and seizing their phone records and e-mails, to trying to deny servicemen and -women the right—which they had put their lives in jeopardy to protect—to share their faith; whether it's trying to take away the citizenry's right to bear arms or drafting a drone policy targeting Americans; or whether it's the NSA not respecting privacy rights and conducting unwarranted searches and seizures, or the IRS targeting those whom the Administration perceives to be their political enemies, "it is a very troubling pattern, and it is one [over which] . . . every American, conservative or liberal, should be concerned when the Federal government arrogates to itself so much power that it admits no limits under the Bill of Rights or the Constitution," Cruz said.[27]

In the confusion of this battle, the president's various opponents were divided over many questions. Perhaps at the top of the list was, how vulnerable was Obama personally to the many scandals swirling around him? Some pointed out that Obama is just a figurehead for a far-left progressive movement that extends vastly beyond the White House. Others speculated that the eruption of domestic scandals might, in fact, have been planned by the administration, to deflect attention away from the Benghazi scandal of executive malfeasance and cover-ups. Still others were divided over whether a particular revelation, such as the massive NSA data-mining operation, was even illegal, or improper, at all.

Our purpose in researching and writing this book has been to go much farther into the misconduct and mis-governance of Barack Obama than the scandals of mid-June 2013. Our work clearly shows that President Obama is deeply and fundamentally subverting the United States Constitution and the powers of his office. We understand quite well that the politically interested public may have difficulty grasping, and then accepting, the disturbing "impeachable offenses" that we have revealed in this book. But we are also heartened that so many Americans are following our work and are rising to do battle against an emerging totalitarian state.

An informed and aroused American public still has a chance to undo the progressive nightmare that has gone beyond the legitimate democratic process. And a scandalized Congress still has the ability to challenge Barack Obama's right to misgovern these United States. ■

NOTES

PREFACE

1. Jon Roland, "Meaning of High Crimes and Misdemeanors," Constitution Society, January 16, 1999, http://constitution.org/cmt/high_crimes.htm.
2. "High Crimes and Misdemeanors" Constitutional Rights Foundation website, accessed May 20, 2013, http://www.crf-usa.org/impeachment/high-crimes-and-misdemeanors.html/#. UYkJ0zb6gqI.

CHAPTER 1. THE REAL BENGHAZI SCANDAL

1. David Alexander, "Pentagon Releases Benghazi Timeline, Defends Response," Reuters, November 10, 2012, http://www.reuters.com/article/2012/11/10/us-usa-libya-pentagon-idUSBRE8A903U20121110.
2. Paul Schemm and Maggie Michael, "Libyan Witnesses Recount Organized Benghazi Attack," Associated Press, October 27, 2012, http://bigstory.ap.org/article/libyan-witnesses-recount-organized-benghazi-attack.
3. "U.S. Studying Benghazi Security Cam Videos," UPI, October 9, 2012, http://www.upi.com/Top_News/World-News/2012/10/09/US-studying-Benghazi-security-cam-videos/UPI-11181349764200.
4. Ibid.
5. "Background Briefing on Libya," Office of the Spokesperson, US Department of State, October 9, 2012, http://www.state.gov/r/pa/prs/ps/2012/10/198791.htm.
6. Bradley Klapper, "Timeline of Comments on Attack on US Consulate," Associated Press, October 27, 2012, http://bigstory.ap.org/article/timeline-comments-attack-us-consulate.
7. "Deputy Asst. Secretary of State Charlene Lamb Testimony before House Oversight Committee," October 10, 2012, http://oversight.house.gov/wp-content/uploads/2012/10/2012-10-09-Lamb-Testimony-FINAL1.pdf; and Jamie Dettmer, "The Truth behind the Benghazi Attack," *Daily Beast,* October 22, 2012, http://www.thedailybeast.com/newsweek/2012/10/21/truth-behind-the-benghazi-attack.html.
8. "US Ambassador Killed in Libya Attack: Chris Stevens 'Given CPR for 90 Minutes,' says Benghazi Doctor," *Telegraph* (UK), September 13, 2012, http://www.telegraph.co.uk/news/worldnews/africaandindianocean/libya/libya-video/9540509/US-ambassador-killed-in-Libya-attack-Chris-Stevens-given-CPR-for-90-minutes-says-Benghazi-doctor.html.
9. Jennifer Griffin, "US Military's Response Questioned in Wake of Deadly Libya Consulate Attack," FoxNews.com, October 25, 2012, http://www.foxnews.com/politics/2012/10/24/us-military-response-questioned-in-wake-deadly-libya-attack/.

10. Daniel Halper, "Panetta: Obama Absent Night of Benghazi," *Weekly Standard*, February 7, 2013, http://www.weeklystandard.com/blogs/panetta-obama-absent-night-benghazi_700405.html.
11. Ibid.
12. Jennifer Griffin, "Sources, Emails Point to Communication Breakdown in Obama Administration During Libya Attack," FoxNews.com, November 2, 2012, http://www.foxnews.com/politics/2012/11/02/sources-emails-point-to-communication-breakdown-in-obama-administration-during.
13. Maggie Haberman, "Officials: No Protests Before Benghazi Attack," Politico.com, October 10, 2012, http://www.politico.com/blogs/burns-haberman/2012/10/officials-no-protests-before-benghazi-attack-137978.html.
14. "State Department Spending $70G on Pakistan Ads Denouncing Anti-Islam Film," FoxNews.com, October 20, 2012, http://www.foxnews.com/politics/2012/09/20/state-department-spending-70g-on-pakistan-ads-denouncing-anti-islam-film/#ixzz2PVJSeb68; "President Obama's 2012 address to U.N. General Assembly (Full text)," *Washington Post*, September 25, 2012, http://www.washingtonpost.com/politics/president-obamas-2012-address-to-un-general-assembly-full-text/2012/09/25/70bc1fce-071d-11e2-afff-d6c7f20a83bf_print.html.
15. "US Embassy Officially Opens Consular Section in Tripoli," *Tripoli Post*, August 28, 2012, http://www.tripolipost.com/articledetail.asp?c=1&i=9095.
16. Ibid.
17. US Department of State, Accountability Review Board (ARB) Report, accessed April 9, 2013, http://www.state.gov/documents/organization/202446.pdf, 1.
18. Ibid., 5.
19. Ibid., 30.
20. Ibid., 13, 21.
21. United Nations, Vienna Convention on Diplomatic Relations of 1961, http://untreaty.un.org/ilc/texts/instruments/english/conventions/9_1_1961.pdf, 3.
22. US Department of State, Accountability Review Board (ARB) Report, 30.
23. United Nations, Vienna Convention on Diplomatic Relations, 5.
24. Aaron Klein, "Sources: Slain U.S. Ambassador Recruited Jihadists," *WND*, September 24, 2012, http://www.wnd.com/2012/09/sources-slain-u-s-ambassador-recruited-jihadists.
25. C. J. Chivers and Eric Schmitt, "Arms Airlift to Syria Rebels Expands, with Aid from C.I.A.," *New York Times*, March 24, 2013, http://www.nytimes.com/2013/03/25/world/middleeast/arms-airlift-to-syrian-rebels-expands-with-cia-aid.html?_r=0.
26. Ibid.
27. Ibid.
28. Mariam Karouny, "U.S.-Trained Syrian Rebels Returning to Fight—Senior Rebel Source," Reuters, reprinted by *Yahoo News,* March 14, 2013, http://uk.news.yahoo.com/u-trained-syrian-rebels-returning-fight-senior-rebel-201214528.html#KZ99cpP.
29. Michael R. Gordon and Mark Landler, "Backstage Glimpses of Clinton as Dogged Diplomat, Win or Lose," *New York Times*, February 2, 2013, http://www.nytimes.com/2013/02/03/us/politics/in-behind-scene-blows-and-triumphs-sense-of-clinton-future.html?pagewanted=all.
30. Ibid.
31. Chivers and Schmitt, "Arms Airlift to Syria Rebels Expands."
32. Gordon and Lander, "Backstage Glimpses of Clinton as Dogged Diplomat."
33. Sharyl Attkisson, "Sources: Key Task Force Not Convened During Benghazi Consulate Attack," CBS News, November 2, 2012, http://www.cbsnews.com/8301-250_162-57544026/sources-key-task-force-not-convened-during-benghazi-consulate-attack.
34. Griffin, "Sources, Emails Point to Communication Breakdown in Obama Administration During Libya Attack."
35. Attkisson, "Sources: Key Task Force Not Convened During Benghazi Consulate Attack."
36. Griffin, "Sources, Emails Point to Communication Breakdown in Obama Administration during Libya attack."
37. Attkisson, "Sources: Key Task Force Not Convened During Benghazi Consulate Attack."
38. Ibid.
39. US Department of State, Accountability Review Board (ARB) Report.

40. U.S. House of Representatives, "Interim Progress Report for the Members of the House Republican Conference on the Events surrounding the September 11, 2012 Terrorist Attacks in Benghazi, Libya," April 23, 2013, http://www.speaker.gov/sites/speaker.house.gov/files/documents/libya-progress-report.pdf, 7. Hereinafter called "Interim Progress Report."

41. Ibid., 6.

42. Aaron Klein, "Hillary Perjured Herself on Benghazi?" *WND*, May 8, 2013, http://www.wnd.com/2013/05/hillary-perjured-herself-on-benghazi/.

43. "Al-Qaeda Confirms Death of Bin Laden Confidant Libi," *Daily Star*, September 11, 2012, http://www.dailystar.com.lb/News/Middle-East/2012/Sep-11/187485-al-qaeda-confirms-death-of-bin-laden-confidant-libi.ashx#ixzz2TwH6Uau4.

44. US Department of State, Accountability Review Board (ARB) Report, 6.

45. "Transcript: Whistle-blower's Account of Sept. 11 Libya Terror Attack," FoxNews.com, May 8, 2013, http://www.foxnews.com/politics/2013/05/08/transcript-whistle-blower-account-sept-11-libya-terror-attack/#ixzz2TwKZKcvm.

46. This quote and the conversation that follows in the remainder of this section are from Terence P. Jeffrey, "Testimony: Stevens Went to Benghazi Mission on 9/11/12 So Clinton Could Announce on Upcoming Libyan Visit It Had Become Permanent U.S. Post," cnsnews.com, May 9, 2013, http://www.cnsnews.com/news/article/testimony-stevens-went-benghazi-mission-91112-so-clinton-could-announce-upcoming-libyan.

47. U.S. House of Representatives, "Interim Progress Report," executive summary.

48. Ibid., 8.

49. Ibid., 19.

50. Tabassum Zakaria and Mark Hosenball, "Shifting Account of CIA's Libya Talking Points Fuels Rice Controversy," Reuters, November 28, 2012, http://www.reuters.com/article/2012/11/29/us-usa-benghazi-rice-cia-idUSBRE8AS03F20121129.

51. "Statement from Senators Graham, McCain, and Ayotte," Senator Graham Press Releases, November 27, 2012, http://www.lgraham.senate.gov/public/index.cfm?FuseAction=PressRoom.PressReleases&ContentRecord_id=44354784-f8c9-664b-6178-c23a24d5c1ee&IsPrint=true; emphasis added.

52. Sharyl Attkisson, "Who Changed the Benghazi Talking Points?" CBS News, November 28, 2012, http://www.cbsnews.com/8301-250_162-57555984/who-changed-the-benghazi-talking-points/.

53. "Statement from Senators Graham, McCain, and Ayotte."

54. Zakaria and Hosenball, "Shifting Account of CIA's Libya Talking Points Fuels Rice Controversy."

55. Attkisson, "Who Changed the Benghazi Talking Points?"

56. U.S. House of Representatives, "Interim Progress Report," 3.

57. Ibid.

58. Ibid., 20.

59. The Hicks dialogue in this section is from "Transcript: Whistle-blower's account of Sept. 11 Libya terror attack."

60. US Department of State, Accountability Review Board (ARB) Report, 25.

61. Ibid., 25, 27.

62. James Risen, Mark Mazzetti, and Michael S. Schmidtt, "U.S.-Approved Arms for Libya Rebels Fell into Jihadis' Hands," *New York Times*, December 6, 2012, http://www.nytimes.com/2012/12/06/world/africa/weapons-sent-to-libyan-rebels-with-us-approval-fell-into-islamist-hands.html?pagewanted=all&_r=0.

63. Mark Hosenball, "Exclusive: Obama Authorizes Secret Help for Libya Rebels," Reuters, March 30, 2011, http://www.reuters.com/article/2011/03/30/us-libya-usa-order-idUSTRE72T6H220110330.

64. Robert Fisk, "America's Secret Plan to Arm Libya's Rrebels," *Independent*, March 7, 2011, http://www.independent.co.uk/news/world/middle-east/americas-secret-plan-to-arm-libyas-rebels-2234227.html.

65. Michael Birnbaum, "France Sent Arms to Libyan Rebels," *Washington Post*, June 20, 2011, http://articles.washingtonpost.com/2011-06-29/world/35235276_1_nafusa-mountains-hans-hillen-libyan-rebels.

66. Michael R. Gordon, "U.S. Steps Up Aid to Syrian Opposition, Pledging $60 Million," *New York Times,* February 28, 2013, http://www.nytimes.com/2013/03/01/world/middleeast/us-pledges-60-million-to-syrian-opposition.htm.

67. Praveen Swami, Nick Squires, and Duncan Gardham, "Libyan Rebel Commander Admits His Fighters Have al-Qaeda Links," *Telegraph,* March 25, 2011, http://www.telegraph.co.uk/news/worldnews/africaandindianocean/libya/8407047/Libyan-rebel-commander-admits-his-fighters-have-al-Qaeda-links.html.

68. Department of Defense, Joint Task Force Guantanamo, APO AE 09360 "Secret//NOFORN//20300609: JTF GTMO Detainee Assessment" (memorandum to the commander, United States Southern Command)" July 5, 2005, available from WikiLeaks at http://wikileaks.org/gitmo/pdf/ag/us9ag-000705dp.pdf, 2.

69. Robert Winnett, and Duncan Gardham, "Libya: al-Qaeda Among Libya Rebels, Nato Chief Fears," *Telegraph,* March 29, 2011, http://www.telegraph.co.uk/news/worldnews/africaand-indianocean/libya/8414583/Libya-al-Qaeda-among-Libya-rebels-Nato-chief-fears.html.

70. Yashwant Raj, "Qaeda Men Amongst Libyan Rebels," *Hindustan Times,* March 30, 2011, http://www.hindustantimes.com/world-news/Americas/Al-Qaeda-present-among-Libyan-rebels/Article1-679511.aspx.

71. Risen, Mazzetti, and Schmidt, "U.S.-Approved Arms for Libya Rebels Fell into Jihadis' Hands."

72. Daniel Wagner, "The Dark Side of the Free Syrian Army," *Huffington Post,* December 31, 2012, http://www.huffingtonpost.com/daniel-wagner/dark-side-free-syrian_b_2380399.html.

73. "News Wrap: U.S. House Votes to Renew Tax Cuts, Including for the Most Wealthy," *PBS News Hour,* August 1, 2012, http://www.pbs.org/newshour/bb/politics/july-dec12/othernews_08-01.html.

74. Hadeel Al Shalchi and Erika Solomon, "Syrian Soldier Executed After Graveside 'Trial'," Reuters, August 1, 2012, http://uk.reuters.com/article/2012/08/01/uk-syria-crisis-justice-idUKBRE8700KJ20120801.

75. Associated Press, "Picture emerges of leaderless, divided Syrian rebel forces," *New York Daily News,* June 21, 2012, http://www.nydailynews.com/news/syria-rebels-divided-violent-rebel-commander-ahmed-eissa-al-sheikh-list-dead-article-1.1100077.

76. "Abuse of the Opposition Forces, 'Ethnic Cleansing' of Christians in Homs, Where Jesuits Remains," Agenzia Fides, March 21, 2012, http://www.fides.org/aree/news/newsdet.php?idnews=31228&lan=eng.

77. "Are Islamists Targeting Christians in Homs? Catholic Groups Dispute Cause of Exodus," *Catholic World News,* March 27, 2012, http://www.catholicculture.org/news/headlines/index.cfm?storyid=13804; David Enders, "Rare inside view of Syria's rebels finds a force vowing to fight on," *Miami Herald,* April 23, 2012 http://www.miamiherald.com/2012/04/23/2764247_p2/rare-inside-view-of-syrias-rebels.html.

78. Laura Rozen, "US Authorizes Financial Support for the Free Syrian Army," *Al-Monitor,* July 27, 2012, http://www.al-monitor.com/pulse/originals/2012/al-monitor/us-authorizes-financial-support.html.

79. "How Safe Are Donations to Syrian Rebels?" NPR, August 9, 2012, http://www.npr.org/2012/08/09/158494219/how-safe-are-donations-to-syrian-rebels.

80. FAQ section of Syrian Support Group website, accessed April 9, 2013, http://www.syriansupportgroup.org/faq/.

81. Aaron Klein, "Ex-Obama Official Funding al-Qaida-Tied Rebels," *WND,* December 18, 2012, http://www.wnd.com/2012/12/ex-obama-official-funding-al-qaida-tied-rebels/.

82. Ibid.

83. Aaron Klein, "Just Lovely: Look Who U.S. is Helping Now," *WND,* May 22, 2012, http://www.wnd.com/2012/05/just-lovely-look-who-u-s-is-helping-now.

84. Risen, Mazzetti, Michael S. Schmidt, "U.S.-Approved Arms for Libya Rebels Fell Into Jihadis' Hands."

85. Ibid.

86. Michelle Nichols, "Libya Arms Fueling Conflicts in Syria, Mali and Beyond: U.N. Experts," Reuters, April 9, 2013, http://www.reuters.com/article/2013/04/09/us-libya-arms-un-idUSBRE93814Y20130409.

87. Ibid.
88. Adam Nossiter, "Some Algeria Attackers Are Placed at Benghazi," *New York Times*, January 23, 2013, http://www.nytimes.com/2013/01/23/world/africa/some-algeria-attackers-are-placed-at-benghazi.html?_r=0.

CHAPTER 2. FROM "FAST AND FURIOUS" TO GUN CONTROL

1. Michelle Saul, "Obama: Some Pennsylvanians 'Bitter'," *Daily News*, April 12, 2008, https://www.nydailynews.com/news/politics/obama-pennsylvanians-bitter-article-1.283600.
2. John Longenecker, "Saturday Special: Answering the Brady Campaign against handgun violence," *Examiner*, February 7, 2009, http://www.examiner.com/article/saturday-special-answering-the-brady-campaign-against-handgun-violence. See Longenecker's profile at http://www.examiner.com/gun-rights-in-los-angeles/john-longenecker.
3. Memorandum: Improving Availability of Relevant Executive Branch Records to the National Instant Criminal Background Check System, Office of the White House Press Secretary, January 16, 2013, http://thehill.com/images/stories/news/2013/01_january/16/2013nics.mem.rel.pdf.
4. Ed O'Keefe and Philip Rucker, "Gun-Control Overhaul is Defeated in Senate," *Washington Post*, April 17, 2013, http://www.washingtonpost.com/politics/gun-control-overhaul-is-defeated-in-senate/2013/04/17/57eb028a-a77c-11e2-b029-8fb7e977ef71_story.html.
5. Michael A. Memoli, "Senate Deals Setback to Gun Bill in Vote on Background Checks," *Los Angeles Times*, April 17, 2013, http://www.latimes.com/news/politics/la-pn-senate-deals-setback-gun-bill-20130417,0,4511607.story; Daniel Halper, "Posted: Full Text of 'The Public Safety and Second Amendment Rights Protection Act'," *Weekly Standard*, April 11, 2013, http://www.weeklystandard.com/blogs/posted-full-text-public-safety-and-second-amendment-rights-protection-act_716249.html.
6. David S. Addington, "Loose Language in Reid's Gun Control Bill Allows the Beginnings of a National Gun Registry," *The Foundry* (blog), April 3, 2013, http://blog.heritage.org/2013/04/03/loose-language-in-reids-gun-control-bill-allows-the-beginnings-of-a-national-gun-registry/.
7. Neil Munro, "Obama Loses 2014 Wedge Issue in Senate Gun Vote," *Daily Caller*, April 17, 2013, http://dailycaller.com/2013/04/17/obama-loses-2014-wedge-issue-in-senate-gun-vote/.
8. "Senate Rejects Democratic Plan to Ban Assault Weapons," Associated Press, http://www.washingtonpost.com/politics/federal_government/senate-rejects-democratic-plan-to-ban-assault-weapons/2013/04/17/1a2faf32-a7a8-11e2-9e1c-bb0fb0c2edd9_story.html.
9. Munro, "Obama Loses 2014 Wedge Issue in Senate Gun Vote."
10. Jonathan Cohn and Eric Kinsbury, "The Angriest Obama We've Ever Seen. After the Senate Failed to Expand Gun Background Checks, the President Flashes Anger," *New Republic*, April 17, 2013, http://www.newrepublic.com/article/112949/senate-fails-expand-gun-background-checks-obama-gets-angry#.
11. Josh Kraushaar, "How Obama Misread the Politics of Gun Control. Reality Check: Gun-Control Opponents Hold the Upper Hand Politically in 2014," *National Journal*, April 18, 2013, http://www.nationaljournal.com/columns/against-the-grain/how-obama-misread-the-politics-of-gun-control-20130418.
12. Alan Fram and David Espo, "Gun Control Backers: Senate Defeat Won't Stop Us," Associated Press, April 18, 2013, http://bigstory.ap.org/article/gun-control-backers-senate-defeat-wont-stop-us.
13. Megan R. Wilson, "Holder Begins Gun-Control Push," *The Hill*, January 25, 2016, http://thehill.com/blogs/regwatch/pending-regs/279345-holder-begins-gun-control-push.
14. Ibid.
15. Awr Hawkins, "Eric Holder Goes Around Congress on Gun Control," Breitbart.com, January 28, 2013, http://www.breitbart.com/Big-Government/2013/01/28/Eric-Holder-Goes-Around-Congress-On-Gun-Control.
16. Ibid.

17. Alan Fram, "NRA Uses Justice Memo to Accuse Obama on Guns," Associated Press, February 23, 2013, http://bigstory.ap.org/article/nra-uses-justice-memo-accuse-obama-guns.

18. Ibid.

19. To read more about the bombing, see Josh Levs and Monte Plott, "Boy, 8, one of 3 killed in bombings at Boston Marathon; scores wounded," CNN, April 15, 2013, http://www.cnn.com/2013/04/15/us/boston-marathon-explosions.

20. Evan McMorris-Santoro, "Biden Pledges More Executive Action on Guns 'Later This Week'," BuzzFeed, April 18, 2013, http://www.buzzfeed.com/evanmcsan/biden-pledges-more-executive-action-on-guns-later-this-week.

21. "Boston Marathon Suspect in No Condition Yet to be Questioned, Boston Police Chief Says," FoxNews.com, April 22, 2013, http://www.foxnews.com/us/2013/04/22/second-boston-bombing-suspect-under-heavy-guard/.

22. William A. Jacobson, "Politically Correct Epistemic Closure Counterattacks Boston Marathon Bombing Reality," LegalInsurrection.com, April 21, 2013, http://legalinsurrection.com/2013/04/politically-correct-epistemic-closure-counterattacks-boston-marathon-bombing-reality/.

23. Deborah Kotz, "Injury Toll from Marathon Bombings Rises to 282," *Boston Globe*, April 23, 2013, http://www.bostonglobe.com/metro/massachusetts/2013/04/22/just-bombing-victims-still-critically-ill-but-count-injured-rises/7mUGAu5tJgKsxc634NCAJJ/story.html; Richard Spencer, "Boston Marathon Bombs: al-Qaeda's *Inspire* Magazine Taught Pressure Cooker Bomb-Making Techniques," *Telegraph* (UK), April 16, 2013, http://www.telegraph.co.uk/news/worldnews/al-qaeda/9998886/Boston-Marathon-bombs-al-Qaedas-Inspire-magazine-taught-pressure-cooker-bomb-making-techniques.html.

24. Rebecca Greenfield, "New Boston Bomb Parts and Crime Scene Photos Provide Early Marathon Answers," Atlantic Wire, April 17, 2013, http://news.yahoo.com/boston-bomb-parts-crime-scene-photos-early-marathon-153654786.html.

25. Department of Health and Human Services, "Obama Administration Moves to Remove Barriers to Firearm Background Check Reporting," news release, April 19, 2013, http://www.hhs.gov/news/press/2013pres/04/20130419a.html.

26. "Bureau of Alcohol, Tobacco, Firearms, and Explosives: 27 CFR Part 447 [Docket No. ATF–50F; AG Order No. 3383–2013], RIN 1140–AA46: Importation of Defense Articles and Defense Services—U.S. Munitions: Import List (2011R–20P)," *Federal Register* 78, no. 77 (April 22, 2013): 23675, http://www.gpo.gov/fdsys/pkg/FR-2013-04-22/pdf/2013-09392.pdf.

27. David Codrea, "After Senate Setback, Obama Quietly Moving Forward With Gun Regulation," *Examiner*, April 22, 2013, http://www.examiner.com/article/after-senate-setback-obama-quietly-moving-forward-with-gun-regulation.

28. James Wesley, Rawles, "Here Come the First of the Executive Actions," *SurvivalBlog.com*, April 22, 2013, http://www.survivalblog.com/2013/04/here-come-the-first-of-the-executive-actions.html. Bold and italics are in the original.

29. "What's in Obama's Gun Control Proposal," *New York Times*, January 16, 2013, http://www.nytimes.com/interactive/2013/01/16/us/obama-gun-control-proposal.html.

30. Eric Krol, "Who Supports Ending Assault Weapon Ban With 10-year Ban Expiring in September, Four Out of Seven Local Lawmakers Want Limits to End," *Daily Herald* (Arlington Heights, IL), May 8, 2004, http://www.highbeam.com/doc/1G1-116459295.html.

31. Editorial, "Who Is Barack Obama?" *Washington Times*, August 2, 2004, http://www.highbeam.com/doc/1G1-120049898.html.

32. Associated Press, "Unremorseful Keyes Takes Shots at Obama; Still Swinging After Controversial Week, He Calls Opponent a 'Marxist Socialist'," *Telegraph-Herald* (Dubuque), August 4, 2004, http://www.highbeam.com/doc/1P2-11140304.html.

33. David Bernstein, *The Volokh Conspiracy* (blog), February 18, 2008, http://www.volokh.com/posts/1203389334.shtml.

34. Ibid.

35. Logan Whiteside, "'Smart Guns' Could Be Next Step in Gun Control. Guns would only fire in the right hands," CNN, April 22, 2013, http://www.wmur.com/news/money/-Smart-guns-could-be-next-step-in-gun-control/-/9857662/19856458/-/ea0gnjz/-/index.html.

36. Ibid.

37. Http://Uscodebeta.House.Gov/View.Xhtml?Req=Granuleid:USC-Prelim-Title20-Section5965&Num=0&Edition=Prelim. See also "Bill Summary & Status, 103rd Congress (1993–1994): H.R.1804," http://thomas.loc.gov/cgi-bin/bdquery/z?d103:h.r.01804:. H.R. 1804, or Goals 2000: Educate America Act, sponsored and introduced by Rep. Dale E. Kildee (MI) with 39 cosponsors, became Public Law No: 103-227, March 31, 1994.

38. "Goals 2000—Enacted into law in 1994," Mediafax Technologies, Inc., 1996, http://www.eskimo.com/~bpentium/articles/goal2000.html.

39. Joel B. Pollak, "The Vetting—Holder 1995: We Must 'Brainwash' People on Guns," Breitbart.com, March 18, 2013, http://www.breitbart.com/Big-Government/2012/03/18/Holder-Fight-Guns-Like-Cigarettes.

40. U.S. Department of Justice, "How to Become a Federal Firearms Licensee," http://www.atf.gov/firearms/how-to/become-an-ffl.html.

41. Ross Arends, "The ATF's iTrafficking Program: Linking Firearms Trace Data with State Fusion Centers," *Police Chief* magazine, September 2012, http://www.policechiefmagazine.org/magazine/index.cfm?fuseaction=display&article_id=2759&issue_id=92012.

42. DiscoverTheNetworks.org, Joyce Foundation profile, accessed June 3, 2013, http://www.discoverthenetworks.org/funderprofile.asp?fndid=5310&category=79.

43. "Michael Savage Attacks Cass Sunstein Obama's Gun Grabbing Czar," YouTube video, from a sound clip by Michael Savage aired on September 9, 2009, posted by imitator777, September 9, 2009, https://www.youtube.com/watch?v=kYuWFm5T378.

44. Cass Sunstein, "The Second Amendment: The Constitution's Most Mysterious Right," University of Chicago, video, October 27, 2007, http://www.law.uchicago.edu/node/76.

45. "Cass Sunstein Predicts Repealing Right to Bear Arms," YouTube video, from a lecture at University of Chicago on October 27, 2007, posted by Kaiser Gerhardt, September 11, 2009, http://youtu.be/6F9eY3rGqEQ.

46. Elizabeth Delaney, "Obama's Czars are Unconstitutional," *Examiner*, September 9, 2009, http://www.examiner.com/article/obama-s-czars-are-unconstitutional.

47. Ibid.

48. Karole Dolen-Proffit, "Cass Sunstein: An Even Bigger Threat Than Van Jones?" *Examiner*, September 11, 2009, http://www.examiner.com/article/cass-sunstein-an-even-bigger-threat-than-van-jones.

49. Ellis Washington, "Cass Sunstein: Regulating America to Death," *WND*, September 12, 2009, http://www.wnd.com/2009/09/109594/.

50. Dave Workman, "Cass Sunstein, Like Van Jones, is an Indicator About How Far Left Obama Leans," *Examiner*, September 10, 2009, http://www.examiner.com/article/cass-sunstein-like-van-jones-is-an-indicator-about-how-far-left-obama-leans.

51. Cass R. Sunstein, "Gun Debate Must Avoid Crazy 2nd Amendment Claims," *Bloomberg View*, December 17, 2012, http://www.bloomberg.com/news/2012-12-17/gun-debate-must-avoid-crazy-second-amendment-claims.html.

52. Torrey Meeks, "Drug Cartels' Guns from beyond Border; Trafficking Deep Inside U.S.," *Washington Times*, March 22, 2009, A01.

53. Aaron Klein, "Is This Why White House Funded 'Guns-to-Drug-Lords' Scheme? Misleading Data Target Gun Owners in Scandal That Could Rock Obama," *WND*, July 10, 2011, http://www.wnd.com/2011/07/320809/.

54. "Statement of William Hoover, Assistant Director for Field Operations Bureau of Alcohol, Tobacco, Firearms and Explosives Before the United States House of Representatives Committee on Foreign Affairs Subcommittee on the Western Hemisphere," press release, ATF, February 7, 2008, http://www.atf.gov/press/releases/2008/02/020708-testimony-atf-ad-hoover-sw-border.html.

55. "Counting Mexico's Guns. President Obama Says 90 Percent of Mexico's Recovered Crime Guns Come From the U.S. That's Not What the Statistics Show," FactCheck, April 17, 2009, http://www.factcheck.org/politics/counting_mexicos_guns.html; Office of the Inspector General, Evaluation and Inspections Division, *Review of ATF's Project Gunrunner, US Department of Justice, November 2010*, http://www.justice.gov/oig/reports/ATF/e1101.pdf.

56. Review of ATF's Project Gunrunner; "'Project Gunwalker' Allegations Bolstered by Project Gunrunner Indictments," Americans for Legal Immigration PAC, February 7, 2011, http://www.alipac.us/ftopict-227383.html.

57. Review of ATF's Project Gunrunner; US Department of Justice, ATF, "Project Gunrunner," fact sheet, http://www.atf.gov/publications/factsheets/factsheet-project-gunrunner.html; accessed June 4, 2013; KenInMontana, "Gunrunner vs Fast & Furious: An overview to separate fact from fiction," *The Right Scoop* (blog), July 11, 2011, http://www.therightscoop.com/gunrunner-vs-fast-furious-an-overview-to-separate-fact-from-fiction/.

58. Office of the Inspector General, Evaluation and Inspections Division, "Working Draft Report: Review of ATF's Project Gunrunner," US Department of Justice, September 2010, http://msnbcmedia.msn.com/i/msnbc/sections/news/OIG_report.pdf.

59. Michelle Malkin, "Good News: House Passes $1.6 billion Border Security, Crime-Fighting Package," *Michelle Malkin* (blog), June 10, 2008, http://michellemalkin.com/2008/06/10/good-news-house-passes-16-billion-border-security-crime-fighting-package/.

60. "Reinvestment Act Money Used for Project Gunrunner," FirearmsAnonymous.com, February 1, 2011, http://firearmsanonymous.com/2011/02/01/project-gunrunner-funded-by-stimulus-money/; no longer accessible. See "H.R.1—American Recovery and Reinvestment Act of 2009," OpenCongress, http://www.opencongress.org/bill/111-h1/text?version=enr&nid=t0:enr:232t. Scroll down to page 16 in the PDF version: "For an additional amount for 'State and Local Law Enforcement Assistance', $40,000,000, for competitive grants to provide assistance and equipment to local law enforcement along the Southern border and in High-Intensity Drug Trafficking Areas to combat criminal narcotics activity stemming from the Southern border, of which $10,000,000 shall be transferred to 'Bureau of Alcohol, Tobacco, Firearms and Explosives, Salaries and Expenses' for the ATF Project Gunrunner." See also "Project Gunrunner Funded by 2009 Stimulus: Obama Signed for It," *Sad Hill News*, July 7, 2011, http://sadhillnews.com/2011/07/07/project-gunrunner-funded-by-2009-stimulus-obama-signed-for-it.

61. Michelle Malkin, "Project Gunrunner: Obama's Stimulus-Funded Border Nightmare," *Michelle Malkin* (blog), March 30, 2011, http://michellemalkin.com/2011/03/30/project-gunrunner-obamas-stimulus-funded-border-nightmare/.

62. "ATF Announces 7 New Gunrunner Groups and Phoenix Gun Runner Impact Teams' Successes," press release, ATF, September 17, 2010, http://www.atf.gov/press/releases/2010/09/091710-atf-announces-seven-new-gunrunner-groups.html.

63. Lori Jane Gleha, "Weapons Linked to Controversial ATF Strategy Found in Valley Crimes," abc15.com (Arizona), June 30, 2011, http://www.abc15.com/dpp/news/local_news/investigations/weapons-linked-to-controversial-atf-strategy-found-in-valley-crimes; Office of the Inspector General, Oversight and Review Division, *A Review of ATF's Operation Fast and Furious and Related Matters*, US Department of Justice, September 2012 (redacted); reissued November 2012 (un-redacted), http://www.justice.gov/oig/reports/2012/s1209.pdf.

64. James V. Grimaldi and Sari Horwitz, "ATF Gunrunning Probe Strategy Scrutinized After Death of Border Patrol Agent," *Washington Post*, February 1, 2011, http://www.washingtonpost.com/wp-dyn/content/article/2011/02/01/AR2011020106366.html.

65. Office of the Inspector General, Oversight and Review Division, *Review of ATF's Project Gunrunner, US Department of Justice, November 2010.*

66. KenInMontana, "Gunrunner vs Fast & Furious."

67. Benjamin Kai Miller, "Fueling Violence along the Southwest Border: What More Can Be Done to Protect the Citizens of the United States and Mexico from Firearms Trafficking," *Houston Journal of International Law* 32, no. 1 (2009): 175, 176, 177.

68. ATF: Bureau of Alcohol, Tobacco, Firearms and Explosives. "Fact Sheet: Tracing Center," February 2013, http://www.atf.gov/publications/factsheets/factsheet-national-tracing-center.html.

69. Dan Noyes, "How Criminals Get Guns," PBS *Frontline*, http://www.pbs.org/wgbh/pages/frontline/shows/guns/procon/guns.html; accessed June 4, 2013.

70. Benjamin R. Hayes, "Officer Safety: The Threat of the Armed Gunman: Using Firearms Tracing to Reduce Armed Violence," *Police Chief* magazine, February 2010, http://www.policechiefmagazine.org/magazine/index.cfm?fuseaction=display_arch&article_id=2009&issue_id=22010.

71. Robert Farago, "ATF Death Watch 16: Show Us the Guns!" The Truth About Guns, June 20, 2011, http://www.thetruthaboutguns.com/2011/06/robert-farago/atf-death-watch-16-show-us-the-guns/.

72. "Hearings Scheduled, Subpoenas to Be Issued in 'Project Gunrunner' Investigation," NRA-ILA, June 10, 2011, http://www.nraila.org/Legislation/Federal/Read.aspx?id=6908; KenInMontana, "Gunrunner vs Fast & Furious."

73. Mary Lu Carnavale, "Grassley, Issa Expand 'Fast and Furious' Investigation," *Wall Street Journal*, September 1, 2011, http://blogs.wsj.com/washwire/2011/09/01/grassley-issa-expand-fast-and-furious-investigation/.

74. "Transcript of President Obama's Townhall," Univision, March 2011, http://vidayfamilia. univision.com/es-el-momento/obama-y-la-educacion/article/2011-03-29/transcript-of-president-obamas-townhall.

75. David Codrea, "Melson 'Sick to Stomach' Over Gunwalker," *Examiner*, July 6, 2011, http://www.examiner.com/article/melson-sick-to-stomach-over-gunwalker.

76. Matthew Boyle, "Issa, Grassley Blast Holder in Letter After Secret Meeting With ATF's Ken Melson," *Daily Caller*, July 6, 2011, http://dailycaller.com/2011/07/06/issa-grassley-blast-holder-in-letter-after-secret-meeting-with-atfs-ken-melson/.

77. Susan Crabtree, "ATF Director 'Sick to His Stomach' When He Learned Details of Fast and Furious," *TPMMuckraker* (blog), July 6, 2011, http://tpmmuckraker.talkingpointsmemo.com/2011/07/atf_director_sick_to_his_stomach_when_he_learned_d.php?m=1.

78. Fred Lucas, "Issa Says He Doesn't Believe Holder's Testimony Was Accurate," CNSNews.com, July 7, 2011, http://cnsnews.com/news/article/issa-says-he-doesn-t-believe-holder-s-testimony-was-accurate.

79. Jerry Seper, "Agents Fight Flow of U.S. Arms to Mexico," *Washington Times*, March 5, 2008, A04.

80. Traci Carl, "Mexico: US Must Battle Cross-Border Gun Trade," Associated Press, February 27, 2009, http://www.highbeam.com/doc/1A1-D96K59C00.html.

81. "Mexico: U.S. Must Stop Gun Trade at Border" CBS News, May 8, 2009, http://www.cbsnews.com/2100-202_162-4835694.html.

82. "Eric Holder Bragged about Operation Gunrunner in 2009," *Sad Hill News*, July 9, 2011, http://sadhillnews.com/2011/07/09/eric-holder-bragged-about-operation-gunrunner-in-2009.

83. "Attorney General Eric Holder at the Mexico/United States Arms Trafficking Conference, Cuernavaca, Mexico," U.S. Department of Justice, April 2, 2009, http://www.justice.gov/ag/speeches/2009/ag-speech-090402.html.

84. Jim Hoft, "Eric Holder Knew of Fast and Furious the Day Border Agent Brian Terry Was Murdered," *Gateway Pundit* (blog), January 29, 2012, http://www.thegatewaypundit.com/2012/01/eric-holder-knew-of-fast-and-furious-the-day-border-agent-brian-terry-was-murdered/.

85. Matthew Boyle, "Latest Friday Night Document Dump Shows Holder Was Informed of Brian Terry's Murder on Day Fast & Furious Weapons Killed Border Agent," *Daily Caller*, January 28, 2012, http://dailycaller.com/2012/01/28/latest-friday-night-document-dump-shows-holder-was-informed-of-fast-and-furious-connection-to-brian-terry%E2%80%99s-murder-on-day-border-agent-died/#ixzz1knPf8Vtq.

86. Katie Pavlich, "The Smearing of Fast and Furious Whistleblower John Dodson," *Townhall.com*, October 3, 2012, http://townhall.com/columnists/katiepavlich/2012/10/03/the_smearing_of_fast_and_furious_whistleblower_john_dodson/page/full/; KenInMontana, "Gunrunner vs Fast & Furious."

87. Gil Guignat, "Obama's DOJ Leads Mexican and American Citizens to Slaughter," *Tea Party Tribune*, June 11, 2011, http://www.teapartytribune.com/2011/06/11/obamas-doj-leads-mexican-and-american-citizens-to-slaughter/.

88. Ibid.

89. Ibid.

90. KenInMontana, "Gunrunner vs Fast & Furious."

91. Sharyl Attkisson, "Documents: ATF Used 'Fast and Furious" to Make the Case for Gun Regulations,'" CBS News, December 7, 2011, http://www.cbsnews.com/8301-31727_162-57338546-10391695/documents-atf-used-fast-and-furious-to-make-the-case-for-gun-regulations/?tag=re1.channel.

92. Office of the Inspector General, Evaluation and Inspections Division, *Working Draft Report: Review of ATF's Project Gunrunner.*"

93. Attkisson, "Documents: ATF Used 'Fast and Furious' to Make the Case for Gun Regulations.'"
94. Ibid.
95. Josh Hicks, "Obama's Univision Denial that Fast and Furious Started on His Watch," *Fact Checker* (blog), September 21, 2012, http://www.washingtonpost.com/blogs/fact-checker/post/obamas-univision-denial-that-fast-and-furious-started-on-his-watch/2012/09/21/7726b4ba-041f-11e2-8102-ebee9c66e190_blog.html.
96. Kevin Benson and Jennifer Weber, "Full Spectrum Operations in the Homeland: A 'Vision' of the Future," *Small Wars Journal*, July 15, 2012, http://smallwarsjournal.com/jrnl/art/full-spectrum-operations-in-the-homeland-a-%E2%80%9Cvision%E2%80%9D-of-the-future; James George, "Obama Seeks to Disarm America With Executive Orders," *Examiner*, January 15, 2013, http://www.examiner.com/article/obama-seeks-to-disarm-america-with-executive-orders-knowing-very-well-that-he; "Top Democrats optimistic Congress will pass gun control legislation, with outside Washington help," FoxNews.com, January 20, 2013, http://www.foxnews.com/politics/2013/01/20/top-democrats-optimistic-congress-will-pass-gun-control-legislation-with/.
97. See ATK Defense Group, http://www.atk.com/business-groups/atk-defense/.
98. "ATK Awarded Contract to Supply Ammo to DHS," Homeland Security Newswire, March 14, 2012, http://www.homelandsecuritynewswire.com/dr20120313-atk-awarded-contract-to-supply-ammo-to-dhs.
99. Mike Adams, "What's the Government Buying These Days? Hollow Point Bullets, Hardened Checkpoint Booths and Radiation Pills," NaturalNews, April 18, 2012, http://www.naturalnews.com/035607_government_checkpoints_Martial_Law.html.
100. Ibid.
101. Jason Samenow, "National Weather Service 'Ammunition' Solicitation Triggers Confusion," *Washington Post*, August 14, 2012, http://www.washingtonpost.com/blogs/capital-weather-gang/post/national-weather-service-ammunition-solicitation-triggers-confusion/2012/08/14/3dc6b67e-e62a-11e1-936a-b801f1abab19_blog.html; Ammunition and Shooting Targets Solicitation Number: DG-1330-12-RQ-1028, National Oceanic and Atmospheric Administration (NOAA), National Weather Service, Department of Commerce, FedBizzOpps.gov, August 9, 2012, https://www.fbo.gov/spg/DOC/NOAA/OCSNWS/DG-1330-12-RQ-1028/listing.html. FedBid Details: https://marketplace.fedbid.com/fbweb/fbobuyDetails.do?token-=%3D%3DwBKxmaVGYR92ezk3E3ONEvQAAAAAHeAAgAgTFCGg%2FFzzqQbJAAyVXBA0Or.
102. Request for Quote for Ammunition Solicitation Number: SSA-RFQ-12-1851, Office of Budget, Finance, and Management, Office of Acquisition and Grants, Social Security Administration, FedBizzOpps.gov, August 7, 2012, https://www.fbo.gov/spg/SSA/DCFIAM/OAG/SSA-RFQ-12-1851/listing.html.
103. Millard K. Ives, "Training Excercise [*sic*] Startles Locals," *Daily Commercial* (Leesburg, FL), January 4, 2012, excerpt available at http://www.freerepublic.com/focus/news/2829048/posts; Operation Shield, Department of Homeland Security, http://www.dhs.gov/operation-shield.
104. "Statement for the Record of Leonard E. Patterson, Director, Federal Protective Service, National Protection and Programs Directorate, Department of Homeland Security, before the U.S. House of Representatives Committee on Homeland Security, Subcommittee on Cybersecurity, Infrastructure Protection, and Security Technologies, Washington, D.C., July 13, 2011," http://homeland.house.gov/sites/homeland.house.gov/files/Testimony%20Patterson.pdf, 2–3.
105. Joel Gehrke, "Obama Launches Bureau of Counterterrorism," *Washington Examiner*, January 4, 2012, http://washingtonexaminer.com/article/1042831.
106. "Establishment of the Bureau of Counterterrorism: Special Briefing, Daniel Benjamin, Coordinator, Office of the Coordinator for Counterterrorism, Washington, D.C.," January 4, 2012, http://www.state.gov/j/ct/rls/rm/2012/180148.htm. Also see Anthony H. Cordesman, "The Quadrennial Diplomacy and Development Review (QDDR). Concepts Are Not Enough," Center for Strategic and International Studies, December 10, 2010, http://csis.org/publication/quadrennial-diplomacy-and-development-review-qddr.
107. Gehrke, "Obama launches Bureau of Counterterrorism."

108. Penny Starr, "Social Security Administration Explains Plan to Buy 174,000 Hollow-Point Bullets," CNSNews.com, August 16, 2012, http://cnsnews.com/news/article/social-security-administration-explains-plan-buy-174000-hollow-point-bullets.

109. Commercial Leaded Training Ammunition Solicitation Number: HSFLGL-12-B-00003, Federal Law Enforcement Training Center (FLETC), Department of Homeland Security, FedBizzOpps.gov, August 10, 2012, https://www.fbo.gov/spg/DHS/FLETC/PDDC20229/HSFLGL-12-B-00003/listing.html.

110. See Commercial Leaded Training Ammunition Solicitation Number: HSFLAR-13-Q-00014, Federal Law Enforcement Training Center (FLETC), Department of Homeland Security, FedBizzOpps.gov, February 5, 2013, https://marketplace.fedbid.com/fbweb/fbobuyDetails. do?token===wBKxmaVGYR9Kcq5Ajq%2BRH6QAAAAAHeAAgAgTFCGg/FzzqQb-JAAyVXBA0Or; and Commercial Leaded Training Ammo (CLTA), Solicitation Number: HSFLAR-13-Q-00020, Federal Law Enforcement Training Center (FLETC), Department of Homeland Security, FedBizzOpps.gov, March 21, 2013, https://www.fbo.gov/index?s=op portunity&mode=form&id=22419062d923f87db4df15c676da7943&tab=core&_cview=0. Some news reports erroneously claimed DHS had ordered 21.4 million rounds. The unit of issue on the requisition form is "MX," which means 1,000. See "Abbreviations for Unit of Issue," http://www.blm.gov/pgdata/etc/medialib/blm/mt/blm_programs/fire/bdc.Par.3103. File.dat/abb.pdf.

111. Federal Law Enforcement Training Center (FLETC) website, accessed February 18, 2013, http://www.fletc.gov/.

112. Lee DeCovnick, "Why does Homeland Security need 1.4 billion rounds of ammunition?" *American Thinker* (blog), September 20, 2012, http://www.americanthinker.com/blog/2012/09/why_does_homeland_security_need_14_billion_rounds_of_ammunition. html.

113. Alicia A. Caldwell, "Homeland Security Explains Plan to Purchase More Than 1.6 Billion Bullets: Buying in Bulk Is Cheaper," *Huffington Post*, February 2013, http://www.huffing-tonpost.com/2013/02/14/homeland-security-bullets_n_2688402.html.

114. Robert Farago, "NSSF: The Truth about Uncle Sam's Ammo Purchases," The Truth About Guns, August 29, 2012, http://www.thetruthaboutguns.com/2012/08/robert-farago/nssf-the-truth-about-uncle-sams-ammo-purchases/.

115. Ibid.

116. Tim Brown, "Congressmen Demand DHS Explain 1.6 Billion Bullets Purchase," *Freedom Outpost* (blog), March 19, 2013, http://freedomoutpost.com/2013/03/congressmen-demand-dhs-explain-1-6-billion-bullets-purchase/.

117. Tim Brown, "Running the Numbers On DHS' Ammo Purchases," *Freedom Outpost*, March 26, 2013, http://freedomoutpost.com/2013/03/running-the-numbers-on-dhs-ammo-purchases/.

118. Ibid.

119. Ibid.

120. *Part I – The Schedule: Section C – Description/Specifications/Statement of Work* (solicitation by Department of Homeland Security, HSCEMS-12-R-00011), http://www.naturalnews.com/files/DHS_Assault_Weapons_bid.pdf.

121. Ryan Keller, "Department of Homeland Security buying 7,000 full auto assault rifles," *Examiner*, January 30, 2013, http://www.examiner.com/article/department-of-homeland-security-buying-7-000-full-auto-assault-rifles.

122. "Sig Sauer OEM Firearms: Solicitation Number: HSCEMS-13-R-00006, Agency: Department of Homeland Security" FedBizzOps.gov, March 7, 2013, https://www.fbo.gov/index?s= opportunity&mode=form&id=c4d7370ac7b6def52479268b5b1c4b65&tab=core&_cview=0; "Heckler & Koch (HK) Weapons Parts: Solicitation Number: HSCEMS-13-R-00005, Agency: Department of Homeland Security" FedBizzOps.gov, March 4, 2013, https://www. fbo.gov/index?s=opportunity&mode=form&id=401b0bf2b6e3921f6a8edaa13356fac5&tab =core&_cview=0.

123. "10--HK UMP40 Submachine gun: Solicitation Number: 20069404: Agency: Department of Homeland Security," FedBizzOps.gov, April 16, 2012, https://www.fbo.gov/?s=opportu nity&mode=form&tab=core&id=91131e392057c6f10ed1c812f702f391&_cview=0.

124. Ken Jorgustin, "Latest Homeland Security Armored Vehicle," *Modern Survival* blog, September 6, 2012, http://modernsurvivalblog.com/government-gone-wild/latest-homeland-security-vehicle-street-sweeper/.

125. Ibid.

126. Rick Moran, "What does DHS need with 2,700 armored vehicles?" *American Thinker*, March 4, 2013, http://www.americanthinker.com/blog/2013/03/what_does_dhs_need_with_2700_armored_vehicles.html.

127. "2008–13 United States ammunition shortage," *Wikipedia*, last modified May 11, 2013, accessed June 8, 2013, https://en.wikipedia.org/wiki/2008%E2%80%9313_United_States_ammunition_shortage.

128. Ben Neary, "Fear of regulation drives gun, ammo shortage," *USA Today*, March 29, 2009, http://usatoday30.usatoday.com/news/nation/2009-03-29-ammo-shortage_N.htm.

129. "News and Press Releases: Ammunition in High Demand," Winchester Ammunition, April 7, 2009, http://www.webcitation.org/5j0uGvCus.

130. Ben Jones, "Gun sales up during Obama's term," *Northwestern*, November 22, 2009, http://www.webcitation.org/5lU3TfTIB.

131. Frank Brunell, "Another Ammunition Shortage?" Ammoland.com, July 3, 2012, http://www.ammoland.com/2012/07/another-ammunition-shortage-frank-talk-about-guns/#axzz2SbyBGcjR.

132. S.843 "A bill to limit the amount of ammunition purchased or possessed by certain Federal agencies for a 6-month period" introduced April 25, 2013, by Sen. James M. Inhofe, http://thomas.loc.gov/cgi-bin/bdquery/D?d113:9:./temp/~bdQDMX::|/bss/|.

133. "Inhofe, Lucas Introduce Bill Limiting Federal Agencies from Stockpiling Ammunition," Office of Sen. James M. Inhofe, press release, April 26, 2013, http://www.inhofe.senate.gov/newsroom/press-releases/inhofe-lucas-introduce-bill-limiting-federal-agencies-from-stockpiling-ammunition. All Inhofe and Lucas quotes in this section are from this press release.

134. Ibid.

135. "Oversight of the Federal Government's Procurement of Ammunition," House Oversight and Government Reform Committee, April 25, 2013, http://oversight.house.gov/hearing/oversight-of-the-federal-governments-procurement-of-ammunition/.

136. Stephanie Condon, "Ammo conspiracy theory inspires new bill," CBS News, May 1, 2013, http://www.cbsnews.com/8301-250_162-57582316/ammo-conspiracy-theory-inspires-new-bill/.

137. Ibid.

138. U.S. Department of Homeland Security Testimony of Nick Nayak, Chief Procurement Officer and Humberto Medina, Assistant Director, Immigrations and Customs Enforcement National Firearms and Tactical Training Unit before the House Committee on Oversight and Government Reform Subcommittee on National Security, Homeland Defense and Foreign Operations and Subcommittee on Economic Growth, Job Creation, and Regulatory Affairs, April 25, 2013, http://oversight.house.gov/wp-content/uploads/2013/04/Nayak-Medina-DHS-Testimony-4-25-Ammunition-COMPLETE.pdf.

139. Drew Zahn, "Inhofe: DHS ammo grab to 'dry up' supply. Claims Obama administration intentionally undermining 2nd Amendment," *WND*, April 6, 2013, http://www.wnd.com/2013/05/inhofe-dhs-ammo-grab-to-dry-up-supply/.

140. Ibid.

141. Ibid.

CHAPTER 3. FORGET CONGRESS! BACKDOOR AMNESTY ALREADY HERE

1. Mark Krikorian, "Obama 'law' helps illegals," *Boston Herald*, August 16, 2012, http://bostonherald.com/news_opinion/opinion/op_ed/2012/08/obama_%E2%80%98law%E2%80%99_helps_illegals.

2. Paul Colford, "'Illegal immigrant' no more," *The Definitive Source* (blog), April 2, 2013, http://blog.ap.org/2013/04/02/illegal-immigrant-no-more/; Noel Sheppard, "Leno: AP Replaces 'Illegal Immigrant' with 'Undocumented Democrat,'" *NewsBusters* (blog), April 3, 2013, http://newsbusters.org/blogs/noel-sheppard/2013/04/03/leno-ap-replaces-illegal-immigrant-undocumented-democrat.

3. Michael Filozof, "If We Took the Constitution Seriously, Obama Would Be Impeached," *American Thinker*, June 16, 2012, http://www.americanthinker.com/blog/2012/06/if_we_took_the_constitution_seriously_obama_would_be_impeached.html.

4. Ibid.

5. Daniel Horowitz, "Congressman Schweikert Takes a Stand Against Obama's Illegal Amnesty," *RedState* (blog), June 19, 2012, http://www.redstate.com/dhorowitz3/2012/06/19/congressman-schweikert-takes-a-stand-against-obama%E2%80%99s-illegal-amnesty/.

6. John C. Eastman, "Obama's Assault on the Constitution" (transcript of panel discussion on February 22–24, 2013), *FrontPage Magazine*, March 14, 2013, http://frontpagemag.com/2013/frontpagemag-com/obamas-assault-on-the-constitution/.

7. Jim Geraghty, "A Long Post: The Complete List of Obama Statement Expiration Dates," *National Review Online*, March 29, 2010, http://www.nationalreview.com/campaign-spot/4701/long-post-complete-list-obama-statement-expiration-dates.

8. "Barack Obama in 2007 Democratic debate at St. Anselm College, sponsored by CNN & WMUR," *On the Issues*, June 3, 2007, http://www.ontheissues.org/Archive/2007_Dem_St_Anselm_Barack_Obama.htm.

9. "Barack Obama in 2007 AFL-CIO Democratic primary forum," *On the Issues*, August 8, 2007, http://www.ontheissues.org/Archive/2007_AFL-CIO_Dems_Barack_Obama.htm.

10. "Transcript: NPR Democratic Candidates' Debate in Iowa," National Public Radio, December 4, 2007, http://www.npr.org/templates/story/story.php?storyId=16898435; Alex Newman, "Obama's Plan for Immigration 'Reform'," *New American*, December 1, 2008, http://www.thenewamerican .com/index.php/usnews/politics/560.

11. "Latinos Pin Hopes of Immigration Reform on Obama. After Helping Barack Obama Win the Election, Latinos Seek to Remind Him to Enact Comprehensive Immigration Reform," McClatchy Newspapers, November 24, 2008; "Patricia Madrid Named to Obama's National Latino Advisory Council," *RootsWire*, August 22, 2008, http://rootswire.org/conventionblog/patricia-madrid-named-obamas-national-latino-advisory-council.

12. See Illinois State Board of Elections online records "Non-Individual Contributions" for Friends of Obama.

13. Soren Dayton, "Is Obama connected to the ACORN-Rathke embezzlement scandal?" *The Next Right* (blog), October 30, 2008, http://www.thenextright.com/category/blog-tags/seiu-880. See Aaron Klein and Brenda J. Elliott's *The Manchurian President* (WND Books, 2010) and *Red Army* (Broadside eBooks, 2011) for details on the ACORN-SEIU-Obama relationship.

14. Peter Nicholas, "Obama's curiously close labor friendship: SEIU chief Andy Stern enjoys unusual access to the White House, but some in the fractious labor movement question its value," *Los Angeles Times*, June 28, 2009.

15. Foon Rhee, "Obama gets big union nod," *Boston Globe*, February 15, 2008.

16. "Eliseo Medina Speaks on Immigrants for Votes [June 2, 2009]," YouTube video from the America's Future Now! Conference on June 2, 2009, posted by keywiki, January 25, 2010, https://www.youtube.com/watch?v=AK7K0itgQt0.

17. "Patricia Madrid Named to Obama's National Latino Advisory Council."

18. "Immigration Policy: Transition Blueprint," Obama-Biden Transition Project, November 16, 2008, http://otrans.3cdn.net/1414e4fb31bb801ef0_wwm6i6uks.pdf.

19. Julia Preston, "Obama to Push Immigration Bill as One Priority," *New York Times*, April 9, 2009.

20. Randy Shaw, "New Immigrant Rights Campaign to Mount Largest March of Obama Era," *Huffington Post*, March 14, 2010; Yani Kunichoff, "Tens of Thousands March on Washington, DC, for Immigration Reform," Truthout, March 23, 2010, http://archive.truthout.org/tens-thousands-march-washington-dc-immigration-reform57911.

21. Jennifer McFadyen, "March for America: Change Takes Courage," DeCosmo LLP, March 21, 2010.
22. Shaw, "New Immigrant Rights Campaign to Mount Largest March of Obama Era"; Kunichoff, "Tens of Thousands March on Washington, DC, for Immigration Reform."
23. Julia Preston, "At Rally, Call for Urgency on Immigration Reform," *New York Times*, March 21, 2010.
24. "The Truth-O-Meter Says 'True': 'As a senator, Barack Obama supported "an amendment that basically gutted the legal temporary worker program,"' PolitiFact.com, July 4, 2010, http://www.politifact.com/truth-o-meter/statements/2010/jul/07/john-mccain/john-mccain-said-barack-obama-voted-against-part-i/.
25. Noel Sheppard, "Obama Helped Kill Immigration Reform In 2007—Will Media Remember?" *NewsBusters.com*, April 29, 2010.
26. Ibid.
27. Michael D. Shear, "Republican immigration position likely to alienate Latinos, Democrats say," *Washington Post*, July 20, 2010.
28. Jennifer Rubin, "Obama Tips His Hand: No Reform, Just an Issue," *Commentary*, July 20, 2010, http://www.commentarymagazine.com/blogs/index.php/rubin/330756.
29. Shear, "Republican immigration position likely to alienate Latinos, Democrats say."
30. A Brief History of Illegal Immigration in the United States," EndIllegalImmigration.com, http://www.endillegalimmigration .com/History_of_Illegal_Immigration_in_US /index .shtml.
31. Rachel L. Swarns, "Failed Amnesty Legislation of 1986 Haunts the Current Immigration Bills in Congress," *New York Times*, May 23, 2006.
32. "A Brief History of Illegal Immigration in the United States."
33. "New INS Report: 1986 Amnesty Increased Illegal Immigration," Center for Immigration Studies, October 12, 2000, http://www.cis.org/articles/2000/ins1986amnesty.html.
34. Ibid.
35. "A Brief History of Illegal Immigration in the United States."
36. Ibid.
37. "New INS Report: 1986 Amnesty Increased Illegal Immigration."
38. H.R.432 Comprehensive Immigration Reform for America's Security and Prosperity Act of 2009, introduced December 14, 2009, by Rep. Solomon Ortiz (D-TX), http://www. opencongress.org/bill/111-h4321/show.
39. Lynn Sweet, "Luis Gutierrez a yes on Obama health care bill," *Chicago Sun-Times*, March 18, 2010; Joshua Hoyt, "Obama risks alienating Latinos with lack of immigration reform," *Washington Post*, March 5, 2010.
40. "*This* is how Obama will grant amnesty to millions of illegals," *WND*, October 25, 2012, http://www.wnd.com/2012/10/this-is-how-obama-will-grant-amnesty-to-millions-of-illegals/.
41. Ibid.
42. Aaron Klein and Brenda Elliott, *Fool Me Twice* (Washington, DC: WND Books, 2012), 45.
43. William Bigelow, "Senate, House Battle Over Immigration Bills," breitbart.com, May 18, 2013, http://www.breitbart.com/Big-Government/2013/05/17/Senate-House-Battle-Over-Immigration-Bills.
44. Matthew Boyle, "Blockbuster Immigration Report Could Derail Gang of Eight," Breitbart. com, April 9, 2013, http://www.breitbart.com/Big-Government/2013/04/09/DeMint-Senate-Gang-of-8-secret-immigration-negotiations-really-disturbing.
45. Wade Rathke, "How Critical is 'Future Flow' to Labor Unions?" *Chief Organizer* (blog), April 1, 2013, http://chieforganizer.org/2013/04/01/how-critical-is-%E2%80%9Cfuture-flow%E2%80%9D-to-labor-unions/.
46. Ibid.
47. Richard Weiner, "Immigration's Gang of 8: Who are they?" *Washington Post*, January 28, 2013, http://www.washingtonpost.com/blogs/the-fix/wp/2013/01/28/immigrations-gang-of-8-who-are-they/.
48. "Business, Labor Get Immigration Deal on Guest Worker Program," Newsmax.com, March 30, 2013, http://www.newsmax.com/Newswidget/Business-Labor-Deal-Immigration/2013/03/30/id/497042.

49. Erica Werner, "Source in Washington, D.C.: Business, labor resolve dispute over worker program that threatened immigration bill," *Peninsula Daily News*, mod. March 30, 2013, http://www.peninsuladailynews.com/article/20130330/NEWS/130339998/source-in-washington-dc-business-labor-resolve-dispute-over.

50. Rathke, "How Critical is 'Future Flow' to Labor Unions?"

51. "Future Flow: Repairing Our Broken Immigration System," Immigration Policy Center, http://www.immigrationpolicy.org/just-facts/future-flow-repairing-our-broken-immigration-system; accessed June 4, 2013.

52. Robert Gittelson, "Immigration reform: Future flow must meet economic need," *The Hill*, March 26, 2013, http://thehill.com/blogs/congress-blog/economy-a-budget/290199-immigration-reform-future-flow-must-meet-economic-need.

53. Humberto Sanchez and Eliza Newlin Carney, "ICE Union Skewers Bill from Immigration 'Gang'," *Roll Call*, April 3, 2013, http://www.rollcall.com/news/ice_union_skewers_immigration_gang_bill-223584-1.html.

54. Gerald F. Seib, "Study Finds High Economic Cost of Immigration System," *Washington Wire*, April 4, 2013, http://blogs.wsj.com/washwire/2013/04/04/study-finds-high-economic-cost-of-immigration-system/.

55. Steven A. Camarota, Center for Immigration Studies website, http://cis.org/Costs.

56. Carrie Budoff Brown and Jake Sherman, "New immigration attack: It's too pricey," *Politico*, April 9, 2013, http://www.politico.com/story/2013/04/immigration-reform-budget-price-tag-cbo-89785.html.

57. See Library of Congress, "Bill Summary & Status: 107th Congress (2001–2002): S.1291," http://thomas.loc.gov/cgi-bin/bdquery/z?d107:S1291:.

58. Cost Estimate for S. 1291 Development, Relief, and Education for Alien Minors Act, Congressional Budget Office (as reported by the Senate Committee on the Judiciary on June 20, 2002), June 20, 2002, https://www.cbo.gov/sites/default/files/cbofiles/ftpdocs/36xx/doc3648/s1291.pdf.

59. See Library of Congress, "Bill Summary & Status: 107th Congress (2001–2002): H.R. 1582," http://thomas.loc.gov/cgi-bin/bdquery/z?d107:H.R.1582:.; Aaron Klein, "History lesson: Congressional Progressive caucus was founded by socialist group. Official website initially hosted by Democratic Socialists of America," *WND*, April 11, 2012, http://kleinonline.wnd.com/2012/04/11/history-lesson-congressional-progressive-caucus-was-founded-by-socialist-group-official-website-initially-hosted-by-democratic-socialists-of-america/. Also see Klein and Elliott's *Red Army*.

60. See Library of Congress "Bill Summary & Status: 109th Congress (2005–2006): S.2075," http://thomas.loc.gov/cgi-bin/bdquery/z?d109:s.02075:.; "Bill Summary & Status: 109th Congress (2005–2006): H.R. 5131," http://thomas.loc.gov/cgi-bin/bdquery/z?d109:HR05131:.; "S.774 DREAM Act of 2007," http://www.opencongress.org/bill/110-s774/show.

61. Sara Hebel, "'Dream Act' Fails to Get Enough Votes for Senate Debate," *Chronicle of Higher Education*, October 24, 2007, https://chronicle.com/article/Dream-Act-Fails-to-Get/39828.

62. "Creating Opportunities for Immigrant Students and Supporting the U.S. Economy," Immigration Policy Center, May 18, 2011 (Update), http://www.immigrationpolicy.org/just-facts/dream-act#do.

63. Kris W. Kobach, Ph.D., J.D., "A Sleeper Amnesty: Time to Wake Up from the DREAM Act," Heritage Foundation, September 13, 2007, http://www.heritage.org/research/reports/2007/09/a-sleeper-amnesty-time-to-wake-up-from-the-dream-act.

64. Ibid. Note that since summer 2012, several universities started granting in-state tuition status to illegals.

65. Justin Akers Chacon and Lee Sustar, "Why was the DREAM Act defeated?" *Socialist Worker* 2 (November 2, 2007): 5, http://socialistworker.org/2007-2/651/651_05_DreamAct.shtml.

66. Mike Lillis, "House passes DREAM Act, but bill faces tough Senate vote Thursday," *The Hill*, December 8, 2010, http://thehill.com/blogs/blog-briefing-room/news/132829-house-passes-dream-act-senate-to-move-next; "Final Vote Results for Roll Call 625," Clerk of the U.S. House of Representatives, December 8, 2010, http://clerk.house.gov/evs/2010/roll625.xml#Y.

67. Congressional Budget Office, "H.R. 6497. Development, Relief, and Education for Alien Minors Act of 2010," cost estimate for the bill as introduced on December 7, 2010, http://www.cbo.gov/ftpdocs/120xx/doc12015/hr6497.pdf; LBG1, "Congressional Budget Office Report: More Than Half of Dream Act Participants Will Drop Out," *Death by 1000 Papercuts*, December 9, 2010, http://deathby1000papercuts.com/2010/12/congressional-budget-office-report-more-than-half-of-dream-act-participants-will-drop-out/; no longer accessible.

68. Tait Trussell, "House Passes DREAM Act," *FrontPage Magazine*, December 9, 2010, http://frontpagemag.com/2010/12/09/house-passes-dream-act/.

69. Ibid.

70. Victor Davis Hanson, "The Road to Lawlessness," *National Review*, September 21, 2010, http://www.nationalreview.com/corner/247301/road-lawlessness-victor-davis-hanson.

71. Mike Riggs, "TheDC Morning: House passes bill aimed at denying stupid immigrants citizenship," *Daily Caller*, December 9, 2010, http://dailycaller.com/2010/12/09/thedc-morning-house-passes-bill-aimed-at-denying-stupid-immigrants-citizenship/.

72. Roy Beck, "House's Last Hurrah for Open Borders Not Too Impressive," NumbersUSA, December 8, 2010, http://www.numbersusa.com/content/nusablog/beckr/december-9-2010/houses-last-hurrah-open-borders-not-too-impressive.html.

73. Michael O'Brien, "Senate's top Dems vow vote on DREAM Act later this month," *The Hill*, December 9, 2010, http://thehill.com/blogs/blog-briefing-room/news/132955-senates-top-dems-vow-vote-on-dream-act-later-this-month.

74. National Public Radio, "Transcript: NPR Democratic Candidates' Debate" (Iowa), December 4, 2007, http://www.npr.org/templates/story/story.php?storyId=16898435

75. John Morton, in a letter to "all ICE Employees," regarding "Civil Immigration Enforcement: Priorities for the Apprehension, Detention, and Removal of Aliens," June 30, 2010, https://www.ice.gov/doclib/news/releases/2010/civil-enforcement-priorities.pdf, pp. 1–2.

76. Ibid., 2n1.

77. Ibid., 2.

78. "The ICE Priority Memos. What do they mean?" National Immigration Forum, September 2010, http://www.immigrationforum.org/images/uploads/2010/FactSheet_ICEPriorityMemos.pdf.

79. Josh Teets, "Morton Memo Authorizes Dismissal of Many Removal (Deportation) Cases!" USVISAInfo.com, August 28, 2010, http://www.usvisainfo.com/news-mainmenu-31/174-morton-memo-authorizes-dismissal-of-many-removal-deportation-cases.html.

80. "When Double Jeopardy Protection Ends," FindLaw.com, http://criminal.findlaw.com/criminal-rights/when-double-jeopardy-protection-ends.html.

81. US Immigration and Customs Enforcement Memorandum #306-112-0026, June 17, 2011, http://www .ice .gov /doclib /secure-communities /pdf/prosecutorial-discretion-memo .pdf.

82. Lynn Stuter, "Obama, John Morton and the Prosecutorial Discretion Memo," NewsWithViews.com, August 24, 2011, http://www.newswithviews.com/Stuter/stuter197.htm.

83. Cecelia Muñoz, "Immigration Update: Maximizing Public Safety and Better Focusing Resources," *The White House Blog*, August 18, 2011, http://www.whitehouse.gov/blog/2011/08/18/immigration-update-maximizing-public-safety-and-better-focusing-resources.

84. Robert Pear, "Fewer Youths to Be Deported in New Policy," *New York Times*, August 18, 2011, http://www.nytimes.com/2011/08/19/us/19immig.html?_r=2&partner=MYWAY&ei=5065.

85. Muñoz, "Immigration Update."

86. Pear, "Fewer Youths to Be Deported in New Policy."

87. Muñoz, "Immigration Update."

88. "Obama to Deport Illegals by 'Priority,'" *Washington Times*, August 18, 2011.

89. Alan Silverleib, "Immigration reform in August: why now?" CNN.com, August 22, 2010, http://edition.cnn.com/2011/POLITICS/08/19/deportation.policy/.

90. Miriam Jordan, "U.S. Alters Policy on Deporting Immigrants," *Wall Street Journal*, August 19, 2011, http://online.wsj.com/article/SB10001424053111903569904576516653574988550.html?mod=WSJ_WSJ_US_News_3.

91. Associated Press, "U.S. undertaking case-by-case review on deportation," ArizonaCentral.com, August 19, 2011, http://www.azcentral.com/12news/news/articles/2011/08/18/20110818feds-to-review-deportation-cases.html.

92. "Comprehensive Amnesty Threat," *NumbersUSA*, August 19, 2011, https://www.numbersusa. com/content/news/august-19-2011/obama-official-illegal-aliens-will-receive-work-permits. html.

93. Jeremy Beck, "How is your local media covering the work-permits-to-illegal-aliens story?" *NumbersUSA*, August 2011, https://www.numbersusa.com/content/nusablog/beckj/august-22-2011/how-your-local-media-covering-work-permits-illegal-aliens-story.html.

94. Federale, "Obama Regime's Administrative Amnesty: Impeachment Is The Only Answer," VDARE, August 27, 2011, http://www.vdare.com/articles/obama-s-administrative-amnesty-impeachment-is-the-only-answer.

95. Michael Shapira, "Illegal immigration: A rising and dangerous tide," *Washington Times*, April 3, 2013, http://communities.washingtontimes.com/neighborhood/truth-hurts-mike-shapira/2013/apr/2/illegal-immigration-rising-and-dangerous-tide/.

96. Aaron Klein, "Obama's New Czar Tied to Occupy, ACORN, MoveOn," *WND*, January 10, 2012, http://www.wnd.com/2012/01/obamas-newczar-tied-to-occupy-acorn-moveon /.

97. Barack Obama, "Remarks by the President on Immigration," Rose Garden, Washington, DC, Office of the White House Press Secretary, WhiteHouse.gov, June 15, 2012, http://www. whitehouse.gov/the-press-office/2012/06/15/remarks-president-immigration; Julia Preston and Josh H. Cushman Jr., "Obama to Permit Young Migrants to Remain in U.S.," *New York Times*, August 15, 2012, https://www.nytimes.com/2012/06/16/us/us-to-stop-deporting-some-illegal-immigrants.html?pagewanted=all&_r=0&gwh=7AF4452FF23A334D62 76A9ACA152225E.

98. Preston and Cushman, "Obama to Permit Young Migrants to Remain in U.S."

99. Nati Carrera, "Immigrants Wary of Deferred Action for Childhood Arrivals Memo," IVN, August 31, 2012, http://ivn.us/2012/08/31/immigrants-wary-of-deferred-action-for-childhood-arrivals-memo/.

100. Executive Orders, WhiteHouse.gov, accessed March 19, 2013, http://www.whitehouse.gov/ briefing-room/presidential-actions/executive-orders.

101. "Deferred Action for Childhood Arrivals (DACA) Federal Policy and Examples of State Examples," National Conference of State Legislatures, February 15, 2013, http://www.ncsl. org/Portals/1/Documents/immig/DACA_2013.pdf.

102. Janet Napolitano, Secretary of Homeland Security, memo to U.S. Customs and Border Protection, U.S. Citizenship and Immigration Services, and U.S. Customs and Immigration Enforcement, June 15, 2012, Department of Homeland Security website, http://www.dhs. gov/xlibrary/assets/s1-exercising-prosecutorial-discretion-individuals-who-came-to-us-as-children.pdf.

103. Ibid.

104. Ibid.

105. "Deferred Action for Childhood Arrivals" (fact sheet), Department of Homeland Security, accessed March 19, 2013, http://www.dhs.gov/deferred-action-childhood-arrivals.

106. "Obamnesty Hits the Streets as Millions of Illegal Aliens Line-up to Claim Legal Status," Judicial Watch, August 16, 2012, http://www.judicialwatch.org/press-room/weekly-updates/ obama-subverts-rule-of-law/.

107. "Consideration of Deferred Action for Childhood Arrivals Fee Exemption Guidance," U.S. Citizenship and Immigration Services, accessed March 19, 2013, http://www.uscis.gov/ portal/site/uscis/menuitem.5af9bb95919f35e66f614176543f6d1a/?vgnextoid=e21adaee785 29310VgnVCM100000082ca60aRCRD&vgnextchannel=fe529c7755cb9010VgnVCM100 00045f3d6a1RCRD. Note that what constitutes "poverty level" differs from state to state and even city to city, depending on the local economy.

108. DHS Memorandum on Deferred Action for Childhood Arrivals, June 15, 2012.

109. "Social Security Number—Deferred Action for Childhood Arrivals," Social Security Admin-istration; accessed March 19, 2013, https://www.socialsecurity.gov/pubs/deferred_action.pdf.

110. "Deferred Action for Childhood Arrivals" (fact sheet).

111. Pamela Constable, "Young illegal immigrants' amnesty could tighten competition for jobs, college," *Washington Post*, June 15, 2012, http://www.washingtonpost.com/local/ young-illegal-immigrants-amnesty-could-tighten-competition-for-jobs-college/2012/06/15/ gJQAmgV4fV_story.html.

112. Obamnesty Hits the Streets as Millions of Illegal Aliens Line-up to Claim Legal Status."

113. Neil Munro, "Obama immigration amnesty to include middle school dropouts," *Daily Caller*, August 15, 2012, http://dailycaller.com/2012/08/15/obama-immigration-amnesty-to-include-middle-school-dropouts/.

114. Alicia A. Caldwell, "Internal documents shows Obama deportation proposal could cost more than $585M," Associated Press, http://www.dailyjournal.net/view/story/a822d4de77c04dbcb-5ba0af5db581166/US--Immigration-Deportations-Halted/.

115. Miriam Jordan, "Immigration-Policy Details Emerge," *Wall Street Journal*, August 3, 2012, http://online.wsj.com/article/SB10000872396390443545504577567441019730890.html?mod=e2tw.

116. "Frequently Asked Questions: Exclusion of People Granted 'Deferred Action for Childhood Arrivals' from Affordable Health Care," National Immigration Law Center, November 26, 2012, http://www.nilc.org/acadacafaq.html.

117. Ibid.

118. "Deferred Action for Childhood Arrivals Process, August 15, 2012–February 14, 2013," US Citizenship and Immigration Services, accessed March 19, 2013, http://www.uscis.gov/USCIS/Resources/Reports%20and%20Studies/Immigration%20Forms%20Data/All%20Form%20Types/DACA/DACA2-15-13.pdf.

119. Wendy Feliz, "Reaching the Six-Month Mark on Deferred Action for Childhood Arrivals (DACA)," ImmigrationImpact.com, February 20, 2013, http://immigrationimpact.com/2013/02/20/reaching-the-six-month-mark-on-deferred-action-for-childhood-arrivals-daca/.

120. Stephen Dinan, "Non-deportation rate drops to 99.2 percent," *Washington Times*, May 18, 2013, http://www.washingtontimes.com/news/2013/may/18/nondeportation-rate-drops-992-percent/.

121. "Deferred Action for Childhood Arrivals Process."

122. Mike Flynn, "Report: DHS Halted Background Checks to Meet Flood of Amnesty Requests," Breitbart.com, June 11, 2013, http://www.breitbart.com/Big-Government/2013/06/11/DHS-Halted-Background-Checks-Due-to-Flood-of-Amnesty-Requests.

123. "Cecilia Muñoz to Stay Second Term, Vows to Continue Push for Immigration Reform," Fox News Latino, February 18, 2013, http://latino.foxnews.com/latino/politics/2013/02/18/cecilia-munoz-to-stay-second-term-vows-to-continue-push-for-immigration-reform/.

124. "FACT SHEET: Fixing Our Broken Immigration System so Everyone Plays by the Rules," Office of the White House Press Secretary, WhiteHouse.gov, January 29, 2013, http://www.whitehouse.gov/the-press-office/2013/01/29/fact-sheet-fixing-our-broken-immigration-system-so-everyone-plays-rules.

125. "AILA section-by-section summary of WH draft bill sections Working Draft," American Immigration Lawyers Association, February 21, 2013, http://www.aila.org/content/default.aspx?bc=6755|37861|25667|43358.

126. Ibid.

127. Ibid.

128. Ibid.

129. Ibid.

130. Ibid.

131. Alison Siskind, *Treatment of Noncitizens Under the Patient Protection and Affordable Care Act*, Congressional Research Service, March 22, 2011, http://www.ciab.com/workarea/downloadasset.aspx?id=2189, 10, Summary.

132. Tom Murse, "The Millions Who Won't Be Covered by Obamacare," About.com, July 3, 2012, http://uspolitics.about.com/b/2012/07/03/the-millions-who-wont-be-covered-by-obamacare.htm.

133. Paul Bedard, "Now they tell us: Obamacare debut will be 'messy'," *Washington Examiner*, March 18, 2013, http://washingtonexaminer.com/now-they-tell-us-obamacare-debut-will-be-messy/article/2524654.

134. "AILA section-by-section summary of WH draft bill sections Working Draft."

135. Ibid.

136. Ibid.

137. Ibid.

CHAPTER 4. REVOLVING DOOR FOR CRIMINAL ILLEGALS

1. Peyton R. Miller, "Why Isn't the Obama Administration Suing 'Sanctuary Cities'? The lawsuit against SB1070 has nothing to do with keeping immigration policy in federal hands," *Weekly Standard*, June 23, 2010, http://www.weeklystandard.com/blogs/why-isnt-obama-administration-suing-sanctuary-cities.

2. Randal C. Archibold, "Arizona Enacts Stringent Law on Immigration," *New York Times*, April 23, 2010, https://www.nytimes.com/2010/04/24/us/politics/24immig.html.

3. Jon Feere, "Is Arizona's SB 1070 Immigration Law Constitutional? Obama Administration Doesn't Want to Enforce the Immigration Laws," *U.S. News & World Report*, April 23, 2012, http://www.usnews.com/debate-club/is-arizonas-sb-1070-immigration-law-constitutional/obama-administration-doesnt-want-to-enforce-the-immigration-laws.

4. "Legal battle looms over Arizona immigration law," *CNN.com*, July 28, 2010, http://www.cnn.com/2010/US/07/28/arizona.immigration.law/index.html?hpt=T2.

5. Robert Barnes, "Supreme Court upholds key part of Arizona law for now, strikes down other provisions," *Washington Post*, June 25, 2012, http://www.washingtonpost.com/politics/supreme-court-rules-on-arizona-immigration-law/2012/06/25/gJQA0Nrm1V_story.html?hpid=z1.

6. "Sen. Sessions Calls for ICE Director John Morton to Step Down," NumbersUSA.com, January 30, 2013, https://www.numbersusa.com/content/news/january-30-2013/sen-sessions-calls-ice-director-john-morton-step-down.html.

7. Feere, "Is Arizona's SB 1070 Immigration Law Constitutional?"

8. Elise Cooper, "Fighting the Immigration Wars," *American Thinker*, March 21, 2013, http://www.americanthinker.com/2013/03/fighting_the_immigration_wars.html.

9. Michael Tarm, "IMPACT: Cartels dispatch agents deep inside US," Associated Press, April 1, 2013, http://bigstory.ap.org/article/ap-impact-cartels-dispatch-agents-deep-inside-us.

10. Mara H. Gottfried, "Drug agents strike cartel in Minnesota, across U.S. 31 arrests in state in crackdown on violent Mexico-based network," *Pioneer Press* (St. Paul, MN), October 23, 2009, http://www.twincities.com/news/ci_13622650.

11. "List of Sanctuary Cities," Ohio Jobs & Justice PAC, accessed March 20, 2013, http://www.ojjpac.org/sanctuary.asp.

12. Editor-in-Chief, "House Passes Walsh Amendment: Sanctuary Cities," *Illinois Conservative Examiner*, May 13, 2012, http://www.ice-news.net/2012/05/13/house-passes-walsh-amendment-sanctuary-cities/.

13. H.R.5326 Commerce, Justice, Science, and Related Agencies Appropriations Act, introduced May 2, 2012, by sponsor Rep. Frank R. Wolf (R-VA), http://beta.congress.gov/bill/112th-congress/house-bill/5326. Latest Action: May 14, 2012, Received in the Senate. Read twice. Placed on Senate Legislative Calendar under General Orders. Calendar No. 397.

14. "Sanctuary Cities: A New Civil War," Claremont Institute, September 7, 2005, http://www.claremont.org/projects/pageid.2022/default.asp.

15. Ibid.

16. Ibid.

17. Ibid.

18. Ibid.

19. Miller, "Why Isn't the Obama Administration Suing 'Sanctuary Cities'?"

20. This blog post from *Talking Points Memo* (http://talkingpointsmemo.com/) is no longer available but was posted by Brenda J. Elliott as part of an RBO blog post about sanctuary cities on July 18, 2010.

21. "Democratic Debate Transcript at Dartmouth College, New Hampshire," August 26, 2007, http://www.cfr.org/us-election-2008/democratic-debate-transcript-new-hampshire/p14313.

22. William Branigin, "INS Pursuing Aliens in Urban Gangs; New Immigration Law Aids Agents in Drive to Put Criminals out of the Country," *Washington Post*, May 2, 1997, http://www.highbeam.com/doc/1P2-729777.html.

23. "Congress Hears Testimony on Border Security; Immigration Officials Crack Down on Illegal Alien Gangs; Tensions Across the," International Wire, March 14, 2005, http://www.highbeam.com/doc/1P3-807764961.html.

24. "Immigration and the Alien Gang Epidemic: Problems and Solutions," Testimony of Heather Mac Donald, Senior Fellow, Manhattan Institute for Policy Research, before the House Judiciary Subcommittee on Immigration, Border Security, and Claims, April 13, 2005, https://www.manhattan-institute.org/html/mac_donald04-13-05.htm.

25. Ibid.

26. "2011 National Gang Threat Assessment – Emerging Trends," FBI website, accessed June 5, 2013, http://www.fbi.gov/stats-services/publications/2011-national-gang-threat-assessment.

27. "MS-13," InSightCrime, accessed March 20, 2013, http://www.insightcrime.org/groups-el-salvador/mara-salvatrucha-ms-13.

28. Alicia A. Caldwell, "U.S. names violent street gang MS-13 as international criminal group," *Denver Post*, October 14, 2012, http://www.denverpost.com/nationworld/ci_21753249/u-s-names-violent-street-gang-ms-13.

29. "2011 National Gang Threat Assessment."

30. Kris W. Kobach, "Deportation and Ban on Entry to U.S. of Non-Citizen Gang: Kris W. Kobach Members" (congressional testimony the House Judiciary Subcommittee on Immigration, Border Security, and Claims), June 28, 2005, http://www.highbeam.com/doc/1P1-110640149.html.

31. Stephen Dinan, "ICE ex-chief: Nondeport rules would've spared 9/11 hijackers," *Washington Times*, February 4, 2013, http://www.washingtontimes.com/news/2013/feb/4/ice-ex-chief-nondeport-rules-wouldve-spared-911-hi/.

32. Ibid.

33. Penny Starr, "Union Leader: 'ICE Crumbling from Within' Because Obama Won't Let Agents Arrest Illegals," CNSNews.com, February 13, 2013, http://cnsnews.com/news/article/union-leader-ice-crumbling-within-because-obama-wont-let-agents-arrest-illegals.

34. Neil Munro, "Arrested illegals who were released charged with 16,226 subsequent crimes," *Daily Caller*, August 9, 2012, http://dailycaller.com/2012/08/09/arrested-illegals-who-were-released-charged-with-16226-subsequent-crimes/.

35. "Mexican, U.S. Media Too Scared to Cover Border Crime," Judicial Watch, March 19, 2013, http://www.judicialwatch.org/blog/2013/03/mexican-u-s-media-too-scared-to-cover-border-crime/.

36. Ibid.

37. Stephen Dinan, "DHS tells Congress it still can't measure border security," *Washington Times*, March 20, 2013, http://www.washingtontimes.com/news/2013/mar/20/dhs-congress-still-cant-measure-border-security/.

38. Judson Berger, "DHS releasing hundreds of illegal immigrants, blaming budget cuts," FoxNews.com, February 26, 2013, http://www.foxnews.com/politics/2013/02/26/dhs-to-release-thousands-illegal-immigrants-blaming-budget-cuts/.

39. Alan Gomez, "Feds free hundreds from immigration detention," *USA Today*, February 26, 2013, http://m.usatoday.com/article/news/1949151.

40. Ibid.

41. Neil Munro, "Obama promises sequester pain until GOP raises taxes," *Daily Caller*, March 1, 2013, http://dailycaller.com/2013/03/01/obama-promises-sequester-pain-until-gop-raises-taxes/.

42. Bob Woodward, "Obama's sequester deal-changer," *Washington Post*, February 22, 2013, http://www.washingtonpost.com/opinions/bob-woodward-obamas-sequester-deal-changer/2013/02/22/c0b65b5e-7ce1-11e2-9a75-dab0201670da_story.html.

43. Alicia A. Caldwell, "DHS official resigns after immigrants are freed," Associated Press, February 27, 2013, http://bigstory.ap.org/article/dhs-official-resigns-after-immigrants-are-freed.

44. Jennifer Epstein, "White House was not involved in ICE's decision to release detainees," *Politico*, February 27, 2013, http://www.politico.com/politico44/2013/02/white-house-was-not-involved-in-ices-decision-to-release-158027.html.

45. Stephen Dinan, "White House: ICE to blame for release of illegals," *Washington Times*, February 27, 2013, http://www.washingtontimes.com/news/2013/feb/27/white-house-ice-blame-release-illegals/.

46. Alicia A. Caldwell, "AP Exclusive: DHS released over 2,000 immigrants," March 1, 2013, http://bigstory.ap.org/article/documents-us-released-more-2000-immigrants.

47. "Update: Policy Guidance on ICE Detainers under the Dec. 21 Morton Memo," Vinesh Patel Law Firm blog, December 21, 2012, http://vpatellaw.com/blog/update-ice-detainers/.

48. Nice Deb, "Backlash: Obama Regime's Decision to Release Illegal Immigrant Prisoners Infuriates Republican Lawmakers," *NiceDeb* (blog), March 11, 2013, https://nicedeb.wordpress.com/2013/03/11/backlash-obama-regimes-decision-to-release-illegal-immigrant-prisoners-infuriates-republican-lawmakers/.

49. Nice Deb, "Video: Jeanine Pirro Rips Obama Regime for Letting Dangerous Illegal Immigrant Criminals Walk—'I Call It the Obama Amnesty Program'," *NiceDeb* (blog), March 9, 2013, http://nicedeb.wordpress.com/2013/03/09/jeanine-pirro-rips-obama-regime-for-letting-dangerous-illegal-immigrant-criminals-walk-i-call-it-the-obama-amnesty-program/.

50. Stephen Dinan, "Sequester do-over: Feds recaptured 4 immigrants released under budget cuts," *Washington Times*, March 14, 2013, http://www.washingtontimes.com/news/2013/mar/14/feds-recaptured-4-immigrants-released-budget-cuts/.

51. Penny Starr, "ICE Director: 'We Have Released Many Individuals Who Have DUI Offenses,'" CNSNews.com, March 14, 2013, http://www.cnsnews.com/news/article/ice-director-we-have-released-many-individuals-who-have-dui-offenses.

52. Mary Chastain, "Rep. Grills ICE Director on Blaming Sequester for Detainee Release," Breitbart.com, March 14, 2013, http://www.breitbart.com/Big-Government/2013/03/19/ICE-Director-Morton-Cannot-Prove-Released-Detainees-Aren-t-Security-Risks.

53. Dinan, "Sequester do-over."

54. Joel Gehrke, "ICE chief admits he could have sought alternatives to releasing illegal aliens, but didn't," *Washington Examiner*, March 19, 2013, http://washingtonexaminer.com/ice-chief-admits-he-could-have-sought-alternatives-to-releasing-illegal-aliens-but-didnt/article/2524794.

55. Penny Starr, "ICE Has Released More Than 8,000 Criminal Illegal Aliens into U.S. Since 2009," CNSNews.com, May 31, 2011, http://cnsnews.com/news/article/ice-has-released-more-8000-criminal-illegal-aliens-us-2009.

56. Edwin Mora, "ICE Allowed the Release of 890 Imprisoned Deportable Aliens, Convicted of Serious Crimes, into U.S. in FY 2009," CNSNews.com, February 9, 2011, http://cnsnews.com/news/article/ice-allowed-release-890-imprisoned-deportable-aliens-convicted-serious-crimes-us-fy.

57. Maria Sacchetti, "Many freed criminals avoid deportation, strike again," *Boston Globe*, December 9, 2012, http://www.bostonglobe.com/metro/2012/12/09/secret-criminals-quietly-released-criminals-who-were-supposed-deported-with-deadly-consequences/864u1YQbUaVcRiSnz6VaxJ/story.html.

58. US House of Representatives, Committee on the Judiciary, Subcommittee on Immigration Policy and Enforcement, "Keep Our Communities Safe Act (H.R. 1932): Hearings before the Subcommittee on Immigration Policy and Enforcement", May 24, 2011, testimony of Gary Mead, ICE executive associate director of enforcement and removal operations, http://www.gpo.gov/fdsys/pkg/CHRG-112hhrg66539/html/CHRG-112hhrg66539.htm.

59. Sacchetti, "Many freed criminals avoid deportation."

60. Mark Motivans, "Immigration Offenders in the Federal Justice System, 2010," Department of Justice, Bureau of Justice Statistics, July 2012, http://www.bjs.gov/content/pub/pdf/iofjs10.pdf, 22.

61. Peter A. Schulkin, "The Revolving Door. Deportations of Criminal Illegal Immigrants," Center for Immigration Studies, November 2012, http://www.cis.org/revolving-door-deportations-of-criminal-illegal-immigrants#36.

62. Deanna Bellandi, "Immigrant Raids: Feds Arrest 370 Illegal Immigrants in 10 States," *Huffington Post*, August 27, 2010, http://www.huffingtonpost.com/2010/08/27/immigrant-raids-feds-arre_n_697355.html.

63. "Immigration raids net 2,900 criminals in largest national crackdown," *Nation Now* (*LA Times blog*), September 28, 2011, http://latimesblogs.latimes.com/nationnow/2011/09/immigration-raids-net-2900-criminals.html.

64. Miriam Jordan, "Fresh Raids Target Illegal Hiring," *Wall Street Journal*, May 2, 2012, http://online.wsj.com/article/SB10001424052702304868004577378042369495780.html.

65. "A Timeline of the Obama Administration's Four Year-Long Conspiracy to Grant Amnesty to Illegal Aliens by Dismantling Enforcement of Our Laws against Illegal Immigration," Judicial Watch, March 1, 2013, http://www.judicialwatch.org/judicial-watch-special-illegal-immigration-report/.

66. Matt Mayer, "Obama Illegal Immigration Silent Work Raid Policy Not Working," Heritage Foundation, May 7, 2012, http://blog.heritage.org/2012/05/07/obama-illegal-immigration-silent-work-raid-policy-not-working/.

67. See "Executive Profile: Nicholas J. Colas," *Bloomberg Businessweek*, accessed June 5, 2013, http://investing.businessweek.com/research/stocks/private/person.asp?personId=30050029&privcapId=1832558.

68. The statistics and quotations from Colas that follow are from Nick Colas, "Ten Fast Facts on the Economics of Immigration," Zero Hedge, April 2, 2013, http://www.zerohedge.com/news/2013-04-02/ten-fast-facts-economics-immigration.

69. "'Catch and release' policy leading to more illegal border crossings," *Examiner*, March 14, 2013, http://www.examiner.com/article/catch-and-release-policy-leading-to-more-illegal-border-crossings.

70. "The new man in the hrad . . . and the old president's disappointments," *Economist*, March 9, 2013, http://www.economist.com/news/europe/21573161-and-old-presidents-disappointments-new-man-hrad.

71. Ibid.

72. Associated Press, "Czech president could face high treason charges for his controversial amnesty," FoxNews.com, February 27, 2013, http://www.foxnews.com/world/2013/02/27/czech-president-could-face-high-treason-charges-for-his-controversial-amnesty/.

73. "Czech President to Join Cato Institute," Cato Institute, February 28, 2013, http://www.cato.org/blog/czech-president-join-cato-institute; Dashiell Bennett, "Czech President Bounced for Treason in Giving Amnesty to Financial Scammers," *Atlantic Wire*, March 4, 2013, http://www.theatlanticwire.com/global/2013/03/czech-president-impeached/62722/.

CHAPTER 5. EMPOWERING ENEMIES DOMESTICALLY AND ABROAD

1. "Leading Sunni Sheikh Yousef Al-Qaradhawi and Other Sheikhs Herald the Coming Conquest of Rome," Middle East Media Research Institute, December 6, 2002, http://www.memri.org/report/en/0/0/0/0/0/0/774.htm.

2. Ibid.

3. "The Muslim Brotherhood in the Arab World and Islamic Communities in Western Europe," Meir Amit Intelligence and Terrorism Information Center (ITIC) at the Israeli Intelligence Heritage and Commemoration Center, January 2012, http://www.terrorism-info.org.il/data/pdf/PDF_11_049_2.pdf.

4. Nonie Darwish, "Sharia for Dummies," *FrontPage* magazine, August 27, 2010, http://frontpagemag.com/2010/nonie-darwish/sharia-for-dummies/.

5. The Meir Amit Intelligence and Terrorism Information Center, "Muslim Brotherhood in the Arab World and Islamic Communities in Western Europe," *Think-Israel*, accessed June 5, 2013, http://www.think-israel.org/itic.muslimbrotherhoodinmeandeurope.html.

6. "Muslim Brotherhood Members to Attend Obama's Cairo Speech," FoxNews.com, June 3, 2009, http://www.foxnews.com/politics/2009/06/03/muslim-brotherhood-members-attend-obamas-cairo-speech.

7. Zvi Bar'el and Avi Issacharoff, "Obama met Muslim Brotherhood members in U.S.," *Haaretz*, June 4, 2009, http://www.haaretz.com/news/obama-met-muslim-brotherhood-members-in-u-s-1.277306.

8. "Egypt's Morsi in 2010: Obama Insincere; We Must Nurse Our Children and Grandchildren on Hatred of Jews," MEMRI, June 10, 2010 http://www.memritv.org/clip_transcript/en/3713.htm.

9. Tim Ross, Matthew Moore, and Steven Swinford, "Egypt protests: America's secret backing for rebel leaders behind uprising," *Telegraph* (UK), January 28, 2011, http://www.telegraph. co.uk/news/worldnews/africaandindianocean/egypt/8289686/Egypt-protests-Americas-secret-backing-for-rebel-leaders-behind-uprising.html.

10. Newscore, "Obama says change must start now, as Egypt's prez vows to step aside," *New York Post*, February 1, 2011, http://www.nypost.com/p/news/international/mubarak_will_not_run_for_president_jUTdxlqRIBPYnd7CbxgjpM.

11. Ibid.

12. Helene Cooper and Mark Landler, "White House and Egypt Discuss Plan for Mubarak's Exit," *New York Times*, February 3, 2011, http://www.nytimes.com/2011/02/04/world/middleeast/04diplomacy.html?pagewanted=all&_r=0.

13. "Egypt unrest: Obama increases pressure on Mubarak," *BBC News Online*, February 5, 2011, http://www.bbc.co.uk/news/world-us-canada-12371479.

14. Christiane Amanpour, Terry Moran, Nasser Atta, and Huma Khan, "Obama Hails Mubarak's Resignation: 'Egypt Will Never Be the Same,'" ABC News, February 11, 2011, http://abcnews.go.com/International/obama-hails-hosni-mubaraks-resignation-egypt/story?id=12891572.

15. *Wikipedia*, s.v. "Egyptian parliamentary election, 2011–12," http://en.wikipedia.org/wiki/Egyptian_parliamentary_election,_2011%E2%80%9312; accessed June 5, 2013.

16. Jack Khoury, "Egypt's Muslim Brotherhood plans to put treaty with Israel to a referendum," Haaretz, January 2, 2012, http://www.haaretz.com/print-edition/news/egypt-s-muslim-brotherhood-plans-to-put-treaty-with-israel-to-a-referendum-1.404987.

17. "Egypt's Morsi in 2010: Obama Insincere; We Must Nurse Our Children and Grandchildren on Hatred of Jews," *MEMRI,* January 20, 2010, http://www.memritv.org/clip_transcript/en/3713.htm.

18. "Hamas chief meets Egypt's Morsi in Cairo, hails 'new era,'" Haaretz, January 19, 2012, http://www.haaretz.com/news/middle-east/hamas-chief-meets-egypt-s-morsi-in-cairo-hails-new-era-1.452281.

19. CNN Wire Staff, "Iranian warships sail into the Mediterranean," *CNN.com*, February 19, 2012, http://edition.cnn.com/2012/02/18/world/meast/iran-warships/index.html.

20. Tom Perry and Yasmine Saleh, "Iran's Ahmadinejad kissed and scolded in Egypt," Reuters, February 5, 2013, http://www.reuters.com/article/2013/02/05/us-egypt-iran-idUS-BRE9140EK20130205.

21. "Egyptian draft constitution to keep sharia as 'main' source of law," *Telegraph* (UK), November 29, 2012, http://www.telegraph.co.uk/news/worldnews/africaandindianocean/egypt/9711879/Egyptian-draft-constitution-to-keep-sharia-as-main-source-of-law.html.

22. "Coptic Egypt: Background Information," Digital Egypt for Universities, University College London, accessed June 11, 2013, http://www.digitalegypt.ucl.ac.uk/coptic/coptic.html.

23. Aaron Klein, "Egypt's Christians face mass slaughter by Islamists," *WND*, September 14, 2012, http://www.wnd.com/2012/09/now-egypts-christians-face-mass-slaughter-by-islamists/.

24. Maxim Lott, "U.S. gift of F-16 fighters headed to Egypt, despite Morsi's harsh rhetoric," FoxNews.com, January 1, 2013, www.foxnews.com/world/2013/01/22/gift-us-f-16-fighter-jets-en-route-to-egypt-amid-criticism/.

25. Michael R. Gordon, "Kerry Announces $250 Million in U.S. Aid for Egypt," *New York Times*, March 4, 2013, http://www.nytimes.com/2013/03/04/world/middleeast/kerry-announces-millions-in-us-aid-for-egypt.html?_r=0.

26. "Statement by the President on Events in Tunisia," White House Office of the Press Secretary, January 14, 2011, http://www.whitehouse.gov/the-press-office/2011/01/14/statement-president-events-tunisia.

27. Ibid.

28. Aidan Lewis, "Profile: Tunisia's Ennahda Party," BBC News Online, October 25, 2011, http://www.bbc.co.uk/news/world-africa-15442859.

29. "Yemen: Hamid al-Ahmar sees Saleh as weak and isolated, plans next steps," *Washington Post*, accessed June 5, 2013, http://www.washingtonpost.com/wp-srv/special/world/wikileaks-yemen/cable12.html.

30. "US urges Yemen's Saleh to transfer power," Al Jazeera, July 10, 2011, http://www.aljazeera. com/news/middleeast/2011/07/201171016636884366.html.
31. Sheryl Gay Stolberg, "Obama Offers Sympathy and Urges No 'Jump to Conclusions," *New York Times*, November 17, 2009.
32. "Fort Hood shootings: The meaning of 'Allahu Akbar,'" *Telegraph* (UK), November 6, 2009.
33. Philip Sherwell and Alex Spillius, "Fort Hood shooting: Texas army killer linked to September 11 terrorists," *Telegraph* (UK), November 7, 2009.
34. "Treasury designates Anwar al-Awlaki key leader of AQAP," *CNN.com*, July 16, 2010.
35. Brian Ross and Rhonda Schwartz, "Major Hasan's E-Mail: 'I Can't Wait to Join You' in Afterlife," ABC News, November 19, 2009, http://abcnews.go.com/Blotter/major-hasans-mail-wait-join-afterlife/story?id=9130339#.Ua9jetJvNCo.
36. U.S. District Court, Eastern District of Michigan, Southern Division, Case 2:10-cr-20005-NGE-DAS Document 7 Filed 01/06/2010, available at http://www.cbsnews.com/htdocs/pdf/Abdulmutallab_Indictment.pdf.
37. "Editorial: Obama denies crotch bomber conspiracy," *Washington Times*, December 29, 2009.
38. Adam Nossiter, "Lonely Trek to Radicalism for Terror Suspect," *New York Times*, January 16, 2010.
39. Matthew Cole, Brian Ross, and Nasser Atta, "Underwear Bomber: New Video of Training, Martyrdom Statements," ABC News, April 26, 2010, http://abcnews.go.com/Blotter/underwear-bomber-video-training-martyrdom-statements/story?id=10479470#.Ua9kvtJvNCo.
40. Editorial, "'Islamic terrorism' and the Obama administration: Critics on the right say the administration is deliberately denying the existence of 'radical Islam' and 'Islamic terrorism,'" *Los Angeles Times*, June 8, 2010.
41. "Obama Bans Islam, Jihad from National Security Strategy Document," FoxNews.com, April 7, 2010.
42. This quote and the remaining Brennan quotes in this section are from Hilary Leila Krieger, "Top US security official: Our enemy isn't terrorism, jihad," *Jerusalem Post*, May 27, 2010.
43. Aaron Klein, "Hagel: Terrorists attack because they lack hope," *WND*, January 9, 2013, http://www.wnd.com/2013/01/hagel-terrorists-attack-because-they-lack-hope/.
44. Ibid.
45. Editorial, "Will Profiling Make a Difference?" *New York Times*, January 4, 2010.
46. Video available at http://www.youtube.com/watch?v=pVP7Y54rdVE; Aaron Klein, "Counter-terror adviser: U.S. should 'never' profile. Declares himself 'citizen of the world,' compares Muslims to 'bias' against Irish, Italians," *WND*, February 18, 2010.
47. Michelle Malkin, "Obama's CAIR-kowtowing, soft-on-jihad CIA Director nominee," *Michelle Malkin* (blog), January 7, 2013, http://michellemalkin.com/2013/01/07/obamas-cair-kowtowing-cia-director-nominee/.
48. "ISNA President Opens Townhall Meeting on the Nation's Security with John Brennan," ISNA, http://www.isna.net/articles/News/ISNA-President-Opens-Dialogue-on-the-Nations-Security-with-John-Brennan.aspx. Though this article is no longer accessible, the following web page states that ISNA "facilitated" the meeting and references this no-longer-existent URL: http://forum.whyislam.org/printer_friendly_posts.asp?TID=26082.
49. "ISNA President Opens Townhall Meeting on the Nation's Security with John Brennan," US 4 Arabs, February 16, 2010, http://www.us4arabs.com/content/view/2546/31/.
50. Discover the Networks, "Islamic Society of North America (ISNA)," http://www.discoverthenetworks.org/printgroupProfile.asp?grpid=6178; Steven Emerson, "New Disclosures Tighten ISNA-Muslim Brotherhood Bonds," Investigative Project on Terrorism (IPT), July 22, 2008, http://www.investigativeproject.org/730/new-disclosures-tighten-isna-muslim-brotherhood-bonds.
51. Aaron Klein, "Soda, Pizza and the Destruction of America," *WND*, March 18, 2003, http://www.wnd.com/2003/03/17795/.
52. Discover the Networks, "Islamic Society of North America (ISNA)."
53. Stephen Schwartz, "Wahhabism & Islam in the U.S.: Two-faced policy fosters danger," *National Review*, June 30, 2003, http://www.nationalreview.com/node/207366/print.
54. Discover the Networks, "Islamic Society of North America (ISNA)."
55. Ibid.

56. Josh Gerstein, "Islamic Groups Named in Hamas Funding Case," *New York Sun*, June 4, 2007.
57. Ron Kampeas, "Holy Land founders get life sentences," JTA: The Global Jewish News Source, May 28, 2009, http://www.jta.org/2009/05/28/news-opinion/united-states/holy-land-founders-get-life-sentences.
58. Aaron Klein, "Obama adviser spoke to Hamas-linked group," *WND*, March 7, 2011, http://www.wnd.com/2011/03/271981/.
59. Ibid.
60. Aaron Klein, "Obama adviser speaks alongside defender of WTC bombers," *WND*, July 5, 2011, http://www.wnd.com/2011/07/319021/.
61. "Leaders of Hamas linked group met with Obama's Transition Team," *Militant Islam Monitor*, January 18, 2009, http://www.militantislammonitor.org/article/id/3820.
62. Josh Gerstein, "Obama prayer speaker has Hamas tie?" *Politico*, January 17, 2009, http://www.politico.com/news/stories/0109/17562.html.
63. Steven Emerson, "Top Obama aide invites head of terrorist-linked org to join administration task force," *Jewish World Review*, June 29, 2009, http://www.jewishworldreview.com/0709/emerson070909.php3#.Ua90VNJvNCo.
64. Jennifer Rubin, "Why Is the Justice Department Cozying Up to Islamic Radicals?" PJ Media, June 22, 2009, http://pjmedia.com/blog/why-is-the-justice-department-reaching-out-to-islamic-radicals/.
65. Hammad Hammad, "Valerie Jarrett Addresses the Islamic Society of North America," White House blog, June 6, 2009, http://www.whitehouse.gov/blog/Valerie-Jarrett-Addresses-the-Islamic-Society-of-North-America.
66. Joseph Klein, "Obama's radical guests," *FrontPage Magazine*, August 19, 2010, http://frontpagemag.com/2013/frontpagemag-com/obamas-radical-transformation-of-america/.
67. Michael A. Fletcher, "Ramadan Dinner at the White House: The Guest List," *Washington Post*, September 1, 2009.
68. Katelyn Sabochik, "President Obama Celebrates Ramadan at White House Iftar Dinner," White House blog, August 14, 2010, http://www.whitehouse.gov/blog/2010/08/14/president-obama-celebrates-ramadan-white-house-iftar-dinner.
69. Rod Dreher, "If She Knew, Would She Care?" BeliefNet.com, August 16, 2007, http://blog.beliefnet.com/roddreher/2007/08/if-she-knew-would-she-care.htm; no longer accessible.
70. "Inside Al-Qaeda," Mideast Web, http://www.mideastweb.org/alqaeda.htm; accessed June 5, 2013.
71. "A Muslim's Nationality and His Belief (By Sayyid Qutb)," posted February 18, 2007, on the 7th Century Generation website, http://www.7cgen.com/index.php?showtopic=8191.
72. Paul Berman, "The Philosopher of Islamic Terror," *New York Times Magazine*, March 23, 2003.
73. Rod Dreher, "Unreliable advice from this Muslim group," *Dallas Morning Views* (blog), November 11, 2009, http://dallasmorningviewsblog.dallasnews.com/archives/2009/11/unreliable-advi.html.
74. Office of the Press Secretary, "Secretary Napolitano Swears in Homeland Security Advisory Council Members," press release, website of the Department of Homeland Security, October 15, 2010, http://www.dhs.gov/news/2010/10/18/secretary-napolitano-swears-homeland-security-advisory-council-members.
75. Mollie, "The long arc of Sayyid Qutb," *Get Religion* (blog), Patheos, December 15, 2009, http://www.patheos.com/blogs/getreligion/2009/12/the-long-arm-of-sayyid-qutb/.
76. Mohamed Elibiary, "OPINION: Mohamed Elibiary: Verdict misinterprets 'material support,'" *Dallas Morning News*, June 24, 2010.
77. "Dallas: A tribute to the great Islamic visionary, Ayatollah Khomeini," Jihad Watch, December 14, 2004.
78. "Sick! Reuters Uses Radical Islamist to Attack Bush Speech!" posted by Jim Hoft on Gateway Pundit website, August 10, 2006, http://www.thegatewaypundit.com/2006/08/sick-reuters-uses-radical-islamist-to-attack-bush-speech/.
79. "Dallas: A tribute to the great Islamic visionary, Ayatollah Khomeini."

80. Todd Bensman and Robert Riggs, "Texas Muslims Host Ayatollah Khomeini Tribute," CBS-11 News, December 17, 2004, http://iranvajahan.net/cgi-bin/printarticle. pl?l=en&y=2004&m=12&d=18&a=1.
81. Ibid.
82. Aaron Klein, "Hillary's chief worked with al-Qaida front man," WND, July 25, 2012, http://www.wnd.com/2012/07/hillarys-chief-worked-with-al-qaida-front-man.
83. Walid Shoebat, "Proof: Huma Has Ties to Muslim Brotherhood—Countless Documents Surface," PDF files posted at http://www.shoebat.com/wp-content/uploads/2012/07/Huma_Brotherhood_Connections_072412.pdf.
84. George Archibald, "Muslim groups want motherhood stressed. Criticize `selfish' U.N. platform," *Washington Times*, August 19, 1995.
85. See Klein, "Hillary's chief worked with al-Qaida front man."
86. Office of Public Affairs, "U.S.-Based Branch of Al Haramain Foundation Linked to Terror," press release, US Department of the Treasury, September 9, 2004, http://www.treasury.gov/press-center/press-releases/Pages/js1895.aspx.
87. "Backgrounder: Muslim World League," Anti-Defamation League website, accessed June 5, 2013. http://archive.adl.org/NR/exeres/A2E75550-9493-4D30-93E8-2A398E6474CB,DB7611A2-02CD-43AF-8147-649E26813571,frameless.htm.
88. David E. Kaplan, "The Saudi Connection: How billions in oil money spawned a global terror network," *U.S. News & World Report*, December 7, 2003, http://www.usnews.com/usnews/news/articles/031215/15terror_3.htm.
89. Aaron Klein, "Weinergate 2: Huma mom tied to boomin' bombers," *WND*, July 13, 2011, http://www.wnd.com/2011/07/321401/. See also the US Court of Appeals for the Ninth Circuit document concerning *Al Haramain v. Department of Treasury*, at http://cdn.ca9.uscourts.gov/datastore/opinions/2011/09/23/10-35032.pdf.
90. Jane Perlez, "Saudis Quietly Promote Strict Islam in Indonesia," *New York Times*, July 5, 2003, http://www.nytimes.com/2003/07/05/world/saudis-quietly-promote-strict-islam-in-indonesia.html.
91. Niles Lathem, "Saudis in New $hame: Embassy Funneled 400G to Osama 'charity,'" *New York Post*, December 2, 2002, http://www.nypost.com/p/news/item_8SdmDGtwsNXLY8tqQ9NahM.
92. Ibid.
93. "Remarks at Dar Al-Hekma College Town Hall," US Department of State website, February 16, 2010, http://www.state.gov/secretary/rm/2010/02/136789.htm.

CHAPTER 6. CRONYISM, CORRUPTION, AND "CLEAN" ENERGY

1. "Transcript of Obama's State of the Union Address," ABC News, February 12, 2013, http://abcnews.go.com/Politics/OTUS/transcript-president-barack-obamas-2013-state-union-address/story?id=18480069#.UWRDEDb6gqI.
2. Klein and Elliott, *Fool Me Twice*.
3. Carol D. Leonnig and Steven Mufson, "Obama green-tech program that backed Solyndra struggles to create jobs," *Washington Post*, September 14, 2011, http://www.washingtonpost.com/politics/obama-green-tech-program-that-backed-solyndra-struggles-to-create-jobs/2011/09/07/gIQA9Zs3SK_story.html.
4. Ivanpah Solar Generating System website, http://ivanpahsolar.com/.
5. "President Obama Highlights Brightsource Energy's Ivanpah Solar Project During Weekly Radio Address," press release, BrightSource Limitless website, October 2, 2010, http://www.brightsourceenergy.com/president-obama-highlights-brightsource-energys-ivanpah-solar-project-during-weekly-radio-address.
6. Scott Martelle, "Utility Infielder. On Obama's Commerce Department pick, business and environmentalists both say meh," *American Prospect*, June 6, 2011, http://prospect.org/cs/articles?article=utility_infielder.
7. "Achievements," Apollo Alliance website; no longer accessible.
8. Ibid.

9. "Brown Announces New Bill Providing $30 Billion in Funds to Help Auto Suppliers, Manufacturers Retool for Clean Energy Jobs," press release, official website of Sen. Sherrod Brown, US Senate, June 17, 2009; no longer accessible.

10. "Apollo Alliance Joins Sen. Sherrod Brown to Introduce Bill to Help Manufacturers Retool for Clean Energy Economy," press release, Apollo Alliance website, June 17, 2009. This article is no longer available.

11. "Sen. Brown IMPACT Legislation: Brown Proposes $30 Billion Plan To Strengthen Green Energy Manufacturers," Apollo Alliance website, no longer accessible. See "Sen. Brown Announces IMPACT Legislation," at the BlueGreen Alliance website, accessed June 5, 2013, http://www.bluegreenalliance.org/apollo/programs/gmap/sen-brown-impact-legislation.

12. "H.R. 3534, Consolidated Land, Energy, and Aquatic Resources (CLEAR) Act," Committee on Energy and Commerce, US House of Representatives, July 30, 2010. See http://www.govtrack.us/congress/bills/111/hr3534/text.

13. See the section titled "Apollo Alliance National Steering Committee," in the post titled "The Apollo Alliance for Good Jobs and Clean Energy," on the *Democratic Underground* blog, posted by pinto on January 1, 2006, http://www.democraticunderground.com/discuss/duboard.php?az=view_all&address=115x37653; and *Wikipedia*, s.v. "Jeff Jones (activist)," http://en.wikipedia.org/wiki/Jeff_Jones_(activist).

14. Federal Bureau of Investigation, "Weather Underground Organization (Weathermen)," FBI Records: The Vault, accessed June 5, 2013, http://vault.fbi.gov/Weather%20Underground%20(Weathermen).

15. "Leveraging the Stimulus," CoLab full report of March 2009, http://web.mit.edu/colab/work-project-stimulus.html.

16. "Tides Foundation and the Tides Center," DiscovertheNetworks.org; "Apollo Alliance," UndueInfluence.com.

17. John P. Holdren et al, "Ending the Energy Stalemate: A Bipartisan Strategy to Meet America's Energy Challenges," National Commission on Energy Policy, December 2004, http://belfercenter.ksg.harvard.edu/publication/4000/ending_the_energy_stalemate.html.

18. Peter Behr, "DOE Delivers Its First, Long-Awaited Nuclear Loan Guarantee," *New York Times*, February 17, 2010, http://www.nytimes.com/cwire/2010/02/17/17climatewire-doe-delivers-its-first-long-awaited-nuclear-71731.html?pagewanted=all.

19. Eric Lipton, "Ties to Obama Aided in Access for Big Utility," *New York Times*, August 23, 2012, http://www.nytimes.com/2012/08/23/us/politics/ties-to-obama-aided-in-access-for-exelon-corporation.html?pagewanted=all.

20. Ibid.

21. Aaron Klein, "Obama czar in 'clean energy' corruption?" *WND*, March 12, 2010, http://www.wnd.com/2010/03/127742/.

22. T. J. Glauthier, Advisory Board, Lawrence Berkeley National Laboratory, http://www.lbl.gov/LBL-PID/Advisory_Board/members.html.

23. Executive Profile: T. J. Gauthier, Union Drilling, Inc., BusinessWeek.com, http://investing.businessweek.com/research/stocks/people/person.asp?personId=22430751&ticker=UDRL:US&previousCapId=7670016&previousTitle=EnerNOC%2C%20Inc.; no longer accessible.

24. "Deployment, Fueled by $100 Million in Stimulus. Demonstrating Smart Charging 3.0 at Plug-In 2009 Conference," press release, GridPoint, August 10, 2009, http://www.gridpoint.com/news/PressReleaseShare/09-08-10/GridPoint%E2%80%99s_Next-Generation_Smart_Charging_Software_to_Support_Largest_U_S_Electric_Vehicle_Deployment_Fueled_by_100_Million_in_Stimulus.aspx.

25. "GridPoint to Provide Solutions for KCP&L's Smart Grid Demonstration Project," press release, GridPoint, December 1, 2009, http://www.gridpoint.com/news/PressReleaseShare/09-12-01/GridPoint_to_Provide_Solutions_for_KCP_L_s_Smart_Grid_Demonstration_Project.aspx.

26. "GridPoint to Provide Software Solutions for SMUD's Smart Grid Solar Project," press release, GridPoint, November 3, 2009, http://www.gridpoint.com/news/PressReleaseShare/09-11-03/GridPoint_to_Provide_Software_Solutions_for_SMUD%E2%80%99s_Smart_Grid_Solar_Project.aspx.

27. Associated Press, "Argonne National Laboratory Gets $99 Million Boost from Stimulus," *Huffington Post*, May 1, 2009, http://www.huffingtonpost.com/2009/03/31/argonne-national-laborato_n_181483.html.
28. "GridPoint Enables U.S. Postal Service to Reduce Energy Costs in Facilities Nationwide with Energy Management Systems. Supports USPS Goal to Achieve 30 Percent Reduction in Facility Energy Usage," press release, Grid Point, May 24, 2010, http://www.gridpoint.com/news/PressReleaseShare/10-05-24/GridPoint_Enables_U_S_Postal_Service_to_Reduce_Energy_Costs_in_Facilities_Nationwide_with_Energy_Management_Systems.aspx.
29. Barack Obama Inauguration Donors 2008 (Top Donors Only), OpenSecrets.org, http://www.opensecrets.org/pres08/inaug_all.php.
30. J. E. Dyer, "Navy buys biofuel for $16 a gallon," *Hot Air* (blog), December 10, 2011, http://hotair.com/greenroom/archives/2011/12/10/navy-buys-biofuel-for-16-a-gallon/.
31. Edgar A. Gunther, "Top 10 Solar 1603 Treasury Grant Awards," Gunther Portfolio, December 10, 2010, http://guntherportfolio.com/2010/12/top-10-solar-1603-treasury-grant-awards/.
32. Michael Scherer, "Inside Obama's Idea Factory in Washington," *Time*, November 21, 2008 http://www.time.com/time/politics/article/0,8599,1861305,00.html.
33. "New York City Mayor Bloomberg's Live in Girlfriend Owns the Park that Wall Street Protesters Occupy and She Won't Ask Them to Go," *Shutking* (blog), October 7, 2011, http://shutking.blogspot.com/2011/10/new-york-city-mayor-bloombergs-live-in.html.
34. Cassandra Sweet, "DOE Guarantees Loans for Several Renewable-Energy Projects," Dow Jones Newswires, September 23, 2011, http://www.foxbusiness.com/industries/2011/09/23/doe-guarantees-loans-for-several-renewable-energy-projects/; editorial, "A NH Solyndra?" *Union Leader* (Manchester, NH), September 28, 2011, http://unionleader.com/article/20110928/OPINION01/709289961.
35. 2011 Lobbying Report: Heather Podesta + Partners, LLC, Senate.gov, http://soprweb.senate.gov/index.cfm?event=getFilingDetails&filingID=CFD1F386-79B8-4CAE-91E0-7DB4F1D82512.
36. Aaron Metha, "Top 5 lobbyist bundlers; power couple Tony and Heather Podesta top the list," iWatchNews.org, July 28, 2011, http://www.iwatchnews.org/2011/07/28/5402/top-5-lobbyist-bundlers-power-couple-tony-and-heather-podesta-top-list.
37. Timothy P. Carver, "Obama's revolving door always open to Podestas," *Washington Examiner*, November 4, 2009, reported in http://romanticpoet.wordpress.com/tag/podesta-obama-relationship-white-house-visits/.
38. Power Plants, Duke Energy, http://www.duke-energy.com/power-plants/nuclear.asp.
39. Timothy P. Carney, "The power company underwriting the DNC for $10M," *Washington Examiner*, February 20, 2012, http://campaign2012.washingtonexaminer.com/blogs/beltway-confidential/power-company-underwriting-dnc-10m/384866; Wynton Hall, "DNC Co-Chairman's Company Landed $230.4M in Obama Stimulus Money," *Big Government*, February 21, 2012, http://www.breitbart.com/Big-Government/2012/02/21/dnc-co-chairmans-company-landed-230-4m-in-obama-stimulus-money.
40. Thomas Mucha, "Obama touts another green company in State of the Union. It immediately goes bankrupt." *Global Post*, January 26, 2012, http://www.globalpost.com/dispatches/globalpost-blogs/macro/obama-names-another-green-company-it-immediately-goes-bankrupt.
41. Bill Vlasic and Matthew L. Wald, "Maker of Batteries Files for Bankruptcy," *New York Times*, October 16, 2012, http://www.nytimes.com/2012/10/17/business/battery-maker-a123-systems-files-for-bankruptcy.html?_r=0.
42. Jim Harger, "Employment is down to 150 at controversial LG Chem plant in Holland, says company spokesman," Michigan Live, February 14, 2013, http://www.mlive.com/business/west-michigan/index.ssf/2013/02/employment_is_down_to_150_at_c.html.
43. "Rentech to Close Product Demonstration Unit," RenTech Inc. press release, http://phx.corporate-ir.net/phoenix.zhtml?c=66629&p=irol-irkitArticle&ID=1790402&highlight=.
44. Aaron Klein, "Now Bush accused in 'green stimulus' madness," *WND*, June 27, 2012, http://www.wnd.com/2012/06/now-bush-accused-in-green-stimulus-madness/.
45. Ibid.
46. "The Cellulosic Ethanol Debacle," *Wall Street Journal*, December 14, 2011, http://online.wsj.com/article/SB10001424052970204012004577072470158115782.html.

47. Klein, "Now Bush accused in 'green stimulus' madness."
48. Jim Angle, "EPA blasted for requiring oil refiners to add type of fuel that's merely hypothetical," FoxNews.com, June 21, 2012, http://www.foxnews.com/politics/2012/06/21/regulation-requires-oil-refiners-use-millions-gallons-fuel-that-is-nonexistent/.
49. Ibid.
50. Klein, "Now Bush accused in 'green stimulus' madness."
51. "U.S. to Help Finance Cellulose Ethanol Plant" *Wall Street Journal*, July 7, 2011, http://online.wsj.com/article/SB10001424052702303365804576431723536395198.html.

CHAPTER 7. BIG BROTHER OBAMA'S SURVEILLANCE REGIME

1. Naomi Gilens, "New Justice Department Documents Show Huge Increase in Warrantless Electronic Surveillance," ACLU.org, September 27, 2012, http://www.aclu.org/blog/national-security-technology-and-liberty/new-justice-department-documents-show-huge-increase.
2. Trevor Trimm, "Congress Disgracefully Approves the FISA Warrantless Spying Bill for Five More Years, Rejects All Privacy Amendments," Electronic Frontier Foundation, December 28, 2012, https://www.eff.org/deeplinks/2012/12/congress-disgracefully-approves-fisa-warrantless-eavesdropping-bill-five-more.
3. Michelle Richardson, "In House Hearing, ACLU Tells Congress to Fix FISA," ACLU *Blog of Rights*, June 1, 2012, http://www.aclu.org/blog/national-security/house-hearing-aclu-tells-congress-fix-fisa.
4. "Senate Reauthorizes Warrantless Wiretapping: After Defeating Moderate Reforms, Senate Extends Unchecked Surveillance Powers for Five Years," press release, ACLU, December 28, 2012, http://www.aclu.org/national-security/senate-reauthorizes-warrantless-wiretapping.
5. Hope Yen, "Hagel: Bush Must Explain Spy Program More," Associated Press Online, January 29, 2006, http://www.highbeam.com/doc/1P1-117895185.html.
6. Ibid.
7. Ibid.
8. H.R. 3773, the "RESTORE Act of 2007 (Responsible Electronic Surveillance That Is Overseen, Reviewed, and Effective Act of 2007)," http://judiciary.house.gov/hearings/pdf/HR3773FISA.pdf.
9. Greg Sargent, "MoveOn and Top Bloggers to Launch Campaign Pressuring Hillary and Obama to Back Dodd on FISA," *Talking Points Memo* "Election Central," October 23, 2007, http://web.archive.org/web/20110226015823/http://tpmelectioncentral.talkingpointsmemo.com/2007/10/moveon_to_launch_campaign_pressuring_hillary_and_obama_to.php.
10. Greg Sargent, "Obama Camp Says It: He'l Support Filibuster of Any Bill Containing Telecom Immunity," *Talking Points Memo* "Election Central," October 24, 2007, http://web.archive.org/web/20080708081806/http://tpmelectioncentral.talkingpointsmemo.com/2007/10/obama_camp_says_it_hell_suppor.php.
11. Paul Kane, "Obama Supports FISA Legislation, Angering Left," *Washington Post*, June 20, 2008, http://blog.washingtonpost.com/44/2008/06/obama-supports-fisa-legislatio.html.
12. Eric Lichtblau, "Deal Reached in Congress to Rewrite Rules on Wiretapping," *New York Times*, June 20, 2008, https://www.nytimes.com/2008/06/20/washington/20fisacnd.html.
13. Matthew Vadum, "We Have Ted Cruz's List: Harvard Law Really Is Littered with Communists," *American Thinker*, March 5, 2013, http://www.americanthinker.com/2013/03/we_have_ted_cruzs_list_harvard_law_really_islittered_with_communists.html. Vadum writes: "Critical legal theory takes the neo-Marxist perspective that the law is concerned with power, not justice. Because the law is a fraud perpetrated on the people, an oppressive tool of capitalism, imperialism, sexism, racism, and whatever other *ism* it is currently fashionable to attack, the legal system should be criticized endlessly as a means of tearing it down. If you're a communist it's natural to embrace critical legal theory as a way of changing American society." Jack M. Balkin, "Critical Legal Theory Today," *Balkinization* (blog), February 7, 2008, http://balkin.blogspot.com/2008/02/critical-legal-theory-today.html.
14. Constitution in 2020, http://www.constitution2020.org/.

15. Aaron Klein, "Sunstein: Obama, not courts, should interpret law. 'Beliefs and commitments' of nation's leader should supersede judges," *WND*, September 18, 2009, http://www.wnd.com/2009/09/110103/.
16. Jack Balkin, "Why Obama Kinda Likes the FISA Bill (but He Won't Come Out and Say It)," *Balkinization*, June 20, 2008, http://balkin.blogspot.com/2008/06/why-obama-kinda-likes-fisa-bill-but-he.html.
17. Kane, "Obama Supports FISA Legislation, Angering Left."
18. Ed Morrissey, "Another one hits the bus: Obama reverses on FISA," *Hot Air* (blog), June 21, 2008, http://hotair.com/archives/2008/06/21/another-one-hits-the-bus-obama-reverses-on-fisa/.
19. Balkin, "Why Obama Kinda Likes the FISA Bill (But He Won't Come Out and Say It)."
20. Ibid.
21. Jim Cook, "Tomorrow, Congress Will Pass a Bill Permitting PHYSICAL SEARCHES without Warrant at its Sole Discretion. Put Down the Chips, Put Down the Remote and Call Your Representative. Now," *Irregular Times*, June 19, 2008, http://irregulartimes.com/index.php/archives/2008/06/19/congress-will-pass-hr6304-physical-searches-no-warrants/.
22. Ibid.
23. Marty Lederman, "The Key Questions about the New FISA Bill," *Balkinization*, June 22, 2008, http://balkin.blogspot.com/2008/06/key-questions-about-new-fisa-bill.html.
24. Martin S. Lederman and David D. Cole, *The National Security Agency's Domestic Spying Program: Framing the Debate, in National Security, Civil Liberties, and the War on Terror* (Amherst, NY: Prometheus, 2011), 306–10.
25. "Senate Passes Unconstitutional Spying Bill and Grants Sweeping Immunity to Phone Companies," ACLU, July 9, 2008, http://www.aclu.org/national-security/senate-passes-unconstitutional-spying-bill-and-grants-sweeping-immunity-phone-comp.
26. Ibid.
27. Jack Balkin, "The Inspector General's Report and the Horse That Is Already out of the Barn Door," *Balkinization*, July 11, 2009, http://balkin.blogspot.com/2009/07/inspector-generals-report-and-horse.html.
28. Sean Lengell, "Obama signs act allowing spying on terrorists. Opponents fear innocent citizens could be caught in investigations," *Washington Times*, December 30, 2012, http://www.washingtontimes.com/news/2012/dec/30/obama-signs-act-allowing-spying-on-terrorists-oppo/?page=all.
29. Glenn Greenwald, "NSA collecting phone records of millions of Verizon customers daily. Exclusive: Top secret court order requiring Verizon to hand over all call data shows scale of domestic surveillance under Obama," *Guardian* (UK), June 5, 2012, http://www.guardian.co.uk/world/2013/jun/06/nsa-phone-records-verizon-court-order.
30. Steven Aftergood, "New FISA Court Judge Appointed," FAS.org, May 24, 2006, http://blogs.fas.org/secrecy/2006/05/new_fisa_court_judge_appointed/.
31. Greenwald, "NSA collecting phone records of millions of Verizon customers daily."
32. Andy Greenberg, "NSA's Verizon Spying Order Specifically Targeted Americans, Not Foreigners" *Forbes*, June 5, 2013, http://www.forbes.com/sites/andygreenberg/2013/06/05/nsas-verizon-spying-order-specifically-targeted-americans-not-foreigners/.
33. Associated Press, "Report: Gov't scooping up Verizon phone records," APNews.myway.com, June 6, 2012, http://apnews.myway.com/article/20130606/DA6O4MG03.html.
34. "State and County Quick Facts," US Department of the Census, http://quickfacts.census.gov/qfd/states/00000.html.
35. Greenwald, "NSA collecting phone records of millions of Verizon customers daily."
36. Cindy Cohn and Mark Rumold, "Confirmed: The NSA Is Spying on Millions of Americans," Electronic Frontier Foundation, June 5, 2012, https://www.eff.org/deeplinks/2013/06/confirmed-nsa-spying-millions-americans.
37. "White House defends NSA order to Verizon to reveal call data," UPI, June 6, 2013, http://www.upi.com/Top_News/US/2013/06/06/White-House-defends-NSA-order-to-Verizon-to-reveal-call-data/UPI-97251370499360/?spt=hts&or=1.

38. Siobhan Gorman, Evan Perez, and Janet Hook, "U.S. Collects Vast Data Trove. NSA Monitoring Includes Three Major Phone Companies, as Well as Online Activity," *Wall Street Journal*, June 7, 2013, http://online.wsj.com/article/SB1000142412788732429910457852911 2289298922.html.

39. Eli Lake, "Phone Records Shared with U.K.," *Daily Beast*, June 7, 2013, http://www.thedailybeast.com/articles/2013/06/07/verizon-data-shared-with-u-k.html.

40. Josh Peterson, "Analysis: NSA Utah Data Center would be world's biggest iPod," *Daily Caller*, April 21, 2013, http://dailycaller.com/2013/04/21/analysis-nsa-utah-data-center-would-be-worlds-biggest-ipod/; James Bamford, "The NSA Is Building the Country's Biggest Spy Center (Watch What You Say)," Wired.com, March 15, 2012, http://www.wired.com/threatlevel/2012/03/ff_nsadatacenter/all/.

41. Rich Miller, "NSA Plans $1.6 Billion Utah Data Center," Data Center Knowledge, July 1, 2009, http://www.datacenterknowledge.com/archives/2009/07/01/nsa-plans-16-billion-utah-data-center/.

42. Bamford, "The NSA Is Building the Country's Biggest Spy Center."

43. Rich Trenholm, "NSA to store yottabytes in Utah data centre," c|net, November 2, 2009, http://crave.cnet.co.uk/gadgets/nsa-to-store-yottabytes-in-utah-data-centre-49304118/.

44. Bamford, "The NSA Is Building the Country's Biggest Spy Center."

45. Utah Data Center, Domestic Surveillance Directorate, NSA.gov, http://nsa.gov1.info/utah-data-center/.

46. Greenberg, "NSA's Verizon Spying Order Specifically Targeted Americans, Not Foreigners."

47. Public Law 112-283, 18 USC § 1385 – Use of Army and Air Force as posse comitatus, http://www.law.cornell.edu/uscode/text/18/1385.

48. "FBI begins installation of $1 billion face recognition system across America, *Russia Today*, September 7, 2012, http://rt.com/usa/fbi-recognition-system-ngi-640/.

49. Ibid.

50. Gene Howington, "The Shame and Waste of Fusion Centers," JonthanTurley.org, October 7, 2012, http://jonathanturley.org/2012/10/07/the-shame-and-waste-of-fusion-centers/.

51. Mark Williams, "The Total Information Awareness Project Lives On. Technology behind the Pentagon's controversial data-mining project has been acquired by NSA, and is probably in use," *MIT Technology Review*, April 26, 2006, http://www.technologyreview.com/news/405707/the-total-information-awareness-project-lives-on/.

52. General Accounting Office, *Data Mining. Federal Efforts Cover a Wide Range of Uses*, GAO-04-548. Report to the Ranking Minority Member, Subcommittee on Financial Management, the Budget, and International Security, Committee on Governmental Affairs, U.S. Senate, May 2004, https://epic.org/privacy/profiling/gao_dm_rpt.pdf.

53. Jeffrey Rosen, "Total Information Awareness," *New York Times*, December 15, 2002, http://www.nytimes.com/2002/12/15/magazine/15TOTA.html.

54. "Data Mining Poses Privacy Challenge" in GAO report on data mining, May 2004, 5.

55. Jeb Babbin, "Merge the 'Terror' Lists to Prevent the Next Attack," *Human Events*, January 4, 2010, http://www.humanevents.com/article.php?id=35044.

56. Ibid.

57. National Counterterrorism Center, "Terrorist Identities Datamart Environment (TIDE)," http://www.nctc.gov/docs/Tide_Fact_Sheet.pdf.

58. Julia Angwin, "U.S. Terrorism Agency to Tap a Vast Database of Citizens," *Wall Street Journal*, December 13, 2012, http://online.wsj.com/article/SB10001424127887324478304578171623040640006.html.

59. National Commission on Terrorist Attacks upon the United States, "Seventh public hearing of the National Commission on Terrorist Attacks upon the United States: Statement of Russell E. Travers to the National Commission on Terrorist Attacks upon the United States," January 26, 2004, http://www.9-11commission.gov/hearings/hearing7/witness_travers.htm; John Brennan, "Testimony: United States Senate Committee on the Judiciary: Information Sharing and Coordination for Visa Issuance: Our First Line of Defense for Homeland Security," September 23, 2003, http://www.globalsecurity.org/security/library/congress/2003_h/030923-brennan.htm.

60. Brennan, "Testimony."

61. "Father of Terror Suspect Reportedly Warned U.S. about Son," FoxNews.com, December 26, 2009, http://www.foxnews.com/story/0,2933,581193,00.html.

62. David Alan Jordan, *Free Course Book for Course 3: Statutory Law and Intelligence 2011* (n.p.: David Alan Jordan, 2011), 224; see also statement of Russell E. Travers to the National Commission on Terrorist Attacks upon the United States, Seventh Public Hearing, January 26, 2004, http://govinfo.library.unt.edu/911/hearings/hearing7/witness_travers.htm.

63. John Markoff, "Pentagon Plans a Computer System That Would Peek at Personal Data of Americans," *New York Times*, November 9, 2002, http://www.nytimes.com/2002/11/09/politics/09COMP.html.

64. Information Awareness Office, DARPA, Internet Archive, August 2, 2002, http://web.archive.org/web/20020802012150/http://www.darpa.mil/iao/.

65. "Total Information Awareness" *SourceWatch*, last modified April 20, 2008, http://www.sourcewatch.org/index.php/Total_Information_Awareness.

66. Ibid.

67. Excluding the TIDE program from the list, we have the National Security Branch Analysis Center dating from 2007, which was suspected of being a reincarnation of TIA. TIA reappeared in various other forms or as part of other personal surveillance data mining programs: ADVISE (2005–2006 or perhaps earlier); MATRIX (2003, terminated 2005); Novel Intelligence from Massive Data (NIMD) (2002); and TALON (Threat and Local Observation Notice reports).

68. Inspector General, US Department of Defense, *The Threat and Local Observation Notice (TALON) Program*, June 27, 2007, http://www.fas.org/irp/agency/dod/talon.pdf, 1.

69. Brian McWilliams, "DoD Logging Unverified Tips," Wired.com, June 25, 2003, http://www.wired.com/politics/law/news/2003/06/59365.

70. Inspector General, US Department of Defense, *The Threat and Local Observation Notice (TALON) Program*, June 27, 2007, 1.

71. Jeffrey Richelson, "The Pentagon's Counterspies. The Counterintelligence Field Activity," National Security Archive, September 17, 2007, http://www.gwu.edu/~nsarchiv/NSAEBB/NSAEBB230/index.htm.

72. Walter Pincus, "Defense Facilities Pass Along Reports of Suspicious Activity," *Washington Post*, December 11, 2005, http://www.washingtonpost.com/wp-dyn/content/article/2005/12/10/AR2005121000893.html.

73. Richelson, "The Pentagon's Counterspies."

74. Inspector General, US Department of Defense, *The Threat and Local Observation Notice (TALON) Program*, 2: USNORTHCOM's mission was "to conduct operations to deter, prevent, and defeat threats and aggression aimed at the United States, its territories, and interests within its area of responsibility."

75. Ibid., 1, 2, 4–5, 8.

76. Ibid.

77. Richelson, "The Pentagon's Counterspies."

78. "Privacy Impact Assessment for the eGuardian Threat Tracking System," FBI.gov, https://www.fbi.gov/foia/privacy-impact-assessments/eguardian-threat.

79. Williams, "The Total Information Awareness Project Lives On."

80. Public Law 112-283.

81. Jay Stanley, *The Surveillance-Industrial Complex: How the American Government is Conscripting Businesses and Individuals in the Construction of a Surveillance Society*, ACLU, August 2004, http://www.aclu.org/files/FilesPDFs/surveillance_report.pdf, 1.

82. Ibid., 2.

83. Ibid., 3.

84. "If You See Something, Say Something," Department of Homeland Security, http://www.dhs.gov/if-you-see-something-say-something.

85. Lisa Simeone, "TSA expands beyond airport screening," *TSA News Blog*, November 22, 2011, http://tsanewsblog.com/112/news/tsa-expands-beyond-airport-screening/.

86. Ibid.

87. "Secretary Napolitano Announces Expansion of 'If You See Something, Say Something' Campaign to Walmart Stores Across the Nation," Department of Homeland Security, December 6, 2010, http://www.dhs.gov/news/2010/12/06/secretary-napolitano-announces-expansion-if-you-see-something-say-something-campaign.

88. Stanley, *The Surveillance-Industrial Complex.*

89. Ryan Gallagher, "'Google for spies' draws ire from rights groups," *Sydney Morning Herald*, February 11, 2013, http://www.smh.com.au/digital-life/consumer-security/google-for-spies-draws-ire-from-rights-groups-20130211-2e75y.html#ixzz2KY9r4cJJ.

90. "How Raytheon software tracks you online—video," UK *Guardian*, February 10, 2013, http://www.guardian.co.uk/world/video/2013/feb/10/raytheon-software-tracks-online-video.

91. Gallagher, "'Google for spies' draws ire from rights groups."

92. Ibid.

93. Suzanne Choney, "Super search engine tracks terrorists—and you—via social networks," NBC News, February 2013, http://www.nbcnews.com/technology/technolog/super-search-engine-tracks-terrorists-you-social-networks-1B8327842?ocid=msnhp&pos=7.

94. "NSA slides explain the PRISM data-collection program," *Washington Post*, June 6, 2013, http://www.washingtonpost.com/wp-srv/special/politics/prism-collection-documents/m/.

95. Barton Gellman and Laura Poitras, "U.S. intelligence mining data from nine U.S. Internet companies in broad secret program," *Washington Post*, June 6, 2013, http://m.washingtonpost.com/investigations/us-intelligence-mining-data-from-nine-us-internet-companies-in-broad-secret-program/2013/06/06/3a0c0da8-cebf-11e2-8845-d970ccb04497_story.html.

96. "NSA slides explain the PRISM data-collection program."

97. Gellman and Poitras, "U.S. intelligence mining data from nine U.S. Internet companies in broad secret program."

98. Ibid.

99. Siobhan Gorman, "U.S. Plans Cyber Shield for Utilities, Companies," *Wall Street Journal*, July 8, 2010, http://online.wsj.com/article/SB10001424052748704545004575352983850463108.html?mod=WSJ_hpp_MIDDLETopStories#articleTabs%3Darticle.

100. "Perfect Citizen" file, Electronic Privacy Information Center, https://epic.org/privacy/cyber-security/nsa-perfect-citizen/default.html.

101. "EPIC Obtains Documents on NSA's 'Perfect Citizen' Program," Electronic Privacy Information Center, January 2, 2013, https://epic.org/2013/01/epic-obtains-documents-on-nsas.html; Gorman, "U.S. Plans Cyber Shield for Utilities, Companies."

102. Nathan Ingraham, "NSA's secret 'Perfect Citizen' cybersecurity program detailed by recently-released documents," The Verge, January 4, 2013, http://www.theverge.com/2013/1/4/3835796/nsa-perfect-citizen-cyber-security-program-confirmed.

103. Lance Whitney, "NSA offers explanation of Perfect Citizen. Claiming that a *Wall Street Journal* story about Perfect Citizen was inaccurate, the federal agency offers its own take on the project but serves up few details," C|Net.com, July 9, 2010, http://news.cnet.com/8301-1009_3-20010155-83.html.

104. Aliya Sternstein, "DHS secret network at the forefront of nationwide intelligence sharing," NextGov.com, March 12, 2012, http://www.nextgov.com/defense/2012/03/dhs-secret-network-at-the-forefront-of-nationwide-intelligence-sharing/50806/; Executive Order 13549 of August 18, 2010, Classified National Security Information Program for State, Local, Tribal, and Private Sector Entities, http://www.archives.gov/isoo/policy-documents/eo-13549.html.

105. Executive Order 13549; National Security Information Program for State, Local, Tribal and Private Sector Entities Implementing Directive, Department of Homeland Security, February 2012, http://www.dhs.gov/xlibrary/assets/mgmt/mgmt-classified-national-security-program-implementation-directive.pdf; Sternstein, "DHS secret network at the forefront of nationwide intelligence sharing."

106. Quintan Wiktorowicz, "Working to Counter Online Radicalization to Violence in the United States," White House Blog, February 5, 2013, http://www.whitehouse.gov/blog/2013/02/05/working-counter-online-radicalization-violence-united-states.

107. "Sovereign Citizens," FBI, http://www.fbi.gov/news/stories/2010/april/sovereigncitizens_041310.

108. Wiktorowicz, "Working to Counter Online Radicalization to Violence in the United States."

109. Ibid.
110. Eric Engleman, "Cybersecurity Bill Killed, Paving Way for Executive Order," Bloomberg. com, November 14, 2012, http://www.bloomberg.com/news/2012-11-15/cybersecurity-bill-killed-paving-way-for-executive-order.html.
111. Jennifer Martinez, "Sources: White House to issue cybersecurity order Wednesday," *The Hill* (blog), February 11, 2013, http://thehill.com/blogs/hillicon-valley/technology/282269-white-house-poised-to-release-cybersecurity-executive-order-on-wednesday.
112. Aaron Klein, "Obama czar proposed government 'infiltrate' social network sites. Sunstein wants agents to 'undermine' talk in chat rooms, message boards," *WND*, January 12, 2012, http://www.wnd.com/2012/01/obama-czar-proposed-government-infiltrate-social-network-sites/.
113. Mark Hosenball, "Homeland Security watches Twitter, social media," Reuters, January 11, 2012, http://www.reuters.com/article/2012/01/11/us-usa-homelandsecurity-websites-idUSTRE80A1RC20120111.
114. Ibid.
115. Charlie Savage, "Federal Contractor Monitored Social Network Sites," *New York Times*, January 13, 2012, https://www.nytimes.com/2012/01/14/us/federal-security-program-monitored-public-opinion.html?_r=0.
116. A Wiki of Social Media Monitoring Solutions, accessed February 13, 2013, http://wiki. kenburbary.com/social-meda-monitoring-wiki.
117. Angwin, "U.S. Terrorism Agency to Tap a Vast Database of Citizens"; Charlie Savage, "U.S. Relaxes Limits on Use of Data in Terror Analysis," *New York Times*, March 22, 2012, https://www.nytimes.com/2012/03/23/us/politics/us-moves-to-relax-some-restrictions-for-counterterrorism-analysis.html.
118. Savage, "U.S. Relaxes Limits on Use of Data in Terror Analysis."
119. Angwin, "U.S. Terrorism Agency to Tap a Vast Database of Citizens."
120. Open Data Sites, http://www.data.gov/opendatasites.
121. Savage, "U.S. Relaxes Limits on Use of Data in Terror Analysis."
122. Ibid.
123. "More About FBI Spying," ACLU, January 22, 2013, http://www.aclu.org/spy-files/more-about-fbi-spying.
124. Ibid.

CHAPTER 8. THE TRUTH ABOUT FUSION CENTERS

1. Gene Howington, "The Shame and Waste of Fusion Centers," JonthanTurley.org, October 7, 2012, http://jonathanturley.org/2012/10/07/the-shame-and-waste-of-fusion-centers/.
2. Gregory Patin, "Fusion centers: Invading your privacy at your expense (Photos)," *Examiner*, October 14, 2012, http://www.examiner.com/article/fusion-centers-invading-your-privacy-at-your-expense.
3. Wendy McElroy, "An American Stasi? The surveillance state," *Freeman*, February 2010, http://www.informationliberation.com/?id=31577.
4. Howington, "The Shame and Waste of Fusion Centers."
5. McElroy, "An American Stasi? The surveillance state."
6. Public Law 107–56—Oct. 26, 2001, Uniting and Strengthening America by Providing Appropriate Tools Required to Intercept and Obstruct Terrorism (USA PATRIOT ACT) Act of 2001, http://www.gpo.gov/fdsys/pkg/PLAW-107publ56/html/PLAW-107publ56.htm.
7. "Obama Signs Last-Minute Patriot Act Extension," FoxNews.com, May 27, 2011, http://www.foxnews.com/politics/2011/05/27/senate-clearing-way-extend-patriot-act/|date.
8. Decree of the Reich President for the Protection of the People and State (Reichstag Fire Decree), February 28, 1933, http://germanhistorydocs.ghi-dc.org/pdf/eng/English%203_5. pdf.
9. See Michael German, "FBI Official Agrees with ACLU: Suspicionless Surveillance is Ineffective and Counterproductive," ACLU *Blog of Rights*, March 9, 2012, http://www.aclu.org/blog/national-security-religion-belief/fbi-official-agrees-aclu-suspicionless-surveillance.

10. Eric J. Schmertz, et al., *President Reagan and the World* (Westport, CT: Greenwood Press, 1997), 181; *July 1985, President Reagan's Cabinet-Level Task Force Chaired by Vice-President George Bush—George Bush, Combating Terrorism: The Official Report of President Reagan's Cabinet-Level Task Force* (n.p.: Diane Publishing, 1987), 4.

11. NSDD 179, Task Force on Combatting Terrorism, July 19, 1985, established a task force, to be headed by Vice President George Bush, to review and evaluate U.S. policy and programs in the counterterrorism area. In particular, the task force was to assess national priorities assigned to combat terrorism, especially concerning intelligence responsibilities; to assign responsibilities after a terrorist incident; and to evaluate laws and law enforcement programs concerning terrorism (http://www.gwu.edu/~nsarchiv/NSAEBB/NSAEBB55/nsdd179.pdf).

12. Schmertz, et al., *President Reagan and the World*, 181.

13. Ibid.

14. *Federal Support for and Involvement in State in Local Fusion Centers*, Majority and Minority Staff Report, Senate Permanent Subcommittee on Investigations, October 3, 2012, https://www.govexec.com/media/gbc/docs/pdfs_edit/100312cc1.pdf, 83; Homeland Security Act of 2002 (P.L. 107-296).

15. Michael Scardaville, "Principles for Creating an Effective Dept of Homeland Security," Heritage Foundation, June 12, 2002, http://www.heritage.org/research/reports/2002/06/principles-for-creating-an-effective-dept-of-homeland-security.

16. Sam MacDonald, "Keeping America out of Harm's Way: From a National Health-Surveillance Network to Better Whistle-Blower Protection, Security Experts Provide Their Commonsense Ideas for Improving Homeland Security," *Insight on the News*, May 13, 2002.

17. *The 9/11 Commission Report*, http://www.9-11commission.gov/report/911Report.pdf.

18. United States Senate Permanent Subcommittee on Investigations, Committee on Homeland Security and Governmental Affairs, *Federal Support for and Involvement in State and Local Fusion Centers Majority And Minority Staff Report*, 11.

19. Daniel M. Gerstein, *Securing America's Future: National Strategy in the Information Age* (Westport, CT: Praeger Security International, 2004), 153.

20. *Federal Support for and Involvement in State in Local Fusion Centers*, 12, 13. Charles E. Allen is currently a principal of the Chertoff Group, a global security advisory firm run by his former DHS boss, Michael Chertoff.

21. Marcy Wheeler, "The Senate Report on Fusion Center Fails to Ask or Answer the Most Basic Question," *Emptywheel* (blog), October 5, 2012, http://www.emptywheel.net/2012/10/05/the-senate-report-on-fusion-center-fails-to-ask-or-answer-the-most-basic-question/.

22. Robin Simcox and Emily Dyer, *Al-Qaeda in the United States. A complete analysis of terrorism offenses*, February 2013, http://henryjacksonsociety.org/wp-content/uploads/2013/02/Al-Qaeda-in-the-USAbridged-version-LOWRES-Final.pdf.

23. Ibid., 12.

24. H.R. 1 (110th): Implementing Recommendations of the 9/11 Commission Act of 2007, introduced January 5, 2007, by Rep. Bennie Thompson (D-Miss.) and signed into law by President George W. Bush, August 3, 2007, http://www.govtrack.us/congress/bills/110/hr1.

25. *Federal Support for and Involvement in State in Local Fusion Centers*, 13.

26. Ibid.; Senate Votes on H.R. 1 (110th): Implementing Recommendations of the 9/11 Commission Act of 2007 (On the Conference Report), July 26, 2007, http://www.govtrack.us/congress/votes/110-2007/s284.

27. "Implementing Recommendations of the 9/11 Commission Act of 2007—Conference Report—(Senate, July 26, 2007)," Library of Congress, http://thomas.loc.gov/cgi-bin/query/z?r110:S26JY7-0018:; Barack Obama, speech to College Democrats of America, Columbia, SC, July 26, 2007, transcript, http://www.asksam.com/ebooks/releases.asp?file=Obama-Speeches.ask&dn=College%20Democrats%20of%20America.

28. *National Security Strategy: 2010*, http://www.whitehouse.gov/sites/default/files/rss_viewer/national_security_strategy.pdf.

29. Testimony of DHS Secretary Janet Napolitano before the Senate Homeland Security and Governmental Affairs Committee, "President Obama's Fiscal 2013 Budget Proposal for the Homeland Security Department," March 21, 2012.

30. *Federal Support for and Involvement in State in Local Fusion Centers*, 10; Homeland Security Act of 2002 (P.L. 107-296).
31. "Fusion Centers: Coping with 'Data Crush," FEMA Responder Knowledge Base, February 14, 2012, https://www.rkb.us/newsdetail.cfm?news_id=1200&query=&overridesubtype=998.
32. "The 72 Threat Fusion Centers Were Designed to Threaten You," *Video Rebel's Blog*, February 12, 2012, https://vidrebel.wordpress.com/2012/02/12/the-72-threat-fusion-centers-were-designed-to-threaten-you/.
33. Neil Gordon, "Senate Report Silent on Fusion Center Reliance on Contractors," Project on Government Oversight (POGO) blog, October 3, 2012, http://pogoblog.typepad.com/pogo/2012/10/senate-report-silent-on-fusion-center-reliance-on-contractors.html.
34. Ibid.
35. Admin, "It's time to pull the plug on fusion centers!" Privacy SOS/ACLU, October 4, 2012, http://privacysos.org/node/838.
36. Senate Hearing, Nominations of Robert D. Jamison and W. Ross Ashley III, November 9, 2007, http://www.gpo.gov/fdsys/pkg/CHRG-110shrg38983/html/CHRG-110shrg38983.htm; Profile: W. Ross Ashley III, *Businessweek*, http://investing.businessweek.com/research/stocks/private/person.asp?personId=8866872&privcapId=6637365&previousCapId=2514851&previousTitle=Albright%20Stonebridge%20Group; "Government," uReveal.com, http://www.ureveal.com/Government.
37. Admin, "It's time to pull the plug on fusion centers!"
38. Mark Hoover, "ICF takes on data fusion center support for DHS," *Washington Technology*, October 24, 2012, http://washingtontechnology.com/articles/2012/10/24/icf-wins-18-million-contract-for-fusion-centers.aspx.
39. "What's Wrong With Fusion Centers – Executive Summary," ACLU, December 5, 2007, http://www.aclu.org/technology-and-liberty/whats-wrong-fusion-centers-executive-summary.
40. Ibid.
41. Transcript: First Hour of Rand Paul's Filibuster, March 6, 2013.
42. *Federal Support for and Involvement in State in Local Fusion Centers*, 2, 83, 85, 89.
43. Ibid., 3, 31, 32, 39, 40, 42.
44. Ibid., 2, 35, 57.
45. Wheeler, "The Senate Report on Fusion Center Fails to Ask or Answer the Most Basic Question."
46. Fusion Center Success Stories, Department of Homeland Security, http://www.dhs.gov/fusion-center-success-stories.
47. *Federal Support for and Involvement in State in Local Fusion Centers*, 95.
48. Ibid., 45, 47, 52, 54, 55.
49. Ibid., 3, 62, 64, 71.
50. Admin, "It's time to pull the plug on fusion centers!"
51. Ibid.
52. Becky Akers, "Doggone, They Lied to Us AGAIN," LewRockwell.com, October 4, 2012, http://lewrockwell.com/akers/akers195.html.
53. *Federal Support for and Involvement in State in Local Fusion Centers*, 93.
54. Ibid., 8.
55. Wheeler, "The Senate Report on Fusion Center Fails to Ask or Answer the Most Basic Question."
56. Jack Kenny, "DHS Fusion Centers Spend Much, Learn Little, Mislead a Lot," *The New American* (blog), October 3, 2013, http://www.thenewamerican.com/usnews/crime/item/13097-dhs-fusion-centers-spend-much-learn-little-mislead-a-lot.

CHAPTER 9. DHS ARMY—THE EMERGING POLICE STATE

1. Abraham Lincoln, "Address before the Young Men's Lyceum of Springfield, Illinois," January 27, 1838, http://constitution.org/lincoln/lyceum.htm.
2. From the United States Constitution:

[Congress is] *To provide for calling forth the Militia to execute the Laws of the Union, suppress Insurrections and repel Invasions; [and] To provide for organizing, arming, and disciplining, the Militia, and for governing such Part of them as may be employed in the Service of the United States, reserving to the States respectively, the Appointment of the Officers, and the Authority of training the Militia according to the discipline prescribed by Congress.*—Article 1, Section 8, pars. 15–16

The United States shall guarantee to every State in this Union a Republican Form of Government, and shall protect each of them against Invasion; and on Application of the Legislature, or of the Executive (when the Legislature cannot be convened) against domestic Violence.—Article 4, Section 4

3. The Aspen Institute Homeland Security Group, "Hearing before the House Permanent Select Committee on Intelligence, 'Homeland Security and Intelligence: Next Steps in Evolving the Mission,'" January 18, 2012, http://www.aspeninstitute.org/sites/default/files/content/docs/pubs/HS-HPSCI-hearing-011812.pdf, 1, 3.

4. Jeff Poor, "Levin: US preparing for societal collapse by buying up billions of rounds of ammo," *Daily Caller*, February 16, 2013, http://dailycaller.com/2013/02/16/levin-u-s-govt-preparing-for-civil-societys-collapse-by-buying-up-billions-of-rounds-of-ammo/.

5. Terrence K. Kelly, et al., *A Stability Police Force for the United States Justification and Options for Creating U.S. Capabilities*, RAND Arroyo Center (prepared for the US Army), 2009, http://www.rand.org/content/dam/rand/pubs/monographs/2009/RAND_MG819.pdf.

6. Joe Wolverton II, "RAND Corporation Calls for a Domestic Stability Police Force," *New American*, January 20, 2010, http://www.thenewamerican.com/usnews/politics/item/2886-rand-corporation-calls-for-a-domestic-stability-police-force.

7. Kelly, et al., *A Stability Police Force for the United States Justification and Options for Creating U.S. Capabilities*, xiii.

8. Ibid.

9. Wolverton, "RAND Corporation Calls for a Domestic Stability Police Force."

10. Joseph Farah, "Obama's 'civilian national security force'," *WND*, July 15, 2008, http://www.wnd.com/2008/07/69601/; text of Barack Obama's Speech, "A New Era of Service," University of Colorado at Colorado Springs, *Rocky Mountain News*, July 2, 2008, http://www.rockymountainnews.com/news/2008/jul/02/text-obamas-speech/.

11. John T. Bennett and Tobias Naegele, *Defense News*, July 7, 2008, cited by Brenda J. Elliott, "More change you can Xerox: Obama's 'public service' plan," July 13, 2008, archived by Zimbio, http://www.zimbio.com/Obamamania/articles/659/More+change+can+xerox+Obama+public+service. See Zimbio.com archived copy for links to SecDef Gates' speeches.

12. Bennet and Naegele, *Defense News*.

13. Department of Defense Directive 1404.10, Emergency-Essential (E-E) DoD US Citizen Civilian Employees, April 10, 1992, http://biotech.law.lsu.edu/blaw/dodd/corres/pdf/d140410_041092/d140410p.pdf.

14. Department of Defense Directive 1404.10, DoD Civilian Expeditionary Workforce, January 23, 2009, http://www.dtic.mil/whs/directives/corres/pdf/140410p.pdf.

15. Doug Ross, "Was Candidate Obama's 'Civilian National Security Force' just established by Directive 1404.10?" *Director Blue* (blog), February 16, 2009, http://directorblue.blogspot.com/2009/02/was-candidate-obamas-civilian-national.html.

16. Gerry J. Gilmore, "Defense Department Establishes Civilian Expeditionary Workforce," American Forces Press Service, January 27, 2009, http://www.defense.gov/news/newsarticle.aspx?id=52840.

17. "Civilian Expeditionary Workforce prepares civilians for the demands of deployment," CampAtterbury.mil, November 16, 2012, http://www.campatterbury.in.ng.mil/PublicAffairs/LatestNewsandMultimediaReleases/tabid/781/articleType/ArticleView/articleId/1157/Civilian-Expeditionary-Workforce-prepares-civilians-for-the-demands-of-deployment.aspx.

18. Frequently Asked Questions, Civilian Expeditionary Workforce, http://www.cpms.osd.mil/expeditionary/cew-faq.aspx#weapons.

19. "Some Government Hot $100K Jobs | DOD Civilian Expeditionary Jobs," HubPages.com, last updated February 12, 2011, http://hmrjmr1.hubpages.com/hub/Some-Government-Hot-100K-Jobs.

20. Summary of Entitlements and Benefits, Defense Civilian Expeditionary Workforce; summary downloadable from: https://www.google.com/url?sa=t&rct=j&q=&esrc=s&source=web&cd=1&ved=0CC0QFjAA&url=http%3A%2F%2Fwww.cpms.osd.mil%2Fexpeditionary%2Fpdf%2FCEW%2520Benefits%2520WEBSITE%2520100110.doc&ei=7sewUZnzKYjl0gGtzIHABw&usg=AFQjCNEMBmf-BBnPoHYOm8RCYT2Ot8LKMA&bvm=bv.47534661,d.dmQ.

21. Traveler Information, http://www.tsa.gov/traveler-information. About, Transportation Security Administration, last updated January 14, 2013; What Is TSA? http://www.tsa.gov/about-tsa/what-tsa. When created, TSA was part of the Department of Transportation and was moved to the Department of Homeland Security in March 2003.

22. "Economic Recovery Money Will Create Jobs While Making America Safer," press release, DHS, March 3, 2009, http://www.dhs.gov/news/2009/03/03/economic-recovery-money-will-create-jobs-make-america-safer.

23. "DHS Recovery Act Aviation Projects to Create 3,000 Jobs," press release, DHS, March 5, 2009, http://www.dhs.gov/news/2009/03/05/dhs-recovery-act-aviation-projects-create-3000-jobs.

24. "The Economic Recovery Act of 2009—In the News," DHS, http://www.dhs.gov/recovery-news.

25. Joe Sharkey, "Playing Simon Says at Airport Security," *New York Times*, March 29, 2011, https://www.nytimes.com/2011/03/29/business/29road.html.

26. Kashmir Hill, "TSA Refuses to Explain Why You Have to Take Your Laptop out of Your Bag but Not Your iPad," *Forbes*, April 2012, http://www.forbes.com/sites/kashmirhill/2012/04/09/tsa-refuses-to-explain-why-you-have-to-take-your-laptop-out-of-your-bag-but-not-your-ipad/.

27. "John Tyner Video Tapes Refusal of X-Ray at San Diego Airport, Civil Suit Pending," *Huffington Post*, November 15, 2012, http://www.huffingtonpost.com/2010/11/15/john-tyner-videos_n_783678.html.

28. Jill Filipovic, "Your tax dollars at work," *Feministe*, October 24, 2011, http://www.feministe.us/blog/archives/2011/10/24/your-tax-dollars-at-work-2/.

29. Mike Masnick, "TSA Security Theater Described in One Simple Infographic," *Techdirt* (blog), April 11, 2012, https://www.techdirt.com/articles/20120405/04390118385/tsa-security-theater-described-one-simple-infographic.shtml. Bruce Schneier, "Harms of Post-9/11 Airline Security," Schneier on Security, March 29, 2012, https://www.schneier.com/blog/archives/2012/03/harms_of_post-9.html.

30. "TSA wastes $1.2 billion a year and causes 1,200 unnecessary deaths annually," Human Events, January 24, 2012, http://www.humanevents.com/2012/01/24/tsa-wastes-12-billion-a-year-and-causes-1200-unnecessary-deaths-annually/.

31. Section 1303, H.R. 1 (110th): Implementing Recommendations of the 9/11 Commission Act of 2007, http://www.govtrack.us/congress/bills/110/hr1.

32. Office of the Inspector General, *Efficiency and Effectiveness of TSA's Visible Intermodal Prevention and Response Program within Rail and Mass Transit Systems (Redacted), Department of Homeland Security*, August 2012, http://www.oig.dhs.gov/assets/Mgmt/2012/OIGr_12-103_Aug12.pdf, 1; S.1447, Aviation and Transportation Security Act, introduced September 21, 2001, by sponsor Sen. Ernest "Fritz" Hollings (D-SC), and signed November 19, 2001, by President George W. Bush, http://www.govtrack.us/congress/bills/107/s1447.

33. Ibid.

34. Kip Hawley, *Permanent Emergency: Inside the TSA and the Fight for the Future of American Security* (n.p.: Palgrave Macmillan, 2012), 122, 176–77, 188, 216.

35. Office of the Inspector General, *Efficiency and Effectiveness of TSA's Visible Intermodal Prevention and Response Program within Rail and Mass Transit Systems (Redacted)*.

36. Office of Inspector General, *TSA's Administration and Coordination of Mass Transit Security Programs*, Department of Homeland Security, June 2008, 6, http://www.oig.dhs.gov/assets/Mgmt/OIG_08-66_Jun08.pdf.

37. Oversight Hearing on the Transportation Security Administration (TSA) – Examining TSA's Efforts and Progression on H.R. 1, "Implementing Recommendations of the 9/11 Commission Act of 2007," Testimony of Kip Hawley, Assistant Secretary, Transportation Security Administration, U.S. Department of Homeland Security, before the US Senate Committee on Commerce, Science, and Transportation, October 16, 2007, http://www.tsa.gov/sites/default/files/publications/pdf/testimony/101607_testimony_scst.pdf.

38. Francine Kerner, ACI-NA Legal Affairs Conference (Slides), Transportation Security Agency, April 18, 2008, http://74.209.241.69/static/entransit/Kerner--Transportation%20 Security%20Administration.pdf.
39. Cathleen A. Berrick, Report to the Chairman, Committee on Homeland Security, House of Representatives, *Transportation Security: Key Actions Have Been Taken to Enhance Mass Transit and Passenger Rail Security, but Opportunities Exist to Strengthen Federal Strategy and Programs*, General Accounting Office, June 2009, http://www.gao.gov/new.items/d09678. pdf.
40. Lori Crouch, "Anti-terrorism exercise held at CBBT," WAVY.com, October 27, 2009, http://www.wavy.com/dpp/news/local_news/local_wavy_vb_cbbt_viper_training_exercise_20091027.
41. Hawley, *Permanent Emergency*, 188.
42. Report to Congressional Requesters: "Aviation Security: A National Strategy and Other Actions Would Strengthen TSA's Efforts to Secure Commercial Airport Perimeters and Access Controls" Highlights, GAO-09-399, U.S. Government Accountability Office, September 2009, http://www.gao.gov/assets/300/296404.html.
43. Sara Kehaulani Goo, "Marshals to Patrol Land, Sea Transport," *Washington Post*, December 14, 2005, http://www.washingtonpost.com/wp-dyn/content/article/2005/12/13/ AR2005121301709.html.
44. Ibid.
45. Ibid.
46. Ibid.
47. Hawley, *Permanent Emergency*, 169.
48. Lynn Freehill, "Joint security team makes surprise check of seaplane passengers," *Virgin Islands Daily News*, March 7, 2008, http://www.highbeam.com/doc/1P2-27449428.html.
49. Lynn Freehill, "TSA leads security checks on Red Hook ferry passengers," *Virgin Islands Daily News*, March 8, 2008, http://www.highbeam.com/doc/1P2-27449402.html.
50. "Amtrak, TSA and Law Enforcement Officers Mobilize for Major Northeast Corridor Rail Security Operation," Transportation Security Administration, U.S. Department of Homeland Security, September 23, 2008, http://www.tsa.gov/press/releases/2008/09/23/amtrak-tsa-and-law-enforcement-officers-mobilize-major-northeast-corridor.
51. "Amtrak, TSA and local law enforcement deploy across Northeast Corridor rail stations," States News Service, September 9, 2009, http://www.highbeam.com/doc/1G1-216150891. html.
52. "Amtrak, TSA and Law Enforcement Officers Mobilize."
53. Ibid.
54. "TSA Teams with Law Enforcement to Keep Super Bowl Fans Safe," Transportation Security Administration, US Department of Homeland Security, February 2, 2009, http://www.tsa. gov/press/releases/2009/02/02/tsa-teams-law-enforcement-keep-super-bowl-fans-safe.
55. Paul Swansen, "VIPR, Visible Intermodal Prevention and Response," *Swansen Report* blog, January 2, 2013, http://swansenreport.com/tag/visible-intermodal-prevention-and-response-team/.
56. "Air Marshals Expand beyond Planes," CBS News, February 11, 2009, http://www.cbsnews. com/stories/2005/12/14/terror/main1124533.shtml. CBS noted this was not exactly the first time that air marshals had "stepped outside of their usual role of flying undercover on airliners [in 2005] after Hurricane Katrina struck New Orleans. They were sent to keep order at Louis Armstrong International Airport, where thousands of evacuees converged after the levees were breached."
57. Rick Steelhammer, "Security ops over city test for transit safety," *Charleston Gazette* (Charleston, WV), March 26, 2009, http://www.highbeam.com/doc/1P2-20044036.html.
58. Ibid.
59. "Transportation Security Administration to begin Metra patrols," Metrarail.com, June 30, 2009, http://metrarail.com/metra/en/home/utility_landing/newsroom/newsroom_archive/ 2009NewsroomArchive/06_30_09_tsa.html.
60. Susan Jacobson, "TSA spot-checks Greyhound terminal," *Orlando Sentinel*, October 23, 2009, http://articles.orlandosentinel.com/2009-10-23/news/0910220205_1_bus-terminal-greyhound-bus-greyhound-station.

61. Crouch, "Anti-terrorism exercise held at CBBT."
62. Cindy Clayton, "Checkpoint set up at Bay Bridge-Tunnel," *Virginian-Pilot* (Norfolk, VA), May 13, 2010, http://www.highbeam.com/doc/1G1-226145927.html.
63. Linda A. Moore, "Terror scarers—Tight security at transportation hubs designed to deter threats," *Commercial Appeal* (Memphis, TN), November 18, 2009, http://www.highbeam.com/doc/1P2-21882027.html.
64. "Memorial Day weekend quiet for CBP at International Bridge," States News Service, June 4, 2010, http://www.highbeam.com/doc/1G1-228310445.html.
65. Rick Steelhammer, "First responders pool resources in drill. W.Va., Ohio agencies use time to network," *Charleston Gazette* (Charleston, WV), June 17, 2010, http://www.highbeam.com/doc/1P2-25228786.html.
66. Public Law 112-283.
67. Steelhammer, "First responders pool resources in drill."
68. Ibid.
69. Pamela Brust, "TSA holds field exercise in area," *Parkersburg News and Sentinel*, June 16, 2011, http://www.newsandsentinel.com/page/content.detail/id/549067/TSA-holds-field-exercise-in-area.html?nav=5061. The Fotenso quote that follows is also from this article.
70. Tara Servatius, "TSA Now Storming Public Places 8,000 Times a Year," *American Thinker*, June 20, 2011, http://www.americanthinker.com/2011/06/tsa_now_storming_public_places_8000_times_a_tear.html.
71. Bob Barr, "TSA's 'VIPER' program stumbles again," *Barr Code* (blog), March 4, 2011, http://blogs.ajc.com/bob-barr-blog/2011/03/04/tsa%E2%80%99s-%E2%80%9Cviper%E2%80%9D-program-stumbles-again/.
72. Jen Quraishi, "Surprise! TSA Is Searching Your Car, Subway, Ferry, Bus, AND Plane," *Mother Jones*, June 20, 2011, http://www.motherjones.com/mojo/2011/06/tsa-swarms-8000-bus-stations-public-transit-systems-yearly.
73. "Department of Safety and Homeland Security partners with Federal and State Agencies in Statewide Security Operation," *ClarksvilleOnline.com*, October 19, 2011, http://www.clarksvilleonline.com/2011/10/19/department-of-safety-and-homeland-security-partners-with-federal-and-state-agencies-in-statewide-security-operation/; Cynthia Hodges, "It's Official: VIPR formally debuts in first U.S. State [Tennessee]," *Examiner*, October 19, 2011, http://www.examiner.com/article/it-s-official-vipr-formally-debuts-first-u-s-state.
74. Hodges, "It's Official."
75. Ibid.
76. Statement of John Pistole, TSA, Senate Committee on Transportation Security Administration, June 14, 2011, http://www.dhs.gov/news/2011/06/14/statement-john-s-pistole-administrator-transportation-security-administration-senate.
77. Thomas Frank, "TSA chief John Pistole to put priority on rail, subways," *USA Today*, July 17, 2010, http://usatoday30.usatoday.com/news/washington/2010-07-16-tsa16_ST_N.htm.
78. "TSA's power grope; Rogue agency reaches out and touches people outside airports," *Washington Times* (Washington, DC), October 27, 2011, http://www.highbeam.com/doc/1G1-270918791.html.
79. "DHS to support security operations for 57th presidential inaugural," States News Service, January 18, 2013, http://www.highbeam.com/doc/1G1-315571234.html.
80. Ibid.
81. Tom Engelhardt, "The American Lockdown State," TomDisatch.com, February 5, 2013, http://readersupportednews.org/opinion2/277-75/15884-focus-the-american-lockdown-state.
82. Video: *NBC Nightly News*, January 21, 2013, http://www.nbcnews.com/id/3032619/#50529127.
83. Engelhardt, "The American Lockdown State."
84. Christopher Elliott, "Mission Creep at the TSA?" *National Geographic Traveler*, February/March 2013, http://travel.nationalgeographic.com/travel/traveler-magazine/the-insider/tsa/.
85. Ibid.
86. Ibid.
87. Michael V. Hayden, "Obama administration takes several wrong paths in dealing with terrorism," *Washington Post*, January 31, 2010, http://www.washingtonpost.com/wp-dyn/content/article/2010/01/29/AR2010012903954.html.
88. Ibid.

89. Anne E. Kornblut, "Obama Approves New Team to Question Key Terror Suspects," *Washington Post*, August 29, 2009, http://www.washingtonpost.com/wp-dyn/content/article/2009/08/23/AR2009082302598.html.

90. Transcript, CNN: "CIA Interrogation Threats Revealed," International Wire, August 24, 2009, http://www.highbeam.com/doc/1P3-1844986291.html.

91. Siobhan Gorman, "U.S. Weighs Special Team of Terrorism Interrogators," *Wall Street Journal*, July 18, 2009, http://online.wsj.com/article/SB124787391051060705.html.

92. Spencer Ackerman, "Obama Task Force on Torture Considers CIA-FBI Interrogation Teams," *Washington Independent*, June 24, 2009, http://washingtonindependent.com/48411/obama-task-force-on-torture-considers-cia-fbi-interrogations-teams; Executive Order 13491–Ensuring Lawful Interrogations, WhiteHouse.gov, January 22, 2009, http://www.whitehouse.gov/the_press_office/EnsuringLawfulInterrogations.

93. Ibid.

94. Ibid.

95. Ibid.

96. Ibid.

97. Lee Speigel, "Two Presidential Task Forces on the War on Terror Fail to Meet Deadlines," *Political Punch* (blog), July 20, 2009, http://abcnews.go.com/blogs/politics/2009/07/two-presidential-task-forces-on-the-war-on-terror-fail-to-meet-deadlines/.

98. Detention Policy Task Force, Preliminary Report, US Department of Defense and US Department of Justice, July 20, 2009, http://a.abcnews.go.com/images/Politics/Determination_of_GITMO_Cases.pdf. See a detailed explanation in the recent Congressional Research Service report, *Comparison of Rights in Military Commission Trials and Trials in Federal Criminal Court* by Jennifer K. Elsea, legislative attorney, February 28, 2013, https://www.fas.org/sgp/crs/natsec/R40932.pdf.

99. David Danzig, "What Do We Lose by Mirandizing Nigerian Who Sought to Blow Up Plane on Christmas Day?" FireDogLake.com, January 6, 2010, http://my.firedoglake.com/david-danzig/tag/abdulmutallab/.

100. Tom Eley, "Obama task force backs indefinite detention without trial," World Social Web Site, July 22, 2009, https://www.wsws.org/en/articles/2009/07/inte-j22.html.

101. Spencer Ackerman, "New Interrogation Unit Unlikely to Question Ft. Hood Suspect," *Washington Independent*, November 20, 2009, http://washingtonindependent.com/68479/new-interrogation-unit-unlikely-to-take-part-in-fort-hood-investigation.

102. Even Perez and Siobhan Gorman, "Interrogation Team Is Still Months Away," *Wall Street Journal*, January 22, 2010, http://online.wsj.com/article/SB10001424052748704423204575017760430119880.html.

103. Ibid.

104. Ibid.

105. David Usborne, "US Set to Investigate Abuse of Terror Suspects by CIA," *Independent* (UK), August 25, 2009.

106. Perez and Gorman, "Interrogation Team Is Still Months Away."

107. Ibid.

108. Ibid.

109. Salaries and Expenses, House Report 112-169 Commerce, Justice, Science, and Related Agencies Appropriation Bill, 112th Congress (2011–2012), http://thomas.loc.gov/cgi-bin/cpquery/?&sid=cp112hl6f5&r_n=hr169.112&dbname=cp112&&sel=TOC_124531&.

110. Carol Cratty and Pam Benson, "Special terror interrogation group used 14 times in last two years," *CNN.com*, March 7, 2012, http://security.blogs.cnn.com/2012/03/07/special-terror-interrogation-group-used-14-times-in-last-two-years/.

111. Ibid.

112. Mark Hosenball, "Special Interrogation Unit Plays Limited Role in Times Square Investigation," *Daily Beast*, May 17, 2010, http://www.thedailybeast.com/newsweek/blogs/declassified/2010/05/17/special-interrogation-unit-plays-limited-role-in-times-square-investigation.html.

113. Ibid.

114. Ibid.

115. Cratty and Benson, "Special terror interrogation group used 14 times in last two years."
116. "Bond: Administration fumbled Christmas Day terror case," State News Service, January 20, 2010, http://www.highbeam.com/doc/1G1-216996721.html.
117. Ibid.
118. Robert Burns and Devlin Barrett, "Intel chief concedes errors in Christmas bomb case," Associated Press, January 20, 2010, http://www.highbeam.com/doc/1A1-D9DBOUF00.html.
119. "Statement of Senators Feinstein and Bond on Senate Intelligence Committee Hearing into Christmas Day," States News Service, January 21, 2010, http://www.highbeam.com/doc/1G1-218044997.html.
120. "Who made call on Abdulmutallab decision?" States News Service, January 21, 2010, http://www.highbeam.com/doc/1G1-217055071.html.
121. "Congressman Joe Pitts: Recent Commentary: Reinventing the Wheel," States News Service, January 22, 2010, http://www.highbeam.com/doc/1G1-217822589.html.
122. "Gregg reacts to intel that an attack by Al-Qaeda in U.S. is expected within 3 to 6 months," States News Service, February 3, 2010, http://www.highbeam.com/doc/1G1-218160784.html.
123. "Hoekstra Statement on Obama Administration's Failures on Guantanamo Bay Closure and HIG Implementation," States News Service, January 22, 2010, http://www.highbeam.com/doc/1G1-217212656.html.
124. "Wolf pushes for answers on status of interrogation unit," States News Service, February 2, 2010, http://www.highbeam.com/doc/1G1-218073650.html.
125. "'Permission' needed to kill American terrorists," Washington Times, February 4, 2010, http://www.highbeam.com/doc/1G1-218215686.html; Walter Pincus and Carrie Johnson, "Interagency teams now can question terror suspects; but questions about intelligence-gathering, other issues remain," Washington Post, February 6, 2010, http://www.highbeam.com/doc/1P2-21226602.html.
126. Pincus and Johnson, "Interagency teams now can question terror suspects."
127. Ibid.
128. Ibid.
129. Cratty and Benson, "Special terror interrogation group used 14 times in last two years."
130. Ibid.
131. Intelligence Interviewing and Interrogation Research, Solicitation Number: BAA-202200, Department of Justice, Federal Bureau of Investigation, February 11, 2013, https://www.fbo.gov/index?_cview=0&id=0f11cc9ef04f799f3998e054af57f3ce&mode=form&s=opportunity&tab=core.

CHAPTER 10. THE DRONE NATION

1. Ed Peaco, "Unseen, Unheard, Unmanned: CBP Office of Air and Marine uses Predator aircraft for border security and emergency response," Inside Homeland Security, Spring 2012, http://www.abchs.com/ihs/SPRING2012/ihs_articles_2.php.
2. Ibid.
3. Justification for Other Than Full and Open Competition, US Customs and Border Protection, Department of Homeland Security, https://www.documentcloud.org/documents/516222-uas-o-amp-m-j-amp-a-redacted.html.
4. Katherine McIntire Peters, Chris Strohm, and Justin Rood, "Wasted Year. From in-house bickering to a fumbled national crisis, the Homeland Security Department is still a mess," Government Executive, March 1, 2006, https://www.govexec.com/magazine/features/2006/03/wasted-year/21283/.
5. Ibid.
6. Richard Whittle, Predator's Big Safari (Air Force Association/Mitchell Institute Press, August 2011), 15, http://www.afa.org/mitchell/reports/MP7_Predator_0811.pdf.
7. Ibid.

8. Adam J. Hebert, "Smaller Bombs for Stealthy Aircraft. The Small Diameter Bomb is emerging as one of the Air Force's top weapon priorities," *Air Force Magazine*, July 2011, http://www.airforce-magazine.com/MagazineArchive/Pages/2001/July%202001/0701small.aspx.
9. Ibid.
10. Interview with Michael C. Kostelnik, *Defense Systems Journal* (Fall 2010), http://www.dsjournal.com/kostelnik.html.
11. Ibid.
12. "'Reaper' moniker given to MQ-9 unmanned aerial vehicle," US Air Force, September 14, 2006, http://www.af.mil/news/story.asp?storyID=123027012.
13. Ibid.
14. Interview with Michael C. Kostelnik.
15. Peters, Strohm, and Rood, "Wasted Year."
16. CBP Press Release: "GA-ASI Unmanned Aircraft Arrives in North Dakota. First Deployment expands Use of CBP's Predator B UAS to the Northern Tier," GA-ASI.com, December 6, 2008, http://www.ga-asi.com/news_events/index.php?read=1&id=179.
17. Randal C. Archibold, "U.S. Adds Drones to Fight Smuggling," *New York Times*, December 7, 2009, https://www.nytimes.com/2009/12/08/us/08drone.html.
18. Mary Lochner, "Send in the drones," *Anchorage Press*, February 24, 2012, http://www.anchoragepress.com/news/send-in-the-drones-oil-companies-want-them-government-wants/article_11f833aa-5e81-11e1-b603-001871e3ce6c.html.
19. Interview with Michael C. Kostelnik.
20. Lochner, "Send in the drones."
21. Presentation by Michael C. Kostelnik, Assistant Commissioner, U.S. Customs and Border Protection, Office of Air and Marine,"Unmanned Aircraft in Homeland Security Role" to High Altitude Near Space Symposium, Colorado Springs, CO, September 30, 2010, http://presentations.rmtech.org/haans_2010/Kostelnik.pdf.
22. Ibid.
23. Presentation by Michael C. Kostelnik.
24. Interview with Michael C. Kostelnik.
25. Evan Munsing and Christopher J. Lamb, *Joint Interagency Task Force–South: The Best Known, Least Understood Interagency Success*, Center for Strategic Research, Institute for National Strategic Studies, National Defense University, June 2011, http://www.ndu.edu/inss/doc-uploaded/Strat%20Perspectives%205%20_%20Lamb-Munsing.pdf.
26. Peaco, "Unseen, Unheard, Unmanned."
27. Ibid.
28. Ibid.
29. Ibid.
30. "Domestic Drones Are Already Reshaping US Crime-Fighting," Reuters, March 3, 2013, http://www.cnbc.com/id/100515357.
31. Declan McCullagh, "DHS built domestic surveillance tech into Predator drones. Homeland Security's specifications say drones must be able to detect whether a civilian is armed. Also specified: 'signals interception' and 'direction finding' for electronic surveillance," CNET, March 2, 2013, http://news.cnet.com/8301-13578_3-57572207-38/dhs-built-domestic-surveillance-tech-into-predator-drones/.
32. Clay Dillow, "Army Developing Drones That Can Recognize Your Face from a Distance. And even recognize your intentions," *Popular Science*, September 28, 2011, http://www.popsci.com/technology/article/2011-09/army-wants-drones-can-recognize-your-face-and-read-your-mind.
33. Ibid.
34. Richard M. Thompson II, *Drones in Domestic Surveillance Operations: Fourth Amendment Implications and Legislative Responses*, Congressional Research Service, September 6, 2012, https://www.fas.org/sgp/crs/natsec/R42701.pdf, 4.
35. Declan McCullagh, "Homeland Security: Let's be clear about aerial drone privacy. A privacy review, intended to 'clarify any misunderstandings that exist' about the controversial unmanned aircraft, comes as concern grows about limited restraints on police use of drones," CNET, February 22, 2013, http://news.cnet.com/8301-13578_3-57570751-38/homeland-security-lets-be-clear-about-aerial-drone-privacy/.

36. Sara Reardon, "FBI launches $1 billion face recognition project," *New Scientist*, September 7, 2012, http://www.newscientist.com/article/mg21528804.200-fbi-launches-1-billion-face-recognition-project.html.

37. John Guillen, "Ohio collects millions selling driving records with your personal information," *Plain Dealer* (Cleveland), July 11, 2010, http://www.cleveland.com/open/index.ssf/2010/07/ohio_collects_millions_selling.html.

38. Michael George, "I-Team: State made $62 million by selling Florida drivers' license information," ABC Action News, June 21, 2011, http://www.abcactionnews.com/dpp/news/local_news/investigations/i-team%3A-state-made-$62-million-by-selling-florida-drivers%27-license-information.

39. Reardon, "FBI launches $1 billion face recognition project."

40. Dillow, "Army Developing Drones That Can Recognize Your Face from a Distance."

41. McCullagh, "Homeland Security."

42. Dillow, "Army Developing Drones That Can Recognize Your Face from a Distance."

43. Ibid.

44. Richard Chirgwin, "Congress report warns: drones will track faces from the sky. I am the eye in the sky, looking at you," *Register* (UK), September 13, 2012, http://www.theregister.co.uk/2012/09/13/congress_warns_on_drones/.

45. Conor Friedersdorf, "Cliffs Notes for the Filibuster: Rand Paul in His Own Words," *Atlantic*, March 7, 2013, http://www.theatlantic.com/politics/archive/2013/03/cliffs-notes-for-the-filibuster-rand-paul-in-his-own-words/273787/.

46. Andrew Becker, "Border agency looks to expand drone fleet," California Watch, November 19, 2012, http://californiawatch.org/dailyreport/border-agency-looks-expand-drone-fleet-18678; "Justification for Other Than Full and Open Competition, U.S. Customs and Border Protection," Department of Homeland Security, https://www.documentcloud.org/documents/516222-uas-o-amp-m-j-amp-a-redacted.html.

47. "Justification for Other Than Full and Open Competition, U.S. Customs and Border Protection."

48. Ibid.

49. Darren Quick, "Upgraded Predator B UAV completes development and testing," GizMag.com, September 6, 2012, http://www.gizmag.com/block-1-plus-predator-b-upgrade/24037/.

50. "MQ9 Reaper Enhances Capabilities with new 'Block I Plus' Configuration," *Defense Update*, September 5, 2012, http://defense-update.com/20120905_predator-b-plus-1.html.

51. McCullagh, "Homeland Security."

52. David Uberti, "Rise of the machines: domestic drones take off," Medill National Security Zone, April 3, 2012, http://nationalsecurityzone.org/site/rise-of-the-machines-domestic-drones-take-off/; David Uberti, profile, *Boston Globe*, http://daviduberti.com/tag/boston-globe/.

53. Ibid.

54. McCullagh, "Homeland Security."

55. Mathew J. Schwartz, "FAA Promises Privacy Standards For Domestic Drones," InformationWeek, February 15, 2013, https://www.informationweek.com/security/privacy/faa-promises-privacy-standards-for-domes/240148698?cid=nl_IW_daily_2013-01-17_html.

56. "Reps. Zoe Lofgren and Ted Poe Introduce Bipartisan Bill to Protect Americans' Privacy Rights from Domestic Drones," February 2013, website of Congresswoman Zoe Lofgren, http://lofgren.house.gov/index.php?option=com_content&view=article&id=785:reps-zoe-lofgren-and-ted-poe-introduce-bipartisan-bill-to-protect-americans-privacy-rights-from-domestic-drones&catid=22:112th-news&Itemid=161. A section-by-section summary can be read at http://lofgren.house.gov/images/stories/pdf/sbs%20-%20preserving%20american%20privacy%20act%20-%20%20021413%202.pdf.

57. Eric Schmitt, "U.S. Weighs Base for Spy Drones in North Africa," *New York Times,* January 28, 2013, http://www.nytimes.com/2013/01/29/us/us-plans-base-for-surveillance-drones-in-northwest-africa.html?_r=0

58. Greg Miller, "Plan for hunting terrorists signals U.S. intends to keep adding names to kill lists," *Washington Post*, October 23, 2012, http://articles.washingtonpost.com/2012-10-23/world/35500278_1_drone-campaign-obama-administration-matrix.

59. Chris Calabrese, "The Biggest New Spying Program You've Probably Never Heard Of," ACLU blog, accessed April 18, 2013, http://www.aclu.org/blog/national-security-technology-and-liberty/biggest-new-spying-program-youve-probably-never-heard.
60. Ibid.
61. Peter Finn, "Holder says Obama plans to explain drone policy," *Washington Post*, March 6, 2013, http://www.washingtonpost.com/world/national-security/holder-says-obama-plans-to-explain-drone-policy/2013/03/06/0d9a64b8-867b-11e2-999e-5f8e0410cb9d_story.html.
62. Josh Voorhees, "Eric Holder's Two-Sentence Response to Rand Paul's 13-Hour Filibuster," *Slate*, March 7 2013, http://www.slate.com/blogs/the_slatest/2013/03/07/eric_holder_s_43_word_response_to_rand_paul_s_13_hour_filibuster.html.
63. Michael Isikoff, "Justice Department memo reveals legal case for drone strikes on Americans," *Open Channel* (blog), February 4, 2013, http://openchannel.nbcnews.com/_news/2013/02/04/16843014-justice-department-memo-reveals-legal-case-for-drone-strikes-on-americans?lite&preview=true.
64. Ibid.
65. Ibid.
66. Department of Justice White Paper, "Lawfulness of a Lethal Operation Directed against a U.S. Citizen Who Is a Senior Operational Leader of Al-Qa'ida or an Associated Force," made available by MSNBC Media at http://msnbcmedia.msn.com/i/msnbc/sections/news/020413_DOJ_White_Paper.pdf.
67. Ibid.
68. Cora Currier "Everything We Know So Far about Drone Strikes," ProPublica, February 5, 2013, https://www.propublica.org/article/everything-we-know-so-far-about-drone-strikes.
69. Scott Shane, "Election Spurred a Move to Codify U.S. Drone Policy," *New York Times*, November 24, 2012, http://www.nytimes.com/2012/11/25/world/white-house-presses-for-drone-rule-book.html?pagewanted=all&_r=1&#p[BbmTit],h[BbmTit,1]).
70. Currier, "Everything We Know So Far about Drone Strikes."
71. Michael Zenko, "Politics, Power, and Preventive Action," Council on Foreign Relations website, retrieved April 18, 2013, http://blogs.cfr.org/zenko/2013/02/20/how-many-terrorists-have-been-killed-by-drones/).
72. Adam Entous, Siobhan Gorman, and Evan Perez, "U.S. Unease over Drone Strikes," *Wall Street Journal*, September 26, 2012, http://online.wsj.com/article/SB10000872396390444100404577641520858011452.html.
73. Mary Ellen O'Connell, "When are drone killings illegal?" *CNN.com*, August 16, 2012, http://edition.cnn.com/2012/08/15/opinion/oconnell-targeted-killing.
74. Dana Hughes, "US Drone Strikes in Pakistan Are Illegal, Says UN Terrorism Official," ABC News, March 15, 2013, http://abcnews.go.com/blogs/politics/2013/03/us-drone-strikes-in-pakistan-are-illegal-says-un-terrorism-official/
75. Eric Posner, "Obama's Drone Dilemma," *Slate*, October 8, 2012, http://www.slate.com/articles/news_and_politics/view_from_chicago/2012/10/obama_s_drone_war_is_probably_illegal_will_it_stop_.html.
76. Charles Krauthammer, "In Defense of Obama's Drone War," *National Review*, February 14, 2013, http://www.nationalreview.com/articles/340747/defense-obama-s-drone-war-charles-krauthammer.
77. Ibid.

CHAPTER 11. OBAMACARE: UNAUTHORIZED EXPANSION OF POWER

1. Ken Klukowski, "An Obamacare Shocker," FoxNews.com, January 13, 2010, http://www.foxnews.com/opinion/2010/01/13/ken-klukowski-tenth-amendment-democrat/.
2. "National Health Care," The 10th Amendment Foundation, http://www.10thamendmentfoundation.org/National_Healthcare.html; site temporarily suspended as of June 6, 2013. See "List of Constitutional Violations in Healthcare bill," in the document titled "Preface to Constitutional Analysis of The Patient Protection and Affordable Care Act" from the 10th Amendment Foundation, March 22, 2010, http://www.10thaf.info/CONSTITUTIONAL_ANALYSIS_HR_3590.pdf, 2–3.

3. Jennifer Haberkorn and Josh Gerstein, "5 takeaways on health law arguments," *Politico*, March 27, 2012, http://dyn.politico.com/printstory.cfm?uuid=61230D8C-5899-49E6-8512-EE824B8E1A77.
4. Dick Morris, as heard on Fox News Channel's *Fox & Friends* morning show, March 28, 2012.
5. Lee Ross, "Supreme Court sets up doubleheader finale on ObamaCare hearing," FoxNews.com, March 28, 2012, http://www.foxnews.com/politics/2012/03/28/supreme-court-sets-up-doubleheader-finale-on-obamacare-hearing/.
6. Adam Liptak, "Supreme Court Upholds Health Care Law, 5-4, in Victory for Obama," *New York Times*, June 28, 2012, https://www.nytimes.com/2012/06/29/us/supreme-court-lets-health-law-largely-stand.html; The Supreme Court's Obamacare Decision: Full Text, June 28, 2012, http://www.theatlantic.com/politics/archive/2012/06/the-supreme-courts-obamacare-decision-full-text/259102/.
7. Liptak, "Supreme Court Upholds Health Care Law."
8. Ibid.
9. Matt Negrin, "Supreme Court Health Care Ruling: The Mandate Can Stay," ABC News, June 28, 012, http://abcnews.go.com/Politics/OTUS/supreme-court-announces-decision-obamas-health-care-law/story?id=16663839.
10. Peter Suderman, "Another IRS Attempt to Rewrite Another Unworkable Part of ObamaCare?" *Reason* (blog), August 7, 2012, http://reason.com/blog/2012/08/07/another-irs-attempt-to-rewrite-an-unwork.
11. Jonathan H. Adler and Michael F. Cannon, "Another ObamaCare Glitch. Congress made a legal mistake while rushing through the health law. Now it's come back to haunt the administration," *Wall Street Journal*, November 16, 2011, http://online.wsj.com/article/SB10001424052970203687504577006322431330662.html.
12. Julian Pecquet, "Healthcare reform penalizes married couples, says report," *The Hill*, October 27, 2011, http://thehill.com/homenews/house/190105-healthcare-reform-penalizes-married-couples-says-report.
13. Julian Pecquet, "IRS warned healthcare law could leave millions without insurance," *The Hill*, November 17, 2011, http://thehill.com/blogs/healthwatch/health-reform-implementation/194367-irs-gets-earful-on-health-law-subsidies.
14. Ibid.
15. Adler and Cannon, "Another ObamaCare Glitch."
16. Ibid.
17. Ibid.
18. Ibid.
19. Ibid.
20. Phil Kerpen, "IRS Health Care Power Grab Tramples States," *Townhall.com*, July 10, 2012, http://townhall.com/columnists/philkerpen/2012/07/10/irs_health_care_power_grab_tramples_states/page/full/. Kerpen is president of the American Commitment, a nationally syndicated columnist, a contributor to Fox News Opinion, chairman of the Internet Freedom Coalition, and author of the book *Democracy Denied*.
21. Ibid.
22. Ibid.
23. Kirsten Anderson, "26 states opt out of ObamaCare's state-run insurance exchanges," LifeSiteNews.com, February 18, 2013, http://www.lifesitenews.com/news/26-states-opt-out-of-obamacares-state-run-insurance-exchanges/.
24. Kerpen, "IRS Health Care Power Grab Tramples States."
25. Ibid.
26. David Catron, "The IRS Illegally Expands Obamacare Tax Credits," *American Spectator*, July 23, 2012, http://spectator.org/archives/2012/07/23/the-irs-illegally-expands-obam.
27. Ibid.
28. Ibid.
29. Michael F. Cannon and Jonathan H. Adler, Testimony: "The Illegal IRS Rule to Increase Taxes & Spending under ObamaCare," before Committee on Oversight and Reform, U.S. House of Representatives, August 2, 2012, http://www.cato.org/publications/congressional-testimony/illegal-irs-rule-increase-taxes-spending-under-obamacare-1.
30. Ibid.
31. Ibid.

32. Robert Book, "The IRS Employer Mandate Loophole," *Forbes*, August 6, 2012, http://www.forbes.com/sites/aroy/2012/08/06/the-irs-employer-mandate-loophole/.
33. Ibid.
34. Ibid.
35. "Oversight Committee Asks IRS to Explain Recent Rule That Expands Obamacare's Reach in a Way Not Authorized in Law," House Oversight and Government Reform Committee, August 22, 2012, http://oversight.house.gov/release/oversight-committee-asks-irs-to-explain-recent-rule-that-expands-obamacares-reach-in-a-way-not-authorized-in-law/.
36. Ashton Ellis, "IRS Rewrites Obamacare to Increase Taxes," Center for Individual Freedom, September 13, 2012, http://cfif.org/v/index.php/commentary/56-health-care/1573-irs-rewrites-obamacare-to-increase-taxes.
37. "Oversight Committee Asks IRS to Explain Recent Rule that Expands Obamacare's Reach in a Way Not Authorized in Law."
38. Scott Garrett, "Top Ten Reasons ObamaCare is Unconstitutional," official website of U.S. Congressman Scott Garrett, accessed June 6, 2013, http://garrett.house.gov/top-ten-reasons-obamacare-unconstitutional.
39. Jonathan Adler and Michael Cannon, "If ObamaCare survives, legal battle has just begun," *USA Today*, June 25, 2012, http://usatoday30.usatoday.com/news/opinion/forum/story/2012-06-24/obamacare-healthcare-supreme-court-unconstitutional/55796730/1.
40. Ibid.
41. Ibid.
42. Ibid.
43. Ibid.
44. Jonathan H. Adler and Michael F. Cannon, "Taxation without Representation: The Illegal IRS Rule to Expand Tax Credits under the PPACA," *HEALTH MATRIX: Journal of Law-Medicine* 23, no. 1 (Spring 2013): 119, http://law.case.edu/journals/HealthMatrix/Documents/23HealthMatrix1.5.Article.Adler.pdf.
45. Profile: Trevor Burrus, Cato Institute, http://www.cato.org/people/trevor-burrus.
46. Trevor Burrus, "Supreme Court Decision: Obamacare Is Taxation without Representation," PolicyMic, June 28, 2012, http://www.policymic.com/articles/10422/supreme-court-decision-obamacare-is-taxation-without-representation.
47. John Hayward, "ObamaCare and Taxation without Representation," *Human Events*, June 28, 2012, http://www.humanevents.com/2012/06/28/obamacare-taxation-without-representation/.
48. Editorial, "Obamacare's Hidden Taxes," *Investor's Business Daily*, June 28, 2012, http://news.investors.com/ibd-editorials/062812-616549-supreme-court-confirms-obamacare-massive-tax-burden.htm.
49. Burrus, "Supreme Court Decision."
50. "About the Tenth Amendment," Tenth Amendment Center website, http://tenthamendmentcenter.com/about/about-the-tenth-amendment/#.UbHudedvNCo.
51. Anderson, "26 states opt out of ObamaCare's state-run insurance exchanges."
52. Klukowski, "An Obamacare Shocker."
53. Ibid.
54. Ibid.
55. Tim Brown, "Obama Ignores Nullification, Says Federal Agents Will Enforce Obamacare," *Freedom Outpost* (blog), March 25, 2013, http://freedomoutpost.com/2013/03/obama-ignores-nullification-says-federal-agents-will-enforce-obamacare/.
56. Ibid.
57. Ibid.
58. Valerie Richardson, "Lawsuit over health care tax could kill 'Obamacare,'" *Washington Times*, March 31, 2013, http://www.washingtontimes.com/news/2013/mar/31/obamacare-lawsuit-over-health-care-tax-will-test-c/.
59. Ibid. The foundation's response in the next paragraph is also from this source.
60. "List of Constitutional Violations in Healthcare bill."
61. Garrett, "Top Ten Reasons ObamaCare is Unconstitutional."
62. Ilya Somin, "Why the health care reform law is unconstitutional," *CNN Opinion*, March 26, 2012, http://www.cnn.com/2012/03/26/opinion/somin-health-supremes.

63. "Is the Obama Health Care Reform Constitutional? Fried, Tribe and Barnett debate the Affordable Care Act (video)," Harvard Law School, March 28, 2011, http://www.law.harvard.edu/news/spotlight/constitutional-law/is-obama-health-care-reform-constitutional.html.

64. "Obama's Healthcare Bill Unconstitutional?" Alliance for Natural Health, January 12, 2010, http://www.anh-usa.org/obama%E2%80%99s-healthcare-bill-unconstitutional/.

65. Garrett, "Top Ten Reasons ObamaCare is Unconstitutional."

66. Debra Smith, "The Main Reason Obama-Care Is Unconstitutional Is Being Missed," Western Center for Journalism, October 10, 2012, http://www.westernjournalism.com/the-main-reason-obama-care-is-unconstitutional-is-being-missed/.

67. Ibid.

68. Ibid.

69. Garrett, "Top Ten Reasons ObamaCare Is Unconstitutional."

70. R. Cort Kirkwood, "Legal Foundation: ObamaCare Still Unconstitutional," *New American*, September 17, 2012, http://www.thenewamerican.com/usnews/constitution/item/12859-legal-foundation-obamacare-still-unconstitutional.

71. Scott P. Richert, "Earl Warren Rides Again," *Chronicle Magazine*, June 28, 2012, http://www.chroniclesmagazine.org/2012/06/28/earl-warren-rides-again/.

72. Office of the Speaker of the House, "Pelosi Remarks at the 2010 Legislative Conference for National Association of Counties," news release, PRNewswire, March 9, 2010, http://www.prnewswire.com/news-releases/pelosi-remarks-at-the-2010-legislative-conference-for-national-association-of-counties-87131117.html.

73. Peter Roff, "Pelosi: Pass Health Reform So You Can Find Out What's In It," *U.S. News & World Report*, March 9, 2010, http://www.usnews.com/opinion/blogs/peter-roff/2010/03/09/pelosi-pass-health-reform-so-you-can-find-out-whats-in-it.

74. Ibid.

75. Aaron Klein, "More evidence of 'death panels' in Obamacare," *WND*, January 5, 2013, http://www.wnd.com/2013/01/more-evidence-of-death-panels-in-obamacare. Wording quoted from ObamaCare text in the remainder of this chapter is from this article.

76. See "Comparative Effectiveness Research Funding" on the government's Health and Human Services/Recovery page, accessed April 18, 2013, http://www.hhs.gov/recovery/programs/cer.

77. Michael F. Cannon, "A Better Way to Generate and Use Comparative-Effectiveness Research," CATO Institute, Policy Analysis no. 632, February 6, 2009, http://www.cato.org/publications/policy-analysis/better-way-generate-use-comparativeeffectiveness-research.

78. David Gauvey Herbert, "Comparative Effectiveness," *National Journal*, January 1, 2011, http://www.nationaljournal.com/njonline/comparative-effectiveness-20090728.

79. Sally Pipes, "Obamacare's Cruel War on Patient-Centered Healthcare," *Forbes*, December 10, 2012, http://www.forbes.com/sites/sallypipes/2012/12/10/obamacares-cruel-war-on-patient-centered-healthcare/.

80. Aaron Klein, "Obama adviser admits: 'We need death panels,'" *WND*, October 1, 2012, http://www.wnd.com/2012/10/obama-adviser-admits-we-need-death-panels.

81. Steven Rattner, "Beyond Obamacare," *New York Times*, September 16, 2012, http://www.nytimes.com/2012/09/17/opinion/health-care-reform-beyond-obamacare.html?_r=2&.

CHAPTER 12. "ANTI-WAR" PRESIDENT'S UNCONSTITUTIONAL WAR?

1. "We came, we saw, he died: What Hillary Clinton told news reporter moments after hearing of Gaddafi's death," *UK Daily Mail*, October 21, 2011, http://www.dailymail.co.uk/news/article-2051826/We-came-saw-died-What-Hillary-Clinton-told-news-reporter-moments-hearing-Gaddafis-death.html.

2. "Letter from the President regarding the commencement of operations in Libya," White House Office of the Press Secretary, March 21, 2011 http://www.whitehouse.gov/the-press-office/2011/03/21/letter-president-regarding-commencement-operations-libya.

3. "The Debates in the Federal Convention of 1787 reported by James Madison: August 17," Avalon Project, Yale Law School, see http://avalon.law.yale.edu/18th_century/debates_817.asp.

4. John Samples, "Why the Libyan War Is Unconstitutional," Cato Institute website, March 22, 2011, http://www.cato.org/publications/commentary/why-libyan-war-is-unconstitutional.
5. Terence P. Jeffrey, "Joe Biden: 'Framers Intended to Grant Congress Power to Initiate All Hostilities, Even Limited Wars,'" CNSNews.com, March 21, 2011, http://cnsnews.com/news/article/joe-biden-framers-intended-grant-congress-power-initiate-all-hostilities-even-limited.
6. Charlie Savage, "Barack Obama's Q&A," *Boston Globe*, December 20, 2007 http://www.boston.com/news/politics/2008/specials/CandidateQA/ObamaQA/.
7. Samples, "Why the Libyan War Is Unconstitutional."
8. Ibid.
9. Jack Goldsmith, "War Power: The president's campaign against Libya is constitutional," *Slate*, March 21, 2011, http://www.slate.com/articles/news_and_politics/jurisprudence/2011/03/war_power.html.
10. Rand Paul, "Obama's unconstitutional Libyan war," *Washington Times*, June 5, 2011, http://www.washingtontimes.com/news/2011/jun/15/obamas-unconstitutional-libyan-war/.
11. Michael Lind, "The Libyan war: Unconstitutional and illegitimate," *Slate*, March 21, 2011 http://www.salon.com/2011/03/21/lind_libya_war/.
12. Kate Hicks, "Panetta: We'd Seek 'International Approval,' Not Congress, to Act in Syria," *TownHall.com*, March 8, 2012, http://townhall.com/tipsheet/katehicks/2012/03/08/panetta_wed_seek_international_approval_not_congress_to_act_in_syria.
13. Chris Lawrence, "Official: Panetta misinterpreted on 'permission' for Syria intervention," *CNN.com*, March 8, 2012, http://edition.cnn.com/2012/03/07/politics/panetta-u-s-intervention-syria.
14. President Barack Obama, "Remarks by the President in Address to the Nation on Libya," delivered at National Defense University, Washington, DC, March 28, 2011, http://www.whitehouse.gov/the-press-office/2011/03/28/remarks-president-address-nation-libya.
15. International Commission on Intervention and State Sovereignty, *The Responsibility to Protect*, December 2001, at http://www.iciss.ca/pdf/Commission-Report.pdf.
16. Peter Beaumont, "Israel may face war crimes trials over Gaza. Court looks at whether Palestinians can bring case. International pressure grows over conflict," *Guardian* (UK), March 2, 2009, http://www.guardian.co.uk/world/2009/mar/02/israel-war-crimes-gaza; Daniel Schwammenthal, "War Crimes: The International Criminal Court claims jurisdiction over U.S. soldiers in Afghanistan," *Wall Street Journal*, November 26, 2009, http://online.wsj.com/article/SB10001424052748704013004574519253095440312.html.
17. See "Donors" page of Global Center for the Responsibility to Protect website, accessed July 26, 2011, http://globalr2p.org/whoweare/donors.php.
18. "Patrons," Global Center for the Responsibility to Protect, http://globalr2p.org/whoweare/patrons.php.
19. "About the Elders," the Elders website, http://www.theelders.org/elders.
20. Kofi A. Annan, "Two concepts of sovereignty," *Economist*, September 18, 1999, http://www.un.org/News/ossg/sg/stories/kaecon.html.
21. "Advisory board," Responsibility to Protect website, http://www.iciss.ca/advisory_board-en.asp.
22. "Annan Calls for Responsibility to Protect," International Commission on Intervention and State Sovereignty website, n.d., http://www.iciss.ca/menu-en.asp; no longer accessible.
23. "Advisory Board," International Commission on Intervention and State Sovereignty, http://www.iciss.ca/advisory_board-en.asp.
24. George Soros, "The People's Sovereignty: How a new twist on an old idea can protect the world's most vulnerable populations," *Foreign Policy*, January 1, 2004, http://www.foreignpolicy.com/articles/2004/01/01/the_peoples_sovereignty.
25. Ramesh Thakur, "Toward a New World Order," *Ottawa Citizen*, March 1, 2010, reprinted at http://www.cigionline.org/articles/2010/03/toward-new-world-order. The remaining Thakur quotes in this chapter are also from this article.
26. Evan McMurry, "Ted Cruz Fires at Obama Administration: 'They View Constitution as a Pesky Obstruction,'" Mediaite.com, June 6, 2013, http://www.mediaite.com/tv/ted-cruz-fires-at-obama-administration-they-view-constitution-as-a-pesky-obstruction/.
27. Ibid.

INDEX

A

ABC News, 210, 251
Abdulmutallab, Umar Farouk, 120–21, 159, 207, 210, 212, 214, 216, 217
Abedin, Huma, 128–29, 130, 131, 261
Abedin, Saleha (aka Saleha Mahmoud), 128–29, 130–31
Abedin, Syed, 128–29
Abengoa Bioenergy, 144
Accountability Review Board (ARB) probe/report on Benghazi affair, 6–7, 12, 13, 15, 19
Ackerman, Spencer, 208–11, 212
ACLU (American Civil Liberties Union), 148, 149, 153, 164, 165, 172, 181, 182, 185, 230, 232–35
ACORN (Association of Community Organizations for Reform Now), 62, 70, 137, 286n13
Adams, David, 197–98, 200
Adler, Jonathan H., 243, 244–245, 246–47, 249–50
ADVISE (Analysis, Dissemination, Visualization, Insight, and Semantic Enhancement), 306n67
Affordable Care Act (ObamaCare). *See chapter 11*
Afghanistan, 8, 10, 21, 50, 111, 192, 210, 231, 236, 237, 261, 268
 War in, 72, 237
African Extremist Network, 21
Agenzia Fides, 23–24
Ahrar al-Sham, 23
Aid to the Church in Need, 23–24
Air Force Magazine, 220
Air Force Office of Special Investigations, 161

air marshals, 195, 197, 200, 202, 315n56
al-Ahmar, Hamid, 118
al-Asi, Muhammad, 127
al-Assad, Bashar, 7, 8, 20, 22–25
al-Awlaki, Anwar, 120, 233, 239
Algeria, 3, 119, 268
Algerian gas complex siege, 27
Al-Haramain Islamic Foundation, 129–30
al-Hasidi, Abdel-Hakim, 21
Allen, Charles E., 176, 178, 310n20
al-Libi, Abu Yahya, 12–13
Allied Assets Advisors Fund, 25
Al-Muqaddasi (Muhammad ibn Ahmad Shams al-Dīn al-Muqaddas), 117
Al-Nour Party, 115
Al-Nusra Front, 23
al-Qaeda, iv, 2, 3, 8, 11–13, 15–18, 20–27, 33, 112, 115, 118, 120–22, 128, 129, 130, 149, 179, 195, 207, 219, 231, 233, 235, 238–39
 arming, 20–22
Al-Qaida and Taliban Sanctions Committee. *See* United Nations Security Council Committee 1267
al-Qaradawi, Yusuf, 111, 124
Alvarez, Mayra, 87
al-Zawahiri, Ayman, 12–13
Amazon reviews, private website monitoring of, 170
amendments to the United States Constitution
 First Amendment, 156
 Second Amendment, 30, 38–40, 44–45, 48, 55, 56, 57, 230
 Fourth Amendment, 149, 156, 171, 227, 230
 Fifth Amendment, 227–28, 230
 Tenth Amendment, 188, 251, 252, 253
 Sixteenth Amendment, 249

American Civil Liberties Union. *See* ACLU
American Recovery and Reinvestment Act of
    2009 (ARRA) (*aka* "the stimulus"), 42,
    67, 134, 135, 139, 280n60
American Revolution, iv, 241
American Spectator, 246
AMMO Act of 2013, 55–56
Ammunition Management for More Obtain-
    ability (AMMO) Act of 2013. *See*
    AMMO Act
ammunition shortage in U.S., 2008–2013,
    54–55
amnesty, iv, 59–88, 107
    "executive amnesty," 79, 85
Amtrak, 196, 97, 199, 200, 201, 204
Anderson, Kirsten, 246
Angelides, Phil, 136
anger management training, 36, 37
Angwin, Julie, 171
Annan, Kofi, 266
Ansar al-Sharia, 3, 4, 12, 19, 27
Anti-Defamation League, 129
anti-government extremists (sovereign citizens),
    168–69
AOL, 166, 167
A123 Systems, 143
Apollo Alliance, 135–37, 139, 141
Apple Inc., 166
Arab League, 266
ARB report on Benghazi affair, 6–7, 12, 13,
    15, 19
Arizona Senate Bill 1070 (SB 1070), 90
Armatix, 36
Arms Trade Treaty, 34
Army Field Manual, 212, 216
Asbahi, Mazen, 25
Ashley, W. Ross, III, 182
Ashrawi, Hanan, 266–67
Aspen Homeland Security Group, 188
assault rifles, 3, 29, 53
Associated Press, vi, 30, 32, 44, 54, 78, 91,
    93, 155
Association of Community Organizations for
    Reform Now. *See* ACORN
AT&T Inc., 156
ATF (Bureau of Alcohol, Tobacco, Firearms,
    and Explosives), 34, 41–47, 280n60
ATK (Alliant Techsystems Inc.), 48
Atkinson, Rick, 200–1
atrocities, 262, 266
Attkisson, Sharyl, 46
Australia, 156, 260, 266
Authorization for Use of Military Force (2001),
    238
Aviation and Transportation Security Act,
    194–95

Axelrod, David, 139
Ayers, Bill, 136
Ayotte, Kelly, 16–17

B

Babbin, Jed, 159
Babeu, Paul (Pinal County, AZ, sheriff), 99,
    101–2
backdoor amnesty, iv, 59–88
background checks, 29–33, 35, 36, 55, 80, 84,
    171, 252
BAIF Granite Holdings, 141–42
Balkin, Jack M., 151–52, 153
Bamford, James, 157–58
Baradar, Abdul Ghani, 213
Barnett, Randy, 255
Barr, Bob, 203–4
Bayoumi, Rashad, 116
Beck, Roy, 75
Beck, Jeremy, 78
Becker, Andrew, 228
Ben Ali, Zine al-Abidine, 117–18
Benghazi scandal, iv, vi, 2–27, 268, 269
Benjamin, David, 50
Bennet, Michael (D-CO), 70
Bennett, John T., 190–91
Bensman, Todd, 127
Biden, Joe, 32–33, 262–63
BigGovernment.com, 45, 141
Bill of Rights, 269. *See also* amendments to the
    United States Constitution
bin Laden, Osama, 50, 126, 129, 206, 238
biofuel, 141, 144
bitly, private website watching of, 170
Blackwell, Kenneth, 252
Blair, Dennis C., 209, 211–12, 214, 216
blogs, government monitoring of, 170
Bloomberg, Michael, 141
*Blueprint: Obama's Plan to Subvert the Constitu-
    tion and Build an Imperial Presidency, The*
    (Blackwell and Klukowski), 252
BlueGreen Alliance. *See* Apollo Alliance
bombings, 11, 32, 125, 130, 136, 214, 265,
    277n19
Bond, Kit (R-MO), 208, 214
Bonner, T. J., 223
Book, Robert, 248
Border Communities Liaison Office, 68, 86
border security, the minimizing of, 68
Bosnia, 104, 130, 220
Boston Globe, 39, 103, 229, 263
Boston Marathon terrorist bombing, 32–33,
    277n19

Boyle, Matthew, 69–70
Brady Act, 252
Brennan, John, 118–19, 121, 122–23, 124, 183, 213, 214, 215, 216, 232, 233
Brennan, Margaret, 17
Brewer, Jan, 90, 91, 93
bribery, ii, iii, v, 60, 108, 245–46
BrightSource Energy, 134–35
Broder, David, 64
Brookfield Asset Management, 141–42
Brown, Sherrod (D-OH), 135–36
Brown, Tim, 53, 253
Bryson, John, 134
Budget Control Act of 2011, 100
bullets, stockpiling by DHS, 48–54, 56
Bureau of Alcohol, Tobacco, Firearms, and Explosives. See ATF
Bureau of Counterterrorism, 50
Burke, Dennis, 43
Burrus, Trevor, 250–51
Burton, Bill, 150
Bush, George H. W., 176
Bush, George W., v, 41, 123, 127, 136, 144, 148–50, 151, 152, 153, 175, 177, 179, 186, 190, 194, 206, 216, 231, 235, 309n11, 313n32
Butler, Pierce, 262–63

C

Calabrese, Chris (ACLU), 232
Calderón, Felipe, 44
Camarota, Steven A., 72
Camp Atterbury Joint Maneuver Training Center, 192
Canada, 88, 97, 104, 123, 156, 260, 266
Cannon, Michael F., 243, 244–45, 246–47, 249–50
cap and trade, 137, 142
capitalism, 304n13
Carabinieri (military police of Italy), 189
Carney, Jay, 101
Carr Center for Human Rights Policy, 266
Carter, Jimmy, 119, 266
Casey, Bill, 176
"catch and release" policy (Obama's), 89, 104–5, 106
Cate, Fred, 207
Cato Institute, 108, 243, 250, 259, 262
Catron, David, 248
Cavanagh, Ralph, 139
CBS News, 11, 17, 46, 47, 56, 127, 200, 261, 315n56
Cello Energy, 144

cellulosic ethanol, 143–45
Center for American Progress (CAP), 87, 141
Center for American Progress Action Fund, 63
Center on Budget and Policy Priorities, 244
Center for Community Change, 64
FIRM (Fair Immigration Reform Movement), 63
Center for Consumer Information and Insurance Oversight, 253
Center for Immigration Studies, 67, 72, 90
Centers for Disease Control and Prevention, 174, 178
Centers for Medicare and Medicaid Services (CMS), 253
Central Intelligence Agency. See CIA
Chambliss, Saxby, 39
Charter of the United Nations. See UN Charter
chat rooms, infiltration of/data gathering from, 167, 169
Chertoff, Michael, 168, 178, 188, 310n20
CHIP (Children's Health Insurance Program), 83
Chirgwin, Richard, 227
Christensen, Gillian, 99
Christians, 120
in Egypt, 115, 116–17
in Syria, persecution of, 23–24
Chu, Steven, 144
CIA, 8, 9–10, 15, 16–17, 21, 130, 159, 174, 178, 183, 195, 207–8, 212, 214, 215, 217, 231, 235–36
annex in Benghazi, 2–4, 22
Civilian Expeditionary Workforce, 191–92
Clapper, James R., 16, 162–63
Claremont Institute, 94
"clean" energy. See chapter 6
Cleveland, Michael, 202
Clinton, Bill, 37, 162, 191, 263
Clinton, Hillary, 4, 5, 8, 9–15, 34, 50, 128, 131, 150, 151, 261
coal technology, 137, 138, 142
Coalition for Comprehensive Immigration Reform, 79
Coast Guard (US), 52, 81, 198, 201, 202, 203, 205, 223, 224
Coburn, Tom (R-OK), 52, 183
cocaine, 91, 106
Codexis, Inc., 144
Codrea, David, 34
COINTELPRO, 172
CoLab, 137
Colas, Nicholas, 105–6
Collier, Sean, 33
Collins, Doug (R-GA), 14
Commerce Clause, 242, 254–55, 256

Committee on Oversight and Government Reform. *See* House Oversight and Government Reform Committee

Community Comprehensive National Cybersecurity Initiative Data Center (aka Bumblehive), 157

"community organizing," Obama's, vi, 62

Comprehensive Immigration Reform for America's Security and Prosperity Act of 2009, 67

Condon, Stephanie, 56

Congressional Budget Office (CBO), 74, 255

Congressional Progressive Caucus, 72, 288n59

Congressional Research Service, 98, 144, 227, 248–49

Conservatives for Comprehensive Immigration Reform, 71

Consolidated Land, Energy, and Aquatic Resources Act of 2009 (CLEAR Act), 236

conspiracy theory, 56, 169, 188

Constable, Pamela, 82

constitution, Egyptian, 115, 116

Constitution, U.S. *See* United States Constitution

Constitutional Convention (1787), ii, iii

convicted criminal illegal aliens released 2009–2011, 102

Cook, Jim (*Irregular Times*), 152

Coptic Christians, 116–17

Cordell, Jenny, 6

corruption, v, 107, 108. *See also chapter 6*

Corsell, Peter L., 140

Council on American-Islamic Relations (CAIR), 126

Counterintelligence Field Activity (CIFA), 162

counterterrorism, *passim*
  agencies, radical Islamic ties to, 126–27
  fusion centers working beyond, 180
  task force to review U.S. policies and programs regarding, 309n11

Counterterrorism Security Group (CSG), 11

Crane, Chris, 71–72, 98

Crime Expressway, 92–93, 106, 107

crimes against humanity, 266

criminal aliens
  convicted and released 2009–2011, 102
  Level 1, 102–33

critical legal theory, 304n13

cronyism, v. *See chapter 6*

Cruz, Ted, 269

Customs and Border Protection (CBP). *See* United States Customs and Border Protection (CBP)

cyber attacks/intrusion, 167, 169, 184, 188

D

DACA (Deferred Action for Childhood Arrivals), 80–85

Daily Beast, 156, 213

Daily Caller, 74–75, 82–83

Dallas Morning News, 126

databases (compiling,tapping, and/or sharing), v, 160–61, 163–64, 171–72, 174, 175, 226

data collection, 154, 164, 185, and passim. *See generally chapters 7 and 8*

data.gov, 171

data mining, 147, 159, 161, 163, 166, 173, 174, 177, 181, 186, 232–33, 269, 306n67 *(see generally chapters 7 and 8)*

death panels, 257, 259, 260

Defense Advanced Research Projects Agency (DARPA), 161

Defense Department. *See* United States Department of Defense

Defense Department Directive 1404.10, 191

Deferred Action for Childhood Arrivals (DACA). *See* DACA

Delaney, Elizabeth, 39

Demand Letter 3 (firearms regulation), 47

DeMint, Jim, 69–70

Democratic Alliance for Egypt, 115

Democratic National Convention, 142, 206

Democratic Socialists of America, 73

Department of Energy. *See* United States Department of Energy

Department of Homeland Security (DHS), iv, v, 30, 45, 56, 60, 61, 75, 77, 80–86, 88, 90, 99, 100, 101, 104–7, 159, 164, 165, 168, 169–70, 174–75, 181, 193, 204, 219, 225–28
  drone program history, 220–24
  emerging police state, 187–217
  fusion centers, 177–80, 183–86, 224, 226, 228
  stockpiling of weapons and ammo by, 48–54, 56

Department of Justice (DOJ), vi, 1, 32, 34, 41–45, 47, 90, 93–94, 124, 125, 148, 164, 153, 156, 182, 208, 209, 212, 213, 233, 234, 237, 254

deportation, 67, 77–79, 83, 86, 91, 94–95, 98, 100–6

Detention Policy Task Force, 210

DHS. *See* Department of Homeland Security

Dillow, Clay, 225, 226

Dinan, Stephen, 98, 99

"diplomatic mission," explained, 6

disabled, ObamaCare and the, 258–59

Discover the Networks (DTN), 37–38, 123, 124
"disposition matrix" to determine drone strike targets, 230–31
Dixon, Peggy, 51–52
Doak, John, 253
Dodd, Chris (D-CT), 150
Dodson, John, 45
Doherty, Glen, 3, 4
Dohrn, Bernardine, 136
Dolen-Proffit, Karole, 40
DREAM Act (Development, Relief, and Education for Alien Minors), 60–61, 70, 72–74, 87
    DACA: Dream Act "Lite," 79–85
Dreher, Rod, 126
Drevna, Charles, 144
drone campaign, Obama's international, v, 220, 231–34, 236–238
    connection with domestic spying, 231–33
drones, v, 48, 188, 219, 222–32, 237
Drudge Report, government monitoring of the, 169
drug cartels, 2, 42, 43, 44, 47, 91–92, 99, 106
Drug Enforcement Administration (DEA), 92, 198
drugs, 37, 93, 103, 106, 184, 198, 199, 224
due process, 97, 175, 228, 230, 239
Duke Energy, 142
Durbin, Dick (D-IL), 70, 72, 180

E

Eagle Eyes program (USAF), 161
"earned citizenship" for illegal aliens, 85–86
Earnest, Josh, 155
Eastman, John, 60–61
eavesdropping (telephone) by government, 147, 150, 152–53, 157, 168, 195
Economist, 108
ecstasy (drug), 106
elderly, ObamaCare and the 258–60
Electric Transportation Engineering Corporation (eTec), 140
electric vehicles (EVs), 140, 143
Electronic Frontier Foundation (EFF), 155
Electronic Privacy Information Center (EPIC), 166, 167, 227
el-Erian, Essam, 114
Eley, Tom, 210–11
Elibiary, Mohamed, 126–27
el-Katatni, Mohamed Saad, 113
Elliott, Brenda J., ii, 293n20
Elliott, Christopher, 206

e-mail surveillance, 147, 149, 150, 153, 157, 159, 167, 186, 195, 269
Emanuel, Rahm, 139
Emerald Cities Collaborative, 137
Emerson, Steven, 124
Emmerson, Ben, 237
Energy Department. *See* United States Department of Energy
Energy Independence and Security Act of 2007, 144
Energy Security Trust, 133–34
Enerl (battery company), 142–43
Engelhardt, Tom, 205–7
England, Gordon, 191
Ennahda Movement, 118
Environmental Protection Agency (EPA), 143–44
EPA. *See* Environmental Protection Agency
eTec (Electric Transportation Engineering Corporation), 140
ethanol, 143–45
ethnic cleansing, 266
eTrace system, 41–43, 46
Evans, Gareth, 268
Examiner, 29, 34, 39, 174, 204
"executive amnesty," 79, 85
Executive Order 13549 (Classified National Security Information Program for State, Local, Tribal, and Private Sector Entities), 168
Exelon, 138–39
explosives, 27, 120, 195, 198, 201, 230

F

Facebook, 165, 169
facial recognition, 158, 159, 184, 225–26
Farouq Brigades, 23
"Fast and Furious" (F&F), v, 1–2, 28, 30, 34, 35, 43–47, 54
FBI, 10, 11, 16, 17, 31, 41, 45, 90, 155, 158, 159, 160, 163, 168–69, 172, 174, 177, 178, 207, 208, 211–13, 216, 217, 226
    statistics on gang membership, 97
Federal Air Marshal Service, 197–98
Federal Aviation Administration's Modernization and Reform Act, 229–30
Federal Bureau of Investigation. *See* FBI
Federale (blogger on VDARE.com), 78–79
Federal Firearms License (FFL), 37
Federalist Papers, iii
Federal Law Enforcement Training Center (FLETC), 50–52
Federal Protective Service (FPS), 49–50, 52–53

Federation for American Immigration Reform (FAIR), 79
Feere, Jon, 90, 91
Fein, Robert A., 209
Feingold, Russ (D-WI), 149–50, 161
Feinstein, Dianne (D-CA), 214–15
Fifth Amendment, 227–28, 230
file transfers, information gathering from, 167
filibuster, 150, 183, 237
Filipovic, Jill, 194
Filozof, Michael, 60
fingerprint identification, 158, 159, 160, 226
First Amendment, 156
First Observers, 164
FISA (Foreign Intelligence Surveillance Act), 148–56, 166, 175
Fisker Automotive, 143
Flake, Jeff (R-AZ), 70
Flickr, private website watching of, 170
Flynn, Mike, 84–85
Fool Me Twice (Klein and Elliott), 67, 133–34, 140, 242, 265
Foreign Emergency Support Team (FEST), 11
Foreign Intelligence Surveillance Act (FISA), 148–56, 166, 175
Fort Hood massacre, 119, 160, 211, 216
forums, government monitoring of online, 170
Fotenso, James M., 203
Foursquare (social networking website), surveillance of, 165
Fourth Amendment, 149, 156, 171, 227, 230
Fox News, vi, 4, 11, 45, 85, 99, 140–41, 144, 242, 322n20
France, 21, 209
Fredrickson, Caroline, 153
Freedom of Information Act, 84, 234
Freedom of Information requests, 167, 171
Free Syrian Army (FSA), 8, 20–25
Fried, Charles, 255
Friends of Obama, SEIU contribution to, 62
fusion centers, v, 172, 173–75, 181–83, 188, 219, 224, 226, 228
    DHS's, 177–80, 183–86, 220, 224, 226, 232
    history, 176–77
    role of private contractors in work of, 181–83
    truth about, 173–86

G

Gaddafi, Muammar, v, 7, 8, 13, 50, 20–22, 119, 261–62, 265
Gallagher, Ryan, 165–66
Gang of Eight, 69–70, 71–72

gangs
    gun-running and, v, 41
    of illegal aliens, 61, 76, 89–90, 96–98, 104
    number and membership of street, motorcycle, and prison (FBI statistics), 97
    weapon of choice for, 35
GAO. *See* Government Accountability Office
Gates, Robert M., 190–91, 192, 209
Gaza, 26, 110, 266
Gellman, Barton, 166–67
Gendarmerie Nationale (French military law enforcement), 189
General Accounting Office (GAO), 159
General Atomics Aeronautical Systems Incorporated (GA-ASI), 220–21, 228
General Motors, 143
genocide, 266
Geraghty, Jim, 61
Gerard, Leo, 139
Gerstein, Daniel M., 178
Gettysburg (blogger at Talking Points Memo), 95
Gibbons, Bill, 204
Giffords, Gabrielle "Gabby," 184
Gittelson, Robert, 71, 72
Glauthier, T. J., 139–41
Global Centre for the Responsibility to Protect, 266
Goals 2000: Educate America Act, 36–37
Goldsmith, Jack, 263
Gonzalez, Barbara (ICE), 100
Google, 166
"Google for Spies," 165
Gordon, Neil, 181
Gottlieb, Alan, 230
Government Accountability Office (GAO), 34, 41, 55, 159, 197, 205
Government Communications Headquarters (GCHQ) (UK), 156
Government Executive magazine, 206
Graham, Lindsey (R-NC), 16–17, 70, 236
Grassley, Charles (R-IO), 43, 46, 233
Green, Adam, 150
Greenberg, Andy (*Forbes*), 155, 158
green cards, 66, 67, 73
green energy projects, 142
"green fuel," 143–45
Green Manufacturing Action Plan (GreenMAP), 136
Greenwald, Glenn (*Guardian*), 154–55, 156
Gregg, Judd (R-NH), 215
Greyhound Bus, 200
GridPoint Inc., 140
Guantánamo Bay, 21, 210, 216
Guardian (UK), 154, 165
Guardian drones, 223–24, 228

Guardian Threat Tracking System, 163
Guignat, Gil, 45
Gulf oil spill crisis, 136
gun control, iv, v, 28, 29–57, 252
  executive actions, 31–35
  Fast and Furious. See Fast and Furious
  Obama's sweeping antigun template, 35–38
  Sunstein and, 38–40
Gun Control Act of 1968, 37
gun registry, 29, 30, 32
Gun Runner Impact Team (GRIT) initiative, 42
gun-running. See "Fast and Furious"; Project Gunrunner
Gun Violence Prevention Program, 37
Gutierrez, Luis (D-IL), 64, 67, 72

H

Hagel, Chuck, 122, 149
Haitian Refugee Immigration Fairness Act, 65
Hamas, 25, 110, 115, 116, 124, 126, 266
Hamilton, Alexander, iii
Hanson, Victor David, 74
Harvard University, vi, 38, 209
Hasan, Nidal Malik, 119–21, 160, 211
Hasbrouck, Edward, 207
Hatch, Orrin (R-UT), 72
Hawkins, A. W. R., 32
Hawley, Kip, 195–98
Hayden, Michael V., 207
Hayward, John, 251
Health Affairs Blog, 247
health care reform. See ObamaCare
health insurance
  constitutionality of requirement to obtain, 242
  exchange(s), 84, 87, 244–47, 250, 252
  for illegal aliens, 83–84, 87
  ObamaCare. See chapter 11
  penalty for not obtaining, 255
Health Insurance Portability and Accountability Act. See HIPAA
Heckler & Koch, 53–54
Henry Jackson Society, 178
Heritage Foundation, 69–70, 73, 98, 104, 141, 177
Heymann, Philip B., 209
Hezbollah, 22, 176
Hicks, Gregory, vi, 13–15, 19
"high crimes and misdemeanors," ii–iii, 60
High-Value Detainee Interrogation Group (HIG), 207–8, 210–17

hijacking of TWA Flight 847 from Cairo to London (1985), 176
Hijazi, Ahmed, 233
Hindenburg, Paul von, 175
Hindustan Times, 22
HIPAA, 33–34
Hispanic Caucus, 70
HMS (security firm), 165
Hodges, Cynthia, 204
Hoekstra, Pete (R-MI), 215
Holder, Eric, 31, 32, 34, 37, 44–45, 47, 54, 95, 170, 209–12, 234
Holdren, John, 137, 138, 139
Holy Land Foundation, 25, 124, 126
Homeland Secure Data Network (HSDN), 168
Hoover, William, 41
Horowitz, Daniel (Madison Project), 60
Hosenball, Mark, 213
Hot Air (blog), 141, 151
House appropriations subcommittee, 216
House Committee on Homeland Security, 196
House Intelligence Committee, 215
House Judiciary Committee, iii
House Judiciary Subcommittee on Immigration, Border Security, and Claims, 96
House Oversight and Government Reform Committee, 56, 244, 247, 248
House Permanent Select Committee on Intelligence, 188
House Resolution 3590, 254. See ObamaCare
Howington, Gene, 159, 174
H.R. 3590, 254. See ObamaCare
Huffington Post, 23, 169
Hulu, monitoring of, 169
human right to life, 237
Hurricane Katrina, 188, 310n56
Hurricane Sandy, 188
Hyde Park Herald, 122

I

ICE (Immigration and Customs Enforcement), 42, 48, 52, 53–54, 71, 75–77, 81, 82, 90–91, 96, 98–104, 106–7, 204, 205
Idaho National Laboratory, 140
"If You See Something, Say Something" (campaign), 164–65
illegal aliens, iv, 59, 66, 67, 73, 74, 78, 79, 82, 183
  arrest-free zones for (proposed legislation), 68
  convicted and released 2009–2011, 102
  criminal, 89–107. See also backdoor amnesty
  "earned citizenship" for, 85–86

Illinois Conservative Examiner, 93
Illinois Sustainable Technology Center, 140
Immigrations and Customs Enforcement, 198
Immigration and Naturalization Service (INS), 66–67
Immigration Policy Center (IPC), 71
immigration raids, 104–5
immigration reform, 59, 61, 63–67, 69, 72, 85–87, 96, 98–99, 107
Immigration Reform and Control Act of 1986 (IRCA), 65–66
impeachable offense, defined, iii
impeachment
    constitutional reasons for, ii, 60
    process, iii
imperialism, 127, 136, 304n13
Independent (UK), 21
individual mandate (health insurance), 84, 242, 250, 256
information gathering on citizens. *See chapters 7 and 8*
Inhofe, James (R-OK), 55–57
INS (Immigration and Naturalization Service), 66–67
Inside Homeland Security, 224
Insight on the News, 177
Institute of Muslim Minority Affairs, 128–29
Institute for Policy Studies, 264
intelligence gathering, 210 and passim. *See generally chapters 7–9*
Intelligence Science Board, 209, 210
intelligence-sharing, 177. *See generally chapter 8*
Interagency Working Group to Counter Online Radicalization to Violence, 168–69
Internal Revenue Service. *See* IRS
International Commission on Intervention and State Sovereignty, 266
International Committee of the Red Cross, 12
International Covenant on Civil and Political Rights, 236
International Crisis Group, 15, 268
International Islamic Relief Organization (IIRO), 129–30
International Law Enforcement Academies (ILEAs), 51
International Traffic in Arms Regulations (ITAR), 34
interrogation, 27, 178, 207–17
Investments for Manufacturing Progress and Clean Technology Act (IMPACT), 134–35
Investor's Business Daily, 251
Iogen Energy Corp., 144
Iranian Revolution, 116, 119, 127
Iraq, 8, 14, 21, 25, 50, 54, 104, 111, 231, 236, 239, 268

Iraq War (*aka* Operation Iraqi Freedom), 221, 239
IRCA (Immigration Reform and Control Act of 1986), 65–66
iris scans, 226
IRS (Internal Revenue Service), iv, vi, 171, 194, 241, 243–50, 269
Islah Party (Egyptian Reform Party), 118
Islamic fundamentalism, v, 109, 122
Islamic Horizons (magazine), 124
Islamic Jihad, 124, 175
Islamic Society of North America (ISNA), 25, 123–25, 298n48
Issa, Darrell (R-CA), 43–46, 244, 248–49
ISX Corporation, 182
Ivanpah Solar Electric Generating System, 134
IxReveal, Inc., 182

J

Jabhat al-Nusra (JaN), 23
Jacobson, William A., 33
Jaffer, Jameel (ACLU), 235
Jarrett, Valerie, 125
Jay, John, iii
Jews, 116, 120
jihad, 20, 22, 33, 112, 115, 120, 121, 129
jihadists, 13, 22, 27, 121
    arms to, 8–9, 22, 25. *See also chapter 5*
Johnson, Bart, 180
Johnson, Carrie, 216
Johnson, Jim, 152
Joint Committee on Taxation, 244
Joint Protection Enterprise Network (JPEN), 162
Jones, Ben (Gannett), 55
Jones, James L., 216
Jones, Jeff, 136
Jones, Van, 136
Jordan, 119
Jorgustin, Ken (*Modern Survival* blog), 54
Journal of Muslim Minority Affairs, 128
Joyce Foundation, 37–38
Judicial Watch, 81, 82, 84, 99
Jund al-Sham / Jund al-Islam / Jund Ansar Allah, 25–26
Justice Department. *See* Department of Justice
Justice with Judge Jeanine (show), 101–2

K

KCP&L (Kansas City Power and Light Company), 140
Keane, Larry (National Shooting Sports Foundation), 52
Kennedy, John F., 206
Kenny, Jack, 186
Kerner, Francine, 196
Kerpen, Phil, 245–46, 322n20
Kerry, John, 117
Keyes, Alan, 35
Khan, Samir, 233
Khomeini, Ruhollah (ayatollah), 127
Kirkwood, R. Cort, 256
Klaus, Václav, 107–8
Klein, Aaron, 8, 9, 25, 56–57, 113, 123, 135, 169, 257, 265, 268
Klukowski, Ken, 241, 252
Kobach, Kris W., 73, 98
Koh, Harold, 236
Korean War, 263
Kornblut, Anne E., 208
Kosovo, 220, 263
Kostelnik, Michael C., 220–25, 227, 228
Kraushaar, Josh, 31
Krauthammer, Charles, 238–39
Krikorian, Mark, 59
Kyl, Jon (R-AZ), 259

L

La Familia Michoacana, 92
Laird, Douglas, 197
Lake, Eli, 156
Lankford, James (R-OK), 14
La Raza. *See* National Council of La Raza
Lawful Prospective Immigrants (LPIs), 86–88
Lederman, Martin "Marty" S., 152–53
Leiter, Michael, 214
Leno, Jay, 59
Levin, Carl (D-MI), 183
Levin, Mark, 189
Lew, Jack, 100
LG Chem Michigan, 143
Libya, v, 119, 237, 261–65
    Benghazi. See Benghazi scandal
    constitutionality of Obama's use of force in.
        See chapter 12
    globalist doctrine used in, 265–66, 268
Libyan Islamic Fighting Group, 21–22
Lichtblau, Eric, 150–51
limitless powers, 256–57
Lincoln, Abraham, 187, 206
Lind, Michael, 264

LinkedIn, private website watching of, 170
Lofgren, Zoe (D-CA), 230
Longenecker, John, 29, 276n1
Loughner, Jared, 184
LPI status, 86–88
    groups of people to be excluded from, 86
Lucas, Frank (R-OK), 55–56

M

Mac Donald, Heather, 96–97
MacGaffin, N. John, III, 209
Madison, James, iii, 262
Maghreb, 3, 27
Magid, Mohamed, 124
Mali, 22, 26
Manchin, Joe (D-WV), III, 30
Manchurian President, The (Klein and Elliott), vi
Mara Salvatrucha (MS-13) street gang, 96, 97
March for America (2010 protest march), 63–64
marijuana, 106, 201
married couples, ObamaCare's penalization of, 243–44
MARTA public transit system (Atlanta), 203
Martyrs' Brigade, 3, 12
Marzook, Mousa, 124
MATRIX (Multistate Anti-Terrorism Information Exchange Program), 306n67
Mattson, Ingrid, 125
Mayer, Matt, 104–5
McCabe, Andrew, 211–12
McCain, John, 16–17, 70
McCall, Ginger, 166, 227
McConnell, Mitch, 215
McCullagh, Declan, 226, 229
McDonough, Denis, 124–25
McElroy, Wendy, 174, 175
McKellar Corporation, 192
McMahon, Colleen, 234
Medicaid, 83, 171, 243
Mead, Gary, 100
Medicare, 260
Medina, Eliseo (SEIU), 62–63
Meir Amit Intelligence and Terrorism Information Center (ITIC), 112
Melson, Kenneth, 43
Memphis Area Transit Authority, 200
Menendez, Robert (D-NJ), 70
Mérida Initiative, 41–42
Meshal, Khaled, 116
message boards, government infiltration and monitoring of, 169, 170
Metra commuter trains, 200

Mexican drug cartels, 2, 42, 43, 44, 46–47, 91–92, 99, 106

Mexico, 40–42, 44–46, 68, 84, 88, 93, 96, 97, 106

Miami Herald, 24, 86

Microsoft, 166

Military Police Corps (US Army), 190

Miller, Greg (*Washington Post*), 231

Miller, Matthew, 212

Miller, Peyton R., 90, 95

Miller, Sunlen, 210

minimum wage, 62, 71

Minority Report (film), 170

misuse of public funds, v, 145

Mohammed, Khalid Sheikh, 213

Mohammed VI of Morocco (king), 119

Mora, Eduardo Medina, 44

Moran, Rick (*American Thinker*), 54

Morell, Mike, 15–17

Morris, Dick, 242

Morrissey, Ed, 151

Morsi, Mohamed, 113, 115, 116, 131

Moseley, T. Michael, 222

Morton, John, 75–77, 90, 101, 102

Mother Jones, 204

Moussa, Amr, 266

MoveOn, 137, 150

MQ-9 Reaper, 221–23, 225, 228. *See also* Predator drone

MS-13 (street gang), 96, 97

Mubarak, Hosni, 112–17

Mueller, Robert, 212

Mukasey, Michael, 44

Muñoz, Cecelia, 77, 79, 85

Munro, Neil, 82–83

Murse, Tom, 87

Muscatatuck Training Range, 192

Muslim Brotherhood, v, 20, 25, 27, 109, 118–19, 128, 131, 261
  brief background on, 110–12
  Obama and Egypt's, 112–17
  official motto, 112
  in the White House, 122–25

Muslim NGO Caucus, 128–29

Muslim Sisterhood, 131

Muslim Students Association (MSA), 25, 123, 125

Muslim World League (MWL), 128–30

MySpace, private website watching of, 170

N

Nabors, Rob, 100

Naegele, Tobias, 190–91

Napolitano, Janet, 45, 46, 61,77–78, 80–81, 99, 101, 102, 120, 126, 165, 168, 180, 205, 214

NASDAQ, 174

Naseef, Abdullah Omar, 128

Nasr, Vali R., 10

National Council of La Raza, 63, 65, 79, 85

National Counterterrorism Center (NCTC), 16, 170–72, 214, 231–33

National Education Goals, 37

National Fusion Center Association (NFCA), 181–82

National Immigration and Customs Enforcement Council 118, 98

National Instant Criminal Background Check System (NICS), 31, 33–34

National Lawyers Guild, 63

National Marine Fisheries Service Office of Law Enforcement, 49

National Public Radio (NPR), 24, 62

National Rifle Association (NRA), 31, 32, 33

National Security Agency (NSA), 153, 154–58, 159, 167, 168, 174, 269

National Security Agency's Domestic Spying Program, The (Lederman), 153

National Security Branch Analysis Center, 306n67

National Security Council, 4, 10, 26, 208, 212, 213, 232, 265

National Weather Service, 49

NATO, v, 3, 14, 15, 20, 21, 53, 262, 268

naturalization, 59–60, 74, 171

Natural Resources Defense Council, 134–35, 139

Navistar Defense, 54

Nayak, Nick, 56

NBC Nightly News, 206

NCTC (National Counterterrorism Center), 16, 171–72, 214, 231–33

New America Foundation (NAF), 260, 264

Next Generation Identification (NGI) program, 158, 226

New Party, 137

New Republican, 31

New York Post, 130

New York Times, 9–10, 20, 22, 26, 27, 77, 79–80, 114, 130, 139, 143, 149, 151, 170, 234, 235–36, 242–43, 259, 260

New York v. United States, 252

New Zealand, 156, 260

NFCA (National Fusion Center Association), 181–82

NGI (Next Generation Identification) program, 158, 226

Nicaraguan Adjustment and Central American Relief Act, 65

9/11, v, 12, 72, 122, 123, 124, 130, 136, 148, 159, 165, 172, 188, 206, 213, 238

9/11 Commission, 177, 179, 195

1979 Islamic Revolution in Iran, 116, 119, 127

Nissan Motor Company, 140

non-deportation, 62, 75–79, 83, 95, 98

nongovernmental organizations, 25, 129, 181

North American Islamic Trust (NAIT), 25, 123

North Atlantic Treaty Organization. See NATO

Northwest Airlines, 197, 200

Novel Intelligence from Massive Data (NIMD), 306n67

NPR (National Public Radio), 24, 62

NRA, 31, 32, 33

NSA (National Security Agency), 153, 154–58, 159, 167, 174, 269

NSDD 179 (Task Force on Combatting Terrorism), 309n11

nuclear power plants, 138, 139, 142

NumbersUSA, 75, 78

O

OAM (Office of Air and Marine), 221–24, 227–29

Obama, Barack, i, ii, iv, *and throughout*
  antigun template of, 35–38
  "catch and release" program of, 89, 104–5, 106
  and community organizing, vi, 62
  drone campaign of, v, 220, 231–34, 237–238
  and the Muslim Brotherhood, 112–17
  speech in Cairo (2007), 113
  surveillance regime of, 147–72

Obama-Biden Transition Project, 63

ObamaCare, iv, 67, 69, 72, 84, 86, 87, 148, 241–60 (*chap. 11*)
  an example of "taxation without representation," 249–51
  financial roots, 253–54
  "glitches" found in, 243–45
  health-care rationing and death panels in, 257–60
  number of constitutional violations, 241

O'Connell, Mary Ellen, 236–37

O'Connor, John, 199

Office of Air and Marine (OAM), 221–24, 227–29

Office of Foreign Assets Control, 24

Office of Information and Regulatory Affairs, 38

Ohio State Highway Patrol, 202, 203

Olsen, Matthew, 16

online forms, government monitoring of, 170

OOIDA (Owner-Operator Independent Drivers Association), 164–65

Open Society Foundations, 151, 265, 266

Operation ALERTS (Allied Law Enforcement for Rail and Transit Security), 199

Operation Glidepath, 195

Operation Iraqi Freedom (Iraq War), 221, 239

Operation Shield, 49–50

Ortiz, Solomon (D-TX), 67

Overseas Security Policy Board (OSPB), 7, 15

P

Pacific Legal Foundation, 254

Padilla, Belinda, 36

Pahlavi, Mohammad Reza (shah), 119

Pakistan, 5, 10, 13, 50, 213–14, 231, 235–38

Palestinian Liberation Organization (PLO), 267

Palestinians, 116

PalTalk.com, 166

Panetta, Leon, 4, 264–65

Patel, Eboo, 125

Patient-Centered Outcomes Research Institute, 258

Patient Protection and Affordable Care Act (ObamaCare). *See chapter 11*

PATRIOT Act, 155–56, 175

Patterson, Leonard, 49

Paul, Rand (R-KY), 183, 227–28, 234, 263–64

Peacekeeping and Stability Operations Institute (PKSOI) (US Army), 189

Pear, Robert, 77

Pecquet, Julian, 244

Pelosi, Nancy, 257

Perfect Citizen (infrastructure vulnerability assessment program), 167–68

persecution of Christians in Syria, 23–24

Persian Gulf War, 239

Petraeus, David H., 9–10, 16

Pew Hispanic Center, 87, 105

photos, data gathering from, 167, 226

physical search, 152

Pickens, Amber, 19

Pickering, Thomas, 6, 13, 15, 268

Pincus, Walter, 216

Pipes, Sally, 259

Pistole, John, 204–5, 206

Pitcher, Whitney, 141

Pitts, Joe (R-PA), 215
Podesta, Heather, 141, 142
Podesta, John, 141, 142
Podesta, Tony, 142
POET LLC, 114
Poe, Ted (R-TX), 230
Poitras, Laura, 166–67
Politico, 72, 253
Posner, Eric, 238
Posse Comitatus Act (1878), 158, 163, 190, 202
Power, Samantha, 265–66
Predator drone (now known as MQ-9 Reaper), 220–23, 224, 228. *See also* MQ-9 Reaper
Pre-Existing Condition Insurance Plan (PCIP), 83
Preserving American Privacy Act, 230
presidential directive, 21, 162. *See also* NSDD 179
Printz v. United States, 252
PRISM (surveillance program), 166–67
Privacy Act of 1974, 165, 184
privacy concerns re: government use of surveillance drones to monitor citizens, 229–31
private contractors, role in work of fusion centers, 181–83
probable cause, 97, 171–72
profiling, 69, 122, 159, 175, 179, 193–94, 201
Project Coronado, 92
Project on Government Oversight (POGO), 181
Project Gunrunner, 40–45, 47, 280n60
ProPublica, 235–36
Pyle, Tom, 144

Q

Qatar, 8, 20, 22, 23, 26
Qteros, Inc., 143, 144
Qumu, Abu Sufian Ibrahim Ahmed Hamuda Bin, 21
Quraishi, Jen, 204
Qutb, Sayyid, 126

R

racism, 304n13
radical Islamic ties to counterterrorism agencies, 126–27
Radicals in Robes: Why Extreme Right-Wing Courts are Wrong for America (Sunstein), 39
Ramadan, Tariq, 125
RAND Corporation, 189

Rathke, Wade, 70–71, 137
rationing (health care), 257–60
Rattner, Steven, 259–60
Rawles, James Wesley, 34–35
Raytheon Company, 165–66
Reagan, Ronald, 65–66, 141, 161, 176, 177
Red Army (Klein and Elliott), 64, 65, 67, 75, 111, 264, 265, 286n13
Reichstag Fire Decree, 175
"responsibility to protect" doctrine (R2P), 15, 265–68
Responsible Electronic Surveillance That Is Overseen, Reviewed, and Effective Act of 2007 (RESTORE), 149
Reuters, 9, 16, 21, 26, 170
Rice, Susan, 5, 16–17
Richardson, Michelle (ACLU), 149
Richert, Scott P., 256–57
Ridge, Tom, 177
RIOT (Rapid Information Overlay Technology), 165
Riggs, Mike, 74–75
Riggs, Robert, 127
right to life, 237
Roberts, John, 242, 254, 256
Robinson, Mary, 266
Rockford Institute, 257
Roff, Peter, 257
Rogers, Jim, 142
Rogers, Joel, 136, 137
Rogers, John W., Jr., 139
Roosevelt, Franklin, 206
Ross, Doug (blogger), 191–92
Rowe, John, 138, 139
Royal Dutch Shell, 144
R2P. *See* "responsibility to protect" doctrine
Rubin, Jennifer, 65
Rubio, Marco (R-FL), 70
Ruckus Society, 137
Rudd, Mark, 136
Rumsfeld, Donald, 162
Russert, Tim, 96
Russia Today, 158–59

S

Sacramento Municipal Utility District (SMUD), 140
Said, Jamal, 25
Saleh, Ali Abdullah, 118
Samples, John, 262, 263
sanctuary cities, 90, 93–96, 106–7
Sandefur, Timothy, 254

Sandy Hook Elementary School (Newtown, CT) massacre, 30, 40
Sargent, Greg, 150
Saudi Arabia, 8, 21, 23, 118, 123–24, 128, 129, 130, 131
Savage, Charlie, 170
Savage, Michael, 38
Sayers, Brian, 24
SB 1070, 90
Scardaville, Michael, 176
Schulkin, Peter A., 103
Schumer, Chuck (D-NY), 70
Schwartz, Stephen, 124
search and seizure, 156, 158, 171
Sebelius, Kathleen, 33
Second Amendment, 30, 38–40, 44–45, 48, 55, 56, 230
Secret Internet Protocol Router Network (SIPRNET), 168
Secure Embassy Construction and Counterterrorism Act of 1999 (SECCA), 6–7, 15
Security Clearance (CNN blog), 265
SEIU (Service Employees International Union), 62–63, 70, 137
self-defense, 38, 39, 237, 238
Senate Armed Services Committee, 264
Senate Finance Committee, 25
Senate Homeland Security Committee, 214
Senate Intelligence Committee, 208, 233
Senate Judiciary Committee, 98
Service Employees International Union (SEIU), 62–63, 70, 137
Service Members Home Ownership Tax Act, 254. See ObamaCare
Sessions, Jeff (R-AL), 264
sexism, 304n13
shah of Iran. See Pahlavi, Mohammad Reza
Shahzad, Faisal, 213
Sharia law, 22, 23, 112, 115, 116, 126
Shays, Christopher (R-CT), 179
Shear, Michael D., 64, 65
Shell (Royal Dutch Shell), 144
Sheppard, Noel, 64
Shoebat, Walid, 128, 131
"signature strikes" (targeted killing), 235. See targeted killing; see generally chapter 10
Simeone, Lisa, 165
Single-payer health care, 242
Sixteenth Amendment, 249
Skype, 166
Small Smart Bomb, 220
Smart Grid projects, 135, 137, 140
"smart guns," 36
Smith, Debra (Western Center for Journalism), 255–56
Smith, Sean, 3, 4

smuggling of guns. See "Fast and Furious"; Project Gunrunner
social engineering, 255
Socialist Worker, 73–74
social media, monitoring of, 166–67, 170, 181
Social Security Administration (SSA), 49, 50, 82, 87–88
solar power, 134–35, 140
Solazyme Inc., 141
Somalia, 130, 231, 235, 236
Somin, Ilya, 255
Soros, George, 70, 137, 143, 144, 150, 151, 260, 265, 266, 267, 268
Soros, Jonathon, 260
"sovereign citizens" (antigovernment extremists), 168–69
Special Task Force on Interrogation and Transfer Policies, 209–10
Sprint Nextel, 156
spying by government. See chapter 7, esp. 152–53
Stability Police Force (SPF), 189–90
Stanley, Jay, 163, 164
State Department, 5–7, 11–16, 18–20, 50, 51, 113, 114, 118, 137, 191, 235, 236
penetration by Islamic extremists and terrorist organizations, 127–31
states' rights, iv, 241, 251–53
Stavridis, James, 21–22
Stephanopoulos, George, 149, 250–51
Stevens, Christopher, iv, 3–4, 5, 7, 8, 12–15, 19
stimulus bill (aka American Recovery and Reinvestment Act of 2009), 42, 67, 134, 135, 139, 280n60
stored data and file transfers, information gathering from, 167
straw purchasers, 1, 35, 43, 46
Strickland, Scott, 4
Students for a Democratic Society (SDS), 70
subsidies, 86, 87, 142, 244–47, 250
Suderman, Peter, 243
suicide attack, 120, 179
Sunrun Inc., 141
Sunstein, Cass, 38–40, 151, 169–70, 265
Supreme Court. See United States Supreme Court
Surveillance, Obama's regime of, 147–72
Surveillance-Industrial Complex, The (Stanley), 163, 164
Sydney Morning Herald (AU), 165–66
Syeed, Sayyid, 125
Syria, 8–10, 20–27, 104, 264, 265
persecution of Christians in, 23–24
Syrian rebels 9, 27
Sayers and fund-raising for, 24–26
U.S. arming of, 9, 10, 20, 22, 27
Syrian Support Group, 24–25

T

Taliban, 50, 213
Talking Points Memo, 95, 150
TALON (Threat and Local Observation Notice reports), 158, 161–63, 306n67
targeted killing, 233, 234, 237. *See generally chapter 10.*
Tarm, Michael, 91–92
taxation without representation, iv, 241, 246, 248, 249–51
Taxation without Representation (Adler and Cannon), 246
tax credits, 83, 86, 243–45, 247, 250
Telegraph (UK), 113
telephone call surveillance, 147, 149, 150, 152–53, 157, 168, 195
telephone records seizure, 154–56, 269
Templar Corporation, 182
Tennessee Office of Homeland Security, 204
Tenth Amendment, 188, 251, 252, 253
Tenth Amendment Center, 251
10th Amendment Foundation, 241
terminally ill, ObamaCare and the, 258–59
terrorism (-ists). *See generally chapters 1 and 5; also:* iv, 32, 35, 50, 60, 72, 76, 107, 147, 149, 153, 157, 159–64, 166, 168, 172, 175–81, 184, 188, 195, 197–99, 201, 202, 204, 207–11, 213–17, 230–33, 235, 237, 267, 309n11
   Department of State penetration by supporters of extremists and terrorist organizations, 127–31
   radical Islamic ties to counterterrorism agencies, 126–27
   White House minimizing of Islamic, 119–22
   war on, 117, 159, 177, 183
Terrorism Information and Prevention System (TIPS), 164
Terrorist Screening Center/Database (FBI), 160, 177
Terrorist Threat Integration Center, 177
terror lists, merging of, 159–61
Terry, Brian, 42–43, 45–46
Thakur, Ramesh, 267–68
This Week with George Stephanopoulus (ABC), 149
Thompson, Bennie (D-MS), 179
Thompson, Richard M., II, 227
THOR (Target Hardening Operational Response), 203
TIDE (Terrorist Identities Datamart Environment) database, 160, 172, 306n67
Tides Center / Tides Foundation, 70, 137
Tierney, Susan, 138
Time magazine, 38, 141

TIPOFF program, 160, 163
TIPS (Terrorism Information and Prevention System), 164
Toomey, Patrick J. (R-PA), 30
torture, 125, 208, 209, 211, 216
Total Information Awareness (TIA) (data-mining and profiling program), 159, 161, 163, 306n67
trafficking
   drug, 92, 93, 97, 101, 104, 184, 280n60
   firearms, 42, 44–45, 47, 97. See generally chapter 2
   human, 184
transportation, TSA's hyper-securing of all modes of (air, ferry, et al.), 194–204
Transportation Security Administration (TSA), 52, 164, 179, 187, 193–207, 313n21
Travelocity, private website monitoring of, 170
Treasury Department. *See* United States Department of the Treasury
Trenholm, Rich, 157
Tribe, Laurence, 255
TriggerSmart, 36
Tripoli, Libya, 5–7, 13, 19–20
truckers as watchdogs and informants, 165
Truman, Harry S., 263
Trussell, Tait, 74
TSA (Transportation Security Administration), 53, 164–65, 179, 187, 193–207, 313n21
Tsarnaev, Dzhokhar, 33
Tsarnaev, Tamerlan, 33
Tunisia, 117–18, 268
Turkey, 7, 8–10, 23, 24
Tutu, Desmond, 266
Tyner, John, 194
Twitter, 19, 165, 169

U

Uberti, David (*Boston Globe*), 229–30
UN. *See* United Nations
UN Charter (Charter of the United Nations), 237–38
"underwear bomber." *See* Abdulmutallab, Umar Farouk
unemployment, 60, 70, 78
United Arab Emirates (UAE), 22, 26
United Nations (UN), 7, 12, 23, 26, 27, 34, 128–29, 189, 237–38, 264, 266–67
United Nations Charter, 237–38
United Nations General Assembly, 5, 268
United Nations Security Council, 26, 238
United Nations Security Council Committee 1267, 129
United States Air Force, 161–62, 220, 221–23

United States Army, 55, 56, 119, 160, 189, 225, 226
United States Army Corps of Engineers, 224
United States Army Field Manual, 212, 216
United States Citizenship and Immigration Services (USCIS), 76, 81–82, 84, 88
United States Coast Guard, 53, 81, 198, 201, 202, 203, 205, 223, 224
United States Congress, ii, 13, 16, 18, 30, 31, 35, 40–41, 52, 54, 55, 67, 69, 71–75, 93, 98–100, 102, 105–6, 110, 134, 135, 143, 148, 150, 152, 153, 163, 164, 167, 174–75, 178, 183, 185, 196, 208, 228, 229, 233–34, 238–39, 241–51, 254–57, 260, 262–65, 270
  bypassing of, iv, v, vi, 29, 34, 59–60, 76–80, 193, 215–17, 241, 243–50, 262–65
United States Constitution, i–vi, 38–40, 44, 48, 79, 90, 97, 149, 156, 187, 234, 239, 241, 242, 246, 248, 249, 253, 255, 256, 262–63, 264, 269, 311n2
  Amendments. See Amendments to the U.S. Constitution
  Article I, Section 1, 246
  Article I, Section 7, 253
  Article I, Section 8, 59, 254, 262, 311n2
  Article I, Section 9, 249
  Article II, Section 3, 60
  Article II, Section 4, ii, 60
  Article IV, Section 5, 311n2
  Bill of Rights, 269. See also amendments to the United States Constitution
  Origination Clause, 254
  Supremacy Clause, 95
United States Customs and Border Protection (CBP), 52, 68, 81, 99, 105–6, 198, 205, 221
  budget and staff increase, FY 2002 to FY 2012, 105
United States Department of Commerce, 39, 134
United States Department of Defense, 55, 158, 159, 161–63, 168, 191, 192, 212, 221, 227, 228.
United States Department of Energy, 134, 138, 139, 140, 141, 143, 144
United States Department of Health and Human Services (HHS), 33, 83, 245–46, 250, 252–53
United States Department of Homeland Security. See Department of Homeland Security
United States Department of Justice. See Department of Justice (DOJ)
United States Department of State. See State Department

United States Department of the Treasury, 24, 97, 129, 130, 141, 244, 245, 260
United States House Committee on Oversight and Government Reform. See House Oversight and Government Reform Committee
United States House of Representatives, iii, 35, 41, 50, 56, 67, 69, 72, 74, 75, 93, 151, 152, 180, 246, 253, 254, 264. See also House Judiciary Committee, et al
United States Marshals Service, 190
United States Munitions Import List (USML), 34
United States Navy, 140–41
United States Postal Service, 140
United States Senate, iii, 4, 22, 30, 35, 62, 69, 73, 75, 94, 96, 121, 136, 148, 149, 151, 153, 169, 180–85, 196, 204, 215, 246, 254, 257, 259, 262, 264. See also Senate Finance Committee; Senate Homeland Security Committee; Senate Intelligence Committee; Senate Judiciary Committee
United States Supreme Court, 38, 39, 90, 103, 241–43, 248–52, 254–56
University of Chicago, vi, 38
Univision, 43, 47
Urban Institute, 250
USA Today, 86, 205
U.S. Immigration and Customs Enforcement (ICE). See ICE
US News and World Report, 129
US Northern Command (and TALON reports), 162, 163
USS Cole, 11
US Treasury. See United States Department of the Treasury

V

Vadum, Matthew, 304n13
Vanterpool, Mel, 198–99
Verizon Communications, 154–56
video, anti-Muhammad (on YouTube), 5, 16, 19
videos and video conferencing, data gathering from, 167
Vienna Convention on Diplomatic Relations (1961), 7
Vietnam War, 263
Vietor, Tommy, 4, 10–11
Vinson, Roger (judge), 154
Visible Intermodal Prevention and Response (VIPR) program, 187, 195–207
VoIP, data gathering from, 166
"vulnerable population," 68

W–X

Wagner, Daniel, 23
Wahhabism, 129
Wahhaj, Siraj, 125
Wall Street Journal, 25, 144, 156, 167, 171, 208, 211–12, 236, 243
war, the power to initiate, 262–63
War in Afghanistan (2001–), 72, 237
war crimes, 266
War Powers Resolution, 263–64
war on terror(ism), 117, 159, 177, 183
Washington, Ellis, 39
Washington Post, 64, 82, 100, 166–67, 197, 198, 207, 208, 216–17, 231–32, 238–39
Washington Times, 44, 98, 99, 128, 205
waterboarding, 216
weapons and ammo, stockpiling by DHS, 48–54, 56
Weather Underground Organization (formerly Weatherman), 136–37
websites, government monitoring of public, 170
Wheeler, Marcy, 178, 186
White House Atrocities Prevention Board, 266
White House Domestic Policy Council, 79
Whiteside, Logan, 36
Wikileaks, 21, 113, 118, 169
Wikipedia, 54–55
Wilson, J. Douglas, 209
Winchester Ammunition, 55
wind power, 134, 141
wiretapping, 149–51, 152, 153, 175
Wisner, Frank, 114
Wolf, Frank (R-VA), 216
Wolfowitz, Paul, 161
Wolverton, Joe, II, 189, 190
Wood, Andrew (Lt. Col.), 12
Woods, Tyrone, 3, 4
Woodward, Bob, 100
Workman, Dave, 39–40
World Trade Center bombing of 1993, 125, 130
Wright, Jeremiah, 151
"W" visas, 70
Wyden, Ron (D-OR), 161

Y

Yahoo!, 166
Yelp, private website monitoring of, 170
Yemen, 26, 118–19, 120, 231, 233, 235–37
YouTube
    data collection and monitoring of, 166, 170
    "Don't Touch My Junk" (Tyner) video protesting airport patdowns
    video disparaging Muhammad, 5, 16, 19

Z

Zahn, Drew, 56–57
Zenko, Micah, 236
Zionism, 127
Zionists, 113, 116

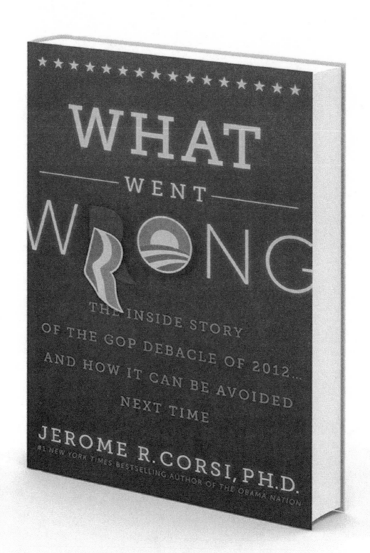

PRESENTS

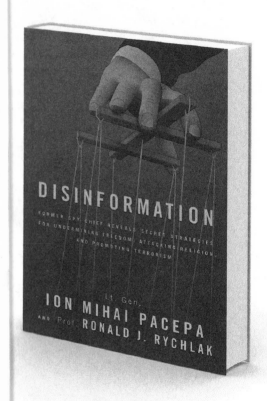

['Disinformation'] will change the way you look at intelligence, foreign affairs, the press, and much else besides."

— **R. JAMES WOOLSEY**, FORMER DIRECTOR OF CENTRAL INTELLIGENCE

"A powerful DVD companion to the book that will bring light into the darkness."

— **JOSEPH FARAH**, WND.COM

Today, living in the United States under a protective identity, the man credited by the CIA as the only person in the Western world who single-handedly demolished an entire enemy espionage service—the one he himself managed—takes aim at an even bigger target: the exotic, widely misunderstood but still astonishingly influential realm of the Russian-born "science" of disinformation.